Christian Social Principles

Sr. Mary Consilia O'Brien, O.P., Ph.D.

Christian
Social Principles

Introduction by
Archbishop Fulton J. Sheen

SOPHIA INSTITUTE PRESS
Manchester, New Hampshire

Sophia Institute Press
Box 5284, Manchester, NH 03108
1-800-888-9344

www.SophiaInstitute.com

Sophia Institute Press® is a registered trademark of Sophia Institute.

paperback ISBN 978-1-64413-616-4

ebook ISBN 978-1-64413-617-1

Library of Congress Control Number: 2021953506

First printing

Presented to Catholic students
through
Mary, Mother of Good Counsel,
on the occasion of
the fiftieth and tenth anniversaries, respectively,
of the encyclicals on labor and on the social order

Contents

Introduction

The sickness of the world is due less to a dearth of new ideas than to the rejection of old truths. And among these old truths none has had more disastrous consequences than the abandonment of the true nature of man. Liberalism and Collectivism, for example, are both distortions of the truth about man. The first bred economic slaves through individual selfishness and by isolating man from society; the second bred political slaves through collective selfishness and by the absorption of man into society.

Somewhere between these extremes is the golden mean of the Christian doctrine of man which alone can serve as the foundation of a new social order. First of all give the true definition of liberty. Liberty is not the right to do whatever I please, nor is liberty the necessity of doing whatever the dictator dictates; rather liberty is the right to do what I ought. In these three words: *please*, *must*, and *ought*, are given the choices facing the modern world. Of the three we choose *ought*.

That little word *ought* signifies that man is free. Fire *must* be hot, ice *must* be cold, but a man *ought* to be good. *Ought* implies morality, that is, a moral power distinct from a physical power. Freedom is not the power to do anything you please, so often expressed by the modern youth as: "I can do it if I want to, can't I? Who will stop me?" Certainly you *can* do anything if you please or want to. You can rob your neighbor, you can beat your wife, you can stuff mattresses with old razor blades, and you can shoot your neighbor's chickens with a machine gun, but you *ought* not to do these things because ought implies morality, rights, and duties.

The Christian doctrine of man furthermore affirms that you cannot have any rights without corresponding duties. Rights and duties are correlative, like the concave and convex sides of a saucer. I have a right to life, but I have inseparably the duty to respect the life of others. Since there are no rights without duties then rights and duties have a social character. That is why in

Christianity, the highest expression of personality is not in the egotistic assertion of rights but in the service of our fellowmen. Politically and economically this implies that the "right" gives way to "role" or "function." This is the Church's solution: Reconstruct society not on selfish "rights" but on the basis of *function*, for, "men must be bound together not according to the position they occupy in the labor market" (i.e., not by their income) "but according to the diverse *functions* which they exercise in society."

The difference between a society founded on rights and founded on function is basic. Rights, in the modern sense, are individual; functions are social in the sense that they look to the good of all, and yet both are inseparable, for many rights depend on functions. For example, my eye has a right to see, but it cannot exercise that *right* except by recognizing its *duty* to remain part of the body. So long as the eye *functions* in the organism, it enjoys its rights. My heart has the right to blood, but it cannot exercise that function unless it so loves the common good of the organism as to fulfill its duty of sending blood through all the other members of the human body. What is true of the human order *physically*, is true of the social order *vocationally*. Capital and labor, from this point of view, are related and made inseparable from the common good of society. This is the foundation of *social justice*.

Finally, the Christian doctrine of man is intrinsically bound up with the problem of property. There are three possible solutions of the problem of property. One is to put all the eggs into a few baskets, which is Capitalism; the other is to make an omelet out of them so that nobody owns, which is Communism; the other is to distribute the eggs in as many baskets as possible, which is the solution of the Catholic Church.

The right to property flows directly from my personality, and the more intimately things are associated with my person, the more personal is my right to them; the more they receive the impress of my rational nature, the more they are my own. That is why writings which are the immediate creation of a mind, and why children, which are the immediate products of a body, are so very much man's own. That is why the State will protect an author by copyright laws, and why the State recognizes that the right of education belongs to the parents rather than to the State itself. Man's right to have, then, follows from his right to be himself or to his own life.

Personality thus becomes a center around which there are a number of zones of property, some very close, some very remote; in the proximate zones of property come our body, food, clothing, habitation, literary products, artistic products of one's own brain and hands, and so forth. In the outer zones are the superfluities and luxuries of life. The right to own property, therefore, does not apply equally to all things; rather the right to property varies in direct ratio with proximity or remoteness to personality; the closer things are to our person, the more profound the right of having; the nearer things are to our inner responsibility, the stronger our right to ownership, as the nearer we get to fire the greater the heat. That is why a millionaire's right to his second million is not at all the same kind of right as that of a poor worker to some share in the profits, management, or ownership of the industry where he labors; that, too, is why a man's right to a yacht is not as primary as a man's right to a living wage. The capitalist who invokes the right to property against the state taxing his superfluous wealth for the sake of the needy, is not appealing to the same basic right as that to which the farmer appeals in claiming his cows are his own. Because property is the extension of personal responsibility, it also follows that five shares of stock in a billion-dollar corporation is not the same kind of property, nor is title to it as sacred as the widow's right to five bushels of potatoes in her back yard. In other words, the right to property is not absolute and invariable. The right to it increases with its relatedness to personality; the right decreases with its unrelatedness to it.

These and other applications are simply and effectively made in this needed work of Sr. Mary Consilia. Written so anyone can understand it, there will no longer be an excuse for ignorance of those basic principles upon which the Church reposes her social teaching. There is no incompatibility between the social philosophy of the Church and the modern world; there is only want of knowledge. That want this book seeks to correct. By so doing, it incidentally re-establishes the old truth that man needs to be rediscovered, not the animal man of whom we know so much, but the *rational* man of whom we know so little. That discovery is conditioned upon knowing Him according to whose image and likeness man was made, for only when God is relevant does man begin to be free.

— Archbishop Fulton J. Sheen, Ph.d., D.D., LL.D., Litt.D.

Preface

Catholic Students, meet St. Thomas!

Should this work need an apology for its nature, I hasten to let Pope Leo XIII defend my action. Should it need apology for its shortcomings, I myself must undertake to make it.

"There is nothing more earnestly desired and wished for by Us," writes Pope Leo, "than that you supply for the benefit of young students, plentifully and abundantly, those purest streams of wisdom that flow from the Angelic Doctor as from an inexhaustible and precious fountain.... Let masters strive to imbue the minds of their pupils with the doctrines of Saint Thomas, and to place clearly before them his superiority over others in solidity and excellence."

Written sixty-two years ago, these words must be the justification of the present work, for without doubt it is a departure from the customary textbooks on principles and problems of the social order. Answering the pleas of Pope Leo and Pope Pius, I have striven to give St. Thomas to young students. *Christian Social Principles* is hereby presented to them.

It is now two years since *Catholic Sociology* went to press. Its aim was identical with this one: to introduce St. Thomas to the young. Intended primarily for the very beginners in the study of Christian social principles, it made its way into circles which no optimism of mine might have hoped for. Seminaries, colleges, novitiates, adult discussion clubs, high schools, and Confraternity of Christian Doctrine circles gave it hearty welcome and practical use. They wanted St. Thomas and they took him, although he came to them in such simple guise.

The reception given to *Catholic Sociology* was so cordial that the author was imbued with fresh courage to meet the demands for a similar book for higher levels. *Christian Social Principles*, I hope, will be a gracious response to the earnest invitation received from many to present the social thought of St. Thomas and the Church to Catholic students of the final years of high school and the early years of college.

Intended for more mature minds than *Catholic Sociology*, the present work delves deeper into Thomistic thought and modern problems. Each chapter is supported by direct quotations from St. Thomas and the encyclicals. These are intended for use in discussion and study. Each chapter carries a summary, listing the highlights discussed in the chapter. A variety of questions and topics for discussion, numerous enough to allow a selection, is given with every chapter. A brief list of readings relevant to the chapter and dealing almost exclusively with the Thomistic approach to the question under discussion is found at the end of every chapter. Aids of this kind expedite not only formal teaching in the classroom but also private study and informal group discussions.

A word of explanation is necessary with respect to the manner of citing references to St. Thomas. References are given to the English Dominican Fathers' translation of the *Summa Theologica* and the *Summa Contra Gentiles*. The references are given by volume and page number. This is a departure from the customary and familiar "S. Theol. Ia, Q.-, a.-, ad-." I hope I shall be pardoned should anyone find fault with the method. I am writing with an eye to decreasing difficulties for the prospective users of the book. A second point needs explanation — and perhaps defense. In direct quotations from St. Thomas the long paragraphs have been broken down and other aids to easy reading have been given. For example, St. Thomas's familiar "firstly" and "secondly" and "thirdly" have been disjoined and given emphasis of place and space to aid the eye as well as the mind in what will be for many the first attempt to read St. Thomas directly. In this as well as in the manner of citing the references, I feel no injury has been done to the thought of St. Thomas, whereas in my opinion a decided benefit accrues to the reader who is as yet unacquainted with the style of St. Thomas and the form of his works.

Pope Leo warns masters to take care that, "the wisdom of Saint Thomas shall be drawn from its very source, or at least from those streams which, derived from the original source, still flow clear and pure" therefrom. It has been my unforgettable experience to have contacted teachers and friends who have initiated me into the beauty and vitality of St. Thomas, and who are themselves "streams which flow clear and pure" from the fountain of St. Thomas. There have been not a few ardent Thomistic scholars from whom I have received inspiration, and to them I gratefully express my indebtedness and appreciation. May they see something of their spirit and their teaching in this work.

Among them are names familiar to many: Doctors Ignatius Smith, O.P., Fulton J. Sheen, Charles A. Hart, Donald A. MacLean, John K. Ryan, and Walter Farrell, O.P. May some of the readers of this book have the opportunity of contacting them personally, as the author did, and of finding keenest joy in the experience. May these Thomistic scholars continue to lead others to the source from which they themselves drink — the inexhaustible fountain of wisdom that flows from the Angelic Doctor.

A word of special thanks is due to those friends who took time from many duties to read the manuscript critically and to make suggestions for correction and improvement. Mention must be made of the Rev. Walter Farrell, O.P., S.T.D., of the Dominican House of Studies, Washington, DC; the Rev. William McDonald, Ph.D., of the School of Philosophy, The Catholic University of America; the Rev. Charles J. McFadden, O.S.A., Ph.D., of Villanova College, and the Rev. Anthony L. Ostheimer, Ph.D. of Roman Catholic High School, Philadelphia. Sincere thanks are here given to all who in any way contributed to the completion of this work, especially to my superior, Rev. Mother Mary de Lourdes, O.P., for her constant encouragement.

Profound thanks are due to the universally known and loved Rt. Rev. Msgr. Fulton J. Sheen, Ph.D., D.D., for his graciousness in writing the introduction to this book. Much has been learned from him during student days and it is hoped that this work reflects creditably his tireless teaching.

The issuance of *Christian Social Principles* coincides, not without design, with the golden jubilee of Pope Leo's famous encyclical on labor. May it help to make better known the social doctrines of the Church as they have been given to the world in the great encyclicals of Pope Leo and Pope Pius.

To St. Thomas belongs all the credit for the wisdom of the doctrine contained herein. To Popes Leo and Pius belong the credit for promulgating it so widely in modern times. Only mine the blame if, in my presentation of him, I have made St. Thomas less glorious than he deserves. In his goodness he will overlook the fault in virtue of my sincere desire to have Catholic students meet St. Thomas!

— S.M.C.
Feast of Our Lady of Good Counsel
April 26, 1941

Christian Social Principles

Part 1

Man

1

Plans and Principles

Plan of the Book

This book is about man and society. It has been written to give you a better understanding of the nature and purpose of man, the desires which motivate him, and the tools or means with which he is equipped to fulfill his divinely ordained destiny, to attain his ultimate end.

This book wouldn't be complete if it were about man alone, for man is a *social being*. Nor could it be written if it were about society alone, for it is *men* who constitute society. Society is the grouping of individuals of a rational nature. So this book is about man and society.

It will discuss man and society in the light of very basic principles. It has been carefully planned so that the principles you learn in this book can be and will (it is hoped) be the source of learning for you. Principles are sources like the head waters of a river. They are seeds from which new growth comes, as the seeds in nature from which flowers and fruit are produced. Principles give us new knowledge, which, though it is hidden in the principles, can be brought to light only when the principle is "worked"; that is, only when one *reasons* about the principle. It is our desire to present to you basic principles of man and society that you may "work" upon them and increase your learning, that thereby you may multiply your practice of those specifically human acts which result in the development of truly human perfection.

Man

Man is a dependent being. No man is self-sufficient. Each one of us depends upon others for innumerable things which spell progress, comfort, and advantage for us. Man requires not only human and non-human creatures for the development of his whole nature, but he requires also something more perfect

5

than dependent beings. Not all the creatures of the universe can be the sufficient reason, the adequate cause of man, because all creatures are themselves dependent beings. Man as well as all creation requires a first cause which is, *by its very nature*, self-sufficient. Man's first cause is God, the Supreme Lord and Master of the universe. From Him man derives his being; that is, man receives from God (1) existence and (2) human nature, resulting in existence that is of a high-grade kind; namely, *human existence*.

No number or kind of dependent beings could call man into existence. Only an utterly independent being, one needing no one and nothing, could cause things to exist. God is the uncaused cause of all things; that is, though no other being has caused God to exist (since He existed from all eternity, having neither beginning nor end), He is the cause of the existence of all other things. And thus the universe, including man, is dependent upon God as upon its first cause.

Now God is not only man's first cause, He is also man's last end. Man is destined for God. God made man to know Him, to love Him, to serve Him, and through the knowledge, love, and service of God, man is destined to spend an eternity of enjoyment in God and with God. The chapter on man's last end will develop this point. For the present let us remember that man is not self-sufficient. God is his first cause and his last end; creatures and institutions (the family, the State, the Church, and so forth) are secondary causes of man's happiness, progress, and perfection. And thus the scope of the present work is not only *man*, but *society* as well.

Man is by nature a social being. This is merely to say that man needs the association of others for the perfection of his whole personality. A hermit's life is mere existence; it is not personal development that is distinctly human. It lacks the social contacts which develop the intellectual, moral, religious, physical, and political potentialities of human nature. The very presence in man of the gift of speech argues to his need of companionship. Man has not the gift of speech to enable him to talk to himself! Internal expression, that is, concepts and judgments of the intellect, would be sufficient for a non-social rational being. Man's power of speech is a means of communicating with others of his kind. For this, man requires others; that is, man needs associates.

Society

Among the secondary causes of man's complete and ultimate perfection is the institution called *society*. This book will investigate human personality in the light of Christian principles and standards. It will investigate the nature and role of society as such, and of societies in particular, with regard to man's need of them. It will investigate and apply the norms of right behavior which pertain to man's acts as a moral individual and to his acts as a social being. It will constantly bring before your mind the thought that man is a moral being not only in his private life but also in his social life, whether it be in the public social life of business, commerce, civil government, or the professions, or in the private social life of the home and family. Man by his very nature is a responsible being, both as private individual and as a member of society. Further discussions of this will be made in an appropriate chapter later.

The Intellectual Habits

The subject matter of this work is drawn from several branches of human knowledge. Now knowledge is *natural* when it is attained by the light of human reason alone. It can be achieved in either or both of two ways.

First, man's intellect presents certain fundamental truths as self-evident. They are truths which can be admitted at once, without reasoning, once the mind understands the meaning of the words. For example, the human mind has no difficulty in recognizing and acknowledging that mathematical truth which presents itself to the thinking individual thus: the whole of anything is greater than any one of its parts. This truth is a primary basic law of mathematics; it is a self-evident truth or principle. It requires no proof or demonstration. We know the truth of it merely by knowing what *whole* and *part* mean.

Another instance of a primary self-evident principle which presents itself to the human mind is this, that a thing is itself and not another. This book is this book and not another book or another object. This is the principle of identity. It is self-evident. We know its truth merely by knowing the meaning of *this book*, *is*, and *itself.* Another such principle is that one known as the principle of contradiction. It declares that a thing cannot *be* what it is and *not be* what it is at the same time and in the same view. It declares that this contraption, for example, cannot *be* an airplane and *not be* an airplane at the same time and viewed in the same way. If a thing is an airplane, it *is* an airplane. If it *is* an airplane, it cannot at the same time and in the same way be something else; a screwdriver, for instance.

The principle of identity and its negative form, the principle of contradiction, are the most fundamental of all first principles of knowledge. They mean, when stated in an affirmative way, that everything is itself, that everything has a determined nature. When stated in a negative way, they mean that everything is so wholly itself that it cannot be another thing. A child does not need to be taught this; neither does a child need to be taught that everything must have a sufficient reason for its existence. When a child asks so many whys he is merely trying to find out what is the sufficient reason for the things he sees. That there *is* a sufficient reason for everything, he takes for granted. Unless a child *naturally* knew these basic principles, no teacher could teach him anything. We would say of him that he "has no sense — he does not understand." A "common-sense" person has a firm hold on self-evident first principles. The first principles which are the beginnings of all knowledge cannot be proved; they cannot be demonstrated as one might demonstrate that the union of hydrogen and oxygen results in water. They are naturally known and about them no mistake can be made. For example, it cannot be a mistake to insist that a potato is a potato, or that a pencil cannot be a chair.

Knowledge via Reasoning

Not all human knowledge is self-evident human knowledge. If it were, then with the beginning of the use of reason and the development of a vocabulary, one would acquire all human knowledge for the simple reason that self-evident principles become known merely by understanding the meaning of the words. Much human knowledge is *reasoned* human knowledge. This is the gradual growth in knowledge which comes from study and experience. The human mind starts out with a certain stock of primary principles and by reasoning, that is, by thinking about them and drawing conclusions from them, it arrives at new truths. For example, from the fundamental truth that a father must provide for his offspring, human reason concludes to the following facts: that a man must be provided with the means of supporting his offspring; that the means must be of a reasonably permanent character; that they must be sufficient to enable him to provide adequately for his children; that because of the duty imposed upon him by nature, the father of a family has the primary right to rear his offspring, and that he has the moral right to the *means* and to the *use of the means* to provide for them. These truths are all *reasoned* truths, unfolded, as it were, from that primary truth that a father should care for his offspring.

Science and Wisdom

Human knowledge, therefore, springs from (1) self-evident principles which are the fountain or springs of further reasoned knowledge, and (2) the reasoned knowledge or conclusions which the mind seeks out and develops by means of analyzing, comparing, and applying the basic truths contained in the primary principles. The firm grasp of first principles is the intellectual habit of understanding. When one firmly grasps the truth that the whole is greater than any of its parts, he "understands"; that is, he exhibits the intellectual habit of understanding. One thus possesses the *seed* of possible future human knowledge. The unfolding from primary principles of new truths in a particular branch of study, as, for example, in physics or chemistry, or the seeking of new truths which are understood in the light of the primary principles, constitute the intellectual habit of knowledge. St. Thomas called it *science*. If one has learned by analyzing, comparing, demonstrating, and generalizing the constant reaction of certain chemicals, then one *knows*, that is, one exhibits the intellectual habit of knowledge or science. The fertile seed of understanding any possible human knowledge thus has blossomed into particular facts of knowledge in a given field of human learning; namely, in chemistry.

This is in great part the knowledge which we learn from our teachers and textbooks. It is the knowledge acquired through reasoning and experimentation. It includes the knowledge of the laws and facts of the sciences of biology, of chemistry, of mathematics, of economics, and so on. It should be a stepping stone to the highest reaches of intellectual attainment in man — to the crown of human knowledge.

The crown of human knowledge consists in a firm grasp of final explanations. It knows the root causes and explanations of things. Inquiry goes no further. The last explanation has been given. The human mind, as if it were on a high elevation, sees the streams of human knowledge like so many rivulets, flowing from first principles as from hidden springs, making their way through reasoning and conclusions to new particular truths. Not content with penetrating the sources of human truths (which is understanding), nor with knowing particular truths of the various sciences (which is knowledge), the human mind, through the intellectual habit of wisdom, seeks and holds the answer to the final "Why?" of all these things.

A "wise" man is far more than a chemist, a biologist, a physicist, a mathematician. A man possessed of the habit of wisdom, a truly "wise" man, sees the relation between the truths of biology and of physics and of chemistry and of mathematics and of economics and of all the natural sciences, of all human knowledge. He sees the fundamental causes of these truths. He sees the truths of these limited sciences as being part of the great truth which is infinite truth, which is God's unlimited and unlimitable wisdom. The "wise" man knows with certainty the ultimate or last explanation of man, of human existence, of human destiny, of human purpose and human endeavors. He knows, too, with equal certainty, the goal of humanity, the ultimate goal which is God. He possesses the intellectual habit of wisdom. The seed of *understanding*, which blossomed in *knowledge*, later bears the desirable fruit of *wisdom*.

Thus, the truly wise man, possessed of the intellectual habit of wisdom, is more than a natural scientist limited to a particular field and to particular, demonstrated truths. His field is all truth; his goal is the final explanation of truth. The truly wise man is called the theologian if his search leads him to study the principles of divine truth. He is called the philosopher if he seeks to explain the final causes and reasons of the truths of the created universe.

Primary Principles Involved

We find, therefore, in the acquisition of human knowledge, (1) first principles, then (2) conclusions derived from these first principles, and finally (3) ultimate explanations of things — the final answer which ends any given series of questions. These are, as it were, three grades of perfection in man's knowledge; (1) the thinking but untutored person; (2) the person of education in the arts and sciences; (3) the truly wise person who views all knowledge in perspective — who knows ultimate causes and principles from that apex of intellectual perfection which we call wisdom. We shall have occasion to note all three grades strewn throughout the pages of this work.

Certainly there are first principles to be found or assumed. In addition to the principles of identity and of contradiction, there is that of sufficient reason as well as that of finality. We have the application of the principle of sufficient reason in this, that the existence of dependent beings must have for the adequate reason of their being, an independent being, Him whom we know as God. That every existing thing acts for a purpose, tends to accomplish its work, to attain the perfection of its nature, is an expression of the primary principle of finality. This we shall meet repeatedly in the course of this work.

These principles we have just mentioned are principles of *thinking*. However, the habit of understanding includes also the firm grasp of the first principles of *doing*. With the first dawn of the use of reason, man knows *naturally*, that is, within himself by the light of human reason, that he must *do* good and avoid evil. This principle will be discussed at length in a subsequent chapter. Its spirit pervades the whole of this book. It is the justification for our statement made previously, that man is a *moral* being. We have here discussed the nature of those primary principles of thinking without which no learning could take place, for they are the basis of any and of every branch of intellectual knowledge in human beings.

Now beyond that primitive store of universal principles, each branch of knowledge in particular requires certain particular principles which must be admitted as starting points of a given science before that science can take its first step in quest of truth in its particular field. The first principles of a particular science are not as broad in meaning and interpretation as are the first principles of all knowledge, such as the principles of contradiction, of sufficient reason, of finality, and the like. These latter are valid principles of *all* human knowledge whereas the former principles of particular sciences are valid in the limited field covered by the particular sciences.

First Principles of Particular Sciences

Now it is an axiom of St. Thomas Aquinas that no science proves its own first principles. Every science must start its investigation from certain accepted sources, that is, (1) from self-evident facts or (2) from "borrowed" principles proved by other sciences. These are springboards from which a particular science bounds into a given field of investigation. For example, biologists, in explaining the laws which govern life, take as an accepted fact the existence of life. They do not first attempt to prove that there is such a thing as life. They accept it as a fact (and who does not know that he is alive?) and they proceed to explain its causes, effects, and manifestations.

Postulates Assumed Herein

Every study must start with a greater or lesser number of self-evident truths or principles proved elsewhere. These essential prerequisites are known as the *postulates* of a given study. Hence, we, also, must declare in our study of man and of society the underlying assumptions upon which we build. We must take as proved elsewhere (as natural theology proves on the rational level and revelation does on the supernatural level) the fact of the existence of an infinite God, the Supreme Being. We must further accept beforehand the fact that man has a rational soul and is endowed with freedom of the will. This is proved in rational psychology. We know it, too, from theology and from revelation. We must accept without presenting proof here and now, the truth that man's soul is immortal; that God is the first beginning and the last end of all creatures; that He is the Supreme Lord and Ruler of the universe. We must acknowledge, too, the divinity of the Church and of her Founder, Jesus Christ, for thereon rests her authority and infallibility.

These are the fundamental truths which constitute the springboard from which our study starts. We do not prove them here. We take them for granted, secure in the belief that they can be and, as a matter of fact, are, proved to the satisfaction of the human intellect in other fields of human knowledge, or by divine revelation, or by both.

Christian Social Principles begins with principles knowable to the normal human mind; it advances to conclusions and applications of these principles in the field of human actions; and it hopes to crown its labors by giving to the sincere student a grasp of ultimate explanations, of the answers to the most fundamental of all questions. It will tell man who he is, why he is, whither he is going, and how he ought to go. This basic knowledge constitutes the essence of the acquired intellectual virtue of wisdom.

Contributing Sciences

We have said that several branches of human knowledge have contributed to this work. Certainly theology and philosophy make a definite contribution. From the former we have a fuller understanding of God and God's law than could be derived from human reason alone. It contributes to our understanding also of the nature of the reward which God has prepared for those who attain their life's purpose. It enables us to understand the value of the human soul and the character of the divine help which God gives to it to assist it in attaining eternal beatitude. Theology contributes also to our understanding of the society of the Church, her nature and her role, as also of the divine character and divinely appointed mission of her Founder. Theology aids us in plumbing the depths of the morality of human acts and its attendant problems of rightness and wrongness in particular instances and under certain circumstances. From this study, too, we have the certitude of man's divine origin and destiny and the certainty of reward and punishment.

Philosophy, likewise, contributes much to our study of man and society. (We must recall the point made previously, that the pursuit of divine wisdom is theology and the pursuit of human wisdom is philosophy.)

Human wisdom, or philosophy, which seeks ultimate reasons and supplies answers to basic questions concerning the universe and all its creatures, including man, contributes to our investigation through several of its branches. More particularly it contributes through ethics, the morality of human acts, including the laws which bind man in those acts; through psychology, the study of man's soul with its powers of intellect and will; and through metaphysics, which supplies the basic principles of identity, of contradiction, of sufficient reason, and of finality upon which principles of thought the validity of our whole work rests in its rational basis.

Social philosophy, too, contributes to our study by supplying the basic principles of man's social nature, the necessity of society for human development, the need of authority in human society, the kinds of authority and the limited spheres of the activity of each, the social vices and virtues, and the inalienable natural rights and consequent duties of human beings. These include other principles concerned with the inner nature of the necessary primary, social institutions to which man belongs. That branch of philosophy known as logic will be manifested in the order it imposes upon the thinking which has gone into the writing and, we hope, into the studying of this work.

Finally, sociology, which deals with the social nature of man and the functioning of social institutions in their concrete reality, contributes its share to the following pages of *Christian Social Principles.*

Revelation Enlightens and Confirms

Above and beyond the rational foundation for the principles advanced in *Christian Social Principles,* there is the fortress impregnable which sustains them: only through revelation do we know Jesus Christ. Human reason could never have attained to a knowledge of the Blessed Trinity nor of the redemptive and instructive role played by the second Person. Revelation confirms the conclusions of reason that a Supreme Being must exist and must be responsible for the existence of other things, and must itself be not caused by anything.

Ecclesiastical Approbation

Christian Social Principles likewise carries the *imprimatur* of the Holy Roman Catholic Church testifying to the fact that in it nothing has been found contrary to faith and morals.

The following pages will show to what degree of solidity are welded together revelation, reason, and Catholic doctrine.

Some Original Sources

Here are some quotations from the *Summa Theologica* of St. Thomas. They are taken from his tract on the intellectual virtues. He says:

1. "A truth is subject to a twofold consideration: (1) as known in itself, and (2) as known through another.

"What is known in itself, is as a *principle,* and is at once understood by the intellect: wherefore the habit that perfects the intellect for the consideration of such truth is called *understanding,* which is the habit of principles.

"On the other hand, a truth which is known through another, is understood by the intellect, not at once, but by means of the reason's inquiry and is a result (of that inquiry). This may happen in two ways:

(a) "First, so that it is the last in some particular class" (or field of knowledge as chemistry, mathematics, and so forth)—

(b) "Secondly, so that it is the ultimate term (or end) of all human knowledge" (beyond which there is no further answer, as that God is man's sole sufficient cause—his first cause and the last end).

"Hence that which is last with respect to *all human knowledge* is most knowable in its nature. And about these is *wisdom* which considers the highest causes.... Wherefore it rightly judges all things and sets them in order ...

"But in regard to that which is last in *this* or *that particular field* of knowable matter, it is *science* that perfects the intellect.

"Wherefore according to the different kinds of knowable matter, there are different habits of scientific knowledge; whereas there is but one wisdom." (*Summa Theologica*, vol. 7, pp. 88, 89)

Interpretative Suggestions
 • From the above can you indicate the places in which St. Thomas is speaking of "self-evident principles"? Reread the text on this matter.
 • Reread the text on how the intellect reasons from first principles to conclusions. Select and call attention to the parts of the above quotation that have reference to knowledge in particular sciences.
 • What portions of the above bear reference to the habit of wisdom which seeks final explanations of all truth?

St. Thomas further says:

2. "Science depends on understanding as on a habit of higher degree: and both of these [viz., science and understanding] depend on wisdom, as holding the highest place, and containing beneath itself both understanding and science, by judging both of the conclusions of science [viz., knowledge] and of the principles on which they are based [viz., understanding]." (*Summa Theologica*, vol. 7, pp. 88, 89)

Interpretative Suggestions
 • From this quotation, tell which St. Thomas considered the higher habit or degree of intellectual perfection, whether it was understanding or knowledge.
 • What is the twofold task which St. Thomas here assigns to wisdom?

From Pope Leo we have the following quotations:

"The special glory of Thomas, one which he has shared with no other Doctor of the Church, is that the Fathers of the Council of Trent laid upon the altar together with the

Sacred Scriptures: and the decrees of the Supreme Pontiffs, the *Summa Theologica* of Saint Thomas, in which to seek counsel, reason and inspiration.

"Our most cherished wish is that you should furnish a generous and copious supply to studious youth of those crystal streams of wisdom flowing in a never-ending and inexhaustible stream from the fountain-head of the Angelic Doctor.

"Many are the reasons why we are so desirous of this. Domestic and civil society which, as all see, is exposed to great danger from this plague of perverse opinions, would certainly enjoy a far more peaceful and secure existence if a more wholesome doctrine *were* taught in the schools; one more in conformity with the teaching of the Church such as is contained in the works of Thomas Aquinas." (Encyclical *Aeterni Patris* [The Study of Christian Philosophy], my emphasis)

Summary

, simple exposition of the basic foundations of man living in society. It has to do with man and society.

2. Man is a dependent being, not only in the social order inasmuch as he depends upon others for the necessities of life, but in a higher order. Man's very existence depends upon God for its beginning and its continuance.

3. God is man's first beginning. God is man's origin. Man came from God. God alone is the sole sufficient cause of man's being.

4. God is man's last end. God is man's destiny. Man's whole life is a return to God. God alone is the sole sufficiently satisfying goal of man's activities.

5. Society is a secondary cause of man's human development. Society is a cause operating under the first cause, under God, from whom society receives its nature, its end, its means, and its powers.

6. Man is a moral being as well as a social being. He is guided to his end interiorly by the natural law and exteriorly by human authority acting in accordance with the natural law. Man is a moral being in his private life as well as in his public life.

7. Definite principles of knowledge will be outlined in this work. The aim, of course, is to put these principles to work in practical life. They would be only a load on the memory or the intellect were they to remain static.

8. Principles are sources of new knowledge. The mind takes a principle and by examining it, analyzing it, applying it, and so forth, new truths are drawn out from it. This is the process known as "reasoning."

9. The new truth drawn out from a principle is called a conclusion. Conclusions may be "worked" and give forth other conclusions, and so on. This represents advance in knowledge.

10. Normal human beings are all possessed of "reasoning" powers. These powers would never start to operate unless they had something upon which to work. The human mind supplies a number of bedrock principles on which the human mind can operate before it has acquired very much knowledge or exercise of reasoning.

11. These principles are understood at once by the mind just as soon as the mind knows the meaning of the words employed in the principle. No one needs to *prove* to anyone that a whole apple is bigger than a half of that same apple. Knowing the meaning of *whole* and *half* is sufficient.

12. Likewise when even a little child knows a dog and knows a picture book, no one has to prove to him that the dog can't be the book. He knows without proof that one cannot be the other.

13. Such very basic principles without which human learning can never advance are called first principles. They are extremely important as anyone can see.

14. Among the very important ones are these: of identity: a thing is itself and not something else; of contradiction: a thing cannot be itself and something else at the same time and in the same way; of finality: every thing has been made for a purpose, otherwise it would have no reason for existing; of cause: every finite thing has a cause for its existence, otherwise it could never be brought into existence; of sufficient reason: everything must have an adequate reason for its existence or its activity, as a mother is not the whole reason for the existence of her child, for she is unable to give her child a soul. God alone is the sole sufficient reason for everything, for He alone is infinite and perfect.

15. Each science has its own specific set of "first principles" which apply to that science, but not to all knowledge and activities as do the first principles in number 14 above.

16. Chemistry has its own general laws from which new truths can be deduced. So, too, has biology, and every science.

17. Ultimately all knowledge depends upon the first principles mentioned in number 14. For what good would it do a chemist to say, "This is nitrogen," if a thing could be itself and something else (say, chloride) at the same time and in the same way.

18. The habit of grasping first principles is called *understanding*. "Do you understand?" asks the teacher when she wants to know if you "grasp" her explanation. Understanding is an intellectual habit or virtue. It directs man's knowledge but not his behavior. Other virtues direct his behavior.

19. The ability to reach new knowledge from principles and experiences—the power to "reason" things out and reach conclusions—is called *reasoning*. It results in the intellectual habit called *knowledge*. Solving an original in geometry is an instance of this.

20. The integration of all knowledge is the intellectual habit of wisdom. It relates the findings of all the sciences and all human knowledge into an orderly whole. It explains the final reasons of things; it seeks ultimate causes; it views all human learning from a pinnacle—the heights of wisdom.

21. The intellectual habits (or virtues) are different from the moral habits (or virtues). The former operate in the field of knowing—or speculative things. The latter operate in the field of doing—or practical, human activities, which they direct toward the end of man. Moral principles concern man's behavior. It is they which really perfect a man. Intellectual habits may make him more learned in this or that line of study, but moral habits make him a better and more virtuous man in every human action.

22. A study of *Christian Social Principles* will involve both kinds of principles. Various human sciences have contributed to the making of this book. It is based on the Primary Principles mentioned in number 14. It presents also the code of morality which the Church holds up as the only adequate norm of moral living. Any growth in learning which might take place in the study of this book will depend upon the intellectual habits and their acuity in the individual student.

23. Finally, divine revelation makes its contribution to this work for it is only through the revelation of God that we know Jesus Christ whom He has sent. And know Jesus Christ *we must* for He is the Founder, the Head, the Source of life and merits, of the Church, mankind's *only true society upon which it may draw for the necessary supernatural sustenance* of which it stands in need.

24. Since knowledge should never be sought for itself but always for some further end, the knowledge gained from the study of *Christian Social Principles* should bear fruit in the Christlikeness of the individual in his social relations.

For Study and Discussion

1. Discuss the possibilities of interesting topics implied in the scope of this book, namely man and society. Would "principles governing the regulation of wages" be an appropriate topic? Would "the desire for happiness motivates human activity" be another? What other topics would properly belong to a study of man and society?

2. Can you explain and give illustrations of the steps in the acquisition of the intellectual habit of wisdom? What are the inferior habits? How do they compare one with the others?

3. First principles are wellsprings of thought. Explain this statement. Can you discuss the most primary of all first principles, namely, the principle of

identity? In the order of *doing*—that is, of morality, what is the primary principle? Mention a first principle of mathematics; of chemistry; of biology; of physics. Discuss first principles and show how the search for new truths (for knowledge) depends upon a firm grasp of first principles.

4. Mention at least five of the first principles (derived from other fields of thought) which must be acknowledged before one can begin a profitable study of this book. Does revelation confirm the truth of those particular first principles?

5. What is the author's intention in basing this book on the philosophy of St. Thomas and on the teachings of the papal encyclicals?

6. How do the sciences of ethics, psychology, social philosophy, and others contribute to this book?

7. What is the difference between theology and philosophy?

8. Can you explain why no science proves its own "first principles"?

For the Advanced Reader

St. Thomas Aquinas:
> *Summa Contra Gentiles*, vol. 1, chap. 1
> *Summa Theologica*, vol. 7, pp. 85–99; 100–111

Chesterton, G. K.:
> *Saint Thomas Aquinas*

Farrell, Walter:
> *A Companion to the Summa*, 11, chaps. 8, 9

Grabmann, M.:
> *Saint Thomas Aquinas: His Life and Works*

Maritain, J.:
> *The Angelic Doctor*

Papal Encyclical:
> Pope Leo XIII: *Aeterni Patris,* trans. in vol. 1, *Summa Theologica,* in Maritain's *The Angelic Doctor,* and in *The Great Encyclical Letters of Leo XIII,* by Fr. Wynne, S.J.

2

Man: His First Beginning; His Last End

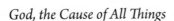

God, the Cause of All Things

We have accepted as a truth or a presupposition to our study of man and society that man has come from the hand of God. Revelation declares this truth with divine certitude. Philosophy can argue to its truth. "Nothing can be the sufficient cause of its own existence," says St. Thomas, "if its existence is caused." But we know that man's existence has been caused. He has been brought into being. He did not always exist, but he began to exist at a given period of time and in a definite place. Therefore, since his existence is a caused existence, he cannot be the one responsible for his own existence.

Everything must have a sufficient reason for its existence, and this is true even of God. But God does not need a *cause*, that is, someone to produce Him, as we need a cause to produce us. He is uncaused. No one brought God into existence. He always was and always will be; otherwise He would not be an infinitely perfect being. It is He who brought all things into existence. He is uncaused in Himself but He is the cause of the existence of all other things. God is the uncaused cause of all things.

God, Man's Beginning and End

God is the cause of man. He is also the only adequate explanation of man's existence and of his nature. God is man's sufficient reason. That is, God made man. God created his specific nature. God endowed that nature with definite powers proper to man. God established man's goal. God directs man toward his goal by means of law. God is man's only adequate explanation; He is the sufficient reason of man.

God is man's first beginning. God is also man's last end.

Christian Social Principles

All Things Tend toward God

St. Thomas tells us that whatever man does, it is true to say that he acts for an end. This means, simply, that man directs his actions to a goal. He has a purpose when he acts. He does a thing for a reason. Action means nothing other than moving toward a goal. A young man who studies medicine is acting; he is moving toward a goal — the goal of the medical profession. His aim is to become a doctor. It is a commonplace remark, therefore, to say that whatever a man does, he does it because of a goal he is striving to reach.

Now this applies not alone to man, but also to all the strivings of nature. When an apple tree blossoms, it is moving toward a goal, the goal of fruit-laden limbs and, ultimately, the production and distribution of new life through the seeds which it produces. Think of the teeming activity of the universe. Think of the multiple natures in the universe. Think of the variety of natural capacities in the many different created natures. Think of all these, and you will form some idea of the number and the kinds of motions toward a variety of goals. And yet, despite the multiplicity of goals because of the multiplicity of different natures, there is one supreme goal, one common aim, one supreme objective of all creation. That end or goal of all nature and of every nature is the Author of nature. Everything in the universe, man included, has come from the hand of God, and everything in the universe tends to fulfill its purpose; tends to follow its natural capacities; tends toward its perfection; tends toward God. Each nature acts according to its own special powers; some by merely existing, as minerals; others by living, as plant life; still others by living and feeling, as brute animals, while man reaches his goal by knowing and loving. Knowledge and love, springing from man's reason and will, distinguish him from and elevate him above all other created natures.

There is one source and one goal of all nature's strivings, one starting point and one resting place of all movement. God, the Creator of Heaven and earth, is the Source and the goal of all activity. He is the cause and the sole sufficient reason of all creatures, of all activity, of all movement.

What Is Man's Good?

Every nature acts for its own good. "The good is what all things tend towards," says St. Thomas. Merely to exist would not be good for man. To exist is good for non-living things. Stones, for example, fulfill their purpose by merely existing. They do not live nor feel nor know and love. But it would not be sufficiently good for man merely to live. It is good for plants to live. Trees and flowers, fruits and vegetables attain their goal by living and producing new life, new trees, new flowers, new fruits, new vegetables.

It would not be good for man merely to live and feel. It is, however, good for animals to live and to feel. Animals fulfill their life's goal by living and sensing (feeling). An animal flees for his life, fights to protect his young, and seeks food, drink, and sleep through his sensations such as when he senses danger or feels hungry. Clearly this is not all of man's good. Man could never be satisfied with living like a well-fed lion or racing horse or rat.

Man's crowning good lies in his power to know and to love, to desire and to will. By these he can know the goal which God has ordained for him; he can choose that goal and so take the steps necessary to reach it. Man is the only creature in the physical universe who can know, love, desire, and will. And so man is the only creature in the physical universe who is free to move toward the goal ordained for him by God, or to refuse to move toward it.

All that means nothing more than this: that the universe and every nature in it fulfills its purpose and reaches its goal by acting according to the natural inclinations which God puts into them. For man, this means acting according to the known wants of his nature. And for man alone this *good* of his nature, this yearning for the end, this satisfaction of his natural capacities, is nothing other than happiness. All that a man does, he does for the purpose of being happy. Whatever makes man truly happy, moves him toward his goal. Whatever makes man supremely happy with no more desires to be satisfied, *is* the goal. With its attainment man at that time will have attained his end. He will have found the perfect good which alone satisfies his rational nature. He will have fulfilled his purpose in life. He will then be perfectly a man, without blight or blemish. Only then will he be at rest.

What Is Happiness?

Let us look at the nature of the happiness which alone can bring rest to man. Human happiness consists, essentially, in the attainment of one's desires. Desires are cravings which arise from the knowledge of something which we deem to be good for us. No one of us would deem it good to descend to the nature of a non-feeling, non-knowing, non-loving daisy, and so we do not desire to become a daisy. Neither does any one of us consider it good to live in isolation from the rest of mankind, a kind of modern Robinson Crusoe, and so no one desires such a non-social existence. But how many of us do consider it good to have money, friends, power, wealth, fame, honor, health, virtue! And whatever we consider good, that is what we desire, and the attainment of what we desire, if it be truly good, brings us some happiness. Thus money, friends, power, fame, honor, health, and virtue can all bring us some degree of happiness.

Man's Final End

The happiness which comes to man from the good things enumerated above is not — indeed, it cannot be — perfect, complete, unmixed happiness. For the possession of no one of them, nor, for that matter, the possession of all of them, can bring man's desires to rest. Complete happiness means the acquisition of the last end, the reaching of his goal, the perfection of his human capacities, the attainment of infinite love and truth — the attainment of God.

Now wealth cannot be the last end of man's desires. Neither can friends. Power, fame, honor, wealth, health, virtue, nor life itself cannot be man's last end. These are partial goals, steps toward the final goal, perhaps; movements toward that perfectly satisfying object which answers all man's cravings and which perfects his entire being. But at best they can never be more than steps, for wealth does not perfect man's whole nature; neither does health; neither does power, nor fame, nor honor, nor any bodily goods or mental goods. These things are all sought for the sake of something else.

For example, one man desires wealth that he might live in luxury. Another one desires health that he might be free from pain and enjoy good living. Another one desires fame that he might win the acclaim of others. Still another one desires power for the sake of the prestige it brings. This is nothing more than saying that the goods mentioned above are not final ends in themselves. They do not perfect man. A man does not ordinarily desire power for the sake of power, but for the sake of the prestige and attention it brings to him. Furthermore, a man does not cease to desire when he has acquired one or all of these things. This fact argues that such things are sought on account of something more which is not at present possessed.

We said above that a man does not *ordinarily* desire power or any other finite good for itself alone. It can happen, though, that one *might* seek a partial good for itself. Perhaps a miser seeks wealth for itself alone. One can crave any one of these things — especially power — for itself. This is the subjective aspect of the matter; it views the good thing not from its true worth but from what it means to the individual who strives for it. Under this *subjective* aspect, any one of the goods mentioned might be sought by an individual (erroneously, of course!) as his final end.

However, from the point of view of the object sought, its worth, or its ability to perfect a man, these things cannot be man's final end. Considered *objectively*, then, health, wealth, power, or other finite goods cannot be man's ultimate end because they do not perfect man. They do not make him wholly perfect. At best, they are intermediate ends, objectively considered.

There is, however, an end or object or goal which is not desired for the sake of something else. There is something which is desired for itself alone. This end or object which is desired for itself alone is the reason why all the other goods are desired. In other words, the final end is the reason why a man desires the partial ends. What is this final end which signals "stop" for all man's cravings? What so satisfies him that he rests when he attains it? What so completes his happiness that he seeks nothing beyond it? Let us see.

Man is restless until his desires are fulfilled. Now man would have no peace or happiness so long as he desired things endlessly. There must be some object, some end, some goal which is the final goal, the completely satisfying thing. It is the reason why other things are desired. It is the reason why a person's desires point out the course of his actions. The completely satisfying thing is the *terminus* of all man's strivings.

That last end which satisfies all man's yearnings is not a particular good thing like wealth, for this merely satisfies the desires for bodily comfort or for power and prestige. The last end cannot be a particular good thing like health, for this is only a physical perfection, and not a permanent perfection at that. It cannot be a particular good thing like virtue, for this perfects only the soul of man. It must be a good that perfects the whole man, body, soul, mind, heart, and will. And that good must be not a particular good or any number of particular goods. It must be the universal good, the supreme good which leaves nothing more to be desired in the body, the soul, the heart, the mind, and the will of man.

Now there is only one perfect good, one supreme good, one last end, one object which can perfect the entire man and bring all his desires to rest. That universal good, that supreme good is God. God is man's last end. "In perfect happiness, the entire man is perfected," says St. Thomas. It is the attainment of that goal which brings perfect happiness. Man can be perfectly happy only when he possesses God. He has varying degrees of happiness insofar as he approaches God in this life. St. Thomas expresses this all very neatly when he says: "Naught can lull man's will save the universal good. This is to be found not in any creature, but in God alone.... Wherefore God alone can satisfy the will of man.... Therefore God alone constitutes man's happiness."

Wealth, fame, power, friends, health, virtue, and so forth can be means of attaining God. They can never be the end; that is, they can never substitute for God. They bring partial happiness only insofar as they lead man to God. They are said to be *good* only insofar as they contribute to the acquisition of the universal good. They can never be more than particular *goods* which only partially satisfy, and therefore only partially bring man's desires to rest. They are steps to the final goal and they are of value and importance only because they are leading toward it. If they are broken loose from their connection to the final end of man, then wealth, health, friends, fame, power, honor, and so forth cease to be good. More simply stated, unless wealth, health, friends, fame, power, honor, virtue, and other things lead toward the final end and contribute to its acquisition, they are meaningless or worse than meaningless in human activity. They are positive hindrances. They are obstacles to a man's march toward happiness. They are causes of sorrow, despondency, brutality, jealousy, hypocrisy, deceit, loss of purpose, of peace, of happiness, of God.

Discussing the possibility of created goods satisfying the desires of man, St. Thomas remarks: "It is impossible for any created good to constitute man's happiness. For happiness is the perfect good which satisfies the appetite [i.e., the desires] altogether; else it would not be the last end, if something yet remained to be desired."

St. Augustine expresses this truth when he says: "Our hearts were made for Thee, O God, and they cannot rest until they rest in Thee."

Let us sum up. Objectively considered, that is, as some object outside of man, ultimately desired and attainable by him, as man's final end, is the universal good which is God. Subjectively, that is, within man, that which is ultimately desired by him is the possession and enjoyment of life's goal, and that possession brings to the man who has attained it perfect happiness.

St. Thomas makes clear the difference between looking at man's last end objectively and looking at it subjectively. He explains the difference between the two by illustration. He says (my emphasis):

First, there is the thing itself which we desire to attain ... secondly, there is the attainment or possession, the use or the enjoyment, of the thing desired.... In the first sense, then, man's last end is the uncreated good, namely God, Who alone by His infinite goodness can perfectly satisfy man's will. But in the second way, man's last end is something created, existing in him, and *this is nothing else than the attainment or enjoyment of the last end*. Now this last end is called happiness.

Man's Perfect Happiness

St. Thomas repeatedly tells us that complete happiness perfects the entire man and that happiness is man's supreme perfection. Man's highest faculties are the powers of his soul, because his soul is superior to his body. The powers of intellect and will are therefore man's highest powers. They are higher than his powers to grow and to feel, for these are powers of his lower nature. Man's intellect seeks to know the truth; man's will seeks to possess the good. Therefore only perfect truth can satisfy man's intellect just as only perfect goodness can end the will's ceaseless quest for good.

Man's perfect happiness, therefore, will consist in the intellect's vision of Perfect Truth; in the will's union with Perfect Good, for only thus will man's desires be set at rest. By our intellects we shall see God; by our wills we shall love Him, and in this attainment of our goal does happiness consist.

St. Thomas says: "Final and perfect happiness can consist in nothing else than the vision of the Divine Essence." But with vision alone man would not be satisfied. Knowledge of the goal alone does not bring perfect happiness. Man must be united with the object he desires. "The Vision of the Divine Essence fills the soul with all good things, since it *unites* it to the source of all goodness," says St. Thomas (my emphasis). It is in the attainment of his desired goal that happiness essentially consists. Hence man must be united to God. St. Thomas says: "In the state of perfect happiness, man's mind will be united to God by one, continual, everlasting operation." And again: "The intellect will have its perfection through union with God as with that in which alone man's happiness consists." These are beautiful thoughts, well worth our repeated reflection.

The will of man will be perfected by the delight and the enjoyment which comes from the attainment of his final end. Then will man be in peace because his desires will have been fulfilled; man will have perfect happiness. "When a man has attained his last end," says St. Thomas, "he remains at peace, his desires being at rest."

All the above can well be summed up in the first words of the Baltimore Catechism. Why did God make you? God made me to know Him (the work of the intellect); to love Him (the work of the will); to serve Him in this world (the work of our whole being), so that we might be happy through Him in this life and with Him forever in Heaven. Knowing God, reaching the goal, and enjoying the possession of the final goal, results in happiness. "Man and other rational creatures attain their last end [i.e., happiness] by knowing and loving God," says St. Thomas.

Some Original Sources

Here are some direct quotations from St. Thomas. Can you grasp their meaning?

1. "Those things that lack reason tend to an end by natural inclination, as being moved by another and not by themselves, since they do not know the nature of an end as such, and consequently cannot ordain anything to an end, but can be ordained to an end only by another....

"Consequently it is proper to the rational nature to tend to an end as directing and leading itself to the end;

"Whereas it is proper to the irrational nature to tend to an end as directed or led by another." (*Summa Theologica*, vol. 6, p. 5)

2. "It is impossible for one man's will to be directed at the same time to diverse things as to last ends ... because since everything desires its own perfection, a man desires for his ultimate end, that which he desires as his perfect and crowning good. It is therefore necessary for the last end so to fill man's desires that nothing is left beside it for man to desire. But this is not possible if something else be required for his perfection. Consequently it is not possible for the appetite so to tend to two things, as though each were its perfect good." (*Summa Theologica*, vol. 6, p. 11)

(How does this compare with our Lord's words: "[A man] cannot serve ... God and mammon" [Matt. 6:24]?)

3. "It is impossible for man's happiness to consist in wealth. For wealth is twofold: viz., natural and artificial. Natural wealth is that which serves man as a remedy for his natural wants such as food, drink, clothing, cars, dwellings, and such like things; while artificial wealth is that which is not a direct help to nature, as money, but is invented by the art of man for the convenience of exchange, and as a measure of things saleable.

"Now it is evident that man's happiness cannot consist in natural wealth, for wealth of this kind is sought for the sake of something else, viz., as a support of human nature; consequently it cannot be man's last end, rather is it ordained to man as to its end....

"And as to artificial wealth, it is not sought save for the sake of natural wealth; since man would not seek it unless because, by its means, he procures for himself the necessaries of life. Consequently much less can it be considered in the light of the last end. Therefore it is impossible for happiness, which is the last end of man, to consist in wealth." (*Summa Theologica*, vol. 6, p. 18)

4. "Our end is twofold. First, there is the thing itself which we desire to attain: thus for the miser, the end is money. Secondly, there is the attainment or possession,

the use or enjoyment of the thing desired; thus we may say that the end of the miser is the possession of money; and the end of the intemperate man is to enjoy something pleasurable.

"In the first sense, then, man's last end is the uncreated good, namely, God, Who alone by His infinite goodness can perfectly satisfy man's will.

"But in the second way, man's last end is something created, existing in him, and this is nothing else than the attainment or enjoyment of the last end.

"Now the last end is called happiness. If therefore, we consider man's happiness in its cause or object, then it is something uncreated; but if we consider it as to the very essence of happiness, then it is something created." (*Summa Theologica*, vol. 6, p. 35)

5. "Perfect and true happiness cannot be had in this life ... for since happiness is a perfect and sufficient good, it excludes every evil, and fulfills every desire.

"But in this life every evil cannot be excluded, for this present life is subject to many unavoidable evils: to ignorance on the part of the intellect; to inordinate affection on the part of the will; and to many penalties on the part of the body.

"Likewise neither can the desire for good be satiated in this life. For man naturally desires the good which he has, to be abiding.

Now the goods of the present life pass away, since life itself passes away, which we naturally desire to have and would wish to hold abidingly, for man naturally shrinks from death.

"Wherefore it is impossible to have true happiness in this life." (*Summa Theologica*, vol. 6, p. 73)

6. "It must be said that every being in any way existing is from God." (*Summa Theologica*, vol. 2, p. 214)

Summary

1. Man is not the cause of himself. Man is not the adequate explanation of his existence. Man's existence has been caused by someone other than man.

2. God is the only adequate explanation of the existence of things. God is man's sufficient reason. God is man's cause.

3. No being is the cause of God. God needed no one to cause Him to exist. God always existed. No being existed prior to God in order to be the cause of God. God is uncaused. He is the cause of everything else. He is the uncaused cause.

4. God is man's first cause because man came from God. God is man's last end because man is destined for God. Man is the most noble of earthly creatures because he is destined for an eternity of happiness with God.

5. Everything in the universe seeks its own good. This is true of both inanimate and animate creatures. Creatures below man are driven to their goal by forces within them implanted there by God.

6. Man is directed toward his goal by reason. The human will, acting deliberately, chooses the actions necessary to reach the goal.

7. There is one supreme goal of all the universe with its many natures. That one supreme goal is, of course, God, for all natures strive toward God as toward their end.

8. Man's crowning good is knowledge and love. When man knows God he knows everything. When he loves God, he loves the most that he can love. God is infinite truth and perfect love. God is the goal of man's intellect and will.

9. God is man's objective final end. Happiness is man's subjective final end. Man will find that perfect happiness only in God who is supremely good and lovable in Himself.

10. Lesser things than God can never be man's final end. They never satisfy all his desires. They leave him with desires unfulfilled. Wealth, power, fame, honor, health, virtue, and the like cannot be man's complete satisfaction. They cannot perfect man wholly.

11. All good things are means to the supremely good being: God. Finite good things are stepping stones to the Infinitely Good Being. Finite things bring us happiness in proportion as they bring us closer to God.

12. The intellect of man will have its perfection through union with God. The will of man will have its perfection by the delight and enjoyment it will experience in its union with God.

For Study and Discussion

1. Explain why nothing can cause itself "if its existence is caused," as St. Thomas says. Can a man bring himself into existence? Explain.

2. Who brought God into existence? Discuss.

3. Everything about God can be explained by the fact that He is an infinitely perfect being. Tell why.

4. Man's dependence is acknowledged by saying that man was created by God. Explain.

5. A sufficient reason is a completely adequate explanation of something. Is God His own sufficient reason? Is man his own sufficient reason? Explain.

6. Explain: Whatever a man does, he does it for an end.

7. What is the end toward which all things tend? What is the perfection of such a thing as a fruit tree?

8. Does each nature in the physical universe tend toward its own specific end? What is the one end toward which the physical universe as a whole

tends? How can you account for this unity of striving toward a common goal?

9. How do minerals tend toward their perfection? plants? brute animals? man?

10. What is man's crowning good? Which are his highest powers?

11. Explain: God has implanted natural inclinations in every nature in the universe. Discuss the reasons for this.

12. List some of the things which attract man as desirable and good. Explain their value in the light of man's final end.

13. What is the difference between an intermediate goal and the final goal?

14. Explain this statement of St. Thomas: "It is necessary for the last end so to fill man's appetite, that nothing is left beside it for man to desire." Discuss this point: Must the last end be *one* or can it be *more than one* desirable thing?

15. What does St. Thomas mean by this: "That in which a man rests as in his last end, is master of his affections, since he takes therefrom his entire rule of life." How is it possible to lose one's soul?

16. Why cannot health or wealth or friends or fame and the like completely satisfy man? Why do they not perfect man's whole nature?

17. Explain St. Augustine's prayer: "Our hearts were made for Thee, O God, and they cannot rest until they rest in Thee."

18. What is man's ultimate end objectively considered? What is man's ultimate end subjectively considered? How can God be said to be man's perfect happiness?

19. How is the will of man perfected? Quote St. Thomas. In what will the intellect of man have its perfection? Quote St. Thomas.

20. Why should each of us strive to know and to love God in this life?

For the Advanced Reader

St. Thomas Aquinas:
   Summa Contra Gentiles, vol. 3, chaps. 1–2, 16–18, 25–32, 37, 48, 63
   Summa Theologica, vol. 6, pp. 1–85

Farrell, Walter:
   A Companion to the Summa, II, chap. 1

Any good book on Christian ethics

3

Man: His Acts

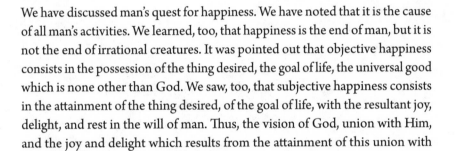

We have discussed man's quest for happiness. We have noted that it is the cause of all man's activities. We learned, too, that happiness is the end of man, but it is not the end of irrational creatures. It was pointed out that objective happiness consists in the possession of the thing desired, the goal of life, the universal good which is none other than God. We saw, too, that subjective happiness consists in the attainment of the thing desired, of the goal of life, with the resultant joy, delight, and rest in the will of man. Thus, the vision of God, union with Him, and the joy and delight which results from the attainment of this union with God, constitute man's ultimate end. Man was made for happiness; man was made for God.

Now that is all very good with respect to man's end or purpose. To attain that end is a personal matter. Each man must reach it for himself. Eternal beatitude is not handed out in gift packages to anyone. A man must plan for it and work toward it throughout his entire rational life. Infants and the insane, of course, can do nothing, while they remain in those conditions, to attain their final end because they have not the use of reason which is absolutely necessary in this endeavor. The only activity possible in infants and in the insane is activity on the sense level. They live and feel and know on the sense level only. They have sensations of pain and pleasure, of sight, hearing, taste, touch, and smell. They have no intellectual knowledge. Therefore their activities cannot be strictly human activities — actions for which they are accountable. They are not accountable until their actions are directed by reason and a deliberate will. No amount of physical strength of itself can bring one even a step nearer to one's eternal reward. A man must labor and by his own deliberate actions win or lose the goal of life.

Directed Activity Is Human

Our present discussion therefore will be the activity which man puts forth in search of his goal of happiness. We mentioned earlier that all activity is motion toward a definite end or goal. We must realize that motion toward a definite goal presupposes the action is performed by an intelligent being. Haphazard movements, like a feather flying in the wind, are not *directed* movements. They are not planned, not guided, not done for a purpose — with an end in mind.

Let us look at activity in the movement of all nature toward its goal. You would not say that the sun had an intellect and a will and so deliberately chose to shine, would you? Or that the stars directed their own twinkling as officers direct traffic? Or that plants directed the development of future new plants contained in the seeds they produced? And yet all these things are activities directed toward definite goals; all these are activities or movements done for a purpose; but the direction of these creatures does not come from the creatures themselves. Rational movements can never come from irrational beings. That would be asking of them more than they could do.

It is God who directs all created natures, including man, to their proper goal. Man, however, because of his free will, may follow the promptings of his nature or he may refuse to follow them. If he follows them, he will attain the supreme good of his nature, the universal good which is God. If he refuses to follow nature's inclinations toward its proper end, man fails to reach the supreme good; he may fail to attain even partial goods; he falls short of reaching his goal. His life becomes a tragic failure.

Perhaps we can make this point more clear. It is so important that one ought not to miss its meaning. For a man, by his own actions, either achieves his proper end or he fails miserably. Is there one of us who *wants* failure in life's ultimate purpose? One who considers it a good thing, desirable and worthy of being pursued? One would speak foolishly who says he does.

Have you ever desired something very much? Did you obtain the object of your desire? Was there joy in its possession and use? For each of us, this is a common enough experience. First there is a desire for something. Finally there is happiness in its possession, enjoyment in its use. But between these two stages, there are other steps. The desire for a car arises because of the desirability of a car: we can go places; we can see things; we can have fun; we can save time; we can conserve energy; and the like. But certainly no degree of intensity in our desire can actually give us the car. If we want the car we must do something about getting it; we must jump into action, go to work, decide upon possible ways and means of getting it, but even then our work is not finished. Once we have chosen the most suitable means of procuring the car, we must actually use those means to procure it. Only then will we be happy, satisfied, and at rest, at least with respect to this particular desire. Only then can there be happiness in the attainment of our object; joy in its possession and use.

All this is saying that between the desire and the satisfaction of the desire, man must act. He has something to do. He must plan and deliberate and judge and choose and execute. And this is precisely the kind of movement, of activity, which we call human activity, human acts.

Human acts are deliberate actions undertaken by the free will of man, under the control of man's reason which prompts the action. They are done for a purpose, with a definite end in view, a precise object to attain, and from the attainment of which man hopes to derive happiness.

Human versus Nonhuman Actions

Human actions, therefore, differ from the actions of non-human beings. This point ought to be very clear on a number of scores. First, happiness is the peculiar goal of man and this is obtained (or lost) through human acts. Creatures below man have neither intellect nor will, and so they cannot desire an end or choose the means thereto. Furthermore, the will of man seeks the universal good. He accepts partial goods (such as money, friends, fame, glory, health, and so forth) only as installments of the universal good which is the completely satisfying object, because it leaves nothing more for man to desire. Non-human beings, however (angels are not considered here), seek only particular good things to satisfy particular present needs. They are not, and indeed they cannot be, aware of the universal good which is capable of satisfying all desires. A dog seeks food because he is hungry. A tree sends out rootlets because it requires water. Neither tree nor dog thinks of these things as means to life and life's purposes. Indeed, they cannot even think!

Man desires particular good things only because they lead him to the ultimate good thing which is wholly satisfying, which satiates all his desires, which leaves nothing more to be sought, which excludes unhappiness and which brings man's will to rest. Man knows and wants the good without limit. Others, the lower natures, seek things that are limited goods.

The Good in Particular

There is a vast difference between these two *goods*. All nature, we have said again and again, is directed toward God as toward its last end. Man, therefore, is directed toward God, since he is part of nature. Each nature, however, tends or moves toward God according to the capacities of its nature. We do not expect an average fifth-grade child to solve problems in geometry. Nor do we expect an infant to swing an axe or wield a sword. These things are beyond the capacity of the persons in question. Neither do we expect a tree to know that it exists, and why it exists, and how it can accomplish its purpose. It is sufficient for a tree to respond to the inclinations of its nature, to move according to the forces of nature which are within it, producing blossoms, fruit, and seeds. It does not *know* anything about these things. It cannot even *feel* the loss of a limb, smell the fragrance of its blossoms, or enjoy the chatter of gay birds nested in its bosom. It can only act blindly, unknowing and unfeeling, following the impulses of physical nature. To do all these things constitutes its *good* and to this *good* it is impelled by nature.

Neither do we expect a dog to know its goal, although it may know physical pain, pleasure, hunger, thirst, and similar sense knowledge. For a dog, it is sufficient to answer the instincts of its nature, to eat when it is hungry, to sleep when it is tired, to drink when it is thirsty, to run from pain, to preserve its life, and so on. It does not know the *reason* for these things. It is prompted by nature to do them and it senses that it is *good* to eat, to drink, to flee, to fight, to sleep, and so forth. These things constitute particular good things for a dog.

Man Knows End and Means

But we do expect man to know his goal, to know the reason why he exists, and to know the steps necessary to reach his end. We expect this because man has an intellect which knows reasons, causes, goals, means, purpose, and so forth. Man can see that finite things like food, clothes, friends, fame, wealth, health, and others are particular good things bringing only partial happiness. These things can be possessed with unhappiness. For example, are all healthy people serenely satisfied? Are all wealthy people happy? Are all well-fed and well-clothed people without anxiety? Man can recognize the insufficiency of these imperfectly good things. He can see that each of them is desirable, not in itself but for a further purpose; as when he wants a car, not just to have a car, but in order to take trips; as when he seeks money, not for the sake of having money, as does a miser, but that he might procure food, drink, and pleasures for himself.

Partial goods, in other words, are sought as a means to an end; they are wanted for some other purpose than just the mere possession of them. They do not and they cannot bring man perfect satisfaction of his desires precisely because they are wanted, not for themselves but for an end beyond themselves.

Immediate Goals

We have learned that whatever a man wants, he wants it because of some final goal or purpose. He wants it either because it *is* the final goal of his life or because it leads to it or *apparently* leads to it. It is a matter of ordinary experience that some men make money or power the ambition of their lives. They seek it, in illusion, as their final end. Others seek money or power because they think it will bring them honor, which is the final ambition of their life. In this sense such things are not even partially good things. They seduce a man, they draw him away from his real purpose, from the perfectly satisfying good, from complete happiness, from God.

An illustration will clarify this all-important truth. Restating it, it runs thus: the end or purpose directs and calls forth all movements. A man acts because he wants something. A man desires the means to the end because he desires the end. And he desires a series of means which might be called intermediate ends because of the one final end or goal or purpose he has in mind. For example, I desire with a very great longing a tour through South America. That is my goal. Because I desire that trip, I desire also the means I must use to make that trip not only possible but actual. I must act. I must procure passports, money, clothes; I must pack, bid farewell, secure reservations, choose companions, and so on, all of which might be very annoying to me, but which I nevertheless consent to because I so heartily desire the trip. This is an example of having an end and of pursuing the activities which make the attainment of the end not only possible but actual.

Now let us press this further. Let us say that I desire the trip to South America not merely for itself, but because I want a raise in my salary as a teacher. The tour of South America will make me eligible for the increased pay. Here we have the case of an end which is desired, not for itself, but for a further purpose — for an increase in pay. Because of this further purpose, the tour of South America is not an end in itself. It is a means to a further end, and in itself it might be considered at most an intermediate end. But I desire the increase in pay because I have aged parents whom I must support. Now we see that the increase in pay is not wanted for itself, but for a further purpose, and so it, too, becomes a means to a further end, and is seen now as merely an intermediate end. It is after every intermediate end has led to a further imperfect end until there is no further end to be sought, that one has reached the final end, the reason why all the other partial ends were sought.

It is this final end, on account of which all other things are undertaken, that we have termed, in the preceding pages, man's ultimate goal, which is the possession of the perfect good, and that is none other than God.

And once more let us say that it is only man, among all earth's creatures, who can know and desire the supreme good because of which he directs all his energies to its attainment.

Now a proper understanding of this is vital to each of us, precisely because it is by those deliberate actions, those willed movements directed by the intellect in the pursuit of the good, that man reaches the goal of life or falls short of it. In other words, man's acts of intellect and will, those movements by which man tends to fill his capacity for happiness, are responsible for a man's saving or losing his soul.

Acts of Man versus Human Acts

Actions such as these are called human actions. Other actions performed by man are known as acts of man. They are actions such as breathing, digesting, growing, and so forth which are spontaneous acts of nature. They are not acts under the control of reason and moved by the will. Man cannot will the beating or the non-beating of his heart. That is beyond his control. He cannot will to digest and assimilate his food or not to do so. These things are taken care of by nature apart from the will of man. A man is not held responsible in the sense of sinning if, without interference with the ordinary process of nature, his food is not assimilated or his breathing becomes difficult and spasmodic or he remains a midget all his life. Ordinarily speaking, these things are not under the control of the intellect and the will.

In speaking of human acts, we have used such expressions as these: under the control of reason; moved by the will; direction to a goal; and so forth. Because it is precisely in these activities that man differs from lower creatures, human acts differ from the movements of lower natures. It is a principle that we must never lose sight of, that all nature tends toward the good of nature according to the individual capacities of the different natures which comprise the universe. Thus man tends toward good under the direction of reason and upon the choice of his free will.

The Universal Good

As lower natures seek a particular good thing, the higher nature of man seeks not a particular good as its ultimate satisfaction but a good that is broader, fuller — a good that is so abundant that it overflows man's whole being and brings him complete satisfaction. A brute is tied down, as it were, to this or that good thing, as sleep, food, rest, drink, escape, and so forth. Man is not so tied down. He can reject such particular good things for the sake of a higher good. To fast during Lent is within the power only of man. He can abstain from eating (a particular good) in view of a higher good, namely, self-mortification and merit. A brute could not do this. It is driven to particular good things by its senses. Only man can be master of himself in the presence of finite *goods.*

The unlimited good is what wholly attracts man. Limited goods are only partially attractive. Thus he can *choose* among a number of particular good things, always keeping his eye fixed, as it were, on their relation to his ultimate good to which his rational nature impels him. So that, since man is bound only to seek his ultimate good, the particular goods are for him a matter of choice — means to his final end.

It is because man's intellect seeks all truth and man's will seeks the perfect good, that man himself can be satisfied only with perfect truth and with universal good. Infinite truth and supreme goodness are found only in God who alone is man's last end as He is his first beginning.

Reason and the Will

Let us look into the activity of the intellect and of the will to see the part played by each in those movements *of* man which we have called human acts. Reason is the captain; will is the crew. Reason sights a desirable particular good thing and calls it to the attention of the will. The will may choose it or reject it. If it chooses the desirable particular good thing which the intellect presents to it, the deliberate will (i.e., the will acting on the command of reason) then starts the activity which results either in the possession of its object with joy, or in its loss with sadness. Going back to St. Thomas's statement of the nature of human acts, we recall that a human act is one undertaken under the direction of reason with a knowledge of the end to be attained.

It is the work of the intellect to single out the possible good things which may make an appeal to the will. All things that a man wants must first be known before they can be wanted; they must first be known to the intellect before they can be desired by the will. When the intellect recognizes a particular thing as good and desirable, it introduces or presents it to the will which then either chooses it as desired or rejects it as not wanted.

Let us take an illustration. My intellect knows that food is a desirable thing. Nay, it is a necessary thing to living beings. My intellect, therefore, presents to the will the suggestion of a juicy steak as a desirable, particular good thing. The will considers the suggestion. Though desirable, it is not at this moment desired by the will. The suggestion is rejected. Free will has chosen not to have the juicy steak. This is but the beginning of the will's movement. Let us suppose the will had chosen the steak as desirable and as immediately desired. That choice would not be enough. It would not bring the steak to my plate. The will must be moved to act to cause the steak to be brought to me. Following upon the choice of my will, reason issues the command and I am moved to take the required means. I deliberately call the waiter and order steak.

Have you ever been satisfied just with *ordering* steak? Did you not want to see it, have it, taste it, enjoy it? The point is this: the will does not rest, it will not be satisfied, unless it attains the object it desires. In this illustration the will is unsatisfied unless and until the steak is put in my possession and I derive pleasure from its proper use.

Briefly, now, in summary, let us say that the intellect recognizes a thing as good and presents it as such to the will. The will, upon the recommendation of the intellect, desires it (or not). Commanded by reason, the will moves to get it (or not). Still under reason's direction, the will attains the good and enjoys its possession (or not).

This is what we might call the mechanism behind the deliberate acts of man. There must be knowledge of the goal and of the various means to reach the goal. There must be choice of the goal and of the suitable means to the goal. This constitutes a deliberate act — an act under the control of reason, directed toward a definite end, and sought after by the will on the command of reason.

Common Goal of Human Actions

If human nature is found in every human being (and it is) then every human being must desire the same goal of human nature. Whatever it is that sufficiently attracts man, so as to be the sole cause of all his efforts, must be the same for all of them. This cannot be riches for not all human beings desire riches nor place the same value upon them. Neither can it be friends for the same reason. Nor honor. Nor bodily pleasures. Nor virtue. We have seen that that attractive lure which makes man try to get what he wants is the desire for happiness. He seeks what he desires because it will bring him happiness. This is repeated throughout the human race in every individual who has control of his actions. Everything he does is through a desire for happiness. However, we must remember that this desire for happiness is not a free act. Every man desires it *naturally* — just as naturally as he desires food, air, companionship, and so forth. The desire for happiness is part of man's natural equipment. It is a means to his return to God.

Who Performs Them?

We have tried to show the great importance of human acts. Let us now question, to whom are these acts possible? The answer is simple: to every human being who has the *use* of reason. Human acts are not limited to the educated, to the rich, to the mature, to the free. Human acts are possible in every member of the race provided he has a functioning intellect which knows the good, and an unconstrained will to choose the good. A brief glance at human nature will convince anyone of this. Human nature impels man toward the universal good. It gives to man the capacity for knowing and desiring the universal good. Human acts are nothing more than the deliberate movements of the will to seek that good which reason presents to it. Hence human acts are found in all human beings who have the use of reason. Of necessity this must be so. Only deliberate human acts can bring man to the goal of human life, and since all men have a common goal, all men must have common means to the attainment of that distinctively human privilege, the possession of infinite good which is God.

By way of summarizing this chapter, let us recall that human acts are self-directed acts. They aim at a definite goal. They are deliberately planned and executed, and because this is true, a man is responsible for his human acts. They proceed from the will's desire to possess an object it thinks to be truly good. They terminate either in the attainment of the object, accompanied by joy in its possession, or in the frustration of the desire, accompanied by sorrow, discontent, dissatisfaction. Because the will of man seeks the universal good as the needle of the compass seeks the north, man can never be perfectly satisfied with particular good things. For this reason he may choose any given particular good thing inasmuch as it will lead him toward his final goal or he may reject any particular good inasmuch as it does not completely satisfy his desires. Thus a man might wish to become famous inasmuch as he hopes it will bring him honor which, to him, seems a desirable thing. Yet another man will scorn fame, not desiring it at all, because he recognizes that it is but an imperfect good and not completely satisfying. Man is free to choose or not to choose a particular good thing. But by the very movements of his nature he must ever seek the universal good — for that alone will perfect man — make him wholly a man.

Nature demands this. Inasmuch as every nature acts according to its natural tendencies in seeking the good, so man *must* seek the universal good, since his intellect and will can be satisfied with nothing less. Man's will must choose the universal good because the universal good is what man's nature insists upon having. It is that which completely satisfies all the natural tendencies of a human being, which alone can make him happy.

Where Is Rest Found?

Human actions, therefore, are steps in the pursuit of a perfect end. Any step that leads to that end is desirable inasmuch as it leads there. But man cannot find complete rest in any step on the way to his final goal, any more than one can find absolute rest in the course of a journey. Human acts are movements going somewhere, stepping surely along the road to the final end of human life, or else stalking away from the goal of happiness in deliberate repudiation of it. The difference lies in the difference between good and evil human acts.

There can be absolutely no rest in surrendering the goal; there can be no complete rest in halting at one of the intermediate stations; there can only be sad delusion in the attempt to make finite, imperfect, perishable good things the terminal of our quest for the universal good. God is none of them. And since He alone can be the goal of man's life, He alone is the end of man's journey, the reward of his labor, the satisfaction of his restlessness, the cause of his happiness.

Some Original Sources

Here are some quotations from St. Thomas. How many of them can you understand? How many of them can you explain?

1. "Man and other rational creatures [angels] attain to their last end by knowing and loving God: this is not possible to other creatures [irrational creatures], which acquire their last end insofar as they share in the Divine likeness, inasmuch as they exist or live, or even know." (*Summa Theologica*, vol. 6, p. 16)

2. "Of actions done by man those alone are properly called *human* which are proper to man as man. Now man differs from irrational animals in this, that he is master of his actions. Wherefore those actions alone are properly called human, of which man is master. Now man is master of his actions through his reason and will ... therefore those actions are properly called human which proceed from a deliberate will. And if any other actions are found in man, they can be called *actions of a man*, but not properly human actions." (*Summa Theologica*, vol. 6, pp. 2, 3)

3. "A thing tends to an end by its action or movement, in two ways:
   (a) First, as a thing moving itself to the end, as man;
   (b) Secondly, as a thing moved by another to the end, as an arrow tends to a determinate end through being moved by the archer who directs his action to the end.

"Therefore those things that are possessed of reason move themselves to an end, because they have dominion over their actions, through their free-will which is the faculty of will and reason.

"But those things that lack reason tend to an end by natural inclination, as being moved by another and not by themselves; since they do not know the nature of an end as such, and consequently cannot ordain anything to an end but can be ordained to an end only by another." (*Summa Theologica*, vol. 6, p. 5)

4. "It is proper to the rational nature to tend to an end, as directing and leading itself to the end: whereas it is proper to the irrational nature to tend to an end, as directed or led by another, whether it apprehend the end as do irrational animals, or do[es] not apprehend it, as is the case of those things which are altogether devoid of knowledge." (*Summa Theologica*, vol. 6, p. 5)

5. "All things that lack reason are, of necessity moved to their particular ends by some rational will which extends to the universal good, namely, by the Divine Will." (*Summa Theologica*, vol. 6, p. 6)

6. "Of actions done by man, those alone are properly called *human* which are proper to man as man.

"Now man differs from irrational animals in this, that he is master of his actions. Wherefore those actions alone are properly called human of which he is master.

"Now man is master of his actions through his reason and will... therefore those actions are properly called human which proceed from a deliberate will." (*Summa Theologica*, vol. 6, pp. 2, 3)

7. "Man must, of necessity, desire all whatsoever he desires for the last end, because whatever man desires, he desires it under the aspect of good. And if he desire it, not as his perfect good which is the last end, he must, of necessity, desire it as tending to the perfect good." (*Summa Theologica*, vol. 6, p. 12)

In discussing whether all men have the *same* last end, St. Thomas points out that men may be in disagreement as to what actually constitutes their last end. He says:

8. "We can speak of the last end in two ways:
   (a) First, considering only the aspect of last end;
   (b) Secondly, considering the *thing* in which the aspect of last end is realized.

"So, then, as to the aspect of last end all agree in desiring the last end, since all desire the fulfillment of their perfection, and it is precisely this fulfillment in which the last end consists.

"But as to the *thing in which this aspect is realized*, all men are not agreed as to their last end: since some desire riches, as their greatest good; some, pleasure; others, something else." (*Summa Theologica*, vol. 6, pp. 14–15)

9. "Happiness can be considered in two ways:

"First, according to the general notion of happiness, and thus of necessity every man desires happiness. For the general notion of happiness consists in the perfect good, but since good is the object of the will, the perfect good of a man is that which entirely satisfies his will.

"Consequently, to desire happiness is nothing else than to desire that one's will be satisfied. And this everyone desires.

"Secondly, we may speak of happiness according to that in which it consists. And thus all do not know happiness because they know not in what thing the general notion of happiness is found." (*Summa Theologica*, vol. 6, p. 84)

Summary

1. Man *naturally* desires happiness. It is a need of his rational nature just as the need for food and rest are needs of his physical nature.

2. Happiness consists in the attainment of the goal of life. Happiness is perfect when it results from the attainment of the final end of human life. Happiness is partial or imperfect when it results from the attainment of intermediate ends or partial goals of human life.

3. The goal of human nature must meet the needs of man's higher powers. His intellect seeks truth; his will seeks goodness. Man's intellect seeks all truth, infinite truth; his will seeks the highest good, supreme goodness.

4. Man's goal can be nothing less than perfect truth and supreme goodness or else his intellect and his will would remain unsatisfied. Man's goal, therefore, is God who alone is perfect, infinite truth, and perfect, unalloyed goodness.

5. The goal of human life can be attained (or lost) only through deliberate actions. These actions are under the command of reason; they are consented to and executed by the will. When these conditions are present, the action is a human action, a deliberate deed, and one for which the person performing it is wholly responsible.

6. All activity is movement. It is movement from what is considered desirable to the attainment of that desirable thing. It is activity directed toward the attainment of the goal.

7. The intellect and the will control human acts. The intellect suggests the desirability of some *good*; the will acquires and seeks it, and when it has attained it, possesses it with joy. The will may reject the good thing as being not now desirable. This is an instance of the exercise of the will's freedom of choice.

8. Universal good, or unlimited good alone can wholly attract the will. Particular good things can move the will insofar as they are deemed to be installments of the universal good. The will is not necessarily moved to them and it is free to reject them.

9. Man must be perfected through his intellect and will, that is, through his human actions. All nature tends toward the specific perfection of each nature. Some natures are perfected by existing; others by living; others by living and feeling. Man is perfected by knowing and loving the true and the good.

10. All human activity is done for a purpose. An involuntary action, such as breathing, is not considered a *human* action. It is called an *act of man.*

11. The goal or end to be attained is that which calls forth the will into action.

12. Some things are desired for the sake of a further good and not for themselves. They are intermediate ends or purposes.

13. One thing and only one thing must be the last or final thing to be desired. It is desired for itself alone and not for a further end. In its possession man's desires are brought to rest.

14. All human beings have the same ultimate end; they are impelled by the same desires to seek their perfection; they all naturally seek goodness and happiness. They all have the same means to their end: namely, deliberate actions under the control of reason and will.

15. All humanity has God for its end. Only man has God for his end in so intimate a union. Every man inasmuch as he is man has God for his end in the distinctively human way, through union of intellect and will with God.

For Study and Discussion

1. Explain the statement: "Man naturally seeks happiness as the lungs seek air and the body nourishment."

2. Why must there be a "final end"—one on account of which nothing further can be desired?

3. Explain the difference between *end* and *means.*

4. In the human pursuit of happiness, what is the end? What is the means?

5. Explain how a desirable object might be considered as an end and also a means.

6. Discuss the difference between particular goods and the universal good. Which does man seek by nature? In which is he free to choose? Explain.

7. Explain the statement: "*All* nature as a whole, and *every* nature in the universe, tends toward its final end according to natural capacities."

8. Explain the grades of perfection in created natures and indicate how each tends toward the final good of its own nature.

9. Why can only perfect truth and supreme goodness completely satisfy man's desires?

10. What is meant by the expression: "bring man's desires to rest"?

11. Define and explain human acts.

12. Why should a man be held responsible for human acts?

13. How do human acts differ from brute acts and the involuntary acts of man?

14. Can you prove that wealth, power, friends, fame, health, and other goods cannot be man's perfect happiness?

15. What role is played by the intellect and by the will in the execution of a human act?
16. What is the distinctive way in which God is man's last end?

For the Advanced Reader

St. Thomas Aquinas:
    Summa Contra Gentiles, vol. 3, chaps. 24, 64, 65
    Summa Theologica, vol. 6, pp. 1–51

Farrell, Walter:
    A Companion to the Summa, II, chaps. 2–4

Any good book on Christian ethics

4

Man: His Good

In discussing the nature of human acts, those deliberate acts which a man performs in the quest of an end which is known and desired by him, we have used the word *good* in speaking of a particular good and of the universal good. It appears to be desirable (and therefore *good*!) at this point to discuss the precise meaning of the word *good* when it is used in speaking of human activity.

All Things Seek Good

To explain, simply but adequately, the meaning of *good* in the philosophical sense, we must consider once more the whole of nature and natural inclinations. St. Thomas tells us: "The good is that which all things seek." Now everything in the universe has its specific nature and with it the natural tendencies or yearnings of that particular nature. A tree, for example, is different from a rock and the tendencies of a tree are not the tendencies of a rock. A tree is not fully a tree if it merely exists. To be wholly a tree, it must nourish itself, grow, and produce new trees. By nature, a rock does not tend to nourish itself, to grow, or to produce new rocks. To exist is the only capacity of a rock. It fulfills its purpose by merely existing. Animals have some tendencies that are different, and in their way, higher than those in plants and non-living beings. Animals have the capacity for seeing, hearing, tasting, touching, smelling, moving about freely, as well as for deriving pleasure from doing these things. A cow, to be fully a cow, must do more than merely exist.

Nature itself directs each of the various creatures. They can do nothing but submit to nature's promptings. When a dog, for instance, is hungry, he *must* seek food. Nature's promptings are insistent. Nature has this way of seeing to it that every particular thing in the universe fulfills its purpose; otherwise the whole of nature, the universe itself, could not attain its final end. Of course, it is not necessary — is it? — to say that *nature* is not equipped with a reason to know and a will to seek the final goal of the universe. *Nature* is not intellectual. The intellect and will which direct nature in this pursuit of its end are the intellect and the will of God, the Author of nature.

Now that is *good* toward which each thing tends by its nature. It is *good* for a tree to seek water, to produce roots, to feed, to grow, and to reproduce new trees. It is *good* for a dog to eat, to sleep, to walk, to hear, to see, and so forth. It is *good* for a rock merely to exist. That is what St. Thomas means when he says that all nature tends to God as to its final good; that is, irrational beings by existing, by living, and by knowing on the sense level, but rational beings, like men and angels, by knowing and loving, which is a higher level. That last point merely means that man seeks his last end through knowledge of the end to be attained and choice of the means to it.

It is this precise point which is the distinctive mark between man and non-human beings. Plants and minerals seek their end, prompted by natural tendencies, without knowledge of any kind. Nature and the God of nature see to that. Animals seek their end, prompted by natural tendencies, with nothing higher than sense knowledge. They have no intellectual knowledge of the final end nor of the means to the final end of their existence. They have no choice of the end nor of the means to the end. A dog cannot choose not to get hungry, neither can he choose not to eat when nature inclines him to eat. Moreover, animals have no knowledge of the relation which exists between end and means. A dog does not know, for instance, that food is the means to self-preservation. It takes more than sense knowledge to understand such a relationship. And more than sense knowledge an animal does not have.

Man Differs from Lower Creatures

Man, on the other hand, has intellectual knowledge, and thus he can know (1) the nature of an end, (2) the nature of the means to it, and (3) the relationship which exists between the end and the means. Man can choose to take his own life! Man can choose to acquire an education or to remain in ignorance. Man can choose to follow the natural inclinations of his being or he can interfere with the attainment of his end. God has given man free will. Only in one thing is man not free: namely, his rational nature imposes upon him, without his will, the capacity and the desire for happiness. No matter how hard man may try to escape it (but who really does want to escape happiness?), he cannot free himself from his natural craving for happiness. It is as much a part of his makeup as are his eyes, his heart, his power of speech, his intellect, and his will. Without these, a man would be less than man. So, too, would he be less than man without the natural desire for happiness. On this point St. Thomas writes: "Happiness may be considered as the final and perfect good, which is the general notion of happiness: and thus the will *naturally and of necessity tends thereto.*"

A man can hinder the attainment of that goal of happiness, to be sure. He can put obstacles in the way of its attainment. He might never achieve perfect happiness because he might never seek the complete good of his entire nature. He might refuse to respond to the cravings of his intellect for truth and of his will for the supreme good; he might attempt to satisfy his natural inclinations by means of wealth, of health, of fame, of any partial, particular physical or mental good. A man may interfere with the attainment of his final purpose, but he can neither deny nor obliterate his desire for happiness, for adequate happiness, for complete satisfaction.

It stands to reason that man, having a higher nature, is urged to and requires, by his very nature, a higher end than other creatures. That end must be in accord with man's nature. Man's rational nature requires the rational good to perfect and satisfy it. Man can never be wholly satisfied with good things of the body alone; nor with good things of the soul alone, such as virtue; for the highest desires of man must be satisfied if man is to be perfectly happy. These highest desires of man are for all truth and all goodness: infinite truth and infinite goodness, and they can be found in none other than God. Some creatures there are, therefore, in nature, whose perfection consists in existence; others, whose perfection consists in existing and living; other natures are higher: they perfect themselves only through existing, living, and possessing sense knowledge, as of sights, sounds, odors, pain, pleasure, fear, and the like. But existing, living, and sense knowledge is not perfect enough for man. His inclinations tend toward a higher kind of knowing and toward freedom of choice: they are perfected in knowledge and in love. These are the natural *appetites* or desires of the specific natures in whom they are found. They urge the several natures to each one's appropriate end or goal. It is the attainment or the satisfaction of these *appetites* or desires which is *good* for each nature.

The Good Satisfies

Good in the philosophical sense, therefore, is that which satisfies the appetites or that which leads to the satisfaction of the appetites. What wholly satisfies the desires or inclinations of a nature is the best possible good for that nature. What leads to the satisfaction of the inclinations of any given nature is a partial good for that nature.

Thus, man's greatest appetite or desire is happiness. This desire is implanted in man's very nature by God. It is, therefore, a *natural appetite* and its fulfillment constitutes a *good* for the nature of man. Perfect happiness, therefore, constitutes the perfect good for man. St. Thomas says: "A fitting good, if indeed it be the perfect good, is precisely man's happiness: and if it is imperfect, it is a share of happiness, either proximate, or remote, or at least apparent."

Now let us go back once more to the principle that all things desire their good. It is important to note that everything that a man desires, he desires under the appearance of good. It might be truly good or only apparently good, but it is seen to be *good* to the one desiring it.

A thing is good for man only if it be in conformity with the end of man; only if it be in accord with his natural tendencies; only if it helps man to fulfill his purpose in life. A ball, for instance, is good if it aids in recreation and creates exercise and fun, but not if it is used to break windows or heads. A thing is good if it fulfills its purpose. Thus a fruit tree is good if it produces good fruit, but not good if it produces bad fruit or no fruit. A man might like a steak, in which case it brings temporary satisfaction to a natural desire, and so it constitutes a good for that man. If, however, he is ill and has been forbidden the use of meat, then it would not be good *ultimately* for him to eat it. What would be good only for the palate, would not be good for his general health, and the good of one's health is a good superior to the good of the palate. Therefore the farther-off good demands precedence over the proximate and immediate good. This must be so inasmuch as the nearer or more immediate good is merely a means to a farther and more ultimate good; otherwise it would lead away from, rather than toward, the final good of man, which is perfect happiness.

Apparent Goods

Thus it frequently happens that a man craves a proximate and apparently good thing (remember everything is desired under the aspect of good!) through a mistaken notion of what is really good. The intellect is liable to error in its judgments concerning real and apparent good. The will, you recall, follows the judgment of the intellect. Hence if the intellect is in error, the will makes choice of only an apparent good but not of a true good. This is the reason why man needs the guidance of law, that he might the more readily and accurately judge the nature of real good and present it truly to the power of choice in the will.

It is, for example, good to have money. A man may desire all possible wealth on the plea that it will bring him all possible good. He would have, he thinks, all possible desires fulfilled, or at least the means to their fulfillment. In this instance, however, the intellectual judgment would be in error. Wealth provides at most only material goods; it cannot supply goods of the soul, nor can it purchase man's final goal. Of this St. Thomas writes:

> The definition of happiness given by some, "Happy is the man that has all he desires, or, whose every wish is fulfilled," is a good and adequate definition *if* it be understood in a certain way; but an inadequate definition if understood in another. For if we understand it simply of all that man desires by his natural appetite, it is true that he who has all that he desires, is happy, since nothing satisfies man's natural desire except the perfect good which is happiness. But if we understand it of those things that man desires according to the apprehension of the reason, it does not belong to happiness to have certain things that man desires; rather does it belong to unhappiness insofar as the possession of such things hinders man from having all that he desires naturally.

An infant might think a knife *good* for play, but in that he is in error. That is why parents hide knives or keep them out of reach.

It is precisely in the pursuit of good that man performs those actions which will bring him to the goal of his nature. In the execution of deliberate acts he chooses the good or he rejects the good. In the choice of good things he judges either correctly, and thus attains a true good, or he judges erroneously, and chooses only an apparent good.

Kinds of Good

A thing is physically good if it is in accord with the physical promptings of man's nature, as a good dinner, for example. A thing is intellectually good if it is in accord with the yearnings of man's intellect for truth, as a good education. A thing is morally good if: (1) the action is done under the command or control of reason (not entirely through emotions such as anger, sorrow, despair, hilarity, and the like); and (2) if it leads toward man's final end. Thus it is a morally good act in itself, deliberately to give an alms, but it is not a morally good act if a drunkard squanders his wages to pay for the drinks of his friends.

A moral good, therefore, is any action which is directed by human reason to the goal of human existence, either as the means to the final end, or as the final end itself.

The Good versus Evil

Some actions are always good. Some actions are always evil. We are speaking here of action in itself, in its very nature considering the end or goal of the action. Of course, one's intention changes the goodness of an action. So too the circumstances surrounding the act. These may spoil the best of actions that are otherwise morally good. It is always good to worship God. It is always evil to blaspheme God. To worship God like the Pharisees of old, for exterior show and human praise, renders that particular action bad. An action is good in itself if it leads to one's perfection; bad if it turns one away from perfection.

Some actions as actions neither lead to perfection nor hinder perfection. As actions they are morally indifferent. Circumstances in particular instances make them either good or evil. To read a book, to play a game, to carry a gun, or any such action, is neither good nor bad in itself. It neither helps nor hinders man's perfection. However, taken one by one and done by individuals, such actions may be good or may be bad according to the end, the intention, and the circumstances. To read a book in order to increase one's knowledge and love of God is a good act. To carry a gun in order to shoot a personal enemy is a bad act, but to carry a gun to defend one's country is not a bad act. To play a game for lawful recreation is good, but to play a game for an evil intention makes that act an evil act. Just as it is morally good to eat, so it is morally evil to injure oneself by excessive eating.

It will clarify a notion that is frequently very vague in many minds if we state here the nature of evil. Evil is the absence of the good which we have spoken about in this and the preceding chapter. Evil is the absence of good, as darkness is the absence of light, and sickness is the absence of health, and nothing is the absence of everything. Evil is not something positive but rather the absence of something positive; it is something negative, something lacking, and that which is lacking in evil actions is goodness.

An act is morally evil if it draws one from the good; if it leads away from the pursuit of goodness which is the pursuit of happiness. That is why evil people are unhappy people. Their back is turned to the goal; they are slinking away from the goal of goodness and are heading deeper and deeper into the morass of unhappiness. Their only chance for happiness is to determine their position, find the goal they have missed, and retrace their steps back to the road of goodness — to the ultimate good, to perfect happiness. In proportion as evil persons return to good will, they find happiness; only when they have embraced supreme goodness will they have perfect happiness, for that is the ultimate, the final end of man. Life will be over then and the pursuit of happiness ended, for man can never in this life reach perfect happiness, for not in this life will he have the vision of God and the joy of full (i.e., complete) union with Him.

Characteristics of True Good

Lest we miss the point, let us repeat by way of summary, that a thing is good, first, if it is desired; second, if it is in accord with the inclinations of nature; third, if it brings satisfaction to the one seeking it. As a tree naturally desires water, and an animal food, so man naturally desires the truth. As the desire for water is a natural desire for the tree and food a natural inclination of animal nature; so is truth a natural desire of rational nature. Finally, as water brings natural satisfaction to the tree, so does food to the animal and truth to man. These three conditions must be complied with. St. Thomas expresses this pithily when he says: "Everything is good so far as it (1) is desirable; (2) is the term of the movement of the appetite; (3) the term of whose movement can be seen from a consideration of the movement of a natural body."

When applied to man, the true good must be understood to be more than the good which satisfies man's lower nature. The true good is what perfects the *whole man*. For in man his natural inclinations are found to be a hierarchy of desires. There are first those inclinations of his nature which correspond to the needs and promote the good of his lower nature. But this is not the whole of man. There are also those inclinations which correspond to the needs and promote the good of his higher nature, of his very highest faculties. Now recognizing that hierarchy of natural inclinations, it is evident that man's greatest good is that which is desired for the good of the whole man. It is that good alone which perfects man wholly.

Only the supreme good, God, can be man's complete perfection!

Some Original Sources

We give you here some expressions and statements of St. Thomas regarding the good. Make use of them in your discussions and explanations. How many of the following can you explain or illustrate?

1. "When we say that good is what all desire, it is not to be understood that every kind of good thing is desired by all; but that whatever is desired has the nature of good." (*Summa Theologica*, vol. 1, pp. 67–68)

2. "Goodness signifies perfection which is desirable; and consequently [it signifies] ultimate perfection." (*Summa Theologica*, vol. 1, p. 53)

3. "The essence of goodness consists in this, that it is in some way desirable." (*Summa Theologica*, vol. 1, p. 53)

4. "Perfection implies desirability and goodness." (*Summa Theologica*, vol. 1, p. 57)

5. "All things by their own perfection desire God Himself, inasmuch as the perfections of all things are so many likenesses of the Divine Being.... And so of those things which desire God, some know Him as He is Himself, and this is proper to the rational creature: others know some participation of His goodness and this belongs also to sensible knowledge: others have a natural desire without knowledge, being directed to their ends by a higher intelligence." (*Summa Theologica*, vol. 1, p. 66)

(Read, in connection with this, quotations no. 4 and no. 1, "Some Original Sources," chap. 3.)

6. "Goodness is that which all things desire." (*Summa Theologica*, vol. 1, p. 58)

7. "Everything is said to be good so far as it is perfect, for in that way only is it desirable. Now a thing is said to be perfect if it lacks nothing according to the mode of its perfection." (*Summa Theologica*, vol. 1, p. 61)

8. "All things desire God as their end, when they desire some good thing, whether this desire be intellectual [man's desire for truth], or sensible [an animal's seeking a sensible good], or natural, i.e., without knowledge [as a plant developing flowers and leaves], for nothing is good and desirable except forasmuch as it participates in the likeness of God." (To fulfill one's nature properly is to participate in the likeness of God.) (*Summa Theologica*, vol. 2, p. 221)

Summary

1. The good is what all things seek. Every nature seeks the good of its nature; seeks to fulfill its natural capacities.
2. This is true of things which merely exist; of things which live; of things which live and have sense knowledge; of things which have intellectual knowledge and free will.
3. Nature itself directs each individual nature to its own proper goal. Nature does this by providing each individual thing in nature with natural inclinations which we call appetites or tendencies.
4. These tendencies are *natural* in the sense that a nature cannot be without them. For man it is just as natural for him to seek happiness as it is for a stone to exist, or a plant to feed, or an animal to follow its instinct of self-preservation.

5. Natures possessed of these tendencies cannot act otherwise. Man must seek happiness just as in his physical part his lungs must have air, and as plants must have water.
6. In man, his natural inclinations urge him to desire what is good for his nature.
7. Man's highest good is good in accord with his highest powers, and these are the intellect and will. Man's highest good, therefore, consists in perfect truth and supreme goodness. These alone satisfy man's intellect.
8. Particular good things are desirable only insofar as they lead to the goal of life.
9. The universal good is desirable in itself, for through this is man wholly perfected.
10. Human actions are good or evil according to (1) the end proposed; (2) the intention; and (3) the circumstances. Actions leading to a goal or an end are good if the goal or end is good. This considers the action in itself. Intentions and circumstances may spoil an act whose end naturally is good.
11. Circumstances may change an otherwise good act to one which is evil.
12. Acts which of themselves are indifferent become morally good or bad according to one's intention in performing them.
13. Morally good acts are under the control of reason and directed toward man's ultimate end.
14. A good act must (1) be desired; (2) be in accord with man's nature; and (3) bring rest to his desires and give him joy in the possession of what he desires.
15. Actions are always the fruits of desire. No one acts unless first he desires.
16. Evil acts turn man from his ultimate end. Evil is the absence of goodness. It is a rejection of the goal of life.
17. Life is the pursuit of goodness — the pursuit of happiness.
18. Eternity is the enjoyment of supreme goodness — rest in union with God.
19. Time is given to seek God; death to find Him; eternity to enjoy Him.
20. Man's eternal rest can be had only in God.

For Study and Discussion

1. Explain the natural appetites found in the various natures in the universe.
2. In what does the natural appetite consist? What is its purpose? How is this purpose effected? What is the result of the attainment of the purpose?
3. Discuss the various types of *natural appetites* in man.
4. Explain the presence of so many types of tendencies in one creature.

5. How do his natural tendencies cause man to differ from non-human natures in the universe?
6. Explain: The good is what every nature seeks.
7. Explain the statement: Man *must* seek happiness as the lungs seek air and the body seeks food. Why *must*?
8. Man's happiness is the universal good and to this he is directed by nature. Tell: (1) Is man free to accept or reject partial good things? Explain. (2) Is man free to accept or reject the universal good? (3) Can a man err with respect to what is good? Explain.
9. Explain and discuss: everything a man desires, he desires it under the aspect of good.
10. The *universal* good is desired in itself. Explain, then, in what way one desires the *particular* good.
11. Explain the difference between "a further end" and "a final end." What has this to do with particular good and universal good? Explain what is meant by a physically good act; an intellectually good act; a morally good act.
12. How would you define a morally good act?
13. What may spoil an act morally good in itself; that is, according to the end or goal of the act?
14. Some acts in themselves are always good. Some acts in themselves are always bad; some acts in themselves are indifferent. Explain each kind.
15. Tell how an act which is morally good in itself may be reduced to an evil act.
16. Explain how acts receive their goodness or badness from the goal toward which they lead.
17. Explain how acts become good or bad according to the intention with which they are performed.
18. Name the three conditions required for a good act.

For the Advanced Reader

St. Thomas Aquinas:

Summa Contra Gentiles, vol. 1, chaps. 37, 38, 40; vol. 3, chaps. 3, 16

Summa Theologica, vol. 6, pp. 210–276; vol. 1, passim

Farrell, Walter:

A Companion to the Summa, II, chap. 4

The Thomist: "The Fecundity of Goodness," pp. 226–236, vol. 2, no. 2, April, 1940

5

Man: His Guides

We have discussed, so far, man's last end, his human acts by which he journeys toward that last end, and finally the nature of the *good* which attracts him irresistibly to it.

Law Is Necessary Direction

It remains for us here to discuss the guidance of man to that attractive *good* in which his last end consists. To know a goal that has a strong natural attraction and to know also in general the means to that goal are not sufficient. Man still needs particular guidance all along the way lest he be betrayed and lured from the right path. One may wish to visit Canada and he may know the general direction in which he must go; nevertheless he needs a map to point out to him every mile of the way along the road. Now that detailed direction by which man is directed all along the road of life to the goal of happiness is known as law.

Probably that last statement is a revelation to you. Perhaps you have thought of law as restrictive, as prohibitive, as a killjoy. That law should in its very essence be a direction to a goal might be an entirely new concept to you. This chapter and the succeeding ones will answer the question: Is law a violation of man's freedom or is law a positive guarantee to its inviolability?

A firm grasp on the basic principles which constitute the subject matter of the previous chapters is the best preparation for an understanding of the nature and work of law. As a matter of fact, the work of this chapter has been made comparatively easy in view of the foundation laid in the preceding chapters. For in its simplest expression, law is nothing more than the direction of all nature as a whole, and of each nature in particular in the universe toward its ultimate end, the perfection of its specific being. By now you have acquired some understanding of the meaning of the repeated statement concerning the wonderful order in nature. If the universe were chaotic and unpredictable, the human mind could not calculate the disastrous effects which would follow such an actuality. But it is precisely because all nature has its origin in the wisdom and power of God, and because all nature and every specific nature tends toward God as toward its highest perfection, that the physical universe is stable, is predictable, is a place in which to live and work and pursue happiness. By way of passing, let us note here that it is only in the moral universe, that is, the world of human behavior, that there can reign disorder, upheaval, uncertainty, confusion. A subsequent chapter will explain this statement.

It is law which preserves order in the physical universe, and law was meant to preserve and *would* preserve order in the universe of human beings if all men would exercise their freedom aright, for law's aim is precisely to direct man's intellect and will in the choice of the true good.

Law a Dictate of Reason

We have linked law with order in the universe. We have said that law is the cause of that order. In general terms, law is a dictate or a command. Like all commands, it must come from an intellectual being. To be truly a law it must direct actions to a goal. Further, the command or direction must come from a legitimate lawgiver.

With respect to the order in the universe, therefore, it can be seen that some lawgiver gives to each nature its specific direction toward its individual perfection and toward the collective perfection or the good of the whole universe. The direction is found in the natural inclinations of each nature, as we have already said. The sun is directed in its energies, plant life in its tendencies, and so forth. That direction must be intelligent, that is, it must be given with an understanding of the specific nature of each created thing, through a knowledge of its goal and the means thereto. Now there is only one Lawgiver who is qualified to direct the various natures of the universe to their individual and collective good. It is He who made them; He who is their end; He who knows the nature and the end, the capacities and the means, of each specific creature.

God the Prime Lawgiver

God, the first cause and last end of all creatures, is the prime Lawgiver. He is the intellect which knows intimately and guides intelligently all things to their proper end. God is the Ruler of the universe. His direction is called law. Law, therefore, is movement directed by intelligence toward a goal, with a knowledge of the goal and the means, by one who is qualified to give such direction, for the sake of perfecting the individual natures and attaining the end of the universe. St. Thomas says: "Law is nothing else but a dictate of practical reason emanating from the ruler who governs a perfect community." Later we shall hear another definition of law by St. Thomas.

What Is the Eternal Law?

St. Thomas, continuing the discussion of law, introduces his readers to the first kind of particular law, namely, eternal law. He points out that the perfect community is the universe; the ruler who guides it intelligently is God. Even the very *idea* of the government of things which exists in the mind of God can be called law. Now the idea of government of the universe has always been in the mind of God, and since God is eternal, so too is the idea of the government of the world. This eternal idea or plan of the government of the universe St. Thomas calls eternal law.

More simply, the eternal plan according to which divine wisdom governs the world is what is known as the eternal law.

Let us consider this in the order of human events. A man intends to build a boat. He first draws up the plan. This plan provides for every feature of the boat, for size, strength, endurance, speed, capacity, and the like. The plan is not well drawn up if any details escape the vigilance of the one who makes the plan. He must provide for the operation of the boat as well as for its construction. He must provide for the coordination of all its parts and for smooth moving of the completed boat. Unless the plan is well thought out, ill-success is the necessary result.

But the plan or idea of the boat is not the boat. The boat must be built. In the essential lines and in the details, the plan must be accurately followed. But even a perfectly constructed boat is not the object of the original intention. It was not made for itself but for a further purpose. It must be put in operation, made to do the work it was built to do; made, in other words, to achieve its purpose, to attain its end. The boat was not made for the sake of the plan, nor for the sake of the boat, but for the pleasure or service of its builder. If it fulfills the purpose for which it was made, we can call the boat a good boat.

God made the universe. Now all intelligent beings work according to a plan. Since God is infinite intelligence, He undoubtedly conceived a perfect plan of a good universe. He executed that plan by making the universe. He has set it in operation, put it to work, made it do the task He had ordained it to do. God's universe, planned, created, and operating, is pursuing its purpose, is tending toward its goal, is, in other words, *good*.

In God's plan, He knew the natures He would create. He knew their goals. He knew their inclinations. He knew their capacities. He knew the direction they would need to attain their end — to be good. And why should God not know these things, for are they not the work of His divine wisdom, planned according to an eternal idea conceived in the mind of an infinite and all-powerful God?

St. Thomas, in speaking of the eternal law, says, "The Eternal Law is nothing else than the plan of Divine Wisdom as directing all acts and movements." Or again he speaks of it as "the plan of Divine Wisdom moving all things to their end." The plan, therefore, which existed from all eternity in the mind of God for the rule of the universe, became, in the course of time, at the moment of Creation and thereafter, the law for the operation of the whole universe of creatures. That law still holds. It will continue to exist, to direct, to bind nature in its strivings, until the universe shall be no more.

Natural Law in All Creatures

Now there is a difference between a plan and the carrying out of the plan; between the idea behind a thing and the thing itself. Thus, the eternal plan is not the same thing as the actual fulfillment of that idea. One is found in the mind of God: the eternal law. The other is found in the universe: in the creatures made according to that plan. In each creature there is found the direction to its goal which we call the natural law.

We see the natural law in operation when we see the various natures in the universe striving to attain their goals. When, for instance, we see a tree budding or bearing fruit; when we see the sun and the moon and the stars perform their work; when we note chemical activities, hear sounds, watch clouds float and objects fall; when we see fire giving heat; when we see birds build nests and beasts protect their young; when we see people provide for their offspring, shun ignorance, keep their contracts, live in society, then we see the law of nature at work. For the law of nature is nothing other than the natural inclinations by which nature and all specific natures seek their good. It goes back once more to the point mentioned several times earlier in this book: the whole group of natures in the universe, striving for the goal of their natures by seeking their good, manifests the law of nature commonly called the natural law. It is manifested in man as well as in lower natures. In each nature it acts by means of the natural inclinations of that nature, driving it to act properly according to God's purpose in creating it.

Have you ever heard of a peach tree or any kind of tree hatching from a chicken's egg? or a gold nugget nourishing itself on milk? or a flower building a nest for its seeds? or a bird reading his morning melody from a music staff? or an elephant doing sums in arithmetic? All that, of course, sounds very silly. But it stresses the fixity of the natural law. Each nature acts according to its capacity and its natural inclinations. It cannot cross any boundary and acquire any capacities or inclinations of a different nature. God ordained all the movements of all things from all eternity. In His divine mind the plan fixing these activities is the eternal law. In the actual carrying out of these plans at the moment of Creation and ever since, the government of the universe through natural inclinations is the natural law. And this law is fixed; unchangeable; necessary. Natures must so act. They can do nothing about it except fulfill their natural promptings; submit to the driving power of their specific natures.

In man, this divine direction according to natural inclinations and capacities is of a more elevated type because of man's more dignified nature. Even when man's direction existed only in the divine idea, it was of the more perfect type. The subject of this direction in man will constitute the content of the following chapter.

Everything Subject to Eternal Law

All natures are subject to the eternal law. It is prior in time to all other law. It is the foundation of all other law. "Since the Eternal Law is the plan of government in the Chief Governor," says St. Thomas, "all the plans of government in the inferior governors [e.g., human authority] must be derived from the Eternal Law. But these plans of inferior governors are all other laws besides the Eternal Law. Therefore, all laws, insofar as they partake of right reason, are derived from the Eternal Law." All lesser laws derive their origin and binding power from the eternal law. Not all natures, however, are subject alike to the eternal law.

Irrational creatures are subject to this law by being moved without knowledge of the law; rational creatures have *knowledge* of the law. Man is moved by his natural inclinations as are all lesser natures; but man has this added feature: he knows the law and knows its movements and knows that he is moved by it. "All actions and movements of the whole of nature are subject to the Eternal Law. Consequently, irrational creatures are subject to the Eternal Law, through being moved by Divine Providence but not, *as rational creatures are, through understanding the Divine commandment*" (my emphasis).

Man does not, however, know the eternal law as you know your hand. The eternal law exists in the mind of God, and man does not, indeed he cannot, know that as you know your hand. Man does know the eternal law, however, through its manifestations, chiefly through the order in the universe; for the eternal law produced its effect at the moment of Creation; from created natures, therefore, man can know the existence and the nature, at least in part, of the eternal law. St. Thomas says: "No one can know the Eternal Law as it is in itself except the blessed who see God in His Essence. But every rational creature knows it in its reflection, greater or less.... We cannot know the things that are of God as they are in themselves, but as they are made known to us in their effects." Thus man knows the eternal law through knowing the natural law which is closer to him, because it is in him, and therefore it is more knowable to him.

St. Thomas says:

> Since all things subject to Divine Providence are ruled and measured by the Eternal Law, it is evident that all things partake somewhat of the Eternal Law, insofar as, from its being imprinted on them, they derive their respective inclinations to their proper acts and ends. Now among all others, the rational creature is subject to Divine Providence in the most excellent way.... This is a prerogative of rational beings, of men and angels. Because of the dignity of their natures, God extends special guidance over them that they might be the more firmly assured of the attainment of their end. It is, indeed, a mark of the great goodness of God.

Eternal Law and Providence

Before closing this chapter, it might be well to include a brief discussion of divine providence. It seems advisable because throughout the chapter we have spoken of and quoted St. Thomas on the government of the world and on providence.

In our first chapter, we discussed primary principles. We saw that they were *seeds* from which might be drawn new truths, new knowledge. The principles were very broad, general truths, universal in scope. The conclusions were more restricted, more specific, particular in scope.

St. Thomas used that likeness to tell us the difference between the eternal law and divine providence and government. Eternal law is the root. Divine providence and government of the universe spring from that root. Eternal law is the seed (as a universal principle) and providence and government are contained in it (as particular conclusions). Let us see how this is.

Eternal law is the precept (or command) of God's intellect ordering all things in the universe to the common good of the universe. It is "the plan of Divine Wisdom moving all things to their end." Now this plan is very extensive.

It covers the whole universe of things. From this general (St. Thomas speaks of it as *universal*) plan, a detailed plan taking care of even the very smallest particular things must be drawn. The details are part of and flow out of the very general plan. The details are like conclusions from a seed principle. The detailed plan of the government of the world which exists in God's mind and which directs the universe is called *divine providence*.

The actual carrying out of God's eternal precept (the eternal law) according to the detailed plan in God's mind (divine providence) is called *divine government*. "The Eternal Law is the plan of government in the Chief Governor," remarks St. Thomas.

Some Original Sources

In addition to the passages already cited from St. Thomas, here are others. Are you able to explain their meaning?

1. "The eternal concept of the Divine Law bears the character of an Eternal Law insofar as it is ordained by God to the government of things foreknown by Him." (*Summa Theologica*, vol. 8, p. 10)

2. "It is evident, granted that the world is ruled by Divine Providence, that the whole community of the universe is governed by Divine Reason. Wherefore the very Idea of the government of things in God the Ruler of the universe, has the nature of a law. And since the Divine Reason's conception of things is not subject to time but is eternal ... therefore it is that this kind of law must be called eternal." (*Summa Theologica*, vol. 8, p. 10)

3. "Under the Divine Lawgiver various creatures have various natural inclinations, so that what is, as it were, a law for one, is against the law for another; thus I might say that fierceness is, in a way, the law of a dog but against the law of a sheep or another meek animal.

"And so the law of man, which ... is allotted to him, according to his proper natural condition, is that he should act in accordance with reason." (*Summa Theologica*, vol. 8, p. 20)

4. "There are two ways in which a thing is subject to the Eternal Law:
   • by partaking of the Eternal Law by way of knowledge
   • by way of action and passion, i.e., by partaking of the Eternal Law by way of an inward moving principle
"In this second way, irrational creatures are subject to the Eternal Law.

"But since the rational nature, together with that which it has in common with all creatures, has something proper to itself inasmuch as it is rational, consequently it is subject to the Eternal Law in both ways;

"Because while each rational creature has some knowledge of the Eternal Law, it also has a natural inclination to that which is in harmony with the Eternal Law." (*Summa Theologica*, vol. 8, pp. 37–38)

5. "As God is the cause of all existent things by giving them their very being, the order of His providence must include all things: because to those things to which He has given being, He must grant a continuance of being, and perfection by attaining their last end." (*Summa Contra Gentiles*, vol. 4, chap. 94)

6. "Since God is the end of all, we may conclude that by His providence He governs or rules all.

"For whenever certain things are ordered to a certain end, they are all subject to the disposal of the one to whom chiefly that end belongs. This may be seen in an army: since all the parts of the army and their actions are directed to the good of the general, namely, to victory as their ultimate end, for which reason the government of the whole army belongs to the general. . . .

"Since all things are directed to the divine goodness as to their last end, it follows that God to whom that goodness belongs chiefly . . . must be the Governor of all.

"Whoever makes a thing for the sake of an end makes use of it for that end. . . . Now God makes all things for an end which is Himself. Therefore He uses everything by directing it to its end. But this is to govern. Therefore God, by His providence, is the Governor of all.

"God is the cause of the entire order of things. Consequently He is the Governor of the whole universe by His providence." (*Summa Contra Gentiles*, vol. 3, chap. 64)

7. "The Eternal Law is the type of the Divine government. Consequently whatever is subject to the Divine government, is subject to the Eternal Law: while if anything is not subject to the Divine government, neither is it subject to the Eternal Law.

"The application of this distinction may be gathered by looking around us. For those things are subject to human government which can be done by man, but what pertains to the nature of man is not subject to human government; for instance, that he should have a soul, hands, or feet. Accordingly all that is in things created by God, is subject to the Eternal Law." (*Summa Theologica*, vol. 8, p. 34)

8. "Since providence has the ordering of things to their end, it follows that to providence belong both the ends and the things directed to the end. Therefore . . . individuals are subject to divine providence.

"Whatever exists, no matter in what way it exists, is subject to God's providence. . . . Therefore divine providence is concerned about individuals.

"Creatures are subject to divine providence, as being directed to their end, which is the divine goodness. Therefore participation in the divine goodness by creatures is the work of divine providence.... Therefore divine providence must extend also to them [i.e., to individuals]." (*Summa Contra Gentiles*, vol. 3, chap. 75)

Summary

1. The universe follows an orderly course. Its happenings are uniformly predictable.
2. The order in the universe results from a plan according to which the universe was made. Perfect sustained order could not result from chance.
3. Only an infinite mind could plan and effect the ordered universe.
4. God is the Creator of the universe, the Author of the plan according to which it was made.
5. The plan of the universe and its many different natures, which existed in the divine wisdom from all eternity, is the eternal law.
6. In creating the various natures, God gave definite inner natural inclinations directing each to the proper goal of its nature.
7. By means of these inner directive tendencies, all nature obeys God's creative plan.
8. By these inner tendencies, the proper actions of each nature are assured. Thus nature's actions are always predictable.
9. The inner direction in each nature, and in the whole of nature, is the law of nature, the natural law.
10. The eternal law is prior to any other law. It is the source and reason of all other law. It is the standard by which human laws are judged.
11. All beings are subject to the eternal law.
12. Man knows the eternal law through its effects which are evident in the universe. He does not know it perfectly. The blessed in Heaven know the eternal law more fully than men on earth because they know God in His essence.
13. Irrational creatures are subject to the eternal law by being moved by it without knowledge. Man is subject to the eternal law with a knowledge of it.

For Study and Discussion

1. Explain the essential notion of law.
2. Why is law an indispensable aid and not a hindrance to the universe, including, of course, man?
3. In what does the eternal law consist? How does St. Thomas define it?
4. Explain the presence and the workings of the natural law in the universe.

5. Are the eternal law and natural laws known to creatures? Explain.
6. The eternal law, imprinted on the various natures, gives to each nature specific inclinations to its proper end. Explain this statement.
7. How is the eternal law the source of all other laws? Explain St. Thomas's statement regarding the chief governor and the inferior governors.
8. What reasons can you give for the fact that in man there is a more noble imprint of the eternal law than in inferior natures? In what capacities or powers of human nature would you expect to find the more noble imprint?
9. Why is God the only being qualified to direct each and all of the various natures in the universe?
10. Can you illustrate the fixity of the law of nature?
11. Discuss the possible effects one would expect if the law of nature were unstable.
12. Mention at least six manifestations of the natural law. Include some from various levels of creation.

For the Advanced Reader

St. Thomas:
> *Summa Theologica*, vol. 8, pp. 1–39
> *Summa Contra Gentiles*, vol. 3, chaps. 64–94

Farrell, Walter:
> *A Companion to the Summa*, II, pp. 363–411

Any good book on Christian ethics

6

Man: His Personal Inner Direction

In discussing the eternal and natural laws in the preceding chapter, we have been setting the stage for the present one. It was indicated in chapter 5 that since man has a more dignified nature, escaping the limits of the sense knowledge which binds the brute to a low level of knowing, it is consonant with his greater dignity to have within him a more perfect imprint of the eternal law.

In addition to this reason, we must note, too, that since man has a destiny far superior to that of the lower natures, he must of necessity require a superior type of direction to his goal. He has this superior direction in what is known as the natural *moral* law. Of course, it is found only in human beings, for the reasons given above.

Principles Govern Knowing and Doing

In the first chapter of this book we discussed the nature of principles — those sources or seeds of knowledge. We saw that the most basic principle which directs all human thinking is that one by which man knows naturally, without study, that a thing cannot be what it is and be something else at the same time and in the same respect. A piano, while it is a piano, cannot be a tree. Without this basic principle by which a thing is declared to be what it is, man could not take his first step forward toward the knowledge of truth. Note, however, that this basic principle governs the field of *knowing*.

Besides *knowing* things, man *does* things. He acts. There is included in his capacities a sphere of *doing*, and just as he can go wrong in his knowing and arrive at false knowledge, so man can go wrong in his doing and so perform evil acts. To prevent wrong doing, nature provides man with basic first principles which govern his doing, just as to prevent wrong thinking, it provides him with basic first principles to safeguard his thinking. The study of this chapter will give the earnest student a thorough grasp of those principles and their proximate conclusions which make it possible for man to attain his ultimate end without fear of going tragically astray.

The Natural Moral Law

We have said that man's goal has been fixed by nature and ultimately by the God of nature. That goal of all man's strivings is the good: man seeks the good of his nature through natural inclinations. The good of man's nature is not a single physical good nor all the physical goods in the universe. Man's rational nature seeks the rational good, and that is the universal good, which, when possessed, constitutes man's perfect happiness. It is the end of the journey for man.

It is precisely that goal of the rational good which is determined for man by another; namely, by his Creator. He is not free to set his own goal. His freedom, as we shall see later, consists in the free choice or rejection of the established goal and of the steps leading thereto. This goal, to which man's rational nature inclines him as surely as his physical nature inclines him to food, is the basis of the natural moral law in man. What leads to that end, is good; what deters man from that end is evil. This is merely to repeat what was said in a previous chapter, that what is in accord with his natural inclinations, what conduces to man's end, is good; and what is not in accord with his natural inclinations is therefore not conducive to his nature, and so is evil. Upon this principle rest the dictates of the natural moral law. Its source is in the eternal law; its direction is toward the good.

Elements of the Natural Moral Law

In investigating the nature of the natural moral law, we must first consider the essential elements which comprise it. The natural moral law has three elements or necessary parts. First, there is that group of tendencies which we have called the natural inclinations. Second, there is in man the light of reason by which he recognizes those inclinations of his nature. Third, there is the command or dictate of the intellect proposing to man that he do good and avoid evil. This command proposed by reason is nothing other than the proposition to act according to his nature. Since man's nature is rational, man is thus urged by the prompting of his intellect to act rationally, and that means to let reason be his guide, be the master of his actions.

Only Man Is Moral

Man, therefore, alone of all the natures in the universe (excepting the angels) directs himself through reason, to his goal. Beasts do not. Plants do not.

Minerals do not. Chemicals do not. Man does. Remember, however, man does not establish his goal; he does not decide what goal he wants. He finds the goal already established by God in his nature; his job is to attain it. In attaining it, he directs himself by the light of reason and the command of reason, to act according to the promptings of his reasoning nature. Those promptings urge him toward the good, toward happiness, toward God. Man therefore is empowered to direct his activities toward God and happiness, or (and this is tragic when it happens) he may use his free will to reject the goal; he may use his free will to refuse to take the steps leading to it. If he does, he has freely chosen not to have the goal. He has freely chosen to act contrary to the promptings of his nature. He has freely chosen to be unhappy. He has freely chosen to be without God. Man's freedom is at the same time his greatest glory because it so closely resembles the freedom of God; it is also his greatest responsibility because it puts the blame of his defeat fairly and squarely on his own shoulders.

Knowledge of the Moral Law

Before discussing the proposition of reason, which is the very essence of the natural moral law, let us consider the stages by which man comes to a knowledge of the natural moral law. We have said that man alone knows the end toward which his natural inclinations tend. He knows this because he is possessed of the light of reason. However, though every human being possesses these natural capacities for knowing and willing, it is only with the use of reason that he actually comes into the possession of the knowledge of end and of means. Hence babies, though they have all the natural capacities of any other human being, do not know their inclinations as such, nor do they know the end to which they are tending. However, babies are capable of knowing these things later when impediments to the operation of reason are removed at that time which we commonly speak of as *the age of reason*.

In addition to knowing the end by the light of reason, and recognizing the end as *good*, there must be also the natural desire of the will for the good. Let us consider the aspects of the natural moral law in a given situation. Man's intellect desires truth (1. This is the natural tendency). Through his natural faculty of reason (2. The light of reason) he recognizes this tendency (3. Knowledge of the end). The tendency, however, existed and manifested itself long before he was seven years of age. Every young child asking "Why?" exhibits the tendency of the mind to grasp the truth. Now knowledge brings satisfaction. It banishes ignorance. It constitutes a partial good for a man, and so it furthers him on his quest for perfect truth. It brings him nearer his goal. But the will naturally desires whatever will perfect man (4. The desire of the will for good), and thus it desires knowledge.

Reason, then, issues its command (5. The proposition of reason) ordering the will to pursue the end proposed. The will, always desirous of the good, accepts the intellect's proposal and moves to acquire the knowledge. The deliberate will sets in motion all those activities which direct the means and which terminate in the acquisition of the end, namely, of truth. Considered in itself, that is, in relation to the end of man, such an act as outlined is morally good. Bad intentions or circumstances can spoil it, however, but we are considering the act here only in relation to the end of man.

The following things, therefore, must be thought of in considering the steps:

1. Knowledge of natural inclinations, furnishing a knowledge of good (for good is what is in accord with the inclinations).
2. The will's natural inclination to good or to its end. For this no reasoning is necessary, merely the knowledge of good.
3. The dictate of reason: do good. This means: act for your end.

The Proposition of Reason

The general proposition which the intellect makes is a *natural* proposition; that is, it is from within; spontaneous; unmistakable; that is, man understands its command as soon as he understands the meaning of *good* and of *evil*. It is so insistent that no one can miss its prompting. The first time a child feels guilty when stealing a cookie or doing any other wrong act marks the time when he first ignores the proposition of reason and so commits his first conscious misdeed.

It is this first general proposition of reason which declares that some acts are good and therefore to be done, and others are evil and therefore to be avoided. It is this which constitutes the dictates of the natural moral law; which subjects the human mind to the will of God in the government of the universe; which establishes the goodness or badness of human acts; which, in other words, establishes *morality*.

We have said that the moral law is *natural* in man; that this proposition of reason is *inborn*. To grasp the full significance of the meaning of this and to enable us to understand the succeeding paragraphs, we will turn our attention once more to the nature of first principles. First principles are seeds of knowledge. They acquire their truth not from any other previous truth (except infinite truth, which is God) but they are the immediate source of other truths. First principles are self-evident; they are grasped by the mind just as soon as the mind understands the meaning of the terms or expressions used. For example, just as soon as the mind understands what is meant by the terms *whole* and *part*, it understands the principle that the whole is greater than any of its parts.

Primary Principle of Doing

Now there are first principles in the two kinds of activities of the human reason. There are the first principles of the speculative activity of the human mind. That is the activity of the intellect which focuses its attention on new facts of *knowledge,* when the mind operates in the field of *knowing* things. Then there are first principles of the practical activity of the human mind when the mind operates in the field of *doing* things. That is the activity of the intellect which directs the *actions* of man. The first principle which the practical activity of the intellect proposes to man for the direction of his actions is the principle that he must do good and avoid evil. It is a seed principle because from it the standards of right behavior are drawn; upon it, as upon a firm foundation, a fixed morality is established — a morality fixed on the natural reason of man and the wisdom of God, instead of on the shifting sands of changing customs and ungrounded opinion.

This primary principle of morality contains conclusions which are discovered when a person reasons about the statement: do good; avoid evil. The conclusions which one reaches from reasoning thus are called the *secondary* principles or standards of behavior. *Secondary* doesn't mean that they are less important, but that they are drawn out of the first; they follow as consequences of the first as when, for instance, incomplete learning is the consequence of faulty habits of study, or to provide all the necessities of life follows as a consequence from nature's prompting that a father must provide for his offspring.

Knowability of the Primary Principles

St. Thomas tells us that the natural moral law imprints itself radically (i.e., it is rooted) in the depth of every created nature. Its various principles are known to the minds of men in varying degrees of clearness. However, the primary principles are immediately known, as we have said before. They are known by everybody having the light and the use of reason. They are the same in every human being existing wherever there is a human heart beating in a body. They are known equally well by all. This must be so, for the primary dictates of the natural moral law flow from human nature itself. They are man's primary guide to his end; all men and every man requires their guidance. Nature teaches everyone, without the aid of teacher or book, that good must be done; that we must harm no one, and so forth. The primary principles cannot be erased from the hearts of men. That they need no external pronouncement — no teacher or textbook knowledge — before being known to man is expressed by St. Thomas when he says that primary principles "need no further promulgation after being once imprinted on the natural reason to which they are self-evident; as, for instance, that one should harm no man and other similar precepts."

Knowability of Secondary Principles

In addition to the universally known primary principles or propositions of reason there are others, the secondary ones, which are contained in the first ones and which are revealed by only slight study. Even unlearned persons can recognize their promptings after but slight consideration of the primary principles. These secondary principles flow from nature readily as do the primary principles. "Some matters connected with human actions are so evident," says St. Thomas, "that after very little consideration one is able at once to approve or disapprove of them by means of the general first principles." Among these secondary principles are the standards of behavior easily recognized by us as belonging to the subject matter of the Ten Commandments.

Let us take an illustration. The natural moral law in its primary precept dictates that good should be done and evil avoided. We see in this command at once and without long consideration the proposition: harm no one. Human reason, by reflecting on the command not to harm, readily comes to the conclusion that one must not kill another; that one must not steal; that one must not lie, and so forth, for to do any of these things is to harm another. These standards of behavior are what we have called above, immediate conclusions from the first principles of good behavior; they are the secondary precepts of the natural moral law.

Secondary precepts are easily recognizable; they are known and observed by all mankind in general. No one of these secondary principles is neglected by all people. In fact, the majority of them are observed by everyone. That one must care for one's parents and provide for one's offspring are universally accepted facts of right human behavior. That this is so, proves how easily they flow from human nature since they make themselves clear to the mind of mankind generally.

Their Universality

Like the primary precepts, the secondary ones are the same in everyone; that is, the same commands are dictated by reason and they are recognized by mankind as such. There is this difference, however, between the universality of the primary and of the secondary principles: the primary principles are absolutely universal whereas the secondary precepts are only morally universal. That is, everyone without exception, knows the first principles; the vast majority of mankind know the secondary principles. All of the people know most of the precepts. Many of them know all of the precepts. There can be some very few exceptions. A small minority lacks knowledge of one or other of the precepts, but no precept is unknown everywhere. These exceptions hinder the secondary precepts from having absolute universality. They are morally universal.

By *know* we here mean *know naturally*, that is, merely by the light of reason and by reflection upon its first general commands. Education and experience, of course, complete what may be lacking through inexperience, dullness of intellect, and so forth. Despite the fact that the subject matter of the Ten Commandments is impressed by nature upon the heart of man, God undertook to reveal, in definite words at a definite time and place, the ten basic commands which nature urges man to obey. Why did God do this? That man might understand more readily and grasp more clearly and know more surely those things to which his intellect, through reasoning and experience, would have eventually led him. God thus graciously confirmed nature's constant urge to goodness, and at the same time brought man to a quicker, fuller, firmer, clearer knowledge of nature's good, sooner than an individual man could otherwise have attained it.

Secondary precepts of the moral law are for the most part easily reasoned, proximate conclusions. They are *proximate* inasmuch as they follow quite closely on the heels of the dictates of the primary principles. There are, however, other conclusions that are more remote; more difficult to grasp; more liable to error in their dictates. Of these St. Thomas remarks: "Some matters cannot be the subject of judgment without much consideration of the various circumstances, which all are not competent to do carefully, but only those who are wise.... Such belong to the law of nature, yet [they belong to it] so that they need to be inculcated [by teachers], the wiser teaching the less wise."

The remote conclusions, therefore, are not so universal. All will not be in agreement concerning them, even though all be in agreement concerning the primary and secondary principles from which the remote ones are derived. This is because in particular matters there are different circumstances surrounding otherwise similar acts; because the human mind is more likely to err in regard to details; and because several judges are not always of the same mind in regard to particular circumstances and details. Not only are remote precepts far less universal than the others but they are neither everywhere the same nor equally known by all. Moreover, it is a fact that they can be and often are lost sight of.

Recalling St. Thomas's comment that only the wise are competent to judge of certain matters, it can easily be understood that it is in the remote principles of the natural moral law that authority operates through the passage of laws made by "the wise"; that is, by the legislators of a community. These judge the way in which the primary and secondary precepts are to be applied in particular cases, and their judgments constitute what is known as *positive law*. Positive law — whether divine or human — has its foundations in the propositions of reason which constitute the natural moral law. The consideration of this kind of law will have our attention in the next chapter.

Permanence of Primary Precepts

It will be undoubtedly profitable at this point to consider the question as to whether or not the dictates of the natural moral law are changeable. Is the answer difficult? Not if we consider that human nature in itself is constantly human nature; that is, human equipment is always human equipment. Man has an intellect; man always has had and always will have an intellect. Man has a will; man always has had and always will have a will. Man has natural promptings toward the good of his nature: some of these promptings are in common with promptings of every other creature, as, for instance, the prompting of self-preservation. Everything wants to keep itself in existence; nothing wants annihilation! Man also has promptings in common only with living natures. These are, for example, desires for food, pleasures of the senses, and so forth. Man has promptings, too, that are utterly his own, unshared by lower natures. An example is his yearning for truth or his desire for the good of his nature. Man is always man. A man always carries the whole of human nature around with him.

Hence man is always and constantly prompted by nature to seek his own good. He is prompted to seek his good on all three levels of inclinations mentioned above. Therefore the first principles of the natural moral law are constant principles. They are unchangeable and unchanging. It is of these that St. Augustine remarks that they can never be erased from the heart of man. Of course they cannot, because man's nature can never be erased from the depths of man's being. No matter how like an animal a man may act, or no matter how like a stone he may merely exist, unknowing and unfeeling, a man is a man nevertheless. He cannot cross the boundaries of natures and become another nature.

Thus the primary precepts of the natural moral law are immutable. Good is always to be sought. One should always act for his end. Evil should always be avoided. Conclusions drawn from the primary principles share the immutability of the principles from which they are drawn. Variability in conclusions would mean variability in the principles, but we have just shown that the principles are invariable. The law of honesty, for instance, which is a secondary precept (a proximate conclusion of the primary principles) can never become a law of dishonesty. The laws prompting one to care for the old and for offspring can never cease to be laws. In a particular act, however, the proposition or command of reason may be said to be blotted out. This might be due, in the first place, to the fact that one's reason does not grasp the connection between the command and one's action. This dullness of reason can be due to an evil life, to anger, lack of attention, forgetfulness, and the like.

So, too, secondary precepts may cease to apply in particular cases due to circumstances. One would not, for example, be obliged to return a borrowed knife to a madman, nor a rope to a demented person. Variations might occur, too, because of the want of clarity or readiness with which men recognize the secondary precepts. For example, through evil practices and corrupt habits, the conscience might be dulled and the dictates of reason thus be enfeebled or drowned out. In this way secondary precepts, in their application, can be blotted out of the human heart by evil persuasions, corrupt habits, and vicious customs. For such causes among some men theft was not considered wrong.

Stability of Remote Precepts

Remote precepts of the natural moral law, being conclusions drawn from the primary precepts, share, as do the secondary ones, the immutability of the principles in which they are contained. It stands to reason that if the principles are stable, constant, so must be the conclusions drawn from them.

Subjectively, however, that is, on the part of individuals, changes might occur in the remote precepts even as in the secondary precepts for causes mentioned in the preceding paragraph. Since the remote precepts deal with the details of human behavior, there is a possibility of much admixture of error in man's reasoning. Dull intellects will not see some of the remote conclusions. Only the wise do, in an adequate way, says St. Thomas. The farther away one moves from the primary principles which are *general* commands, universal in application, the more one is likely to fall into error. Therefore for the details of human life, far removed from the universal primary precepts, the more direction man needs in his conduct. Positive law supplies this necessary direction.

Without entering into a discussion of positive law here, for it will be presented in the following chapter, let us note that its work is in the more proximate things of life — the details of daily living. Positive law is not derived by way of conclusions from the primary principles of the natural moral law. Since it is concerned with the details of human behavior under varying circumstances and times, it is necessarily *variable*. But we saw that the primary principles and their conclusions were invariable.

Positive law is derived from the natural moral law by way of determination. That is, positive law determines *means* of attaining the end proposed by the natural moral law. The many human laws which are made daily by human legislators are determinations of the natural moral law applied to particular situations. It is sufficient in this chapter to show the relation of this kind of law to the natural moral law, and to show that it is — indeed it must be — variable. We shall discuss it in detail in chapter 7.

Universal Norms of Morality

It should be evident that there is and must be a universal norm of morality. This means that there are certain norms of right behavior which are binding upon all. This is so in virtue of the eternal law of God whereby the whole of nature and each nature individually must seek its good and attain its perfection.

Let us see what relation conscience bears to the natural moral law.

We have said repeatedly throughout this work thus far that man must direct himself to his goal under the eternal direction of God. That direction of God is the eternal law and divine providence. The point is this, that man must direct himself while keeping his eye fixed, as it were, upon God's law which indicates the proper course. Man's reason is his personal director. His acts must be under the control of reason.

The direction of reason, God's and man's, brings man to his goal. It should not be surprising, therefore, to learn that conscience, which judges the rightness or wrongness of human actions, is an act of reason. It is an act of human reason. It is an act of the practical aspect of human reason. Conscience is not reason. It is a particular act of reason. The difference between reason and conscience is the difference between a man and that man's action. Conscience applies the precepts of the natural moral law to particular cases and judges of the rightness or the wrongness of the act performed or about to be performed.

Let us see somewhat how the process goes. Man's practical intellect presents him with self-evident moral principles. On these principles man reasons to discover the goodness or the evil of his particular human acts. The judgment which follows the thinking declares something to be morally good or morally bad. Conscience is that judgment. Conscience is a norm of morality. It helps us to see our particular deliberate actions in relation to the requirements of the moral law. Naturally, since it is a dictate of man's judgment, conscience is an internal norm of morality. It is also a proximate or immediate norm because it tells us here and now what relation our conduct bears to the moral law requirements.

Conscience is said to be the subjective norm of morality because it is internal. The objective norm of morality, that is, that which exists outside of man as the rule or measure of his conduct, is the eternal law of God. The eternal law, as a standard of morality, is not proximate. It is remote. However, both conscience and the eternal law are norms within easy reach of man because they are rooted in man's nature as his director and judge. They are the same for all human beings. They will bring each individual to his goal and so perfect his nature if the individual will have it so. They cannot direct man if his free will chooses otherwise. Man's reason and his free will are at the same time his great glory and his inescapable responsibility.

Some Original Sources

This page contains additional statements of St. Thomas to challenge your thinking capacity. How many of them could you explain? How many of them can you link up with definite statements on the preceding pages? Try it. Select a statement or series of statements in this chapter and find a comment of St. Thomas which would substantiate the text.

1. "There are certain things which, after a more careful consideration, wise men deem obligatory." (*Summa Theologica*, vol. 8, p. 115)

2. "The practical reason is busied with contingent matters, about which human actions are concerned: and consequently, although there is necessity in the general principles, the more we descend to matters of detail, the more frequently we encounter defects ... [hence] in matters of action, precept is not the same for all as to matters of detail, but only as to the general principles: and where there is the same precept in matters of detail, it is not equally known to all." (*Summa Theologica*, vol. 8, p. 47)

3. "The Natural [Moral] Law, as to general principles, is the same for all both as to the precepts and the knowledge of the precepts.

"But as to certain matters of detail which are conclusions of those general principles, it is the same for all in the majority of cases, both as to the precept and as to the recognition of the precept, and yet in some cases it may fail:

1. As to the precept by reason of certain obstacles,
2. As to the recognition of the precept.

"Since in some [persons] the reason is perverted by passion, or evil habit, or an evil disposition of nature; thus formerly, theft, although it is expressly contrary to the Natural Law, was not considered wrong among the Germans, as Julius Caesar relates." (*Summa Theologica*, vol. 8, p. 48)

4. "The first thing that falls under the apprehension of the practical reason, which is directed to action, is 'good,' since every agent acts for an end under the aspect of good.

"Consequently the first principle in the practical reason is one founded on the notion of good, namely, that good is that which all things seek after. Hence this is the first precept of law, that good is to be done and ensued, and evil is to be avoided.

"All other precepts of the Natural Law are based upon this: so that whatever the practical reason naturally apprehends as man's good [or evil] belongs to the precepts of the Natural Law as something to be done or to be avoided." (*Summa Theologica*, vol. 8, p. 43)

5. "There belong to the Natural Law,

1. First, certain most general precepts, that are known to all; and
2. Secondly, certain secondary and more detailed precepts which are, as it were, conclusions following closely from first principles.

"As to those general principles, the Natural Law in the abstract, can nowise be blotted out from men's hearts.

"But it is blotted out in the case of a particular action insofar as reason is hindered from applying the general principle to a particular point of practice on account of concupiscence or some other passion.

"But as to the other, i.e., the secondary precepts, the Natural Law can be blotted out from the human heart either by evil persuasion ... or by vicious customs and corrupt habits, as among some men, theft, and even unnatural vices were not esteemed sinful." (*Summa Theologica*, vol. 8, p. 52)

6. "Sin blots out the law of nature in particular cases, not universally, except perchance in regard to the secondary precepts of the Natural Law in the way stated above." (See no. 5.) (*Summa Theologica*, vol. 8, p. 52)

7. "A change in the Natural Law may be understood in two ways:

"(1) First, by way of addition.

"In this sense nothing hinders the Natural Law from being changed: since many things for the benefit of human life have been added over and above the Natural Law, both by the Divine Law and by Human Laws:

"(2) Secondly, a change in the Natural Law may be understood by way of subtraction, so that what previously was according to the Natural Law, ceases to be so.

"In this sense, the Natural Law is altogether unchangeable in its first principles: but in its secondary principles, which are certain detailed proximate conclusions drawn from the first principles, the Natural Law is not changed so that what it prescribes be not right in most cases. But it may be changed in some particular case of rare occurrence, through some special causes hindering the observance of such precepts as mentioned above." (See no. 3.) (*Summa Theologica*, vol. 8, p. 50)

8. "It may happen that a man has some knowledge in general and yet he does not know in particular that this act must not be done....

"Again it must be observed that nothing prevents a thing which is known habitually from not being considered actually; so that it is possible for a man to have correct knowledge not only in general but also in particular, and yet not to consider his knowledge actually; and in such a case it does not seem difficult for a man to act counter to what he does not actually consider.

"Now that a man sometimes fails to consider in particular what he knows habitually, may happen through mere lack of attention ... sometimes on account of some hindrance supervening, e.g. some external occupation, or some bodily infirmity; and in this way a man ... fails to consider in particular what he knows in general." (*Summa Theologica*, vol. 7, pp. 361–362)

9. "Now among all others, the rational creature is subject to Divine Providence in the most excellent way insofar as it partakes of a share of Providence....

"Wherefore it has a share of the Eternal Reason whereby it has a natural inclination to its proper act and end: and this participation of the Eternal Law in the rational creature is called the Natural Law." (*Summa Theologica*, vol. 8, p. 11)

Summary

1. Man's superior nature requires a superior type of direction. This special direction proper to man's rational nature is known as the natural moral law.
2. The natural moral law has fundamentally three basic notes, the third one of which is the very essence of the natural moral law:
   1. The natural inclinations of man toward his proper end.
   2. Knowledge of these through the light of human reason.
   3. The proposition of reason commanding that in the light of man's end good ought to be done and evil avoided.

3. The natural moral law is that dictate of reason whereby man is impelled to seek his perfection.

4. The natural (physical) law is imposed on all creation. The natural moral law is specially given to man for his proper guidance.

5. Of all physical creatures (angels are not considered here), only man directs his activities toward his goal. He alone can be master of his actions.

6. The natural moral law impresses itself upon the heart of every human being. It impresses itself with varying degrees of clarity, based on how close to man's natural good are the things it commands.

7. The first and most general proposition of human reason is that good must be done and evil avoided.

8. This is the seed principle from which other rules of human behavior are drawn forth.

9. In this primary proposition are contained other propositions which man can very easily know by simple reasoning.

10. There are also propositions which are not so easily recognized or clearly known. These are the remote propositions. They are known only by long study or by being taught. St. Thomas says only "the wise" know them.

11. The primary propositions are unchangeable; they are in every human being; they are knowable by all; they are self-evident; they are innate.

12. The secondary propositions—the Ten Commandments—are known by the vast majority of mankind. No precept is unknown everywhere.

13. Those who do not know the secondary precepts of the moral law fail to grasp them through such reasons as imperfect reasoning, bad habits, vicious customs, and so forth.

14. The remote precepts are subject to change because they deal with the details of human existence which are constantly subject to new regulations.

15. All the propositions of reason which constitute the natural moral law draw their force from their connection with the eternal law. No proposition of the moral law can contradict or deny the eternal law.

16. Conscience is an act of man's reason. It is a judgment passed by his practical reason made upon the rightness or wrongness of man's actions.

17. The eternal law and conscience are the universal norms or standards of morality.

18. The eternal law is the objective measure of the morality of human acts; conscience is the subjective measure of human acts.

For Study and Discussion

1. Explain the following statement: Man *must* seek the universal good.

2. How do the goodness and badness of a human act depend upon the goal of life?

3. Name and explain the three essential features of the natural moral law. In which does the moral law *essentially* consist?
4. Discuss: Only man directs himself to his goal.
5. Why does man need the light of reason before the proposition of reason can be formulated? What else must proceed the proposition?
6. In the process of drawing forth a moral proposition, the intellect needs to know particular facts, present circumstances, and so forth. Can you account for this?
7. What is the difference between the primary and the secondary precepts of the moral law? What is the difference between a principle and its conclusions? Explain.
8. Discuss the knowability of the primary and the secondary precepts.
9. What is meant by the *remote conclusions* of the moral law? How permanent are they? How knowable?
10. Discuss the stability (i.e., immutability) of the primary precepts; of the secondary precepts.
11. The natural moral law cannot be erased from the human heart. Explain this statement. Can it be erased in individuals?
12. Explain conscience: its nature and its work.
13. What is the objective norm of morality? What is the subjective norm of morality?
14. Why does true morality require a *fixed standard* of judgment?
15. Can you explain why customs, opinions, and usefulness cannot be standards of a genuine morality?

For the Advanced Reader

St. Thomas:
Summa Theologica, vol. 8, pp. 9–21, 22–26, 40–52, 76–83

Farrell, Walter:
A Companion to the Summa, II, pp. 363–411

Any good book on Christian ethics

Man: His Extrinsic Guide

The more one descends to details in human affairs, stretching farther and farther from basic principles as from an anchorage, the more liable one is to confusion and error. It is not an isolated fact of high school experience that a boy or girl can explain a geometric theorem with ease, but in the application of it to an *original* finds himself floundering and seeking help. And so it is with man in the direction of his human acts.

Life's goal is clear. The basic proposition of reason is self-evident and insistent. The proximate conclusions are almost immediately evident and likewise lucid. But as to the details — well, that is a different story. That honesty, kindness, care for offspring, life in society with others, and so forth are humanly *good* is very evident; they are immediate conclusions from the principle that good is to be done. The application of these to the fine points of daily life need detailed guidance. They are the *theorems* which must be applied to the *originals* of human existence for an adequate solution of its problems. This is the precise work of positive law. It puts flesh on the skeletal structure of the moral law.

Positive Law

"The general principles of the Natural [Moral] Law cannot be applied to all men in the same way on account of the great variety of human affairs, and hence arises the diversity of Positive Laws among various people," says St. Thomas. The basic reason for the need of positive law over and above the moral law is that natural reason, being human and not divine, is liable to error and doubt, particularly in respect to the details of life. Thus, it is inadequate to enlighten man with respect to the detailed steps to be taken in attaining his goal. The "shortage," so to speak, of the natural moral law is with respect to appropriate *means* to the end. In some things the natural law shines with remarkable clearness; in others, less clearly. It is, for example, more easy to recognize the fact that one must eat in order to live than to recognize the principle that to steal is evil.

A further reason is that the more remote conclusions are not evident to any but the wise who reach them only after much consideration. Again, at times the natural moral law only insufficiently indicates what course is to be taken, as for example, when it commands that one keep his contracts but does not determine the terms of a just bargain between an employer and his employees.

For all these reasons, some law in addition to the moral law is necessary for the direction of man. That further law is positive law. Positive law is a dictate or command of reason in harmony with the natural law and therefore with the eternal law, which determines what has been left undetermined in the natural law. It is promulgated by the one in authority and it must be for the general good. Positive law has a twofold field: (1) viewing the principles of the natural moral law, it determines the particular ways and means best suited for carrying out the precepts of that law; and (2) it makes the detailed and explicit application of the moral law to human acts performed under widely different circumstances and ages.

Kinds: Divine and Human

St. Thomas explains that there are certain things, for example, the interior actions of man, for which only God can supply the proper direction. Other things, like man's exterior actions, can be directed to the general good by human authority. This gives those two divisions of the positive law known as the divine positive law and the human positive law.

There are some things which only God can teach man. Man's supernatural life needs supernatural direction to his goal and no human legislators can give this. "Since man is ordained to an end of eternal happiness which is proportionate to man's natural faculty," says St. Thomas, "it was necessary that besides the Natural and the Human Law, man should be directed to his end by a law given by God." If man had only temporary happiness for his final end, then temporal lawgivers would suffice. But man has been made for eternal happiness, and man is brought thereto by interior movements of his heart and will. But human legislators are unable to judge of interior movements because they are hidden from their eyes; they can judge properly only of those movements which appear, which are exterior. Hence in order to perfect man both interiorly and exteriorly, two kinds of positive law are required — one human, which directs and curbs exterior actions; the other, divine, which directs and curbs interior actions. God's direction of men through the Old and the New Law constitutes the divine positive law.

Divine Positive Law

The formal, detailed commands enunciated on Mount Sinai by God are precepts of divine positive law. Do not forget that those prohibitions, not to kill, for example, and not to steal, not to commit adultery, and others, are knowable by the light of human reason when it "reasons" on the primary principle that good is to be done and evil avoided. In other words, they constitute also the innate secondary precepts of the moral law, which precepts, as we said in the preceding chapter, are *morally universal*, that is, *knowable* by all as conclusions from the primary principle, and *actually known* by the great majority of the human race. Impediments which we discussed in that chapter told us why the minority did not know all of these commands. The point now is this: that God, by giving to Moses the Ten Commandments, chose to enlighten man's reason more quickly, even though eventually it would have come to know these principles naturally. God thus gave all men a quicker and clearer idea of the moral law through the positive statement of the Ten Commandments which constitute the divine positive law. This reviews the facts that the moral law is innate and natural, while the positive law is from outside man and natural only insofar as it is based on the bedrock of that first principle: do good; avoid evil.

Human Positive Law

Human positive law is that directing force whereby man is directed in his external acts only. The purpose of human law is not *primarily* the individual good, but the general good; not the good of the part, but the good of the whole. That *whole* is the community; the *part* is the individuals who in association with one another make up the *whole*. St. Thomas remarks: "Since every part is ordained to the whole as the imperfect is ordained to the perfect, and since one man is a part of the perfect community, the law must have regard for universal happiness." He concludes (and hereafter we shall use his terminology) that "every law is ordained to the common good."

St. Thomas gives us two striking definitions of law. First he tells us: "Law is a certain ordination [i.e., a command or direction] of reason for the sake of the common good and promulgated by him who has the care of the community." Elsewhere he explains law as "a rule and measure of acts, whereby man is induced to act or is restrained from acting."

A Dictate of Reason

Law is something reasonable, not something emotional such as anger, hatred, fear, despair, pleasure, and the like. Now reason is man's director and so law, which is a command of reason, must point the same way as reason does. But man's reason is his director to his final end, to happiness, to God. Therefore law, which is reason's pronouncement of the way to the final end, must lead man to his final end, to happiness, to God. Unless law does this, it ought to be considered "a perversion of law," "an act of violence," in the words of St. Thomas. It must be noted carefully, therefore, that law has to do with the *means* to man's end. Law is not an end in itself. It is something given to man *for the sake of something else*, and that something else is his final destiny.

Now no law is an exception to the general nature of law. The eternal law is an act of divine wisdom by which God conceived the creative plan of the universe whereby each nature is impelled toward its proper goal and the whole universe toward the good of all natures. We heard in chapter 5 that God was the Lawgiver of the perfect community (the universe), and so the definition of law in this sense fits the particular law called the eternal law.

The natural moral law is also a dictate of reason, the reason of man proximately, and the divine reason ultimately. It directs all mankind toward its proper goal. It is promulgated in the heart of every individual by the Universal Lawgiver who created man.

Human positive law and divine positive law must likewise conform to this definition of law. There is no question of the conformity of the divine law. God cannot contradict Himself. He is perfect, unlimited, and unlimitable truth. Human law, however, may in certain instances, due to ignorance, vice, hatred, and the like, fail to conform to the general notion of law. Unless, however, human law is in conformity with natural law which in turn is the outward manifestation of the eternal law, human law is not law, properly speaking, but violence.

Characteristics of Human Law

Human law, to be law, must be a dictate of reason. It must come from him who is legitimately in charge of those over whom he rules. It must point the way to happiness. It must direct the whole society for the sake of the whole society and not for the sake of a number of individuals in the society. It must never be more than a *means*; it must never attempt to usurp the role of end and set itself up as an end in itself. It can never truly be anything more than a means to the final destiny of the whole group. In other words, it is a means to the common good. Further, law must be promulgated, that is, made known to those whom it binds, before it has power to bind them.

St. Thomas repeatedly says that the purpose of law is to make men good. "The proper effect of law is to lead its subjects to their proper virtue." If the intention of the lawgiver is to foster the common good according to the dictates of the eternal law and divine justice, then law will make men wholly good with respect to acts of virtues which affect the social order. If, however, the lawgiver makes laws for his personal advantage or for pleasure, in opposition to divine justice, then that law is not just, and it does not make men wholly good.

Virtue must characterize those who govern. "The common good of the state cannot flourish," says St. Thomas, "unless the citizens be virtuous, at least those whose business it is to govern. But it is enough for the good of the community that the other citizens be so far virtuous that they obey the commands of their rulers." This is very easy to understand. For rulers are "the wise" spoken of by St. Thomas when he said that the dictates of reason with respect to particulars of human living were such that only the wise after long consideration could judge of them. If "the wise" be not truly good, it is impossible for them to lead others to goodness. Yet this is precisely the work of rulers: to lead men to virtuous living — the life of peace. Hence rulers must be virtuous.

That law has for its purpose to make men virtuous does not mean that obedience to human law will end in canonization. Human law is the directive agency which holds the community to its course of right reason. Canonization is the crown of sainthood, and sanctity belongs to the individual, not to the community. It is not the aim of human law to foster all virtue and to destroy all vice. It aims at peaceful living for the individuals who make up the community, so that these, by their own efforts, advance to the personal goal of every man, woman, and child: eternal beatitude. Human law forbids those vices which would cause the destruction of society or render social living unstable and undesirable: vices such as murder, theft, and the like.

This prohibition of the socially destructive vices is the minimum requirement. For *virtuous* social living, the virtuous among the citizens abstain from all vices. "The purpose of Human Law is to lead men to virtue, not suddenly but gradually," says St. Thomas. "Wherefore it does not lay upon the multitude of imperfect men the burdens of those who are already virtuous, viz., that they should abstain from all evil. Otherwise these imperfect ones, being unable to bear such precepts, would break out into yet greater evils."

As it does not forbid all vicious acts, neither does human law command all virtuous acts. It prescribes only those virtuous acts which foster the common good, as that of justice which ordains that citizens should give to the community those things which are its due, such as taxation, military service, respect and obedience to its laws, and the like; or that justice by which citizens are ordained to give to each other that which is due to each so that they might live in peace, and thus advance the common good of the community.

Good Human Laws

Good human laws should have certain characteristics. They should, for example, (1) be for the good of all the citizens (the common good); (2) they should distribute burdens equally on all; (3) they should be within the power of the lawgiver. Human laws are good when they are useful, planned for no private benefit, and when no injury results from them.

They distribute burdens equally when they are possible to nature, when they are suited to the time and place, and when they are in accord with custom. They are just when they are based on reason and in harmony with the natural law and when consideration is had for the ability of the ones on whom the law is imposed. "The same is not possible to a child as to a full grown man, for which reason the law for children is not the same for adults, since many things are permitted to children, which in an adult are punished by law or at any rate are open to blame," says St. Thomas.

Looking at this from the other side, that is, from the side of bad legislation, laws are unjust when the ruler imposes burdens on his subjects which redound to his own private good rather than for the commonweal; when the lawgiver exceeds the limits of his authority; when the burdens are unequally distributed on the community. "The like are acts of violence rather than laws," says St. Thomas, and he adds, "wherefore such laws do not bind in conscience except perhaps in order to avoid scandal or disturbance, for which cause a man should even yield his right."

Derivation of Positive Law

As to the source of human law, we have noted before that it is derived from and must be in conformity to the natural law and to the eternal law. Recall that the natural law consists of three kinds of precepts or commands. They are: (1) the primary or self-evident principles; (2) the secondary or easily derived conclusions from the primary principles; and (3) the remote conclusions which are difficult to attain. From these, positive law, both human and divine, is derived.

In the first place, positive law is derived from the natural moral law by *determination*. This is not the same thing as saying that it is derived by way of *conclusion* from the natural moral law. Let us make sure of this point. For a command of reason to be derived by conclusion, it must be contained in the primary principle. For example: it is a universal principle of the moral law that one should do no harm to anyone. By reasoning on this principle, we draw from it this truth: that one must not kill another, because to kill another is to do him harm. But to do harm to anyone is forbidden by the natural moral law. Therefore the command not to kill is a conclusion which we reach by reasoning. It is a conclusion drawn from a universal principle. Now this is not positive law. It is still natural moral law, for the conclusion is as much natural moral law as was the principle from which it was drawn. Now even though such commands as "Do not kill" are promulgated by human authority, they do not become human law. They remain precepts of the natural moral law and they have all the force of such precepts.

Positive law, on the other hand, whether it be human or divine positive law, is derived from the primary principles of the natural moral law by way of *determining how the general precepts are to be carried out*. It deals with the *means* to the dictate proposed by the natural moral law. The natural moral law deals with the thing to be done. Positive law determines how that end is to be attained here and now, under this or that set of conditions, with these or those particular people. Thus you see positive law is and must be subject to variation. The command which the natural moral law indicates does not change when positive law begins its work of determination. The end ordained by the natural moral law stands as it is; the means of attaining that end vary.

Let us take an example. The natural moral law dictates that evildoers ought to be punished inasmuch as they act contrary to the primary dictate that evil should be avoided. The natural moral law, however, does not determine *how* evildoers ought to be punished. The manner of punishment is left entirely to the human lawmakers to determine. They do so according to what is best for the community at a given time and place and under given circumstances. Such a decision of human legislators is, therefore, a determination of what was not determined by the natural moral law for particular cases.

Positive law is of this kind. Now if the determination be made concerning the internal conduct of man, his interior acts, then the commands of positive law are known as divine positive law. Only God is competent to give guidance to man for his interior conduct. If, on the other hand, the determination of natural moral law precepts be made concerning man's exterior conduct, then the commands of positive law are known as human positive law. Man is competent to direct the exterior actions of man.

Force of Human Law

All laws promulgated by human authority have not the same force. We mentioned in the preceding section that human legislators at times promulgate commands which are *conclusions* from the natural moral law. Such is the command, "Do not kill." We said, too, that such commands always belong to the natural moral law. They are promptings that arise within man by the operation of his reason. They are therefore *natural* and do not have their origin in legislators other than God who is the Supreme Legislator and the Author of man's nature. Hence these commands have all the vigor of the natural moral law precepts.

Commands promulgated by human authority which have their origin in human authority have the force only of human authority. In other words, human law, derived by determination of how the natural moral law is to be carried out, has the force only of human law. This is important to remember in view of the fact that human law is subject to great variability. Let us take an example.

How ought evildoers to be punished? Human law answers the question variously. Among the penalties we find those which impose a fine, or imprisonment, or death. With respect to fines alone, the amount varies. With respect to imprisonment, the duration varies and even the type of confinement. With respect to the death penalty, the manner varies. Whether death will be by hanging, gas, or the electric chair is subject to the decision of the lawmakers or the judges. Human law determinations of natural moral law precepts are subject to great variety according to circumstances, times, peoples, and so forth. Regardless of the manner in which it carries out the precept, human law is obeying the dictates of the natural moral law when it punishes evildoers.

The Jus Gentium

Before closing our discussion of human law, another type of law should claim our attention. This is called the *law of nations*, but it should not be confused with *international law*, which is very different.

The *law of nations* is in part made up of a very decided element of human law. It is human law insofar as it is a determination of the natural moral law and insofar as it is a human solution telling how the moral law precept is to be carried out. It is distinct, however, from those types of human law mentioned above. The difference lies in this: it is not the dictate of any individual legislator. It is a dictate arising immediately in nature without the intervention of any institution whatsoever. This type of law is based on (1) a natural prompting of man's nature *and* (2) a universal fact.

This type of law is not limited to any given time, place, nation, set of circumstances, or legislative body. It is the common property of all men. St. Thomas says of the *law of nations* that it is "that part of the Positive Law which pertains to the Natural Law and which is publicly acknowledged by all peoples." It is "part of Positive Law" because it is a particular determination as to the best means of doing something demanded by the natural moral law. It "pertains to the Natural Law" because it deals with a natural inclination of man. It is "publicly acknowledged by all peoples" because it is common to all men. It is a natural determination and is not, in its origin, framed by any governing body. It is framed within man, by his reason, when he takes into consideration (1) a natural prompting and (2) a universal fact. An illustration will make this clear.

First of all, it is a natural inclination of man to preserve his life and that of his offspring. To do this, man must possess the things necessary for life. Those things include food, clothing, and shelter. (This is the element of the *jus gentium* of which St. Thomas says that it "pertains to the Natural Law.") Now the possession of the necessary things of life might be held in common, as being free to everybody, *or* they might be held in private, as belonging exclusively to this particular person rather than that particular person. (These are two possible means by which the natural prompting of man can be obeyed.) Considering the fact of man *as he is*, human reason recognizes that disorder would reign in the human family if possessions were common to everybody. (This is the *universal fact* upon which the *jus gentium* is based.)

Human reason, noting both the natural inclination and the universal fact, determines that possession of things necessary to life should not be in common. They should be held in private. Both individual happiness and the common good of society require this. (This is the element of which St. Thomas says that it "is that part of the Positive Law" — it is a positive determination, you see.)

Now this determination can be arrived at by any and all human beings. It isn't only the wise who can grasp the point. It isn't only governments or legislators who can see this. Initially, this command arises in human reason — in any functioning human reason. It does not depend upon any institution for its origin. A natural determination of reason such as that prompting private ownership of goods, while not depending on any institution *for its origin*, does depend upon human institutions *for its protection*. As we shall see in our discussion of private property, human positive law must protect man's natural right to private ownership of goods.

The Jus Gentium *versus Civil Law*

St. Thomas distinguishes thus between the *law of nations* and the civil law. He says:

> It belongs to the notion of Human Law to be derived from the Law of Nature.
>
> In this respect, Positive Law is divided into the "Law of Nations" and Civil Law according to the two ways in which something may be derived from the Law of Nature.
>
> Because to the "Law of Nations" belong those things which are derived from the Law of Nature, as conclusions from principles. For example, just buyings and sellings and the like, without which men cannot live together, which living together is a point of the Law of Nature since man is by nature a social being.
>
> But those things which are derived from the Law of Nature by way of particular determination, belong to the Civil Law according as each state decides on what is best for itself.

In the following chapter we shall discuss man's obligation to obey law and the reconciliation of law and human freedom.

Some Original Sources

From St. Thomas we again cull the more important of his statements regarding law—human law this time. It ought to be a joy to you to read these statements coming as they do from a mind so clear and penetrating as St. Thomas. Can you understand these? explain them? apply them? Make use of these quotations in your study and discussions.

1. "It is from the precepts of the Natural Law ... that the human reason needs to proceed to the more particular determination of certain matters.

"These particular determinations, devised by human reason, are called Human Laws, provided the other essential conditions of law be observed." (*Summa Theologica*, vol. 8, p. 13)

2. "In order that a law obtain the binding force which is proper to a law, it must needs be applied to the men who have to be ruled by it.

"Such application is made by its being notified to them by promulgation. Wherefore promulgation is necessary for the law to obtain its force." (*Summa Theologica*, vol. 8, pp. 7–8)

3. "It must be noted that something may be derived from the Natural Law in two ways:
   1. First, as a conclusion from principles;
   2. Secondly, by way of determination of certain generalities ...

   "Accordingly both modes of derivation are found in the Human Law.

   "But those things which are derived in the first way are contained in Human Law not as emanating therefore exclusively, but have some force from the Natural Law also.

   "But those things which are derived in the second way, have no other force than that of Human Law." (*Summa Theologica*, vol. 8, p. 57)

4. "The end of Human Law is the temporal tranquility of the State, which end law effects by directing external actions as regards those evils which might disturb the peaceful condition of that state.

   "On the other hand, the end of the Divine Law, is to bring man to that end which is everlasting happiness." (*Summa Theologica*, vol. 8, pp. 85–86)

5. "All law proceeds from the reason and will of the lawgiver; the Divine and Natural Laws from the reasonable Will of God; the Human Law from the will of man regulated by reason." (*Summa Theologica*, vol. 8, p. 80)

6. "Laws are said to be just, both from the *end*, as when they are ordained to the common good, and from their *author*, as when the law that is made does not exceed the power of the lawgiver, and from their *form*, as when burdens are laid on the subjects according to an equality of proportion and with a view to the common good." (*Summa Theologica*, vol. 8, p. 69)

7. "Laws may be unjust in two ways:
   "*First*, by being contrary to human good....
   "(a) in respect to the *end*, as when an authority imposes on his subjects burdensome laws, conducive, not to the common good but rather to his own greed or vainglory; or
   "(b) in respect to the *author*, as when a man makes a law that goes beyond the power committed to him; or
   "(c) in respect to the *form*, as when burdens are imposed unequally on the community although with a view to the common good ...
   "*Secondly*, laws may be unjust through being opposed to the Divine Good.
   "Such are the laws of tyrants inducing to idolatry or to anything contrary to the Divine Law." (*Summa Theologica*, vol. 8, p. 70)

8. Read in this connection with item no. 6, "Some Original Sources," chap. 15.

Summary

1. The primary and secondary precepts of the natural moral law are distinct, innate, naturally knowable, but *general* principles of human behavior. They have universal application.

2. Being natural to all mankind, they cannot descend to the details of human living under varying conditions. More definite guides are necessary for varying times, places, and circumstances.

3. Such details are filled in by positive law: divine and human. These constitute positive and detailed direction by legitimate lawmakers for the guidance of man.

4. For the inner guidance of man to his eternal happiness, there is the divine positive law: the Old and the New Testaments and ecclesiastical authority.

5. For the external guidance of man's acts to the common good, there is human positive law: the multiplicity of human laws governing particular peoples, in times, and under circumstances, which vary considerably throughout the world.

6. The *law of nations (jus gentium)* bears characteristics of both the natural law and the human law.

7. It is based on natural promptings which are conclusions from the primary principles of the natural moral law. It is based, also, on a universal fact recognized as a factor to be considered in directing man's activities to his end.

8. The *jus gentium* is a determination of human reason without the necessity of being formulated by any institution. It is knowable to all men.

9. Laws must be just, useful, possible, honest, directed toward the common good, based on the natural law, and flow from legitimate authority within proper limits.

10. Law is an ordination of reason for the common good, made by him who has charge of the community, and promulgated. It is a rule and measure of human acts.

11. Law is a means to an end; it shows the way to the attainment of the goal of reason.

12. Nature and law must point the same way: nature to nature's end which is the universal good. Law indicates how this good can be attained.

13. All law must be derived from the natural law which is, in effect, the eternal law.

14. Laws lack the note of justice when they (1) are used for private gain to the detriment of the common good; (2) are not within the power of the lawgiver to impose; (3) are not equitably imposed on all.

15. Human law is derived from the natural moral law by way of determining what was left indeterminate in that law. It determines the means of fulfilling the natural moral law precepts.

For Study and Discussion

1. Explain the necessity of positive law.
2. Why must there be both divine and human positive law?

3. The *law of nations* (*jus gentium*) cuts across both the natural and the human law. Explain this statement.
4. Explain how some laws promulgated by human legislators are really natural moral law precepts and have the force of the natural law.
5. Explain how some laws promulgated by human legislators are merely positive law precepts and have the force only of human law.
6. What is the difference between *formulating* and *promulgating* a law? Does human authority *frame* any laws? Explain.
7. Explain the derivation of the *jus gentium*.
8. Tell how human law is derived from the natural moral law by determination.
9. Explain the difference between deriving a law *by conclusion* and *by determination* from the natural moral law. Explain the force of each type of law.
10. Discuss St. Thomas's statement regarding the division of human law into the *jus gentium* and civil law. Give the essential differences between the two types.
11. Why must civil laws be of particular things and limited in time, place, and application?
12. Discuss: Unjust laws are acts of violence rather than laws.
13. Discuss: Law and nature ought to be in agreement.
14. Explain part by part St. Thomas's definition of law.
15. Explain the characteristics of good human law.
16. Discuss the derivation of all law and of each kind of law from the eternal law.

For the Advanced Reader

St. Thomas:
> *On the Governance of Rulers*
> *Summa Theologica*: human law, vol. 8, pp. 53–83; divine law, Old and New Laws, vol. 8, pp. 84–319

Farrell, Walter:
> *A Companion to the Summa*, II, pp. 363–412

Sheen, Fulton J.:
> *Whence Come Wars*, chap. 2

Any good book on Christian ethics

8

Man: His Obligation and His Freedom

In the chapters on law we raised the question, "Is law a violation of man's freedom?" By now the answer ought to be evident: law and nature point the same way. Not only are they in accord but their operations are complementary. Nature points out the goal; law leads to it step by step. Nature and law, it must be remembered, operate under divine direction. God is the Author of nature and of man's goal; God is the Source of law and its effectiveness. God is the primary cause, nature and law the secondary causes of the attainment of the goal of life.

But if man is bound by law to act according to his nature, how can he be free? If he has obligations, how can he have freedom? And if he is free, of what purpose then is conscience? This chapter will discuss man's obligation which is a truly real thing in man. It will discuss also man's freedom which is just as truly a real thing in man. It will show that man has both obligations and personal freedom in virtue of his last end. Moreover, it will be seen that obligation and freedom both take root in the eternal law.

Man's Goal Fixed

The explanation of man's obligation goes back, of course, to the fact that man's goal is "fixed." Man did not select it from among other probable goals. Hence God established the goal and made it so absolutely attractive to man's will that no other object can lure it away. There is one and only one true goal of human activity: the goal that is perfect happiness, which means the goal that is the universal good. The good (real or apparent) is the only target at which the human will constantly aims. Nothing else but the good attracts it. The will will have that goal or none. In fact, it *can* have no other, for it knows no other in which it can rest.

It is evident that in this matter of the goal, man is not free because, as we said before, he did not select his goal from among probable goals, but had this one put before him as the only goal. He may be compared to marksmen who participate in a shooting tournament. The marksmen do not choose their target; they aim at the one set up under the conditions of the contest. No marksman can say to the promoters of the tournament: "I'll put up my own target if you please, and aim at that."

But, you say, the marksmen do not have to fire at the target if they don't want to. They can shoot some place beside it. That's right, they *can*. "Can" is really the word; it means they have the physical power to do so if they want to. But at what cost! They lose out. They fail in the contest. Their aim has been purposeless, their effort has been wasted as far as winning in the contest goes. They simply have not achieved their goal.

With man in life it is similar. He is in a kind of tournament. He has a target — the goal of reason, the end of human existence. He is asked to shoot at that goal of life. However, no substitute goal can be put up. He may accept the established goal and aim at it, or he may refuse to accept that goal and not aim at all. He is free to accept or not to accept the goal, but he is not free to make his own goal. It is there for him, ready-made, God-made. It is the specific goal of a rational nature; the highest possible goal a visible creature can have. To want less is to demean oneself; it is to be satisfied with husks and leave the feast untasted. Just remember, now, that man's final end is a necessary end; a fixed end; one about which he can have no other say than to accept it or reject it.

This is the first step in the understanding of man's obligation. Now for the second step.

Means Are Steps to a Goal

We discussed the nature of means earlier. They are the ways man has of attaining his desires. To go out and buy a steak and cook it are means to satisfying that keen appetite for food. To buy a ticket for San Francisco is a means of getting to the Pacific Coast. Means are always wanted because something else is wanted. Means are steps going somewhere; the place where they are going is the place to which our desires have flown and where they are centered. Means are not ends; they lead to ends. Ends are the things that are wanted for themselves. For instance, my palate craves good food, and I want that food because I am hungry. Or perhaps I want to use that end for a further end: to put me in good spirits for the day. And perhaps I want that end for another further end: to make a good impression on a visitor. I could use that end to attain a further end: to be remembered in that person's will, and so on. What was an end in the first instance was not a final end because I wanted it for a further end. Each of the partial ends became means to the further ends. So too, in life. Each thing in life is wanted for a further end, the end of happiness, which is the final end.

Wouldn't it be almost unnecessary to remark, now, that if one wishes to attain the final end he must take the steps that lead to it? Everyone knows a quitter doesn't get to where he started for. That is saying nothing other than that if one wants the goal, one must go to it, which means, of course, one must take steps to it; one must take, as a matter of fact, the very steps that will lead to it, and none other.

Necessity of End and Means

If one wants the end, one must use the means. That is most obvious. The reason, of course, is that there is a connection between the two. It is a connection which we cannot afford to overlook; it is a *necessary* connection. Suppose I am sick. I call in a doctor who prescribes for me. The next day I am better. Is it likely that there was some connection between the doctor's medicine and my recovery? Can it be claimed, however, that as a matter of positive fact, there was some connection between the medicine and my recovery? No. The connection, of course, is only a probable one. It may have been more than a probable one, it may have been an actual one, but we cannot be sure. My day of rest and sleep may have restored me. Other probable causes of my recovery are not hard to think of.

On the other hand, let us suppose someone in perfect health takes a generous portion of deadly poison. He drinks it all. He dies at once. Is it likely that there was some connection between the taking of the poison and the man's death? Is it only a probable connection? Could not one say, as morally certain fact, that there was more than a probable connection between the act and the effect? The connection is such that it can be called a *necessary connection*.

What Is Obligation?

Now there is a necessary connection or relationship between man's final end and the steps toward it. If man wants the end, he must want the means. If he wills to have the goal, he must will to use the proper means of getting it. The reason is the necessary relation which exists between man's final destiny and good human acts which lead to it. Therefore, the principle is this: obligation is the relation existing between the necessary goal and the necessary steps to that goal. Note the predicate substantive: obligation *is* the relation. The end or goal of man is a necessary goal. The steps to it are necessary steps. The relation between these two necessities is obligation.

One is obligated to hear Mass on Sundays. This statement means that the act is a necessary one in the attainment of man's necessary end. One is obligated to care for his offspring. This means, that the care for one's offspring is necessary in the attainment of one's final destiny. One is obligated to speak the truth. This means the act of truthful speaking is a necessary act in bringing man to the necessary goal of life.

If man had only a probable end of such or such a kind, then merely probable means would satisfy to attain it, but *because* man has a necessary end, the necessary steps to it *must* be taken if he will have the end; and if so, then he *ought* to take those steps and none other. The *because* reveals the obligation; the *must* tells us the necessity which creates the obligation; the *ought* tells us how man should react to the obligation.

The sense of obligation is not a physical power; it is not a protest from a man's stomach; not a push in the back; not a strong wind carrying him off his feet. A protest from a man's stomach sends him looking for food; a push in the back sends his fists clenching in self-defense; a strong wind carrying him off his feet makes him shout out for help. These are physical actions and reactions, and they belong to man's physical makeup. Obligation is not a physical power; it does not belong to man's physical makeup. It is of quite a different nature.

Obligation is a moral power. It is an appeal made to man's reason. It is a power urging him to act in this or that way in conformity to his true good. It leaves man still free to follow or not to follow. A man must have air for his lungs; food for his stomach; sleep for his nerves; he *must* because he is not free about things like that. Physical needs drive him to seek their satisfaction. This is expressed by the word *must*.

But a man *ought* to be good because his final end is the universal good; he *ought* to be truthful because his final goal is union with Infinite Truth; he *ought* to provide for his offspring because they have the dignity of human persons; he *ought* because that is what the light of reason prompts him to do, and reason is his director to the final goal of life. And of course he *ought* to do them if he wants to reach that goal because it was for this he was made. This is moral obligation. Physical necessity says "must do"; moral obligation says "ought to do."

Human Dignity and Obligation

What dignity does it add or subtract from the nature of man to be under obligation? Let us look at it this way. You certainly must have heard of *backseat drivers*. They are objectionable people. They are heard from when they ought not to be.

They are trying *to lead* when their very position in the car indicates that they are *to be led*. They should be driven, but they are trying to drive. There is a difference between the two, naturally. *To drive* is not the same as *to be driven*. As a matter of fact, one who is driving cannot at the same time and in the same way be driven. Nor can it be the other way about: *to be driven* means *to be driven* and it cannot mean at the same time and in the same way *to drive*. It's hitching the wagon to the horse and asking the wagon to pull. Actually, the point we are making is this: in the universe most natures are driven; one alone drives. Most are driven because they are not intelligent natures. The one intelligent nature in the universe is the one which drives, and that one is man. Man drives himself to his goal, or away from it if he is foolish enough so to choose. No other nature has this power of choice; no nature in the universe except man can say, "I will" and "I will not." Man can say that because he can see the end and see the means thereto. Seeing the end and the means, man can see the necessary connection between them; between his necessary end and the acts necessary to reach it. But only man can see this. The whole thing rests upon man's more noble nature, as you can see. And so it is that only man can be obliged, only he can know obligation, because only he can see the relationship of means to end of which we spoke.

Obligation, therefore, does not make man lose his dignity, but rather it is because of his dignity that he has obligations; and the obligation he is under is the safeguard of his dignity; it marks him as distinctly human; it keeps him from falling to the level of non-intellectual natures. It keeps him "the driver" instead of "the driven." It is a sign of nobility. It is a badge of mastery.

Between obligation and freedom there exists this link: only free persons can be obliged. An obligation can be put only on those who are dignified by freedom, only on those whose nature cannot be forced. Without freedom of the will there could be no moral obligation! For man could not be obliged to do one act rather than another act unless he were *free to do this act instead of that act*. If someone pushes you into a stream, it would be unjust to blame you for wetting your feet. There was simply nothing you could do about it. You were forced into the water; you were not free to choose to stay out. So, too, if man were forced physically in all his actions (as all lower natures are) then no one could blame him for *any* of his actions. They could neither praise him for good ones nor blame him for bad ones, for none of them would be within his control, and so they would be neither good nor bad. An action is within man's control precisely because he is free to do the act or not to do it. Praise and blame can be given to man only because he is free to choose to do, or not to do, what he ought to do.

The Freedom to Choose God

Now what is this freedom which so dignifies man that moral persuasion, and not physical force, guides him toward his final end? Freedom is the power to choose. That is simple enough to understand. We all have made choices. When a man makes a choice among several alternatives, he is *free*. A man may choose to be a doctor or a lawyer. He may choose between playing tennis and handball. He may make a choice between coffee and tea. He may be free to go out or not to go out. These choices, however, concern rather unimportant things — professions, games, drinks, and so forth.

Some of man's choices are far more important than those. They concern things that have a very important connection with man's final destiny. They concern things belonging to the precepts of the natural law, for instance. When man's choices are concerned with matters that have an important connection with man's final end, then man must use his freedom very carefully. Not everything that it is possible for him to choose will lead him there. He must be careful to choose those actions which will lead him step by step toward his final end. He must be careful to choose not to do those actions which lead him step by step away from his final end.

All this is saying that man is free to choose the *means* to the goal or he is free not to choose them; he is free to choose one means instead of another, if two or more lead toward the goal. He must always remember that if he wants a goal he must choose the proper means to that goal. He can always choose *not to have the goal itself* but that spells tragic failure of life; a life without a true purpose; a meaningless life; a lost life.

Thus, freedom does not mean the power to do *as one pleases*, but the power to choose the good things which will bring one to the wholly good goal, God. That is why animals and plants go down to oblivion at death, whereas man is either condemned to eternal fires or borne into eternal realms and crowned everlastingly.

Binding Power of Human Laws

A final question remains to be answered. The answer is easy to give now, in the light of what we learned in this chapter. Is man obliged to obey the commands of human lawgivers? Do human laws bind men? The answer is yes. Just human laws are means to man's final end. If man chooses to have the end, he must choose the means to it. So just human laws bind man's conscience, obliging him to obey. St. Thomas says: "Laws framed by man ... if they be just, have the power of binding in conscience from the Eternal Law whence they are derived." Unjust laws do not bind in conscience except, as was mentioned earlier, it would cause a scandal or other disturbance out of proportion to the gravity of the injustice. Should the unjust human laws command things contrary to the law of God, then laws of this kind do not bind in conscience and are not to be obeyed. For man must always be free to choose the steps to his final end, and human laws such as one which would forbid him to worship God, cannot be a step toward God. Man is free in the depths of his conscience!

Pope Leo XIII, confronted with many false theories of human liberty, issued an encyclical on *Human Liberty* in which he gives to the world the teachings of the Church. When we consider that it was this same Holy Father who designated the teachings of St. Thomas as the sources from which teachers should draw in their presentation of Christian philosophy, it is not surprising to find in his document a very decided flavor of St. Thomas's teachings.

In this encyclical Pope Leo points out that the liberty natural to man, that is, *natural liberty*, is the source from which flows all other liberties: political, economic, religious, and so forth. This *natural liberty* is due to man's intellectual nature, and so ultimately the source of human liberty is the Creator of man. The Holy Father writes: "Natural liberty, though distinct and separate from moral liberty, is the fountain-head from which liberty of whatsoever kind flows by its own force and of its own accord.... When it is established that man's soul is immortal and endowed with reason and not bound up with material things, the foundation of natural liberty is thus most firmly laid."

Let us attempt to show from this encyclical that the obligatory power of law is not only an abstract principle, food for the mind alone, but a practical fact of Catholic teaching. In presenting St. Thomas's teaching on obligation we said that laws oblige; that law and obligation have their proximate cause in man's rational nature; that freedom is the soil from which obligation draws its nourishment; that the binding power of law is derived ultimately from the eternal law. Of these things Pope Leo writes:

> The binding force of Human Laws lies in this, that they are to be regarded as applications of the Eternal Law.... Since the force of law consists in the imposing of obligations and the granting of rights, authority is the one and only foundation of all law.... In man's free will, or in the moral necessity that our voluntary acts must be in accordance with reason, lies the very root of the necessity of law. Nothing more foolish can be uttered or conceived than the notion that because man is free by nature, he is therefore exempt from law. Were this the case, it would follow that

to become free we must be deprived of reason; whereas the truth is that we are bound to submit to law precisely because we are free by our very nature. For law is the guide of man's actions; it turns him towards good by its rewards; it deters him from evil by its punishments.

Man's rational nature is the proximate source of law and obligation; the eternal law of God is the ultimate source of them.

The note of obligation is struck again in this statement. Watch for it in the meaning of the word *necessity*. The Holy Father writes:

The nature of human liberty, however it be considered, whether in individuals or in society; whether in those who command or in those who obey, supposes the necessity of obedience to some supreme and Eternal Law which is no other than the authority of God commanding good and forbidding evil. And this most just authority of God neither diminishes nor destroys man's liberty but rather it protects and perfects it for the real perfection of all creatures is to be found in the striving after and attaining their end. But the supreme end to which human liberty must ever aspire is God.

We could find great pleasure and profit, if we would, in seeking in the encyclical on *Human Liberty* more and more of the Thomistic teaching. This connection between the papal encyclicals and St. Thomas's principles has been emphasized because first, it is the will of the Church that it be so emphasized, and further, that it may instill among the readers of this book a keen desire for deeper thinking into basic principles; so keen a desire, in fact, that it will give them no rest until they seek the truths at their source. We hope that they will go directly to St. Thomas and find in his writings the sublimity and the simplicity, the depth and the clarity, the wisdom and the guilelessness that can be found only in the mind and the heart of him who in his lifetime journeyed far toward Infinite Truth, and who could say, as Thomas said, to Infinite Love: "Only Thee will I have."

Some Original Sources

You are being introduced here to quotations from the papal encyclicals. Consult the Catholic Encyclopedia to inform yourself on their nature and purpose. Note the great similarity in expression between St. Thomas and Pope Leo, showing how closely Pope Leo studied St. Thomas. It is your great privilege to be studying St. Thomas, too, and at an age and in a way which are uncommon today.

What meaning can you draw from these? How many of them can you interpret for others? How many of them can you apply in substantiation of statements made throughout the chapter?

1. "The word *necessity* is employed in many ways, for that which *must be* is necessary.... A thing is necessary on the part of the end when without it the end is not to be attained or so well attained; for instance, food is said to be necessary for life, and a horse is necessary for a journey. This is necessity of end....

"But necessity of end is not repugnant to the will when the end cannot be attained except in one way: thus from the will to cross the sea, arises in the will the necessity to wish for a ship ... hence the will must *of necessity* adhere to the last end which is happiness." (*Summa Theologica*, vol. 4, p. 136)

2. "We are masters of our own actions by reason of our being able to choose this or that. But choice regards not the end, but the means to the end." (*Summa Theologica*, vol. 4, p. 137)

3. "The will does not desire of necessity everything that it desires.... For there are certain individual goods which have not a necessary connection with happiness, because without them a man can be happy: and to such the will does not adhere of necessity.

"But there are some things which have a necessary connection with happiness, by means of which things man adheres to God, in Whom alone true happiness consists." (*Summa Theologica*, vol. 4, p. 138)

4. "Man has free will; otherwise counsels, exhortations, commands, prohibitions, rewards and punishments would be in vain.

"In order to make this evident, we must observe that some things act without judgment; as a stone moves downwards; and in like manner all things which lack knowledge. And some act from judgment, but not a free judgment; as brute animals. For the sheep, seeing the wolf, judges it a thing to be shunned from a natural and not a free judgment, because it judges not from reason but from natural instinct.

"But man acts from judgment, because by his apprehensive power he judges that something should be avoided or sought. But because this judgment, in the case of some particular act, is not from a natural instinct but from some act of comparison in the reason, therefore he acts from free judgment and retains the power of being inclined to various things....

"For as much as man is rational is it necessary that man have a free-will." (*Summa Theologica*, vol. 4, p. 148)

5. "Man naturally desires his last end which is happiness, which desire is a natural desire and is not subject to free will." (*Summa Theologica*, vol. 4, p. 149)

6. "Those things to which we are naturally inclined are not subject to free will, as we have said of the desire of happiness." (*Summa Theologica*, vol. 4, p. 151)

7. "The proper act of free will is choice: for we say that we have a free will because we can take one thing while refusing another; and this is to choose.... The proper object of choice is the means to the end." (*Summa Theologica*, vol. 4, pp. 152–153)

8. "To choose is to desire something for the sake of obtaining something else: therefore it regards the means to the end." (*Summa Theologica*, vol. 4, p. 155)

All the following are taken from Pope Leo's encyclical on *Human Liberty*:

9. "Liberty is nature's most exalted gift and is the endowment of intellectual and rational beings only" (God, angels, men).

"It confers on man the dignity of having power over his own actions.

"However, it is of the utmost importance to consider how this dignity is to be exercised, for upon the use of liberty depend both man's highest good and his greatest evil.

"Man is free to obey his reason, to seek his good, and to strive unceasingly to attain his last end. However, man is free also to turn aside to other things, so that, by pursuing a false good, he disturbs the true order of things and falls into that destruction which he has freely chosen for himself."

10. "Liberty belongs only to those who have the gift of reason. If we consider what liberty is in its nature, we see that it is the faculty of choosing means fitted to attain the end proposed. He alone is master of his actions who can choose one thing from among many."

11. "Human liberty necessarily stands in need of light and strength to direct its actions to good and to restrain them from evil. Without this strength and light, the freedom of our will would be our ruin.

"First of all, there must be law; that is, a fixed rule of teaching what is to be done and what is to be left undone. This rule cannot affect the lower animals in any true sense, since they act of necessity, following their natural instinct, and cannot of themselves act in any other way.

"On the other hand, as was said above, he who is free can either act or not act, can do this or do that, as he pleases, because his judgment precedes his choice. And his judgment not only decides what is right or wrong of its own nature, but also what is practically good and therefore to be chosen, and what is practically evil and therefore to be avoided.

"In other words, the reason prescribes to the will what it should seek after or shun, in order to attain his last end, for the sake of which all his actions ought to be performed.

"This ordinance of reason is called law."

Summary

1. The basis of man's obligation is rooted, proximately, in man's nature and in the fixity of his final end. Man's final end is a necessary end.
2. A connection or relationship exists between means and end.
3. Between some means and ends there exists a necessary connection: one that *must* be. Between other means and ends there exists only a loose connection: one that *can* be, or *cannot* be; one that *need not* exist.
4. Between going abroad and taking a ship (or plane) there is a necessary connection. If I want the end (a trip abroad) I must use the proper means to it (an adequate mode of transportation).
5. Between getting an education and going to school there is only a loose connection. Education doesn't necessarily result from schooling.
6. Between man's last end and his *human* acts there always exists a relation.
7. Between man's last end and his human acts there exists, in some cases, a necessary connection; in others, only a loose connection.
8. Between man's last end and those human acts which are direct steps to it, and without which man cannot attain his goal, there is a necessary connection.
9. Between man's last end and other human acts which do not directly lead to his goal and which do not hinder him from attaining his goal, there is not a necessary connection.
10. The relation which exists between man's necessary end and the acts necessary to reach that end constitutes *obligation*.
11. Obligation is a moral power; an inner persuasion of man's rational nature. It differs from physical force which drives subhuman creatures to their end.
12. Obligation exists in man because man has free will. If man had no choice, but was driven, as are lower natures, then man could have no obligation. There would be no praise or blame for man on that supposition.
13. Obligation does not destroy man's dignity. It is because man has so noble a nature that he has free will, and it is because of his free will that he is obligated.
14. Free will consists in the power of choice. It pertains to the means and not to the nature of man's final end. Means are things employed for attaining something else. Intermediate ends are means to further ends and all terminate in the final or last end.
15. The eternal law of God is the ultimate source of obligation, as it is also of freedom.

For Study and Discussion

1. Defend the point: law is not only not a violation of man's freedom but is its very protection.

2. Explain Pope Leo's statement: "In man's free will ... lies the very root of the necessity of law."
3. What is moral obligation? How does it differ from physical force?
4. Discuss the following: man's necessary end; freedom of choice; choice of means; relation between end and means; *necessary* relation between end and means; final end; an end for a further end; the nature of human freedom.
5. Give original examples of a necessary relation existing between two things; of a probable relation existing between two things.
6. How does the fixity of man's final end form the proximate reason for his obligation? In what way is the eternal law the source of man's obligation?
7. Discuss this point: to be obliged does not detract from human dignity.
8. Why can only rational creatures be under obligation? Why is obligation an indication of mastery?
9. Man's will is fixed by nature upon a single goal. What freedom has man with respect to this goal?
10. What power has man's will with regard to the means to the end?
11. Explain the relation between obligation and freedom.
12. In what foundation are political, civil, economic, and other liberties founded? Quote Pope Leo.
13. To what supreme end must human liberty ever aspire?
14. On what grounds should you be grateful for your freedom?

For the Advanced Reader

St. Thomas:
  Summa Theologica, vol. 4, pp. 135–155; vol. 8, pp. 63–75

Farrell, Walter:
  A Companion to the Summa, II, pp. 383–385

Sheen, Fulton J.:
  Freedom, part 1, Our Sunday Visitor Press

Papal Encyclical:
  Pope Leo XIII: *Human Liberty*

The New Scholasticism: vol. XV, no. 1, January 1941:
  "Intelligence and Liberty," pp. 1–17
  "Necessity and Liberty," pp. 18–45

The Thomist:
  "The Roots of Obligation," pp. 14–30, vol. 1, no. 1, April 1939

Any good book on Christian ethics

Man

The subject matter of this text is man and society. A study of one without the other would be incomplete, to say the least.

Man is unique among God's creatures. He is not only matter, but spirit. He alone is thus composed. Brutes are all matter; angels are all spirit. Man is matter and spirit: body and soul. He is matchless, unequalled, single of kind in his nature.

Now his nature is the key to his excellence. Sharing, through his body, the existence, the living, and the sense-knowing of the lower natures, he shares, through his soul, the intelligence of angels and of God. Man is made to the image and likeness of God.

Man's destiny, therefore, is in accord with his dignity. That rational soul of man's is immortal. God's image and likeness cannot be consigned to oblivion, but it must live on endlessly even as God's existence is endless. Man's immortal existence will be one of joy or of suffering; of infinite gain or eternal loss, depending on his personal choice. Man is master of his actions, and it is by his actions that he journeys *toward* the goal of life or away from it — to everlasting loss.

God has aided man in making this choice by implanting in his nature certain tendencies which urge man to the good of his nature, to particular good things, and finally, through them, to the ultimate good which is supreme happiness, God Himself. This effective direction of man toward his goal is law. God commands by law. God aids, too, by supernatural help, by the flow of divine grace; by supernatural life which inclines man ever more and more toward God.

Because of the relation which exists between man's final end (which God has fixed for him) and between the acts that lead him to his end (which he is free to choose), man is obliged to make use of the proper means which alone will lead him to his final destiny. To desire the goal necessarily demands the taking of those steps which will invariably and unmistakenly lead to it.

Man's responsibility to his Creator requires that man be free; that he have the power to choose. Unless man were free he could not be praised for his good deeds nor blamed for his bad ones. There would be no good or bad, strictly speaking. The goodness and badness of one's actions receive their character from the goodness or badness of the end to which they are directed. Any act toward the goal of life is good because the goal of life is good. Any act away from the goal of life is not good because it is not good to turn from the goal.

Man's freedom is the freedom to choose the good — ultimately to choose God. It is the power to select those means which are necessary to the attainment of the end of life as well as those means which, though not necessary to the end of life, yet are not opposed to it.

Man's rational nature and his divine destiny confer upon him certain privileges not given to the subhuman creatures. These privileges are known as *rights*. Rights are moral powers, *not physical powers*. It is not *might* which makes *right* but a moral claim which makes right. Rights are rooted in man's nature. No rights exist among subhuman creatures. This is so because rights are expressions of man's spirituality; they exist in man because of his soul and his ultimate destiny.

Man's natural rights, that is, those rights which flow directly from his rational nature, are inalienable by any human power. God is the Author of man's nature, and hence God is the source of natural rights. No human power can legitimately abrogate man's natural rights. Only He who conferred them can take them away and this could be done only by dehumanizing man; but then man would no longer be man, but animal — or less.

Rooted in his spirituality, man's rights are aids to his human development: body, mind, heart, will, emotions, the whole of human personality. Human institutions are, in God's plan of creation, protective agencies which, respecting the sacredness of natural rights, are obligated to be their guardian and defender.

The Declaration of Independence sums up these rights as "Life, Liberty, and the Pursuit of Happiness." In the enumeration of these rights by the late Pope Pius XI, we find him mentioning "the right to life, to soundness of body, to the necessary means of existence, the right to work towards his final goal in the path marked out for him by God, the right of associating with others, and the right to possess and to use property."

These are fundamental; they are God-given. Society cannot cheat man in these God-given natural rights.

Part 2

Society

9

Society: Its Necessity and Nature; Its Material and Formal Causes

Man Is Social

Aristotle had called man a political being. St. Thomas found that characterization of man too limited. He amplified it, broadening it far beyond the restrictions of Aristotle's meaning. St. Thomas said that man is a *social* being. As St. Thomas saw the matter, one had to be a social being first. That is, one had to have a need for society in his natural makeup before he united with other beings into a political society. For St. Thomas, man would not have been politically inclined unless first he were socially inclined. To be social was a broader view; it meant belonging to the human family. To be political was but one of the number of manifestations of man's social nature. It urged man to become a member of this or of that political division. It urged man to form groups known as civil government. But civil governments are limited territorially whereas humanity is worldwide. Therefore St. Thomas declared: "It is natural for man to be a social and political animal, to live in a group, even more than all other animals, as the very needs of his nature indicate."

Man Needs Society

One need not go far into the works of St. Thomas to find other expressions of man's need for society. In every outstanding work the saint has occasion to mention this requirement of human nature.

"It is entirely super-human to stand in need of nothing," he says. "Every man needs in the first place Divine aid and in the second place human aid, because man being naturally a social being, of himself has not all whereby to live." Indeed it is a matter of common experience that we need the association of our fellows in order to live *good* human lives; good morally, economically, politically. That each of us is insufficient in himself to live a truly human life, making use of all human equipment, is self-evident. Why, for instance, has man the gift of speech, if not to communicate ideas to others? No human life can be *complete* without association with other human beings.

The word *complete* in the foregoing sentence is important. The sentence does not read: "No human life *can continue to exist* without association with other human beings." That would be untrue. Did not St. John the Baptist live without human association for many years? Do not prisoners in solitary confinement exist practically without intercourse with humankind? The hermits of the desert, in the early centuries of the Church, all lived solitary lives. Napoleon was banished to the island of St. Helena and St. John to the island of Patmos. The fabled Robinson Crusoe had his island refuge practically to himself. So human beings *can* live in isolation. The point is, they cannot live fully human lives. There is much missing from a human life when it is lived apart from men. It is incomplete. From the natural viewpoint, it is mere existence. It is not personal development. Bodily wants may be met, but without divine intervention the spirit droops. The mind, the will, the heart, the human *person* remains undeveloped. Society is necessary, in the natural order, for the perfection of human personality, for complete human living.

The argument cannot justly be put forward, that St. John the Baptist, St. John the Evangelist, the hermits, and anchorites of the desert were all stunted personalities, blighted lives. The lives of such persons were elevated far above the natural order. By the grace of God they were able to conquer the cravings of human nature for society. They were able to find in God the fulfillment of all their powers, heart, mind, soul, will. This is not impossible to souls who are absorbed in God when, through the grace of God, they are led to withdraw from normal human living. The mode of their lives is no longer normal. The fact remains that the normal development of human beings, the perfection of their nature, is found in society, and that through it, they are led to their final end. Hence man needs society and he needs it by the very deep needs of his nature.

Some subhuman creatures seem to have social life, but it is not the same kind of social life as that of man. The "social life" of animals is natural but not rational. Instinct, but not reason, is the power behind their grouping. Animals do not know the meaning of society nor the advantages of it. Instinct drives them to band themselves together in greater or lesser numbers according to the species. It is man's reason that impels him to live in society, because he recognizes that only in society can he perfect himself and complete his human capacities. Only in society can he meet his material needs adequately, develop his intellect, communicate ideas, strengthen his willpower, exercise self-control, and such like things which raise man to a truly human level of existence. Of himself man cannot supply these things; of himself he is insufficient. Of himself he has not the physical strength, the natural weapons (as tusks, horns, sharp teeth, and the like), the keenness of instinct nor nature's protective covering to guarantee himself protection, food, clothing, and the like material needs of his nature. So intellectually, morally, economically, and politically, man is humanly perfected by social living.

Society Natural to Man

Just as water is the natural environment for fish; just as it is natural for fire to burn; just as it is natural for birds to fly and for dogs to bark, so is it natural for man to live in society. For the fish, fire, birds, and dogs respond to the promptings, nay, even to the needs of their nature, when they do the things which we recognize as *natural* to them. Just so is it with man and social life. Man is inclined to social living by his very nature. To act otherwise would be to frustrate the complete development of his nature. He would be less perfectly, less fully a man. Why is this so? Well, the answer is simple. God gave man the kind of nature that requires social intercourse. God could, had He wished, have made man a different kind of being. He could, had He wished, have made man without his social inclinations so that man could perfect himself by hermit life. But then man would have no need of speech. And then, too, man would have had to be given a different kind of equipment wherewith to make his way in the world. He would probably have had to be naturally endowed with hair instead of clothing for covering; with teeth, horns, and claws as means of defense or else very great speed for ready flight from danger. Man would, as in the case of so many animals who live alone, have had to be supplied by nature with equipment for individual living. He would not be the human person we know.

But God did not choose thus to make man. He gave man a disposition for society. Instead of lower-animal kind of equipment, therefore, God provided man with reason and hands; with reason to prompt him what to do and with hands to do what reason prompts for the procuring of food, clothing, safety, and the like. In addition to reason and hands, God gave man the power to communicate the thoughts which are born in his mind through the action of his senses and his reason. St. Thomas points out that nature does nothing in vain. Whatever nature does, it is done for a definite purpose. That, of course, shows the eternal wisdom of God who is the Author of nature and the director of its course. Then St. Thomas shows that of all the living things in the universe, only man has the power of speech. Lesser things in the universe have only material needs and satisfactions. Their existence is purely temporal existence. But with man it is otherwise. His needs are more than material. His existence is more than temporal. Through the power of speech men communicate with one another and promote the intellectual and moral development of their human powers.

We say, therefore, that man is disposed by nature to live in society, and that he is equipped by nature for social living. So strong is the inclination toward society in man's nature that society is necessary for him if he would live at a level which is above that of mere existence, above that of non-reasoning brutes.

What Is Society?

Society is the grouping of men for the purpose of attaining a common end by common effort. There must, first of all, be a grouping. Clothespins on a line may form a group, but one pin is wholly unrelated to another, even though they might be touching one another. The only thing they share in common is the fact that each is a clothespin and has certain accidental characteristics like shape, size, and color. There is nothing, not even the line on which they stand, that binds them together in a kind of unity.

Birds chattering gaily on a telegraph wire form a group, too. The individual birds are not wholly unrelated to one another as are the clothespins. There is a kind of unity existing among them. Even our language symbolizes this unity by calling the birds a *flock* — a symbol of "many in one." Their unity comes from the fact that nature prompts them to live together. It is natural, that is, it is instinctive for them to do so. Their union is not a perfect union because birds can have no knowledge of means and end. They do not know a goal or the means thereto. They do not understand the advantages of social living. The meaning of cooperation, of the common good, and other abstract terms which they would need to know in order to have common striving for a common end is beyond their powers to comprehend. God is responsible for the *flocking* of birds, since He is the Author of the instinct which drives them to that kind of existence.

Man differs from clothespins and from birds. Man can know a goal. He can recognize the fact that all mankind has an identical goal. He can understand that by common effort the goal can be reached more easily. Man can consider the goal and consider the best means to reach it. Man's grouping thus becomes a well-ordered grouping. It possesses a unity more perfect than the unity found in the flocking of birds or animals. It is a unity of end and of means. It is "a one made up of many" and unified through common purposes arrived at by common effort, both of which are knowable and known to man.

To live thus is natural to man; that is, it is not instinctive as in the birds, but it is *rational* and thus in keeping with man's rational nature. As we said before, reason prompts man to live in company with his fellows. Further characteristics of society will be discussed immediately through a consideration of the causes of society.

Causes of Society

When one sees smoke, he asks, "Where is the fire? How did it start?" He has seen an effect, and he wants to trace it to its cause. A child's insistent questioning concerning a strange object, "What makes it like that?" "Why is it like that?" "What is it made of?" and "What's this for?" seeks to discover the causes of an unfamiliar thing.

So, too, we question concerning society: What is it made up of? What makes it what it is? Who is responsible for social living? Why do we have social living? In seeking answers to these whys and whats we show ourselves to be good philosophers, for among the ancient Greeks, philosophers were called "seekers after wisdom — wise men." The reason, of course, is that philosophers sought to understand the causes and principles of things. The further back into the unknown a philosopher pushed his inquiry, the more of a wise man he was considered to be. He was truly a wise man when he reached the ultimate principles from which the world of knowledge might be surveyed and understood. Do you recall our discussion of understanding, knowledge, and wisdom in chapter 1?

Aristotle has told us that we know a thing when we know its causes. He and outstanding philosophers of the ages tell us there are four causes of things. These causes can be summed up simply thus: what is a thing made up of, that is, its material; what distinguishes it from other things; that is, its nature; who made it, that is, its producing agent; why was it made, that is, its purpose. Let us find out what are the four causes of society. Let us discover its material, its nature, its agent, its purpose.

Material Cause of Society

This is the first of the four causes of anything. It might be likened to the ingredients which a baker puts into the cake. What is the material cause of society? Look once more at the definition of St. Thomas: "Society is the grouping of men for the purpose of perfecting a common end." The material, therefore, of society is men, individual men. It is based, as we saw above, on man's natural inclinations toward society. That gives us a double view of the material cause of society; first, and proximately, the material of which society is made is the individual men who compose society; ultimately, the material cause of society is man's social nature.

Man and society are two indispensable and inseparable elements. Man could not have an adequately human existence without society. Society could not exist without the individuals which compose it. Society lives only through its members but its existence does not terminate with the end of life of the individual members. Society continues in the new individuals who are constantly being born into social life. Society will terminate with the end of human existence on earth, but not with the death of individual members of the race. The need for society will continue until the entire human family has attained (or lost irrevocably) its distinctively human goal: the possession and enjoyment of God.

Society is made up of the individuals but it is more than just the sum of those individuals. The individuals have their specific purpose in life; society has its specific purpose. Ultimately the purpose of the individual and the purpose of society meet in a common purpose but proximately each has its own goal and the means thereto. Each must pursue its proximate end and be throughout the entire pursuit actively conscious that finally, the ends of both society and of man coincide according to God's creative plan. This shall be discussed later under the title "Final Cause of Society."

Formal Cause of Society

This is the second of the four causes of anything. It might be likened to that which makes a cake a cake and which distinguishes a cake from bread or pie. It has to do with the very substance or the nature of a thing. What is the formal cause of society? What is it that distinguishes society from non-societies?

Let us again have recourse to the definition: "Society is the grouping of men for the purpose of perfecting a common end." We have the key to the nature of society from the word *grouping*. In a grouping there is arrangement and order. The thousands of pedestrians which traverse the streets of New York City daily, considered in themselves, are merely walking individuals. Each is going his own way and the diversity of their ways is unlimited. They do not constitute a grouping but rather an unorganized mass of individuals.

Grouping implies a common purpose together with common striving for its attainment. In man, this is a conscious knowledge. Reason dictates to him that he must live in society so that, through the sharing of effort, he might enjoy the attainment of the common goal toward which all mankind is striving: toward distinctly human perfection. The *unity* which exists in society explains why society differs from mere multiplicity in numbers without the oneness necessary to bind them into a unity.

What Is Social Unity?

When we recall that society is composed of individuals who are free by the creative act of God; who are complete human persons, heirs to definite human rights because of their human personality; who have a personal, individual goal to gain (or to lose) eternally, we might wonder if social living — that unity in multiplicity — might not be a hindrance rather than a help to man. We might wonder if man does not necessarily forfeit some of his dignity as a free, complete human individual. We might reflect, for instance, that social living requires a certain amount of subordination, and we would wonder, then, if this would not be an undue surrender of his freedom. We might wonder how that unity is attained without leveling to a single common class individuals possessed of the diversity of gifts and capacities which characterizes human nature. We recall that Communism advocates the leveling of human society and we cannot reconcile this with Christian doctrine. We note the words of Pope Leo in his encyclical on *The Condition of Labor* wherein he says: "Let it be laid down, in the first place, that humanity must remain as it is. It is impossible to reduce human society to a level. The Socialists and Communists may do their utmost, but all striving against nature is vain."

How, then, can social unity be achieved, since without it society would have no formal cause? Without unity even a family cannot survive and how much less could the race?

Social unity, to be brief and concise, is that unity which exists among individuals striving by common effort for a common goal. It entails order, which in turn implies subordination. But neither the unity, the order, nor the subordination take from man his completeness and autonomy as a personal being destined for ultimate happiness with God for all eternity. It unites him to others while at the same time it leaves him his own complete self.

Social Unity and the Common Good

The cause of social unity is the recognition of the common goal of humanity. Insofar as that recognition is dimmed or forgotten, social unity weakens. Though the twentieth century has brought us undreamed-of progress in means of communication and transportation; though the world can be encircled in a matter of minutes, hours, and days respectively by radio and air and ship, it is nevertheless true that at no period of history has there been less social unity than there is in this second quarter of the twentieth century. The cult of *racism* tends mightily to break down the concept of the common brotherhood of humanity, and with the weakening of this latter concept and the strengthening of the former (or any similar partial view of humankind), social unity, as it is found in the race at large, is heading toward disintegration.

However, ideally speaking and as it is in the plan of God for the return of the human race to His bosom, unity is obtained through common effort toward the common goal. The unity we speak of in no way destroys individual autonomy. It allows the individual to pursue his personal goal, his specific end, within the social order. It is through the common good that the individuals achieve personal development and well-being. It is also through the common good that society achieves its purpose and redistributes to the individuals, for their further perfection, the public goods of the commonwealth.

"He who seeks the good of the many seeks his own good," says St. Thomas. Again, he says: "Man is not bound to the commonwealth by all that he is." These two give us the key to St. Thomas's view of the place of the individual in society.

The individual strives to advance the common good and receives in return from the common good those helps he needs to fill up the insufficiency of his human nature and so to attain greater human perfection. Thus, in seeking the good of the many (the common good), he seeks his own good (the individual good) as well. However, man retains the dignity of his human personality throughout all his efforts for the common good. His obligation to work for the common good pertains only to those external actions which affect the good of those with whom he is striving. He is left unbound in heart and mind and will for the pursuit of his personal goal, his inner happiness, his temporal well-being, and life of virtue. Thus, he is not "bound to the commonwealth by *all* that he is." His personal goal goes beyond the direct and immediate end of society. It is individual and personal; it is his eternal happiness and the perfection of his complete nature.

Man contributes to the common good of society, (1) positively, by fulfilling his duties to it in promoting the commonweal, and (2) negatively, by refraining from doing whatever might hinder the advance of his fellow associates and of society as a whole. For in the strength and well-being of the commonweal, the individual finds the storehouse of his temporal needs. Man gives and takes in the social order.

On the other hand, society aims at the individual good *through* the common good. Its primary and chief purpose is the promotion of the good of all. Society has the task of promoting group purposes, that through the good of the whole, it may re-distribute to the individuals the fruits of the common good. It aims to give the individuals the help required by their natures. Its direct goal is the commonweal; indirectly it lavishes upon man the riches (mental, social, physical, moral, and economic riches) of the commonweal of which it is the custodian and dispenser. Society takes and gives in the social order.

Social Unity Involves Order

St. Thomas defines order as the apt arrangement of parts. Certainly in "a one in many" order is prerequisite. It cannot be denied that inequalities exist among individuals. Order, therefore, necessitates the proper arrangements of individuals according to their proper place, as, for instance, according to their importance, their contribution, and the like.

Pope Leo writes of this:

> There naturally exists among mankind innumerable differences of the most important kind; people differ in capability, in diligence, in health, and in strength; and unequal fortune is a necessary result of inequality in condition. Such inequality is far from being disadvantageous either to individuals or to the community; social and public life can only go on by the help of various kinds of capacity and the playing of many parts, and each man, as a rule, chooses the part which peculiarly suits his case.

As a consequence of the natural inequalities in the individuals, there will be inequalities of contribution to the common good and likewise there will be inequalities of returns. Unequal distribution is as natural and as just as unequal contribution.

Social order, therefore, implies first a recognition of this inequality and then the arrangement of the various unequal parts in the common striving for the common end, so that the greatest possible good will be attained. It is order imposed upon the individuals in such actions as affect the common good. It would not, for instance, in normal times, regulate the kind and quantity of food taken; it would, however, regulate such actions as involve injustice toward individuals or the commonwealth, such as matters of life and death or lawbreaking.

Order Demands Subordination

Things must be put in order, that is, in a proper arrangement, because some are of more value and others of less, or because some are of more importance and others of less, or some have greater usefulness and others less, and so forth. In the individuals that constitute society, some things are of more importance and others are of less importance; some individuals make a greater contribution and others make a lesser one, according to their natural capacities. Order, or arrangement, must be introduced into society to regulate these inequalities.

To regulate such things, individuals will have to be satisfied to bow before the common good when their individual will conflicts with the good of the whole. This applies to those things in which the individual is subject to the common good. It does not apply to those things in which the individual good is superior to the common good, as in matters of conscience. In things pertaining to the common striving of the whole society, an individual must yield when it is necessary, provided there be no injustice done to him in his personal liberties and his right to pursue the path marked out for him by God. In his final destiny and in those things which pertain to it, the individual is superior to society. In things which pertain to the temporal well-being of the commonwealth, an individual must yield his personal interests in favor of the common good. The former, with respect to his final destiny, is because of man's completeness as a human person with inviolable natural rights. The latter, with respect to man's temporal well-being, is because of man's insufficiency. He needs society and he needs the contribution to his well-being which society makes. Therefore man must respect the good of society and he must do nothing to injure it, for in society he finds his own temporal well-being. Hence it is that the individual seeks the common good *at least* for his individual personal welfare, for in seeking the good of all he seeks his own good, too. A less selfish view, naturally, is that one whereby a man loves and seeks the common good for *its* sake rather than for his own.

Subordination Not Demeaning

In discussing the question of mastery, St. Thomas tells us there are two kinds. There is, first of all, subjection of one's personality; that is, of one's intellect, will, and all things that a man has. This yields to another what is strictly one's own. It is slavery. This is not the kind of mastery we mean in speaking of man's striving for the common good and his submission to it in exterior matters which pertain to the common good. This was the kind of mastery which Pope Leo condemned in his encyclical on the *Abolition of African Slavery*: "They (pagan philosophers) did not hesitate to say that slaves were very inferior to freemen both in intelligence and in the perfection of bodily development. Hence they concluded that slaves, since they lacked reason and sense, ought to do, in all things however rash and unworthy, the will of their masters."

This is not Christian subordination!

The second type of mastery, explains St. Thomas, is that of subordination. This is the mastery of a free subject, a being of intellect and will, a being of natural rights and eternal destiny. It is not slavery, for it does not require that a man surrender his intellect and will. It means that he accepts the guidance of one appointed to direct him either toward his own welfare or toward the common good.

Pope Leo, in his encyclical on *Human Liberty*, has said: "The true liberty of human society does not consist in every man's doing what he pleases, for this would simply end in turmoil and confusion and bring on the overthrow of the state." And Pope Pius XI in his encyclical entitled *The Reconstruction of the Social Order*, says: "It is true, indeed, that a just freedom of action should be left to individual citizens and families, but the principle is only valid as long as the common good is secured and no injustice is entailed." In his famous *Labor* encyclical, Pope Leo had written: "The State must not absorb the individual or the family; both should be allowed free and untrammeled action as far as is consistent with the common good and the interests of others." In the Christian concept of society, therefore, man is not enslaved, neither is he undisciplined. He is duly subordinated without destroying his personality and dignity. He contributes to social oneness insofar as he is thus subordinated as a part of the whole — as the imperfect to the perfect.

We seem to have gone far from our initial discussion of the formal cause of society. You will recall that we said the distinguishing mark of society was its unity. "A one in many" describes society. It is not just *one*; it is not just *many*. It is "a one in many"; it possesses a unity of external strivings toward a common goal. It reflects a unity of wills joined in common effort. Where there is unity, there must be order or arrangement of the inequalities which exist among the many. That necessitates subordination and direction of the many legitimate authorities representing the "one" and designated for that purpose. On the proper understanding of subordination depends the proper understanding of the place of the individual in the group. The individual is not annihilated. The group is not absolutely supreme. The individuals are united but they still possess and exercise their personal liberty. Social unity, social order, and social interaction are blessings in the social order!

St. Thomas Says

It is interesting to note how St. Thomas speaks of the requisites for social unity. In his work addressed to King Hugh of Cypress, he tells the king (who, by the way, is believed to be a distant relative of his):

> The *unity of society which we call peace,* must be procured through the efforts of the ruler; therefore *to establish virtuous living* in the multitude, three things are necessary:
> (1) the multitude *be established* in the unity of peace
> (2) the multitude thus established *be guided* to good living
> (3) it is necessary that there be at hand *a sufficient supply of the things required* for proper living, procured by the ruler's efforts.

But that is not the whole of the ruler's duty in the establishment of social unity. St. Thomas says that once the life of unity, peace, and virtue is established, it remains for the ruler to look to its preservation.

The duty of establishing the life of virtue, difficult as that may be for a ruler, becomes more difficult when we consider its additional obligation, namely, the permanence of the life of virtue and peace. Without a permanent peace based on virtuous living, no unity can long prevail in the social order.

There are three forces working against this permanence in public virtue upon which depends the preservation of social unity. St. Thomas classifies them thus to King Hugh:

Dangers (1) from nature; (2) from within the social whole; (3) from outside the social whole. First, dangers from nature itself. St. Thomas points out that the good of society should be perpetual, at least relatively so, but, he adds, men die, they lose their vigor, they are not equally suited to perform the same duties throughout the whole span of life and so the common good would suffer, social unity and peace and virtue would not be constant unless the ruler replaced in public office the old, the corrupt, the less vigorous by younger, virtuous, vigorous men.

Second, the danger from within consists in perversity of wills as when individuals are too lazy or too selfish to contribute to the common good or when, through injustice, they disturb the public and private peace.

Third, the danger from without consists in the destruction of peace through the attack of enemies.

This threefold danger lays upon the ruler a threefold duty:

1. The ruler should make reappointments in various offices so that he will insure that the *best* men occupy public offices. In this way, physical and moral corruption will be averted. By the appointment of younger men to refill the places of the aged men, energy will characterize the services rendered to the common good by men in public office.

2. Through laws — rewards and punishments — and through the consequent maintenance of order, the ruler must restrain his subjects from vice and encourage them in the exercise of virtue.

3. The ruler should keep his charges safe from external enemies as well as the internal ones mentioned above.

Thus, St. Thomas sets forth the method for preserving social unity through the life of virtue and of peace in the common strivings of mankind for a common goal.

Some Original Sources

Numerous sources could be tapped in the works of St. Thomas for the subject matter in this chapter. Following the lead of St. Thomas, the Holy Fathers have taken his principles and expounded in their various encyclicals the nature and necessity of human society. What do the following excerpts mean to you?

1. "It is natural for man to be a social and political animal, to live in a group, even more so than all other animals, as the very needs of his nature indicate.

"For all other animals, nature has prepared food, hair as a covering, teeth, horns, claws as means of defense, or at least speed in flight.

"Man, on the other hand, was created without any natural provision for these things. But, instead of them all, he was endowed with reason, by the use of which he could procure them all for himself.

"For one man could not sufficiently provide for life, unassisted. It is, therefore, natural that man should live in company with his fellows.

"Moreover, all other animals are able to discern by inborn skill what is useful and what is injurious; just as the sheep naturally regards the wolf as his enemy. Some animals even recognize by natural instinct certain medicinal herbs and other things necessary for their life.

"Man, however, has a natural knowledge of the things which are essential for his life, only in a general fashion, inasmuch as he has power of attaining knowledge of the particular things necessary for human life by reasoning from universal principles.

"But it is not possible for one man to arrive at a knowledge of all these things for his own individual reason. It is, therefore, necessary for man to live in a group so that each one may assist his fellows and different men may be occupied in seeking, by their reason, to make discoveries, one for example, in medicine, one in this and another in that." (*On the Governance of Rulers*, bk. 1, pp. 30–31)

2. "He who seeks the good of the many seeks his own good for two reasons:

(1) Because the individual good is impossible without the common good of Family, State or Kingdom;

(2) Because since man is part of the home and State he must needs consider what is good for him by being prudent about the many, because the good disposition of parts depends upon the relation to the whole." (*Summa Theologica*, vol. 10, p. 18)

3. "Man is not ordained to the State according to all that he is and has." (*Summa Theologica*, vol. 6, p. 276)

4. "A man is master of a free subject, by directing him either towards his proper welfare, or to the common good." (*Summa Theologica*, vol. 4, p. 333)

5. "It is natural to man to be a social animal, and this is proved by the fact that one man alone does not suffice to procure all the necessities of human life." (*Summa Contra Gentiles*, vol. 4, p. 128)

6. "As the perfection of a whole consists in the union of its parts, a whole cannot exist unless its parts agree.

"Hence any decrees drawn up for the welfare of a State and city ought to be formulated with a view to the advantage of all its members.

"Any statutes which would hinder the unity of a commonwealth, ought to be abolished. For laws are established in order to preserve the concord of a state, and not to promote internal dissension." (*An Apology for Religious Orders*, p. 91)

7. "If one man surpassed another in knowledge and virtue, this would not have been fitting unless these gifts conduced to the benefit of others." (*Summa Theologica*, vol. 4, p. 334)

Interpretative Suggestion:

- In what ways do the natural gifts of certain members of society conduce to the benefit of others? Does this quotation suggest the Socialist-Communist *leveling of society* or the Christian *subordination* based on inequalities in the social order? Discuss.

8. "It is society which affords the opportunities for the development of all the individual and social gifts bestowed on human nature. These natural gifts have a

value surpassing the immediate interests of the moment for in society they reflect the Divine perfection, which would not be true were man to live alone." (Pope Pius XI, in the encyclical *Atheistic Communism*)

9. "Just as in the living organism it is impossible to provide for the good of the whole unless each single part and each individual member is given what it needs for the exercise of its proper functions, so it is impossible to care for the social organism and the good of society as a unit unless each single part and each individual member—that is to say, each individual man in the dignity of his human personality—is supplied with all that is necessary for the exercise of his social functions." (Pope Pius XI, in the encyclical *Atheistic Communism*)

Summary

1. Man is social by nature. The inclinations of his nature toward social living are so pronounced that it makes social life necessary for man. Humanity as a race must live in society. Individuals can live apart from association with others but their life would be mere existence and not full human development and perfection.
2. Every man constitutes a member of society. Society exists and lives in the individual members. It would not be possible for society to continue if the individuals which compose it were all obliterated.
3. Man's need for society pertains not only to his material well-being but also to his intellectual and moral development.
4. Man's nature requires society for the necessities of this life; that is, for the material needs of the body and for the life of virtue. Man's nature came from God and man will return to God. Through society man obtains the help necessary for temporal well-being and the life of virtue; through these he makes his way to God as to his final end in life.
5. Society has for its goal, directly and immediately, the common good; while indirectly and ultimately, the goal is the good of the individual, that thereby he may reach his final end. It helps man to satisfy his desires for God and unending happiness.
6. Man's final end is God. Man's intermediate ends are the common good and individual temporal good which become, for him, means to his ultimate end.
7. Society is the grouping of men to effect a common purpose through common striving. Members of society must be aware of one another and of their own insufficiency. They must recognize a common nature, a common destiny, and common needs in all mankind. This creates the unity in society which constitutes society as such, and which distinguishes it from other kinds of association.

8. The individual good is subordinate to the common good of the society. The common good is subordinate to the final good of man which is eternal. Hence society must not only concentrate on the good of the group, but it must see that this overflows unto the individual who has as his personal destiny the attainment of the final good, of eternal felicity.

9. Every individual in society has its own purpose in life; has its own dignity as a human person; and has its consequent liberties which are sacred and God-given. Society must never, therefore, exercise the mastery of slavedom over the individual members.

10. Subordination is necessary in society because of the natural inequalities which exist among the individual members. Subordination is the recognition of one's proper place according to one's importance, contribution, and so forth. Subordination is proper and just and necessary in the social order.

11. Inequalities in society constitute the basis of social order.

12. When selfishness dominates in society, social unity is weakened because of the disturbance to the proper order of parts in the whole. Individuals must be willing, for the sake of the commonweal, to surrender their will in those things which do not violate their natural liberties and their conscience.

For Study and Discussion

1. Explain how St. Thomas's view of man as a social being is broader than Aristotle's view of man as a political being.

2. How urgent is man's need of society? Could an individual man live apart from the race? Could the human race live apart from social intercourse? In what ways can only society meet man's needs?

3. What did St. Thomas mean by saying that to stand in need of nothing is superhuman? Discuss this in connection with quotation number 1 from the "Some Original Sources" section in this chapter. What is meant by saying that society is *natural* to man?

4. Explain how speech is distinctly human equipment.

5. Discuss the nature of society. In some subhuman creatures, association is *instinctive*; in man, social life is *rational*. Explain.

6. From a study of the definition of society, explain how subhuman associations are not true societies. How may society be said to be "a one in many"?

7. Sum up the paragraphs on causes: How many causes may a thing be said to have? How are they classed? What do they tell about the thing?

8. Individual men constitute the material cause of society. Explain this cause and tell how men constitute the material cause of social life. Explain the proximate as well as the ultimate material cause of society. Is *man* the basis of both aspects of the material cause?

9. Explain: Man and society are two indispensable and inseparable elements.
10. What is the second of the four causes of society? Explain this cause.
11. What bearing has the term *unity* on the formal cause of society? Wherein does a society of men differ from a herd of buffaloes?
12. Is social unity achieved through a denial of man's personality?
13. Is there any direct connection between the vitality of society and the degree of unity therein?
14. How can you reconcile the statement that man, as a free individual, is obligated to pursue the common good of society?
15. Can you explain how the common good is both the cause and the effect of social unity?
16. Why does Pope Leo say that inequalities are *natural*? How can unequal distribution and unequal contribution be "both natural and just"?
17. Explain the difference between subordination and slavery. Which of them might be called *exploitation*?
18. Discuss the interrelation between social order, social unity, social action, and the common good.

For the Advanced Reader

St. Thomas:
> *An Apology for Religious Orders*, chap. 3
> *On the Governance of Rulers, Bk. I*, chap. 1
> *Summa Theologica*, vol. 4, The Mastery of Man, pp. 326–334, esp. pp. 332–333; vol. 10, Of Justice, pp. 113–135, passim; Of the Parts of Justice, pp. 157–167, esp. 158–159; 160–161

Farrell, Walter:
> *A Companion to the Summa*, III, chaps. 8–9, pp. 191–244; chaps. 12–13, pp. 301–353

Sheen, Fulton J.:
> *Whence Come Wars*, chap. 3

Papal Encyclicals:
> Pope Pius XI, *Atheistic Communism*

The New Scholasticism:
> "What Is Social Autonomy?," vol. 13, no. 3, July 1939

The Thomist:
> "Social Unity and the Individual," vol. 1, no. 1, April 1939

Any good book on Christian social ethics

10

Society: Its Efficient Cause; Its Final Cause

We began in the last chapter a study of the nature of society through its causes. We shall continue that subject in this chapter, giving our attention now to the efficient and the final causes of society; namely, to the agent and to the purpose of society.

Efficient Cause of Society

This is the third of the causes of society. It might be likened to that by which society is effected. What agent (if a person) or what agency (if not a person) is responsible for the existence of society?

It may not seem strange to say that "understanding" is considered as one of the efficient causes of society. Through reason, man "understands" the necessity of social living; he grasps the notion and the nature of the common good and recognizing these as advantageous to his personal development, he is disposed to accept social living in response to the inclinations of his nature. A second efficient cause of society, therefore, can be traced to the will of man. Ultimately, God, in His divine plan of the universe, willed society for man, but less remotely, it is traceable to man's free will. In response to the dictate of his reason that social living is the only adequate human living, man willed so to live. Social living, which has been a fact of history from the beginning of human life, came into existence in response to the willed action of man. Early man might have recognized the natural need for society but, being possessed of free will, it is conceivable that he might have not willed to live in social intercourse with others. On that supposition what the condition of the race (if it yet persisted on the earth — which is doubtful) might be at the present era, no one knows. Hence, man's free will is an efficient cause of society.

Further than that, however, we must mention external authority as being also an efficient cause of society. Without the external restraint exercised on man by authority, human selfishness might long ago have broken down the social unity and dragged social living to the depths of mere brute association, if not to complete annihilation.

A later section will be devoted to the discussion of authority, its nature, and its work.

Final Cause of Society

The final cause is the fourth and last of the causes which explain the nature of a thing. It corresponds to the reason or purpose for which a thing is made. The final cause of society, therefore, must answer the question: What is the final end, the goal, of society? Toward what is it directed? What does it hope to attain? The answer, in view of the foregoing pages, is relatively simple to us now. The interaction of the individuals aiming at the common good tells us why society exists. It exists for the individual and the common good of the members of society. It exists primarily for the well-being of the collectivity and secondarily for the well-being of the collected individuals. In other words, *all the individuals* in society are the complete end or purpose of society; *each individual* is the incomplete or partial end of society. If society, through its individual members, is intent upon the well-being of the whole, securing to the whole a good life on the human level, then society is accomplishing its complete or perfect end; it is achieving its primary purpose. If, on the other hand, society concentrates merely on promoting the welfare of selected individuals or lesser groups to the neglect of the whole, then society fails to meet its primary purpose. At best it is accomplishing only a partial goal and it would be guilty of injustice if this neglect of the whole be intentional and avoidable.

The Common Good

The common good is nothing other than the good of the collected individuals, not as individuals, but as *collected*; that is, as a whole. It is the general welfare of the society and its benefits that are distributed *to all* and *to each*. It is another aspect of that axiom of St. Thomas, that he who works for the common good works for his own good, too. The social order, social security, the wealth and resources (not merely economic wealth), the peace and protection, and the common action of the members advance the *good* of the group and, through the greater goodness of the group, advance the individual's good or well-being.

Aspects of the Common Good

The common good represents the good human life, one which includes a sufficiency of intellectual, moral, and economic goods. If man were ordained merely for economic well-being, that is, for an abundance of wealth, then a financier would be the likely ruler of a society. If the end of man were merely life and health of body, then a physician would be the governor. If intellectual knowledge were the end of man, then the ruler would have to be a teacher. But man as an individual, or man as a multitude of men, is ordained for something higher than physical, mental, or economic goods. The common good of society and the individual good of each member should include these goods, but it should not neglect to consider and provide for the good which alone can be man's ultimate end. The common good is the good which contributes to man's perfect development, and this includes moral and religious goods as well.

St. Thomas tells us the common good corresponds to the life of virtue. By the *life of virtue* St. Thomas does not mean that society must make its individuals, one or collectively, *saints*. By *virtue* he includes those virtues which tend to promote well-being and peace among the multitude. The life of charity and of justice, for instance, is absolutely necessary if the social order is to maintain itself. By *virtue* too, St. Thomas means *peace,* and this can be accomplished only through a life of virtue; that is, a life based on charity and justice in the individual and in the collectivity. Through charity and justice, peace is obtained, and social unity is strengthened.

The Common Good as an End

The common good is said to be the end or purpose of society's existence. Let us understand this correctly. Society is not ordained to itself. Society does not exist for its own good but rather for the good of its members. The end of society, therefore, is outside itself. It is *for* something else. It is a means to some further end.

Society, like all the rest of creation, is ultimately ordained to God. Man is likewise ordained to God. Brutes are ordained to God. Plants and minerals are ordained to God. All creatures are ordained (or have an end) outside of themselves. They are all insufficient unto themselves. Society, therefore, finds its ultimate end in God. It has, however, a proximate end.

The direct and proximate aim or purpose of society is to advance the common good. Now since it is only through the common good that the individuals in society can be perfected, each individual is obliged to work for the common good. Each individual must make his contribution to it, since the common good is necessary to the humanly better life of the individuals in the society. It has for its purpose the assurance of the opportunities necessary to live life on earth well.

As subjects of the social order, individuals are ordained to the good of that order. In other words, individuals find in the social order an *end* which they are bound to attain. That end, of course, is the common good. Let us repeat that statement. Individual members are bound to contribute to the common good. They are bound to forego even individual good things for the sake of the common good. The common good takes precedence over the individual when the matter in question is purely a social matter directive of man's temporal happiness. It does not pertain to matters of conscience, or to human personal liberties and natural rights and duties which man has, *not due to his social nature,* but to his character as a human person with a divine origin and destiny. In this way, and in such matters as pertain to the good life of the group, society is man's superior.

Not only does society find in the common good an end or reason for its existence, but man too finds in it an end or purpose. The common good is not man's *final end,* but only an *intermediate end.* Man's final end is God, and for this reason the common good is used by man as a means to his final end. In other words, the common good may be likened (not too strictly) to a re-fueling station wherein man's needs are filled so that he might continue his flight to God. It is not a stopping place for man, but a treasury on which he may draw in passing. Man's ultimate goal, as we know, is not finite existence or temporal happiness. Therefore, he does not come "to rest" in the common good. He uses it for further ends. He uses it as a means to God. In this way, every man in the collectivity transcends society because he has a goal beyond society. In this respect man is society's superior. The temporal is thus made to serve the spiritual.

To sum up then, the common good is the good of the collectivity. In it man finds the means to perfect his life and to attain perfect happiness. The common good is the direct end of society, and, at the same time, it is an intermediate end of the individual who continues onward toward his ultimate goal, using the means placed at his disposal by the common good to which he contributes according to his capacities. Man goes, through the common good and its help, to God.

Some Original Sources

1. "We are not provided with raiment, as other animals are furnished with hides. Neither has nature given us weapons, like the horns which she has bestowed on cattle; nor the claws wherewith lions defend themselves....

"In lieu of the gifts bestowed upon other animals, man is endowed with reason, which teaches him to supply his needs, and [man is endowed] with hands, wherewith he can carry out the dictates of reason." (*An Apology for Religious Orders*, p. 158)

(See also item no. 1, "Some Original Sources," chap. 9.)

2. "If anything is ordained to an end outside itself, it is the governor's duty, not only to preserve the thing unharmed, but further to bring it to its end.

"If, on the contrary, there should be anything whose end is not outside itself, then the governor's endeavors would merely tend to preserve the thing itself undamaged in its proper perfection ... [but] nothing of this kind is found in the world, except God Himself, Who is the end of all....

"One person may perhaps have the duty of preserving a thing in existence, and another the duty of bringing it to a higher state of perfection.

"This is clearly the case in the example of the ship, from which the idea of government is derived. For it is the carpenter's duty to repair anything that is broken in the ship, but the sailor bears the anxiety of bringing the ship to port.

"It is the same with man. The doctor sees to it that a man's life is preserved in health, the tradesman supplies the necessities of life, the teacher takes care that he learns the truth, and the tutor sees that he lives according to reason.

"If a man *were not* ordained to any other end outside himself, the above mentioned cares would be sufficient for him.

"But as long as a man's mortal life endures, there is some good extraneous to him, namely, final beatitude, which is looked for after death in the enjoyment of God....

"Consequently the Christian man ... needs an additional spiritual care to direct him to the harbor of eternal salvation, and this care is provided for the faithful by the ministers of the Church of Christ.

"We must form the same judgment about the end of society as a whole as we do concerning the end of one man.

"If, therefore, the end of man were some good that exists in himself, then the ultimate end of the multitude to be governed would likewise be for the multitude to acquire such good and persevere in its possession.

"If such an ultimate end, either of an individual man or a multitude, were a corporeal one, namely, life and health of body, to govern would then be a physician's charge. If that ultimate end were an abundance of wealth, then some financier would be king of the multitude. If the good of the knowledge of truth were of such a kind that the multitude might attain to it, the ruler would have the duty of teacher.

"But it is clear, that the end of any multitude gathered together, is to live virtuously. For men form groups for the purpose of living well together, a thing which the individual man living alone could not attain. But a good life is a virtuous life. Therefore a virtuous life is the end for which men form groups....

"Only those are regarded as forming one society who are directed by the same laws and the same government to live well.

"Therefore, since man, by living virtuously, is ordained to a higher end, which consists of the enjoyment of God, then human society must have the same end as the individual man.

"Therefore, it is not the ultimate end of an assembled multitude to live virtuously but through virtuous living to attain to the possession of God.

"As the life by which men live here on earth is ordained as a means to the end of that blessed life which we hope for in heaven, so, too, whatever particular goods are procured by man's agency, whether wealth, or profits, or health, or eloquence, or learning are ordained as a means to the end of the common good....

"Since the beatitude of heaven is the end of that virtuous life which we live at present, it pertains to the governor's office to promote such good living among his people, as is suitable for the attainment of heavenly happiness, that is to say, he should command those things which lead to the happiness of heaven and as far as possible forbid the contrary....

"For an individual man to lead a good life two things are required. The first and most important is to act in a virtuous manner (for virtue is that by which one lives well); the second, which is secondary, and, as it were, instrumental (i.e., as a means) is a sufficiency of those bodily goods whose use is necessary for an act of virtue.

"Yet the unity of man is brought about by nature, while the unity of a society, which we call peace, must be procured through the efforts of the ruler. Therefore, to establish virtuous living in a multitude three things are necessary:

1. that the multitude be established in the unity of peace
2. that the multitude thus united in the bond of peace be guided to good deeds
3. that there be a sufficient supply of the things required for proper living."

(It was deemed advisable to quote these passages almost in their entirety because of their lucidity and wisdom. They are taken from St. Thomas's work *On the Governance of Rulers*, bk. 1, chaps. 14–15. Numerous passages might have been quoted from the *Summa Theologica* and others from the *Summa Contra Gentiles*. The above seemed to suffice.)

Summary

1. The efficient cause of society is threefold: (1) understanding its necessity through the light of reason; (2) the will of man moving him to live in association with others; (3) authority which maintains the social unity and promotes social action.

2. The final cause of society is the common good. The common good is the collective well-being. St. Thomas says it is the life of virtue, through which peace is found in the social order and social unity strengthened.

3. The *life of virtue* referred to is not the practice of all virtues, for this is beyond the realm of a human ruler to legislate. The *life of virtue* is the exercise of those virtues which pertain to the social well-being, chiefly charity, justice, and peace. These virtues promote the common good.

4. Individuals in the group desire the common good at least for their own individual welfare. This is not the highest motive possible, however. The normal attitude is an equal interest in the common good and one's own good. A higher attitude is that wherein an individual member considers the personal welfare of others through the success of the group, even at the cost of personal sacrifice. All individuals should strive for the least possible degree of selfishness in his attitude and strivings for the common good.

5. The common good may be viewed as the good of the collectivity or the whole society, and thus it is the complete or perfect end of society. The common good may be viewed as it is distributed unto the collected members of the group, and in this way the individual good is the partial or incomplete end of society.

6. The common good constitutes an end for man as well as for society. Whereas it is the direct end of society, it is only an intermediate end for man inasmuch as man marches on to his final destiny which is above and beyond the group. Each man's goal is personal and eternal; the common good therefore becomes a means which man may and must make use of to perfect his efforts and supply his needs for the attainment of the ultimate end to which he is ordained by God and nature.

7. Each individual, insofar as he is a citizen and is bound to contribute, is ordained to society and is subordinate to the common good of society. Inasmuch as he is a person with a divine destiny, he transcends society, and uses the common good as a means to his ultimate end.

8. Society is ordained to the common good, and through the common good it is ordained to the individual good. Now since the individual good is ultimately perfect happiness in the possession of God, the individual and society are said to have the same end, *ultimately*; the end of society is the end of the individual, namely God.

9. The common good is superior to the individual good in matters pertaining to man as a citizen, as when, for instance, an insane person is deprived of his liberty of action, that others might not suffer.

10. The individual good is superior in matters that pertain to man as a rational being with rights which transcend social control; as when, for instance, authority would attempt to abolish man's right to life, to marriage, to freedom of worship, and the like, the individual may legitimately resist the violation of his personal rights.

For Study and Discussion

1. What is the efficient cause of society? In what way is it said to be threefold?
2. How is authority an efficient cause of social order and social action?
3. What is meant by the expression: "Man is disposed to social life by nature"?
4. What role does the will of man exercise with respect to man's social inclinations?
5. Explain the difference between the complete end of society and the partial end.
6. What is meant by saying that man is at once inferior and superior to society? Upon what basis is man inferior to society? Upon what claims does his superiority rest?
7. Explain how the common good constitutes the direct end of society. In what way can society be said to have the same end as the individual?
8. Society has as its end the common good; however, the common good has a further end. What is it?
9. In what way can the common good be said to be an end for man?
10. Discuss the case if the common good were man's *final* end. What philosophy of government operative in the world today considers the commonweal as man's ultimate end and chief obligation?
11. What obligations has society toward the individual man? What obligations has the individual toward society?
12. What is meant by *the common good*? To what extent does St. Thomas make the common good synonymous with the life of virtue?
13. How is peace said to be the common good? What are its effects upon social unity?
14. Explain, in terms of means and end, the following statements: "Society is for man." "Man is for society." Which is the Christian concept of society? Why?
15. Explain: "Man is not ordained to society in *all* that he is and has." How can you reconcile that statement with this one, also by St. Thomas: "The common good is the end of each individual member of a community, just as the good of the whole is the end of each part."

For the Advanced Reader

St. Thomas:

On the Governance of Rulers, Bk. I, chaps. 14–15

Summa Contra Gentiles, vol. 4, chaps. 111–113, 129

Summa Theologica, vol. 6, pp. 17–51; vol. 8, pp. 4–5; vol. 10, pp. 121–122, 124–125, 127, 130, 198, 200

Farrell, Walter:

A Companion to the Summa, II, "Common Good," pp. 397–403

Philosophy of the State, reprinted 1940 from vol. 15, Proceedings of the American Catholic Philosophical Association, 1939

"The Common Good and Political Action," pp. 119–122

"The Individual and the State," pp. 10–21

Any good book on social ethics

11

Society: Its Authority

We have called society "a one in many" and we have noted that the unity which makes the many "a one" is effected by the human will following the dictates of reason, and by external authority.

St. Thomas tells us: "A social life cannot exist among a number of people unless under the presidency of one to look after the common good; for many, as such (that is, a multitude of individuals) seek many things, whereas one attends only to one thing. Wherefore ... wherever many things are directed to one [end], we shall always find one at the head, directing them." In these words St. Thomas expresses the need of authority in social living.

Why Authority Is Needed

The duty of authority is to govern. Now to govern, says St. Thomas, is "to bring the thing governed in a suitable way to its proper end." A society without government is as a ship without a helmsman or a body without a head. There would be no likelihood of the end of either being achieved, for there would be nothing in the nature of a director to indicate the suitable means and to move each toward its goal.

Quite simply, authority in society is necessary because of human self-seeking. In society there are many wills. Now many wills individually seek the things each desires. Frequently this is not in accord with the common good or it may even be opposed to it. The exercise of one's freedom may infringe upon the equally natural right of another member of the society. Authority, therefore, is needed to establish and maintain harmony between the *self* and the *group*, as well as among the individual *selves* in the community.

Of course, we do not overlook the fact that each human person is endowed with physical freedom (i.e., the lack of physical restraint) to do as he chooses to do. However, the important thing to remember is that, *morally*, he is not free to do so. That means, a human person *can* do anything he is physically able to do and which he chooses to do, but that he *may* not do so, *if* he wishes to lead a morally good life. The freedom of man's will leaves him *physically free* but his obligation to act *humanly*, that is, according to reason and law, leaves man *morally not free* to do certain things, that is, it makes him morally obliged to act according to God's law.

A man, for instance, *can* deliberately maim or murder another or speak unjustly against him. Morally, he *may* not do so without forfeiting the goal of human life. He is obliged by the moral law to respect the rights of others.

Without authority, the common good would not be safeguarded and individuals would fail in their duty toward the commonwealth. St. Thomas writes: "For where there are many men together, and each one is looking after his own interest, the group would be broken up and scattered unless there were also someone to take care of what appertains to the commonweal.... There must exist something which impels towards the common good of the many, over and above that which impels towards the private good of each individual."

Authority directs the society and the individual members to their proper goal. Authority also restrains the society and the individual members from acts of injustice one toward the other. It creates opportunities for the individual to provide for his needs; it secures the necessities of life to the individual; it advances the common good; and finally, it distributes to the individuals the advantages of the whole society, that is, of the common good of the society.

Without authority, there would be no reconciliation of the conflicting views of the individual and the group. There would be, furthermore, no guarantee of man's personal, inalienable, natural rights which are bestowed on him by his Creator and which are beyond the power of individuals or of society to destroy or to abolish. Let us repeat: authority ordinarily is the source of social order, social unity, and social action. As such, it is absolutely necessary to the life and preservation of the social body.

"As the Soul to the Body"

Let us try to understand the functioning of authority. Since authority may be vested in one, or in a number ruling as one, we shall speak of the person or persons in whom authority is vested as *the ruler*, understanding by that term the individual one-man ruler or the ruling body. In his treatise *On the Governance of Rulers*, St. Thomas used several likenesses to express the kingly office. St. Thomas speaks in his work above mentioned of *the kingly office* because he was address-ing himself to a king, to King Hugh of Cyprus. We must understand by *kingly office* the office of any legitimate ruler exercising authority over a social body.

In this work St. Thomas likens the ruler to a sailor who brings the ship to harbor by a direct route and unharmed. He says, again, that the ruler is to the society what the soul is to the body. As reason is the controlling power of the body, so the ruler is the controlling power of the body politic. Now the soul gives life to the body and governs it, moving it by reason and will to its proper end. So, too, must the ruler establish in existence (if it be not already established) a body politic and direct it to its proper end. But even that likeness is not sufficiently noble, for St. Thomas says that the king must recognize that "such is the office which he undertakes that he is to be in the kingdom what the soul is in the body *and what God is in the world.*"

"What God Is in the World"

What a noble ambition is thus laid down for the earthly ruler, that he pattern his ruling after that of the Divine Ruler! And why should it not be thus, for no man rules for himself or in virtue of his own excellence, but in virtue of God's will! Does not the universe of corporal and spiritual creatures come under the divine government "whereby everything is embraced under the rulership of God who governs all things by His Providence"? Thus St. Thomas finds in God the pattern whereby the earthly ruler ought to be formed. His comparison is at once striking and illuminating. We summarize it herewith.

God, firstly, established the world. But what did this imply? It implied (1) the production of things; (2) the orderly distinction of the things produced, whereby one species was distinct from another as plant differs from mineral, and the brute from the human animal; (3) the distribution of the various species to an appropriate locale, as the fish to water, men, brutes, plants, and minerals to the earth, birds to the air, and the sun and moon to the heavens; (4) it implied, lastly, provision for their needs. All this is concerned with the establishment of the world.

A ruler, modeling his direction upon that of God, cannot produce things, not being a creator, but (1) he takes the materials which he finds already pro-duced and uses them wherewith to establish his body politic. He decides upon a certain location as the site of his realm. Then, (2) he lays it out site by site, this for farming, that for trade, that for a center of learning, another for a city, and so forth. (3) He distributes his subjects according to their occupations and the role they play in the social life; this one to be a farmer, that one a teacher, another a merchant, and so on. Finally, (4) the ruler provides for the needs of his subjects according to their particular condition in life.

Thus the ruler establishes his ruling on the pattern of the Divine Ruler of the world.

God not only established the world but He governs it and preserves it in existence. This, particularly, is God's *government*. He directs each nature according to its purpose and He moves the universe as a whole to its end, *which is outside of itself*. If the end of the universe were its own perfection, then God's ruling would be only to preserve it unharmed. But the end of the universe is not the universe itself but God, toward whom all things tend; hence God's government of the world must do more than keep it unharmed; it must move *the universe to its end* — namely, to God Himself.

So, too, must the ruler exercise his powers of government. If the end of the society over which he rules were the good of that society as such, rather than the good of the human beings who compose it, then the ruler would be fulfilling his duty by preserving it unharmed. Since the end of society is not the good of society as such, but the *common good* through which the individual's final good is attained, the ruler must do more than merely preserve the society. The ruler, following the leadership of God, must (1) preserve it unharmed; (2) bring it to its end; (3) be duly solicitous for its improvement which is advanced through its movement toward the proper end.

"The governor," says St. Thomas, "being taught the law of God, should have for his principal concern the means by which the multitude subject to him may live well. Now this concern is threefold: first of all, to establish a virtuous life in the multitude subject to him; second, to preserve it, once established; and third, having preserved it, to promote its greater perfection."

Source of Authority

There is little need of elaborating on this. The point is obvious in view of the above paragraphs. The source of authority is not the ruler, but God. It is not accurate to say authority resides in the people. Authority is an attribute of God, the One and only Creator to whom all creatures — rulers and ruled — are subject. Where the multitude chooses the ruler (as in a democracy) its role is twofold. First, the will of the many determines upon him who shall rule them. Secondly, it pertains to them also to determine the manner in which the ruler shall exercise the authority that is his. The only one capable of *conferring authority* itself is He who is absolute authority, because He is Absolute Lord and Master of the universe. God shares His authority with earthly rulers. He confers it upon them. God, and not the people, confers authority. God, who created man and his social nature, knows that authority is needful. That the purpose for which He created man might not be frustrated, God condescends to permit creatures to share in His rulership over the universe. God does not thus give away His authority but merely shares the exercise of it with His creatures.

Unless authority is rooted thus in God, it has no other basis but human rule which is subject to all kinds of uncertainty. Furthermore, without rooting authority in the spiritual (as in God) there is no basis for man's subjection to it, for one man is as good as another and no one man is privileged to set himself up as ruler over another. Only by the will of God and in participation of His authority, can one man rule other men. Unless it had the spiritual basis, there would be no foundation for man's obligation to work for the good of society as a whole. Without a spiritual basis for authority, there would be only tyranny and force and countless revolutions. Human authority *must* have its roots in divine authority or wither away purposeless.

Functions of Authority

We have already noted a number of general functions of authority in society. To achieve harmony, promote virtue, secure peace, preserve unity, direct all to their proper end, distribute the goods of the community, and provide for the common good have all been discussed. Do you recall the Preamble to the Constitution of the United States? It reads: "We, the people of the United States, in order to form a more perfect union, establish justice, insure domestic tranquility, provide for the common defense, promote the general welfare, and secure the blessings of liberty to ourselves and our posterity, do ordain and establish this constitution for the United States of America." Note how closely it embodies the Christian concept of the functions of authority.

Perhaps you may not have thought much about it before, but it *does* make a difference what concepts or principles underlie one's thinking, either individual thinking or collective thinking.

If one believes in the dignity of the human person, its right to work toward its final goal in the path marked out for it by God; if one believes in the divine origin and destiny of man, it follows that certain modes of conduct will be in order, and other modes entirely out of order, in dealing with the multitude of such human persons. A concept of man as just outlined demands that the virtue of justice be always operative in the social order. Then men will not only give to society what is its due, but also between individual and individual in the social group, justice will constantly direct man's conduct. A pagan concept of man, his nature, goal, rights and consequently, his *value*, would dictate an entirely different line of conduct. In a later chapter we shall see how such a concept works out in practice in the case of particular nations with which we are too sadly familiar.

Duties to Itself

Authority has for its purpose to direct the society and its individual members to their last ends. Ultimately these final ends are one and the same end, namely, God. If we had said that authority *must* do so we would mean that authority *was driven* to perform its purpose as an animal is driven to seek food. We learned earlier in this work that *must* is the expression for necessity and not free choice. Ice *must* be cold, but a man *may* be temperate or otherwise. The ice has no choice in the matter; man freely chooses the one state or the other. To signify man's position in the matter we say that he *ought* to choose temperance in view of his last end (moral obligation), but that he *can* choose intemperance if he so wills (physical freedom).

Now if we were to say that authority must direct men to their final goal we would be denying that authority was a moral being. It would be equivalent to saying that authority could do no right or no wrong. Only moral beings are capable of right and wrong.

But authority *is* a moral being, and it has rights and duties. With what its duties to others are, we are now quite thoroughly familiar. It also has duties to itself. It has the duty, for instance, to preserve itself. This can be done first, by clearly defining its rights so that the subjects know what is expected of them as subjects and, on the other hand, what limits are placed to the exercise of mastery by authority. If the power of taxation is a right of the ruler, to what extent may taxation go? Should it be so excessive as to deprive a man of all his possessions?

A second way of preserving itself is by recognizing its limitations, for there *are* limits beyond which authority ought not go (moral obligation). This implies that the rights of the individuals in the commonwealth must be known and respected. In the question of excessive taxation, for instance, it would be tantamount to destroying the right of private property by making the exercise of this right impossible. But authority cannot do this. Man's right to the possession and use of private property is too deep and sacred for society to abolish or circumvent it.

Limits of Authority

The principle is simple and rational: Authority — any authority — is limited *by its end or purpose*. Authority in the family is limited to commanding and compelling obedience in those things which concern the purpose of the family, the reason why it exists. A family could not, for instance, command and compel obedience to such a law as this: No parking after 6:00 p.m. Laws and ordinances regarding parking are not within the scope of familial authority; it belongs to civic authority to legislate thus.

Civil authority, whose end is the common good primarily in matters of temporal happiness, could not legislate regarding days of fasting and abstinence. This is beyond its scope. Fasting has nothing to do with the end or purpose of civil society. To legislate concerning spiritual matters belongs to a society whose end is spiritual; namely, the Church. It is beyond the limits of the mayor of a city to declare a national holiday, as it is beyond the limits of the authority of a school principal to legislate regarding the quality and quantity of food eaten by the pupils.

Authority is limited, too, by the eternal and natural laws in commanding and compelling obedience in those matters pertaining to their end. Nothing contrary to these laws may be commanded. What authority commands must not violate God's law or the law of nature. "Things which are of human right cannot derogate from divine or natural right," says St. Thomas. Within the scope of the eternal and natural law, authority may legislate only for those things which pertain to the proper end for which it was established. All authority is limited by the eternal law and the law of nature. Each kind of authority — familial, civic, ecclesiastical — is further limited to those things which pertain only to each one's particular goal.

Other Duties of Authority

We already mentioned authority's duty to preserve itself in power. This is done, generally, (1) by defining its rights and (2) by recognizing its limitations which is, of course, nothing more or less than recognizing and respecting the individual's rights. A second duty of authority is to legislate. It has the right to make laws. A third duty is to enforce its laws. For what purpose would it be to have laws if they were not enforced? Either they were not necessary and so should not have been imposed, or they are necessary and should therefore be enforced. Authority has the duty to enforce its just laws. The basis of law enforcement may be twofold: (1) authority may use and carry out threats of punishments, or (2) it may motivate obedience through rewards. "Under penalty of the law" is a familiar warning to us. "Under penalty of fine or imprisonment or both" is another threat justifiably used by social authority to enforce its laws.

Authority does not pin gold, silver, and bronze medals on those who obey. The reward is not so tangible. Its reward is the reward of a smooth-running social order; the reward of peace; of unity; of virtue which compensates the members of the social order for their obedience to authority's rulings. Only a mother, in the small social circle of the family, finds it possible to hand out cookies to reward her subjects' obedience.

Rights of the Individuals

Human rights will receive considerable attention in chapter 12. For the present, in order to complete the picture of authority, it will be sufficient to indicate the more important human rights. In general, and in ordinary circumstances, the individuals which comprise the social order have a right to the fullest possible development of their human personalities. They are entitled to the satisfaction of their innate cravings; that is to the fulfillment of their natural desires, including goods of the body, goods of the soul, and external goods, both natural and artificial. Mentioning several specifically, we note the right to life, to domestic society, to liberty, to labor, and to property, all in the natural order, and, in the supernatural order, the right to religious worship and the pursuit of God.

In extraordinary times, a limitation of the individual's rights may be required. Special surrender must sometimes be made as the forfeiture of life, in capital punishment; of liberty, for crime; a limitation of property, through moderate taxation which, however, does not amount to confiscation. In regard to supernatural rights, the right to worship may at times be suspended as in times of epidemics, when churches are closed.

On all occasions, however, the individuals in society are entitled to justice both on the part of authority and on the part of individuals.

The individual, having rights, has duties also. He is obliged to obey lawful authority in those matters to which the rights of authority extend. Considering the lower authority as human and the higher authority as divine, the following statement of St. Thomas would sum up the individual's just attitude toward authority. The saint writes: "A man should submit to the lower authority in so far as the latter observes the order of the higher authority. If the lower authority departs from the order of the higher, we ought not to submit to it."

Tyranny

St. Thomas, in his tract on law, declares several times that law which is not an act of reason cannot be considered law at all but rather a species of violence. The question might be asked: Can lawfully constituted authority be deposed? The answer is based on the principle that authority, in God's plan, exists to direct society and men to their ultimate goals; it orders society, directly to the common good and indirectly back to the Author of society; it directs men, through the intermediate goal of the common good, beyond it to the final goal — the Author of mankind. Now any authority which does not fulfill its purpose, has no reason for existing. Thus it would seem that lawfully constituted authority may be deposed.

St. Thomas cautions, however, that if the tyranny practiced be not in excess, it would be more expedient to tolerate it, because of greater evils which may result. The tyrant, knowing the opposition against his rule, may increase his violence in order to excite great fear in his subjects. Or perhaps, he being deposed, his successor might be more of a tyrant. It not infrequently happens that the multitude, excited to violence, may know no bounds within which to confine its activities. In all these cases, the results would be more injurious than to tolerate the not-too-excessive tyrant.

A story is told by St. Thomas in this connection. He writes:

> In Syracuse, when there was a time that everybody desired the death of Dionysius, a certain old woman kept constantly praying that he might be unharmed and that he might survive her. When the tyrant learned this, he asked why she did it. Then she said, "When I was a girl we had a harsh tyrant and I wished for his death; when he was killed, there succeeded him one who was somewhat harsher; I was very eager to see the end of his dominion also; then we began to have a third ruler still more harsh — that was you. So if you should be taken away a worse would succeed in your place."

St. Thomas doesn't relate what then happened to the old woman, but the story presses home its meaning nevertheless.

Granted that a given tyrant is excessive in his abuse of rights and the burdens with which he inflicts the subjects, it is not permitted to private individuals to undertake to remove him. To admit a principle that any private individual, on his own initiative and in his own name, has the right to make away with the ruler, would be to make precarious the very position which has been established for man's protection and perfection.

The deposition of one in authority, however, may be undertaken by public authority. If the right to designate a ruler resides in the multitude, then only the multitude may depose him if he abuses his authority. If the right to elect a ruler resides in some other than the multitude, as in an elective body, then such body, being public authority, may depose him.

St. Thomas adds, however, that if no human help be forthcoming, then recourse should be had to God.

No love is lost between a tyrant and his subjects and both are given to fear. How often do we not find tyrannical rulers surrounding themselves with a few satellites (*strong men*) whose favor they curry and upon whose strength they depend to protect them from their subjects. Love between ruler and subjects secures a ruler in his office, for "It is no easy task to shake the government of a prince whom the people so unanimously love," while "the government of tyrants cannot last long because it is hateful to the multitude."

Authority's Reward

Our chapter on the important question of authority would not be complete unless we closed with a brief discussion on a reward suitable to a ruler in return for his services to the commonweal. Surely the services rendered by a just ruler are invaluable. Certainly they have brought with them no small measure of pain, fatigue, worry, and self-sacrifice. What suitable reward may a ruler justly desire in exchange?

In the eyes of a subject, one in authority has an easy life. There is a certain amount of deference paid to him. He is well fed and well clothed and well housed. He is the focus of public attention and of private envy. He meets people and goes places. His office is surrounded by a certain glamor, while glory and honor is his daily diet. Should a ruler seek in these the adequate return for his ruling?

St. Thomas (and your own common sense, too) answers with a long and hearty no. Nothing that depends on the fickle opinion of men is of long duration, and what more depends on mere opinion than the honor and glory paid to a ruler? One whose opinion changes overnight heaps scorn today upon the ruler to whom yesterday he showed greatest respect and deference. Further, to seek in honor and glory the reward of one's ruling, takes away from the ruler the true greatness of soul which should characterize him. It makes of the ruler a slave to his subjects, rather than a servant. In trying to please each and all, he loses his freedom of soul and peace of mind. Honor and praise are not a fitting reward for a ruler, and good men spurn them.

Furthermore, a good man makes no account of glory, but should one seek it, he would endanger the multitude over whom he rules for he is less good than it becomes a ruler to be. Rulers desirous of gaining glory oftentimes plunge their countries into war, seeking in warfare and its spoils the glory they crave. It causes a leader to become a plunderer, presumptuous, abusive, hypocritical, a doer of deeds to be seen by men.

Only to genuine virtue is honor due, and it is extremely difficult to acquire such depth of virtue as is deserving of the honor and glory of men. And so frequently rulers, craving honor, and not being possessed of the virtue to which honor is due, have recourse to deceit, to fraud, to crimes in order to gain it, not knowing that what they gain is not honor, but notoriety.

The only suitable reward, says St. Thomas (and your reason prompts it, too) is to seek something in God. "It is fitting to expect as a reward for virtue that which makes man happy.... Happiness is called the perfect good inasmuch as it comprises in itself all things desirable. But no earthly good is such a good ... and so nothing earthly can make man happy, that it may be a fitting reward for a governor.... It is God alone Who can still the desires of man and make man happy and be the fitting reward for a ruler."

Some Original Sources

In these sources, there will be found some from the Angelic Doctor and some from the writings of Pope Leo XIII and Pope Pius XI. Note the similarity of doctrine. See how closely the popes drank from the stream of St. Thomas in its original purity.

With respect to legislation, which is one of the foremost means used by rulers for the direction of their people toward the common good, St. Thomas has this to say:

1. "Laws framed by man are either just or unjust. If they be just, they have the power of binding in conscience, from the Eternal Law whence they are derived.

  "Now laws are said to be just,

  1. from the end, when, that is, they are ordained to the common good,
  2. from their author, i.e., when the law that is made does not exceed the power of the lawgiver, and
  3. from their form, that is, when burdens are laid on the subjects according to an equality of proportion and with a view to the common good.

  "Wherefore ... on this account, such laws as these, which impose proportionate burdens, are just and binding in conscience, and are legal laws.

  "On the other hand, laws may be unjust in two ways:

  1. by being contrary to human good, through being opposed to the things mentioned above: either
    (a) in respect to the end, as when an authority imposes on his subjects burdensome laws conducive, not to the common good, but rather to his own cupidity or vainglory;
    (b) in respect of the author, as when a man makes a law that goes beyond the power committed to him;

(c)   or in respect of the form, as when burdens are imposed unequally on the community, although with a view to the common good.

"The like are acts of violence rather than laws; wherefore such laws do not bind in conscience, except perhaps in order to avoid scandal or disturbance, for which cause a man should even yield his right.

2. Laws may be unjust through being opposed to the Divine good. Such laws are the laws of tyrants inducing to idolatry or to anything else contrary to the Divine Law: and laws of this kind must in nowise be obeyed." (*Summa Theologica*, Tract on Human Law, vol. 8, pp. 69–70)

From the encyclical of Pope Leo XIII, we quote:

2. "The right to rule is not necessarily bound up with any special mode of government. It may take this or that form provided only that it be of a nature to insure the general welfare. But whatever be the nature of the government, rulers must ever bear in mind that God is the paramount Ruler of the world, and must set Him before themselves as their exemplar and law in the administration of the State.... In civil society God has always willed that there should be a ruling authority, and that they who are invested with it should reflect the Divine power and providence in some measure over the human race.

"They, therefore, who rule, should rule with even-handed justice, not as masters, but rather as fathers, for the rule of God over man is most just, and is tempered always with a father's kindness. Government should moreover be administered for the well-being of the citizens, because they who govern others possess authority solely for the welfare of the State.

"Furthermore, the civil power must not be subservient to the advantage of any one individual, or of some few persons; inasmuch as it was established for the common good of all. But if those who are in authority rule unjustly, if they govern overbearingly or arrogantly, and if their measures prove hurtful to the people, they must remember that the Almighty will one day bring them to account, the more strictly in proportion to the sacredness of their office and preeminence of their dignity.

"Then truly will the majesty of the law meet with the dutiful and willing homage of the people, when they are convinced that their rulers hold authority from God, and feel that it is a matter of justice and duty to obey them and to show them reverence and fealty, united to a love not unlike that which children show their parents.

"To despise legitimate authority, in whomsoever vested, is unlawful, as a rebellion against the Divine Will; and whoever resists that, rushes wilfully to destruction. To cast aside obedience and by popular violence to incite to revolt, is therefore treason, not against man only, but against God." (*The Christian Constitution of States*)

Pope Pius XI has written:

3. "It is true, indeed, that a just freedom of action should be left to the individual citizens and families, but this principle is valid only as long as the common good is secured and no injustice is done. The duty of rulers is to protect the community and its various parts; in protecting the rights of the individual they must also have special regard for the infirm and needy.... The State must not absorb the individual nor the Family; both should be allowed free and untrammeled action as far as is consistent with the common good and the interests of others." (*The Reconstruction of the Social Order*)

4. "Tyrants err in deserting justice for a few earthly advantages; for they are deprived of this great reward [viz., eternal beatitude] which they could have obtained by ruling justly. That it is foolish to sacrifice the greatest and eternal goods for trifling, temporal goods, is clear to everybody but a fool or an infidel." (St. Thomas, *On the Governance of Rulers*, bk. 1, chap. 10)

Summary

1. Society is the grouping of men for the purpose of achieving a common end by common effort. It is "a one in many" without destroying the many or undermining the one.
2. Social living is necessary for human beings, for the full development of their rational nature cannot be effected without intercourse with others of their kind.
3. To preserve the "one in many" there must be a head directing the many to the goal of the group. This is not the final goal of the many, but it is a necessary intermediate goal; otherwise the individuals could not effect their purely personal goal which is beyond the goal of the group.
4. Achievement of the common goal would be impossible without the direct measures of the one in charge, for many as such have many goals and conflict of rights is the logical result. If the need for society can be traced to man's nature, so the need for authority can be traced to man's nature—to his fallen nature, for selfishness and greed make authority necessary. Man ever remains an individual of personal desires and free will.
5. The ruler of the community over which he rules is likened to the sailor who guides the ship; to the soul which vivifies the body; to the rule of God over the universe.
6. The work of authority in society is to harmonize the interests of the individual with individual; of individual with the group; the group with the individual. This is the foundation of the operation of justice in society.

Christian Social Principles

7. The threefold task of the ruler, in general terms, is: (1) to preserve order, unity, and peace in the society; (2) to promote public and private well-being through supplying the opportunities for procuring the necessities of a good life; (3) to stimulate progress. Besides supplying the means to individuals for their temporal well-being, it must concentrate on group purpose because it is only through attaining the common good of the group that the individuals really benefit from association.

8. Authority has its source in God. It draws upon God for the power which it exercises. Only when authority is thus rooted in a being beyond the material universe or any of its parts (such as man or the society itself) can human authority find reason for its existence and justification for its demands upon the subjects.

9. Authority has the right, from God, to command its subjects to act according to the common advantages of the group. It may compel obedience to its commands. It has the right to preserve itself in existence. It may legislate for the common good, promote group strivings, punish offenders, and the like.

10. Human authority must acknowledge the limits beyond which it may not go. Any human authority is limited; it is limited by the very purpose for which it was established. Familial authority is of lesser extent than the public authority of the State. Ecclesiastical authority is not limited by territorial boundaries, because the Church is worldwide and her limits are restricted to matters of ecclesiastical jurisdiction: spiritual concerns, concerns of faith and morals wherever and whenever they present themselves. The principle which it would be well to bear always in mind is this: authority is limited by the purpose for which it was established. It may not act beyond that. Its purpose is determined by its end. This is the extent of its power.

11. Natural human rights must always be respected by authority. Though authority may regulate the exercise of personal rights for the sake of the common good, it may not abolish them or make their use impossible.

12. Human authority, even though legitimately constituted in office, may be deposed from office if the good of the commonwealth necessitates it. The right to depose a ruler does not rest with individuals as private persons. The multitude which constituted the ruler in office is alone entitled to depose him.

13. Authority is a sharing of God's providence over the world. It is a sacred trust. It is given for the good of the group and the good of the individuals in the group. No finite good thing can sufficiently recompense a ruler for enduring the difficulties consequent upon his office. Honor, fame, power, and vanity are insufficient rewards. They make a ruler "small-souled" rather than magnanimous. The only adequate reward of rulers lies in the attainment of eternal beatitude: the possession and enjoyment of God.

For Study and Discussion

1. Explain this statement of St. Thomas: "No man can judge others than his subjects and this in virtue either of delegated or of ordinary authority." Why is this principle a safeguard of human dignity and freedom?

2. "The act of distributing the goods of the community belongs to none but those who exercise authority over those goods." Explain this principle in terms of the need of authority in social living.

3. "One who exercises public authority may lawfully put to death an evildoer, since he can pass judgment on him." Explain how this does not violate man's basic right to life. Explain man's right to life under ordinary circumstances; under extraordinary circumstances. How can capital punishment be justified?

4. What is meant by "look after the common good" when said of the duty of the ruler?

5. Explain the analogy between God as the governor of the universe and the human ruler as the governor of the community. How is the ruler likened to the soul of the body? to the pilot of a ship?

6. Anarchists are opposed to government. Explain what losses would accrue to a society which overthrew legitimate and just authority and accepted the principles and the practices of anarchy. What losses would be sustained in this country if governmental rights were denied and abolished?

7. Why is it forbidden to private individuals to undertake the deposition of authority? Explain how this is not an unjust limitation of man's freedom, but rather a guarantee of it.

8. "In human society no man can exercise coercion except through public authority." Explain how violation of rights must be settled through lawfully constituted authority rather than by recourse to violence between the individuals concerned.

9. What limitation is placed on the exercise of human authority in the various ways in which God shares His authority with human rulers? Why is the principle involved in this discussion a very important one? Give examples indicating the limits of authority in three or more specific grades of human authority: for example, in the family, and so forth.

10. Discuss and give reasons for the reasonableness of the statement: "All public power must proceed from God: for God alone is the true and supreme Lord of the world ... whosoever holds the right to govern, holds it from one sole and single source, namely, God, the Sovereign Ruler of all."

11. Why should tyranny, if it be not excessive, be borne with patience? Why should recourse be had to God if legitimate human means do not avail?

12. Explain the end of authority (its purpose) from these words of Pope Leo: "Civil society, established for the common welfare, should not only safeguard the well-being of the community, but have also at heart the interests of its individual members."
13. Explain fully why honor and glory are ill-becoming rewards for a ruler. Why do good men spurn such rewards? Why are such returns inadequate? What is the adequate reward of rulers? Why?

For the Advanced Reader

St. Thomas:

On the Governance of Rulers, Bk. I, chaps. 6–15.
Summa Contra Gentiles, vol. 4, chaps. 114–117, 146; vol. 3, chaps. 77–78.
Summa Theologica, Tract on Law, vol. 8, human law, pp. 53–83; Tract on Justice, injustice, parts of justice, passim, judgment, etc., vol. 10.

Farrell, Walter:

A Companion to the Summa, II, chap. 19

Sheen, Fulton J.:

Whence Come Wars, chap. 4

Papal Encyclicals:

Pope Leo: *Chief Duties of Christians as Citizens*
Civil Government
Evils of Modern Society
Human Liberty
The Christian Constitution of States
Socialism and Communism

Any good book on Christian ethics

12

Society: Social Virtues

It takes but a moment's glance over the whole range of virtues to determine very accurately those which should hold primary place in social action. Society is a grouping of men. The word *grouping* implies a host of *other* selves; the word *men* tells us that those *others* are *brothers*. In the *other* we enter the field of justice; in *brother* that of charity. Among human individuals there can be no *other* unless he be a *brother*. And thus, the foremost social virtues are justice and charity.

A discussion of social virtues necessarily brings along with it a discussion of the nature of virtue and the nature of rights. Let us take a brief view of each of these.

Virtue Is a Habit

Not infrequently the word *habit* brings to mind such things as a steady consumption of cigarettes; a regular and prompt insistence upon shutting off the alarm and turning over; or a persistent yielding to this or that weakness. Habit is connected in one's thoughts, not infrequently, with indifferent acts or with sinful acts but seldom with good acts. As a matter of fact, *virtue is a habit*.

Man starts off life with a definite nature moving along to a determined goal. He has a certain amount of equipment which is destined to make his progress easier and more certain of successful termination. Upon this original equipment, man builds. By directing his actions along certain lines toward certain ends which he knows and wills, he constructs a *second nature*. He has given his original equipment a battery of habits to facilitate his proper movements.

Some habits are intellectual habits. They develop the mind. They cause easier movement of one's mental powers toward the acquisition of intellectual knowledge. An expert mathematician is a man of habit; his mind moves easily and freely along the tracks of quantities. An outstanding grammarian is a man of habit; his mind moves easily and freely along the tracks of syntax and form. Habits which develop the intellect and send it fairly swinging along its way to goals of knowledge are intellectual virtues. There are five: art, prudence, and the three we discussed under primary principles of thinking — namely, understanding, knowledge, and wisdom.

The fact that prison records show an increasing percentage of college graduates among the convicts of today tells its own story. It shows that men of knowledge are not necessarily *good* men. In fact, if men of knowledge are good men, morally good men, it is not because of their knowledge, but because of another factor which we shall name almost at once. A good mathematician can never attain the goal of human life on that score alone. If he reaches his proper goal it is because he has another set of virtues which do not operate on his intellect. It is a group of virtues that perfect his will.

Man's will brings him to his goal. This is true, in that a man must will to reach his end; that no amount of knowing the end will bring him to it. He must reach it by his own human acts, willed and executed. To do this, man needs the moral virtues. Moral virtues move his will. They direct his conduct. They alone are capable of bringing him to his end. Of a man's *knowledge*, we say that it is true or false, but of a man's *actions* that they are good or bad. A man reaches his goal because he is good and not because he is learned. It is the moral virtues which will facilitate his movements to the goal of life.

The moral virtues are prudence, justice, fortitude, and temperance. They are habits which, when possessed, not only *incline* a man to act virtuously but they are practically a guarantee that he *will act* virtuously. Of course, man has free will and he *can* (and at times he may) act contrariwise, but his normal behavior will be virtuous behavior. The deeper the habit of virtue has taken root in his nature, the less likely he is to act contrary to it because it is the more natural to him. A man who is strongly possessed of the virtue of justice would find it as difficult to be unjust in a given situation, as an unjust man would find it difficult to act with justice. For both it would be a case of "going against the grain"; against the grain of justice for the man possessed of the good habit if he were to act unjustly; against the grain of injustice for the man possessed of the evil habit if he were to act justly.

By virtue, therefore, is meant habits that are morally good because they lead to man's goal. With virtue a man lives rightly as becomes his human dignity. Without virtue a man is turned away from his goal. It is equivalent to being anti-social, because the movement of man is toward the proper goal of man and that is the goal of reason; the goal of the morally good; the goal that is God. Do you recall that the end of human association is "the good life," that is, the life of virtue?

Justice Presupposes Rights

Justice reaches out beyond its possessor into the multitude and finds out there the object of its action. The sole basis upon which justice comes to rest are the rights of others. Destroy or deny rights, and justice would have no role to play in the social order. It is the work of justice to give to everyone what is due to him. It is the payment of a debt. It is the recognition of a right. It is a bowing before that right. It is to recognize in the other, another man; another human personality; another heavenly-bound being; another self.

What Is Right?

Let us look at the question this way. Might is physical force. An army is said to be mighty; a battleship is mighty; the waves of the ocean are mighty; Longfellow's village blacksmith was "a mighty man." *Might* is physical; it belongs to bodies; it is observable by the senses; it makes its appeal to the senses.

Right is power, too, not different *in degree* but different *in kind* from physical power. Right is *moral* power. It belongs only to man, not to an army as an army, to a battleship, or to ocean waves. It belongs to a man's personality, not to his body only. It traces its source to man's spirituality, not to his animality. It is a moral power to do something, to possess something, to acquire something distinctly as his own. The doing, having, or getting something is independent of the weight of his body or the strength of his arm. It is altogether independent of physical force.

Right implies some standard for judging, otherwise what would be the dividing line between one man's moral power to do, to have, and to acquire and another man's moral power to the same things? To be of any use at all to man, a right would have to be inviolable, but must it be unlimited, too? If a man, for instance, has an inviolable right to do as he pleases with his possessions, is that right absolute, that is, is it unlimited? May he, for instance, use his truck to maim and kill his personal enemies? But if one's rights are limited, by what are they limited and on whose authority?

Rights Depend upon Law

Rights are moral powers and must therefore conform to the standards of morality. They are inviolable, which means that no human agent or agency can abolish them or render their exercise impossible. They are, however, subject to limitation; that is, to regulation. Being moral, their limitations are the limits set by the standards of morality. Now the norm of morality is right reason and the eternal law of God. Rights, therefore, trace their origin to the needs of man's nature and ultimately to the Creator; their inviolability is traced to their very necessity for the attainment of man's end; their limitation is traced to whatever is in conformity to God's law and the law of nature as manifested through the light of human reason. All rights, therefore, have their origin and their sanction in the natural and the eternal laws.

Rights Must Be Natural

Man's ultimate goal transcends the goal of society. Man must be guaranteed the freedom to attain his strictly personal goal. His rights must not have their source in society, for then society, at will, could abolish them or prohibit their exercise. Man's rights must come from outside society — from above society. They must come from someone outside of the individual, too, for rights carry with them the power to impose the obligation on others to respect one's rights. One man cannot impose obligations upon another man, as individual on individual. Man's rights are part and parcel of his nature; wherever human nature is found, the same basic rights will be found rooted therein. Though the rights originate in man's nature, they are found there because God so chose to create and endow man. Their source, therefore, rightly is said to be in God.

Rights which thus belong to man by reason of his nature are said to be connatural rights. The right to pursue one's destiny in the path marked out for him by God is the foremost right of man. No one and nothing can interfere with it. The right to life and to liberty are also connatural, but as we noted before under authority, society has some licit power over these extraordinarily, though not ordinarily.

Rights and Duties Correlative

Rights would be useless unless they were safeguarded. Treasures are always protected, and rights are one of the chiefest of man's treasures. Since rights are moral powers to do and to have, they carry with them the moral power to oblige others to recognize and respect them. The obligation or duty must be moral even as the right is moral. If not moral, then it would be physical. The result would be that one could safeguard his rights only by physical force. It would mean the strength of the offended party pitted against the strength of the offending party. In the case of violation of a man's rights by civil authority, what redress could there be?

The correlative obligation which attends every right is a moral persuasion, and it is precisely in the field of these moral rights and duties that the moral virtue of justice goes about its work.

The Virtue of Justice

Justice is a cool, calculating virtue going on its rounds paying debts to creditors. Just as no man contracts a debt with himself, so no man finds himself the object of his justice. Justice speeds from self to others.

Justice is a habit — a moral habit — which means it regulates the actions of a man. Justice is characterized by a firm will to give each one his due. Not only must the will be firm, but it must also be constant, perpetually constant and not constant for a time only. Anything that is due to a person belongs to him. It is his right. Thus a father has the right to the love of his child but not so a jailer to the love of his prisoner. Putting it all very simply, we say that justice is that moral virtue which disposes us and moves us to respect the rights of others. It is that habit whereby we are inclined by a constant and perpetual will to give to another what is due to him. No wonder it is of utmost importance in social living! It renders intercourse in society good, because it perfects the individual possessed of justice. Social life depends upon justice for its continued existence. When justice weakens its hold on individuals or on rulers, peace flees, unity breaks down, and social life is corrupted.

Kinds of Justice

There are three possibilities of rendering just dues in social living. We said earlier that individuals were obliged to contribute to the common good. But that is obligation. What is the correlative *right*? For remember, justice is inexplicable as a virtue without *rights*. In this case, if the obligation be on the part of the individuals, then the society is the creditor. Man owes something to society. Something is due to society and, in justice, the individuals must give society what is due to it. This is one possibility for rendering just dues: the individual to society. St. Thomas called this *legal* justice. He speaks of it as *general* justice because it directs man to the common good.

By legal justice the individual is moved to refrain from hindering the advance of the common good, and he is moved to make his contribution, according to his capacity, to the common good. This kind of justice directs to the common good; it is a payment made by the individual members on the basis of a debt due to society. A very simple illustration of this is in the payment of taxes; another is in giving military service in times when it is required.

Besides general justice, there is also particular justice which is directed toward the individual. Of this, there are two kinds: first, when the community pays its debt to the individuals by reason of their personal rights; second, when individuals pay their social debts to other individuals. Particular justice is directed always to the individual.

When the movement of justice is from the society or the ruler to the individual, it is called *distributive* justice. Quite simply, it directs the distribution of the common good to each and all. Instances of this kind of justice would be the equal distribution of burdens on all, protection from aggression, supplying opportunities for meeting the needs of life, and the like.

Justice rendered by individuals to individuals is *commutative* justice. Under this "individual to individual" movement must be considered also *moral persons* such as corporations or other organizations. This justice governs their interchanges such as in trade, as between the buyer and the seller, as between the workman and his master, and so on. It applies also to such individual goods as one's person, one's character, and one's possessions. Injustices committed in the field of commutative justice strictly require restitution. Defaming one's character and theft require, as you well know, strict restitution as a matter of justice.

Social Justice

Recently much has been heard of the term *social* justice, particularly since Pope Pius XI used it in his encyclicals. What is *social* justice? We said before that without society, justice would be an unnecessary virtue because a man can exercise justice, strictly speaking, only to others. If a man acts what we call *unjustly* toward himself, he does so freely with deliberate will. He does it because he chooses to do it, and this can scarcely be said to constitute a violation of what is *due* him. What is *social* justice and does the term refer to all types of justice or not?

It is quite generally agreed that the social justice of today is the *legal* justice of St. Thomas's century with perhaps a flavoring of another type of justice. In an earlier chapter we spoke of attitudes toward the social group. We indicated one which was a high ideal: the individual's interest was concerned primarily in the personal welfare of others through the well-being of the group, and to this he made his contribution even at the cost of personal sacrifice. This is the ideal citizen in the social order; the one who seeks his individual welfare only in relation to the welfare of the community and his fellowmen.

This implies a two-way action: to the commonwealth and from it to the individuals. It is expressed neatly in the phrase, "the good of all and of each."

Social justice would then seem to be the legal justice wherein the common good as common good is promoted, plus a flavoring of distributive justice wherein the common good is viewed as the good of society's members.

The virtue of justice cancels a debt, pays its dues; and thus it removes the obstacles to peace. It does not, however, beget peace. That is the work of charity, the queen of the virtues. For whereas law directs justice to the payment of its social dues, it is love which prompts charity to give of its goods to supply, not what *is due*, but what *is needful*.

Justice satisfies *rights*; charity satisfies *needs*.

What Is Charity?

Like justice, it is a habit. Because it inclines us to goodness, it is a virtue. Unlike justice, it does not have human actions for its object, and so it differs from the moral virtues. Charity has God for its object; it moves the individual toward his Maker, impelling him to give to his Lord and Master the first place in his life. When God is supplanted by other things, when His rights are ignored or denied, then the life of charity is lost. The soul is in mortal sin.

Charity is a theological virtue, along with faith and hope, because faith, hope, and charity are directed toward God; they have God as their object. Like all habits, they become *second nature*, moving easily, swiftly along their appointed ways, increasing in facility through exercise; waning in vitality through neglect. By faith one believes in God and what He has taught; by hope one expects, through God's help, to reach Him; by charity, one loves God for His own sake.

Charity a Social Virtue

As justice gives to the "other" as "other," charity gives to the "other" as "brother." It has a divine foundation. Loving God for His very self, the individual should love the children and friends of God, not necessarily for their own lovableness, but for the love of God. Certainly a man loves his family, and a friend loves his friend. The love is based on closeness, on enjoyment, on some measure of satisfaction to the one loving. But God is loved because He is so worthy to be loved; He is so lovable in Himself; He is loved for Himself.

In the intimacy of one's heart, one finds God; turning outward through God, one reaches the neighbor. Unless society is based on this triangle of human relationships in contact with and through the Divine, it cannot withstand the inroads of human selfishness. It will crumble and fall. Through reason, one is conscious of the existence of self and the neighbor; through charity, which exceeds reason, one extends his interest out beyond the walls of self to the neighbor but only after having passed through vivifying contact with the Divine Being. Charity is love of God for Himself, and love of neighbor is the overflow of one's love of God.

St. Paul speaks of charity as the bond of perfection. That is precisely what it is: a bond. It unites. It sees in every rational being a neighbor, because it sees in that being a child of God. It constructs a unity out of the multitude. It joins man to man because it sees in each man a brother seeking the same goal of happiness as itself; it sees in each a brother returning to his Father's mansion. Charity is the soul of the social order for it alone can bring about the union of hearts which society absolutely requires.

Justice gives to all men their due; charity, finding the obstacles to union thus removed by justice, proceeds at once to bind hearts together. Justice alone can never bind hearts; payment of debts is too cold and calculating a thing. Charity binds with strongest cords because it is a loving thing, a generous thing, a thing so noble and elevated that human rulers find it beyond their sphere of acting. They simply cannot legislate love. Justice is the most that they can require. A judge is empowered by his office to insist that a debtor pay a just debt to another, no matter how wealthy the other may be, but he simply cannot command that a wealthy man, of his abundance, give in charity to those less fortunate than himself. Charity is practiced in obedience to God and through love of Him.

Charity Cannot Replace Justice

In the social order justice is not infrequently withheld. Instances of it will be brought to your attention in a later chapter. It is sufficient to say right here that families, working men, individuals, are often victims of the injustice of others. Must charity supply for this? Must the State and the Church through organized charity, and individuals through private charity, make up the deficit? Naturally, the first duty of the State is to promote the common good. Now the common good is not strengthened, but weakened, by injustice. The remedy is clearly seen to lie in the establishment of justice. However, this is usually a long process; bodies and souls are suffering in the meantime. Charity steps in to relieve the suffering. But charity can never take the place of justice unfairly withheld. A debt is a sacred thing; it involves rights, and rights are a man's means of forging ahead to his goal of temporal and eternal happiness. No amount of charity can supply for an injustice. Charity can only supply the most needful things out of another's abundance, until the standards of justice have been re-established and are functioning.

St. Thomas enters very fully into the discussion of what obligations one has in the matter of almsgiving. It is only out of the surplus, after due consideration has been given to one's station in life and the cost of keeping up with that station in life, that a man is obliged by charity to give alms. If one were obliged to give in alms all that is over and above the *necessities* of life, there would be no stimulation to raise the standards of living; further, there would be wholesale idleness among certain classes of people. For if one were obliged to give away everything over and above, let us say, the twenty-five dollars needed for the necessities of life in a family for a given week, then what inducement would some men have to work, knowing that those who do work *must* give away the surplus? What ambition could a workman or his family have to raise their condition? Hence, the duty of charity is the duty to give out of the surplus which exists over and above keeping up with one's station in life.

Following St. Thomas's doctrine, Pope Leo, in his encyclical on *The Condition of Labor*, wrote:

> No one is commanded to distribute to others that which is required for his own necessities and those of his household; nor even to give away what is reasonably required to keep up becomingly his condition of life.... But when necessity has been supplied, and one's position fairly considered, it is a duty to give to the poor out of that which is over. It is a duty, not of Justice (except in extreme cases of dire need when life itself is in danger) but of Christian Charity — a duty which is not enforced by Human Laws.

If justice is the body, the framework, upon which society functions, charity is the soul, the breath of life, by which it thrives. When these two virtues form the foundation stones of the social order, it is indestructible. When the foundations weaken, the superstructure totters and falls. The good life, the life of virtue, the life of peace, is the goal of human association. Justice clears the indebtedness; charity binds the hearts; peace flowers on the stalk of that sincere love of neighbor which is in itself a part of one's sincere love of God.

Other Social Virtues

Though justice and charity are the foremost social virtues because they aim directly at man's final goal and the means thereto, they are not the only virtues required in social living. A ruler, for instance, might be a very just and God-fearing man, given to much almsgiving for the love of God, but at the same time be a very reckless ruler. He needs, for instance, the virtue of prudence which enlightens one about the best way of getting things done. Some people are very apt; others blunder everything they attempt. The prudent man takes consideration within himself concerning the fixed end to be attained and how it can best be attained. Then he follows up thought by action. Prudence is the star guiding his thinking and his activity. Prudence, therefore, is necessary in the social order; for a ruler, whose concern is the end of society and the means thereto, plunges into activity heedlessly and causes confusion and loss to the society over which he rules if he does not consider ways and means.

The opposite of prudence in government is rashness and inconsiderate-ness. This shows a lack of the virtue of prudence. On the other hand one who practices prudence to excess until it is no longer a virtue but rather a vice, is guilty of cunning (foxiness), fraud. Neither the excess of prudence nor the lack of prudence is desirable in a ruler, for a ruler must be virtuous as well as his subjects. Political prudence confers upon the ruler facility in governing according to law.

In addition to prudence, and in fact, as the basis of natural prudence, intelligence is needed in social life, especially in the ruler. Practical reason, capable of knowing the meaning and purpose of man, of society, of ends and of means, and such like things, is absolutely necessary. Intellectual develop-ment, of course, might come through understanding of primary principles and the conclusions wrapped up in them, through reasoning, instruction, education, and revelation. Intellectual knowledge is not only desirable but necessary in social living. As for the subjects, St. Thomas, following the light of reason, insists upon a certain degree of knowledge on the part of those who comprise the society. Certainly a fundamental knowledge of their purpose, their rights and duties, the nature of their contribution to the common good, the duty of rulers, and the advantages to be obtained from social living ought to be the minimum requirements, particularly in societies where there is self-government, as in a democracy.

However, all the moral virtues are needed in society. They are the lever which raises society above subhuman levels of association. Fortitude and temperance are therefore necessary, for one of these means great courage and the other, moderation. Fortitude is not the impatience of the peevish man who brooks no contradiction; neither is it the cowardliness of the street bully who attacks a smaller child but runs from one his size. Fortitude is called into play when difficulties surround one. Fortitude surmounts the difficulties rather than succumbs to them or flees from them. That there are difficulties in social living, who does not know? Patience, perseverance, and constancy are virtues which bolster up the courage which faces, battles, and conquers difficulties.

Moderation would be necessary even if man lived alone, but as a social virtue it can with less reason be ignored. Moderation in food and drink are perhaps the most common types of temperance with which you are acquainted. But moderation in pleasures of any kind keeps a man the master over himself. Habitual want of temperance, which is intemperance, results in insensibility, drunkenness, gluttony, anger, pride, lust, and cruelty. An insatiable thirst for power is also intemperance. In that vice, too, is found the source of the cruelties perpetrated upon innocent victims by ruthless, lustful, power-mad demons who may mask as rulers.

Now the possession of the habit of the above virtues is not sufficient for the moral development of individuals or of society. They must be externally, that is, publicly, manifested. They must be the light that shines before men, so that mankind, individually and *en masse*, will find its way safely back to its Father's home.

Group Virtues

Lest it be thought that only individuals as such, and the ruler as a public personage should be possessed of virtue, let us note that society as the group of individuals is a moral person with moral obligations even as are the individual men within its fold. Virtue must be more than private; more than publicly manifested by private individuals. Society as society is obligated to the practice of justice, of obedience, of religion and worship, of truth, and of piety. Public recognition of God as the source of man's nature and of society; recognition of God as the destiny of man and of society; recognition of God as the Supreme Ruler of the universe; recognition of God's rights as holding first place in the individual heart, mind, and will, as well as in the collectivity's heart, mind, and will; these, and the constant public avowal of its dependence upon God, are obligations of society as society.

Pope Leo, in his encyclical on *The Christian Constitution of States*, wrote: "Men living together in society are under the power of God no less than individuals are, and society, not less than individuals, owes gratitude to God, Who gave it being and maintains it, and whose ever-bounteous goodness enriches it with countless blessings."

The *good* life, the life of constancy in virtue, will alone establish human society in lasting peace.

Some Original Sources

Use these quotations from St. Thomas in connection with your discussions and explanations of the contents of this chapter.

1. "The Divine Law aims at the love of our neighbor. For there should be union of affection between those who have one common end. Now men have one common last end, namely, happiness, to which they are directed by God. Therefore men should be united together by mutual love.

"Whosoever loves a man, loves those whom he loves and those who are his kindred. Now, men are loved by God, since He prepared for them a last end consisting in the enjoyment of Himself. Therefore as a man is a lover of God, so must he be a lover of his neighbor.

"Moreover, since man by nature is a social animal, he needs assistance from other men in order to obtain his own end. Now this is most suitably done if men love one another mutually. Hence the law of God, which directs men to their last end, commands us to love one another." (*Summa Contra Gentiles*, vol. 4, chap. 117)

2. "The aspect under which our neighbor is to be loved, is God, since what we ought to love in our neighbor is what he may be in God. Hence it is clear that it is specifically the same act whereby we love God, and whereby we love our neighbor. Consequently the habit of Charity extends not only to the love of God, but also the love of our neighbor.

"It is wrong to hope in man as though he were the principal author of salvation, but not to hope in man as helping us ministerially under God. In like manner it would be wrong if a man loved his neighbor as though he were his last end, but not if he loved him for God's sake, which is what Charity does." (*Summa Theologica*, vol. 9, pp. 308–309)

3. "Since man loves his neighbor out of charity for God's sake, the more he loves God the more does he put enmities aside and show love towards his neighbor: thus if we loved a certain man very much we would love his children though they were unfriendly towards us." (*Summa Theologica*, vol. 9, pp. 322–323)

4. "The proper matter of justice consists of those things that belong to our intercourse with other men ... hence justice is a habit whereby a man renders to each one his due by a constant and perpetual will." (*Summa Theologica*, vol. 9, pp. 114, 115)

5. "Justice directs man in his relations with other men. Now this may happen in two ways:

    (1) as regards his relations with individuals,

    (2) as regards his relations with others in general, insofar as a man who serves a community, serves all those who are included in that community.

"Accordingly justice in its proper acceptation can be directed to another in both these senses.

"Now it is evident that all who are included in a community, stand in relation to that community as parts to a whole; while a part, as such, belongs to a whole, so that whatever is the good of a part can be directed to the good of the whole.

"It follows therefore, that the good of any virtue, whether such virtue direct man in relation to himself or in relation to certain other individual persons, [it] is referable to the common good, to which justice directs:

"So that the acts of all virtues can pertain to justice, insofar as it directs man to the common good.

"And since it belongs to the law to direct to the common good, it follows that the justice which is in this way styled general, is called *legal justice*, because thereby man is in harmony with the law which directs the acts of all the virtues to the common good." (*Summa Theologica*, vol. 10, p. 126)

6. "Besides legal justice which directs man immediately to the common good, there is a need for other virtues to direct him immediately in matters relating to particular goods ... so besides legal justice there is need for particular justice to direct man in his relations to other individuals." (*Summa Theologica*, vol. 10, p. 126)

7. "Now particular justice is directed to the private individual who is compared to the community as a part to the whole. Now a twofold order may be considered in relation to a part:
   (1) There is the order of one part to another, to which corresponds the order of one private individual to another. This order is directed by commutative justice, which is concerned about the mutual dealings between two persons.
   (2) There is the order of the whole towards the parts, to which corresponds the order of that which belongs to the community in relation to each single person. This order is directed by distributive justice, which distributes the common good proportionately.

"Hence there are two species of [particular] justice, distributive and commutative." (*Summa Theologica*, vol. 9, pp. 158–59)

8. "Even as part and whole are somewhat the same, so too, that which pertains to the whole, pertains somewhat to the part also; so that when the goods of the community are distributed among a number of individuals, each one receives that which, in a way, is his own.

"The act of distributing the goods of the community belongs to none but those who exercise authority over those goods.

"It belongs to legal justice to direct to the common good those matters which concern private individuals: whereas on the contrary, it belongs to particular justice to direct the common good to particular individuals by way of distribution.

Christian Social Principles

"Distributive and commutative justice differ not only in respect of unity and multitude, but also in respect of different kinds of 'due' because common property is due to an individual in one way, and his personal property in another way." (*Summa Theologica*, vol. 9, p. 159)

9. "Besides commutative justice, there is social justice with its own set of obligations, from which neither employer nor workingmen can escape. Now it is of the very essence of social justice to demand from each individual all that is necessary for the common good. But ... it is impossible to care for ... the good of society as a unit, unless each single part and each individual member is supplied with all that is necessary for the exercise of his social functions." (Pope Pius XI, *Atheistic Communism*)

Summary

1. Social life requires consideration for the rights of others and a genuine sympathy for them in their needs. This attitude of mind should be a constant one, not flighty. This attitude of mind must go beyond the mind to the will. The will of man must be moved easily and constantly in the direction of his fellows. The attitude of mind and movement of will must be habitual.

2. Ease in acting is a habit. When it inclines man toward good ends, the habit is a virtue. When it inclines man toward evil ends, the habit is a vice. Habits become *second nature*, causing the actions of man to flow easily along to their goal, or away from it, as the case may be.

3. Some habits perfect the intellect, making its movement toward knowledge easier. They are called intellectual habits. There are five of them: prudence and art which concern practical knowledge, that is, the "doing" and "making" of things respectively; and understanding, knowledge, and wisdom which concern speculative knowledge.

4. Intellectual habits (or virtues) are necessary in social life, for the ruler requires prudence to guide him in the selection of means to the end; he needs also intelligence to know the nature, goal, and purpose of his subjects, and so forth. Subjects, too, require them in their own way.

5. Social life could not be preserved in its unity and progress without moral habits: habits which perfect man's will by directing him aright in the production of good acts. They point out the way to the goal. These habits of the will are the moral virtues.

6. The moral virtues are prudence, justice, fortitude, and temperance. Prudence is found in the enumeration of both classes of virtue. This is because it applies right reason (the intellectual aspect) to human action (the moral aspect). Prudence might really be considered in a class by itself. St. Thomas calls it "a special virtue, distinct from all other virtues."

7. In addition to the moral virtues, social life needs a cementing bond: that of charity. Charity is a virtue, too; an infused virtue which makes its first appearance in the human soul at Baptism. It is that virtue which inclines one to God as lovable—perfectly lovable in Himself. It finds in its love of God, love for neighbor, and so charity, in regard to one's neighbor, might be called that virtue whereby one constantly wishes well to one's fellow creatures — *to all of them*, out of love for God.

8. To understand the work of justice, one must understand the true nature of right. Rights are moral powers entitling a human being to something distinctly his own. All human beings are possessed of certain rights because of their human nature. These rights are connatural rights. They are inalienable, inviolable, personal, moral.

9. Because man is social by nature, all individuals are possessed of equally natural and equally personal rights. Authority in society harmonizes the exercise of these rights. It may do this by regulation which, though it imposes a limit on the exercise of the right, leaves the right intact.

10. Human rights are based on law; ultimately they have their foundation in the natural law which is, as we know, the reflection of the eternal law of God.

11. Justice inclines one to give to another his *rights*; namely, *to* give him what is his due, and to give it with a constant and perpetual will.

12. Justice is divided into general and particular justice. General justice is *legal* justice. It regulates the actions of the individuals so that they give to the community what is its due.

13. Particular justice is subdivided into distributive and commutative. Distributive justice has to do with the regulation of the actions of society toward the individuals who compose it. It is the distribution of the goods of the community.

14. Commutative justice concerns the mutual relations of individual with individual as such in the community.

15. Social justice—a new term today—is the legal justice of St. Thomas plus an element of distributive justice. It is expressed by the term: "the good of all and of each."

16. Justice removes the obstacles to peace. Charity, by cementing the hearts of the social individuals, begets peace. "Peace is the tranquility of order." Charity must come to relieve suffering even when it be caused by injustice, but charity can never take the place of justice unfairly withheld. It can never be its substitute but only a temporary remedy.

17. Other social virtues include temperance (moderation) and fortitude (courage in the face of difficulties), truth, obedience, religion, piety (patriotism), knowledge, and public recognition and worship of God.

Christian Social Principles

For Study and Discussion

1. Explain how habits are *second nature*. Mention at least five habits that are directed toward the good of man. Can you tell what virtue each of these five good habits is called?

2. Name the intellectual habits. Name the moral habits or virtues. What is the difference between the object of charity and the object of justice?

3. Does charity find God or neighbor most lovable in very nature? Upon what triangle is Christian social life based?

4. Explain fully the work of justice. How does this differ from the work of charity? Why are the two called the foundation stones of Christian social life? What relation does peace bear to these virtues?

5. Explain the statement: Justice presupposes *rights*. Explain the origin, nature, and purpose of rights. Strictly speaking, only human beings have rights. Can you tell why?

6. What is the relation between rights and man's final end? What is the difference between inalienable rights and alienable rights? What are connatural rights?

7. Are all rights derived directly from the law of nature? What role does human authority play in the matter of natural rights?

8. What is meant by the expression: rights are *moral* powers. To what is the term *moral* opposed? Explain the differences.

9. "Rights *must* be natural." *Must* implies necessity. Explain the statement.

10. Rights do not come single-handed. They carry along with them a moral power called *obligation*. What does this mean? Why are rights and obligations correlative? Of what benefit would rights be without obligations? If you have a right to property, on whom does the correlative obligation rest? If man has the duty to contribute to the common good, whose is the corresponding right?

11. What are the three possibilities of rendering just dues in social living?

12. Justice is divided into two classes: namely, that (1) in which the right is on the part of the community and that (2) in which the right is on the part of individuals. Name the classes of justice and show how the three possibilities of rendering just dues in society fit into this dual classification.

13. Explain *social* justice.

14. Is there any justification for almsgiving? To what extent is one obliged to give alms? What virtue commands almsgiving?

15. Explain the Holy Father's statement: "When necessity has been supplied ... it is a duty to give to the poor out of that which is over." Discuss this principle. How would a contrary principle work out in practice?

16. Discuss prudence, temperance, and fortitude as social virtues. How do they effect the social order? How do they make men virtuous?

17. Why should subjects have an appropriate knowledge of their rights and obligations? Why does St. Thomas think intelligence is a necessary virtue in social living?
18. Discuss the part of the following virtues in social living: obedience, truth, piety (patriotism), patience, constancy, and mercy.
19. Why does society as a whole have the duty of gratitude, dependence, and public worship of God?
20. Why should virtue be publicly manifested?
21. How is "the good life, the life of virtue" the means to man's final end?

For the Advanced Reader

St. Thomas:

On the Governance of Rulers: virtue, pp. 64–108 passim, 126
Summa Contra Gentiles, charity: vol. 4, chap. 128
Summa Theologica, vol. 7, habits: pp. 1–55; good habits (virtues): pp. 63–84, 100–147; vol. 10, prudence: pp. 1–103; right: pp. 104–112; justice, injustice, etc.: pp. 113–185, 342–350; vices opposed to justice: to distributive justice: pp. 186–194; to commutative justice: pp. 195–341

Farrell, Walter:

A Companion to the Summa, II, chaps. 8–11; III, chaps. 3–4, 6, 8, 12–14, 16

Papal Encyclicals:

Pope Leo XIII: *Chief Duties of Christians as Citizens*
   Christian Popular Action
   On the Condition of Labor
Pope Pius XI: *Atheistic Communism*
   Reconstruction of the Social Order
Pope Pius XII: *To the American Hierarchy*
   Unity in Opposing World Evils

Philosophy of the State, reprinted 1940 from the 1939 proceedings, American Catholic Philosophical Association "The Political Philosopher," pp. 1–10

The Thomist

"The Field of Social Justice," vol. 1, no. 3, October 1939, pp. 295–330
"A Thomistic Analysis of Peace," vol. 1, no. 2, July 1939, pp. 169–192

Any good book on Christian ethics

Part 2 Cumulative Summary

Society

Part 1 of this work was concerned with man. Part 2 viewed society. With these two foundations laid, the remainder of the book will consider man in society.

We saw that man is a social being, not by choice but by nature. Man's nature demands social living. This does not imply that any individual man, or for that matter, any number of men, *could not* live apart from society. They could, but their living would not be at the human level. At best it would be mere existence; it would be an animal type of living that is unworthy of man. This is so, because it is precisely in society that man finds the helps he needs to develop his whole personality.

Man is not humanly developed when only his physical needs are fulfilled. Man is an intelligent being and mental development is required to contribute to his perfection. As he is a being of free will, he needs also moral training and direction. And still further, as he is in subjection to God, he requires religious training. None of these could man get by himself. The very power of speech and use of language indicate man's need of someone to whom to talk and to express his ideas. Man, therefore, needs society. It is a natural need; it is implanted in his very nature by the Author of that nature. God constituted man a social being and no human force whatsoever can abolish it from his nature. At best, it can be restricted in some of his manifestations and that but for a time only.

St. Thomas writes: "Reason dictates that man by himself cannot pass through life alone, and so he lives in society whereby different duties are fulfilled by different persons.... This need for society applies not only to the necessities of life but also to seeking his supernatural end."

The causes of society are *material*, or the individuals who comprise it; *formal*, or the unity or grouping; *efficient*, or the will of God, man's nature, and external authority; *final*, or common action in view of a common end; namely, individual happiness and the common good.

Society is more than the sum of the individuals who compose it: over and above the members, society is characterized by the directive power of authority guiding the group toward a common destiny. The note of *common destiny* which is found in the group is something more than the sum of the individual destinies which make up the goal of the parts.

The individual in the community is neither swallowed up by the group purpose, nor is he wholly above the group by reason of his individual destiny. As a *social* individual, he is subject to society and he must contribute to the common good of society. As a *rational* creature destined for a personal goal of eternal happiness, he transcends society and with respect to his final goal, he is superior to society.

Since society represents innumerable free wills, each seeking fulfillment of immediate, personal desires, there is need of a directive force to keep all headed in the general direction of the common good. For society has as its purpose the promotion of (1) the welfare of the group, and (2) the welfare of the individuals in the group.

> Rulers should anxiously safeguard the community and all its individual members — the community, because the preservation of the community is so emphatically the business of the supreme power that the safety of the commonwealth is not only the *first law*, but is a government's *whole reason of existence*. The ruler should safeguard the individuals because ... the object of the administration of the State should be not the advantage of the ruler but the benefit of those over whom he rules. The gift of authority is from God ... it should be exercised as the power of God is exercised — with a fatherly care which not only guides the whole but reaches to lesser things as well.

This is a magnificent statement on social authority. It was made by Pope Leo XIII in his encyclical on *The Condition of Labor*.

Social life is the movement of mankind toward a common goal through association and common effort. It can be seen that justice is needed in order to maintain harmony among the members of society. Were man an isolated being, he would have no need of justice, except, that is, toward God. But as for man himself, St. Thomas tells us that justice does not regulate one's dealings with oneself (as temperance does, for instance) so that one can scarcely be said to be just or unjust toward himself.

Justice pertains to the relations of man to the group, and this is general justice, as for example, that individuals are bound in justice to seek the common good. Justice pertains, also, to the relations of man toward individuals, as for instance, man to man and the society to its members. These constitute particular justice of two species: commutative in the case of man to man, and distributive, in the case of the society as such to its members.

Justice alone cannot weld together a social order. This is done by recognizing in the individuals who comprise it, other selves, brothers, having the same nature, destiny, equipment, and paths to travel. The virtue which regulates this is charity — love.

Peace is consequent upon virtue, so that the goal of society, namely, the common good, the peace and preservation of the community, requires the public and private practice of virtue in its citizens as well as in the community as such. Almsgiving is a duty upon those who have a superfluity of goods. It demands that after the requirements of their station in life have been met, that they distribute alms to the poor from the surplus.

Morality is the bulwark of society. Without it society could not retain its unity. When morality breaks down in social living, to that extent the social fabric is weakened. The reason is evident. Moral living leads to a right end. It demands that all the actions performed by man lead to that end. It demands, too, that the use of means be proportionate to the end. It offers as rewards, individual happiness and common temporal happiness in this life, plus perfect happiness for the individual hereafter — *for all the individuals*; it offers, that is, common eternal happiness. Moral living points to God as the only adequate end of man. It demands the exercise of habits directed toward the good (toward virtue), and it gives rise to the concept of duty, whereby men recognize the important fact that proper steps must be taken to reach a given goal; that godly living alone will lead to God. But this is the life of virtue; this is the aim of social living: the *good* life; the life of virtue; the life of peace here, and hereafter — eternal beatitude.

Part 3

Man in Society

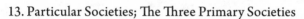

13

Particular Societies; the Three Primary Societies

We have reached the third part of our book. We shall enter upon a discussion of the particular societies to which man belongs. If we consider the meaning of society, namely, that it is an association of men gathered together for the accomplishment of some specific work by common effort, we shall see that there are many possible kinds of societies. Naturally, not all associations of men for a common purpose have equal importance in man's welfare. Baseball associations, for instance, have not the significance that labor unions have, and these latter are not necessary to man as are the family and civil society. In this chapter we shall discover which societies are necessary and what their characteristics are.

Particular Societies

Since the value of a thing can be judged from the purpose for which it exists, let us investigate the purpose of particular associations of human beings and so learn something of their importance and necessity.

Associations of human beings can be public ones or private ones. Civil society, for instance, is a public one. The family is a private one. We do not mean by this that the public societies have no relation to the private ones, or that the private ones are unrelated to the public ones. There is a relationship between the two, for the same human beings are members of each society. The relationship between the two is sometimes very close, at other times, less close and immediate. In fact, St. Thomas writes that a private society is part of a public society as a house is part of a city. Speaking with particular reference to the family and civil society, St. Thomas tells us: "The fact that a man forms part of a family causes him to form part of a city which is composed of many families." See how Pope Pius expressed the same thought in his encyclical on *The Christian Education of Youth*: "The children ... enter into and become part of civil society, not directly by themselves, but through the Family in which they were born."

Particular societies, therefore, bear a relation to each other, the ties of the bond between them being proportionate to the need which man has for the different kinds of particular societies.

Again, particular societies may be perpetual or temporary. Marriage is a perpetual contract, and therefore it constitutes the family as a perpetual society. Business partnerships, however, as well as study and pleasure associations, have only a temporary existence. Civil society, therefore, is both public and permanent. The family is both private and permanent. The 1939–1940 World Fair Committee constituted a public but only temporary society. Business partners form a private and temporary society. Obviously all these are not *necessary* to man.

Necessary Societies

A society is *necessary* when some law of human nature, or of the Author of human nature, requires it. For example, the family is necessary because it is in and through the family that new members of the human race are brought into existence. The law of nature (the natural law) demands the association of the family for the adequate upbringing of offspring. Thus the family is a necessary society. Because human nature demands association, and because the family is a necessary society, a further necessary society is demanded; namely, that of civil society. This consists of the association of *families*. Civil society is the necessary association required for the promotion of the common welfare of all the families and the individual members that compose them.

The family and the State (domestic and civil societies) are therefore necessary societies, fulfilling the demands of the natural law for the attainment of their purposes. They are *natural* also, as distinct from the Church which is a *supernatural* society. A society is natural when it is demanded by human nature; that is, when nature decrees that one must live in association. This is true of human association and so human society, such as the family, is not only necessary but natural. A society can be necessary without being natural, as in the case of the Church. The Church is *supernatural* because it is demanded by super-nature; that is, it is required by the human soul, for the Church alone dispenses spiritual nourishment and growth.

Other societies are not necessary in the way that the three societies mentioned above are necessary. Labor unions, for instance, are beneficial to the laboring man for the protection of his labor rights, but they are not absolutely necessary for his total human perfection. It is only through the domestic society, however, that the new members of the race are properly reared as they come into existence. No substitute can be found for the family. We shall understand this better when we enter more deeply into the nature of the family in a subsequent chapter (14). Likewise civil society is necessary for the promotion of the general welfare of the smaller units: the family and the individual. No substitute for civil society can be found. We shall discuss this, too, more fully later. Again, no supernatural society can be found for the attainment of man's supernatural end other than the Church. Therefore these three societies are necessary societies. All other societies have not this note of *necessity*.

The need for domestic society and civil society are so deeply rooted in man's very nature that they are the heritage and common lot of all men. Not only is it natural that they be born into domestic and civil societies, but men actually are so born. You recall, do you not, that St. Thomas remarked that by being born into the family, one is born also into civil society? That is because civil society is the greater unit of which the families are the lesser component parts. On the other hand, a person is not actually born into the Church when he is born into the family and the State. One is born into the supernatural society by the Sacrament of Baptism. However, every human being has the right to belong to the Church; nay, has the duty to belong to it, if he knows the Church to be the true Church.

To escape from domestic society, one would have to live completely apart from the members of his family. To escape from civil society, one would have to live in complete isolation from every other human being. To do either of these things, however, is not the normal human conduct. Family and civil circles are too precious to be readily thrust aside, for the advantages they bring affect man's natural (i.e., temporal) welfare too greatly. Matters of food, clothing, shelter, companionship, and the like are daily human necessities, and living in partial or complete solitude deprives one of too many natural human pleasures and advantages.

Unfortunately for them men at times permit the natural needs of the body to take precedence over the supernatural needs of the soul. They become blinded to the importance of the supernatural, probably because a starving soul does not clamor for nourishment loudly three times a day as does a starving body. The grave hunger is there in the soul, but it is not a physical pain and hence it can, unfortunately, be drowned out by the clamor and bustle of the body, the external senses, the imagination, and the sense memory. It can be neglected, stifled, starved, but for a long time it will resist this ill treatment. Eventually, after it has been thwarted and choked down times without number, the craving for spiritual nourishment ceases and the loss to that man is irreparable. His nature is now doomed to exist with atrophied organs. His being is now nothing more than a frustrated nature. And though such individuals would not for anything leave the domestic and civil societies which meet only their temporal needs, they either forsake or refuse to enter that society which *alone* can provide the more important, because the eternal, needs of their souls. If the need which man experienced for the Church were a physical gnawing as is the need of his stomach or any part of his physical nature, then the Church would physically be just as inescapable as domestic society and civil society. For these latter concentrate on temporal advantages, whereas the Church has for its aim and object, eternal life.

Primary Societies

These three, therefore, are said to be *primary* or basic societies: (1) the family — necessary, natural, private, perpetual; (2) the State — necessary, natural, public, perpetual; (3) the Church — necessary, supernatural, public, perpetual. All are necessary for the attainment of a necessary end. Two are required by the natural law; one by the God of nature and the Source of that law. All are perpetual; that is, they will exist throughout the course of human history.

After that, the family will no longer be required for the procreation of new beings; civil society will no longer be required for the promotion of the common temporal welfare; the Church will have passed into eternity, not as Church Militant but as Church Triumphant, and will be at peace. For all three societies are *means* to a further end — the eternal destiny of individual men. The three primary societies will have completed their work; they will have made men virtuous or failed to do so; they will have helped men to their only true goal or have been wanting in this respect; they will have fulfilled their purpose or failed it utterly. At the end of the world there will be no further need for their existence. They will pass out of existence as "associations of men for a common purpose." They will be found only in the effect they have produced on the individual, immortal, human souls enjoying the blessedness of Heaven or undergoing the torments of Hell eternally.

Perfect and Imperfect Societies

We noted, a few paragraphs back, that because the family is a necessary society, a further necessary society is demanded: namely, that of civil society. The reason for the second necessary society (civil society) emphasizes the distinction between a perfect and an imperfect society.

Everything that exists has its purpose. A pencil has a purpose and so there is reason for its existence. A typewriter has a purpose, and likewise a reason for its existence. A purposeless thing, like a badly smashed hat, no longer has a reason for existence. What do we do with it? We put it out of existence. We burn it or throw it away or otherwise reduce it to non-existence as a hat. A purposeless thing has no reason for its existence. A thing of purpose has a reason for its existence. That explains the reason why we hold on to some things but other things we discard.

Now society also has a purpose. Its purpose is the reason why society exists. If God had not a definite purpose in mind, if His eternal plan did not call for a specific end for society to accomplish, well, we just would not have had society. All societies have a purpose; the common striving of the members of an association is directed toward the fulfillment of that purpose, the attainment of the end is that for which it exists. Not all societies, however, reach all the way to man's ultimate goal. One sends him only part of the way; in other words, it contributes only partly to his final perfection. Another sends him somewhat farther along the paths of human development en route to his goal. Still another one gives him other kinds of help which it alone can give. This is another way of saying that each particular society has an object which it must accomplish, and that, in accomplishing its object, it has contributed according to its own kind and degree to the perfection of the whole human personality.

It is evident that the civil society cannot do for man what the domestic society can do. It is equally evident that civil society cannot do what the supernatural society of the Church can do for man.

Besides having its own goal at which to aim, each society is equipped with the means of reaching that goal. Some means are adequate; other means are inadequate. Some societies can reach their goal without help. They have within themselves the power to attain their goal. Other societies must depend upon outside help to do their work completely. A society that has within itself all that it needs to attain its specific end is called a self-sufficient society. A society that lacks sufficient means to accomplish its end, one that must call upon other societies for help in its work, is called an insufficient society. Can you give an example of each?

Two Perfect Societies

There are two necessary, primary societies that are self-sufficient. There is one necessary, primary society that is not self-sufficient. Civil society or the State is a self-sufficient society. It is called *perfect* because it is self-sufficient; because it has within itself the means necessary to accomplish its end. Note, however, it has not the means to accomplish the end or purpose of any other society, but only its own end. It could never accomplish the work of the family even though both itself and the family work on the natural level, aiming directly at temporal happiness. But what is more, civil society can never accomplish the work of the Church, for the Church is on an entirely different level. The Church works on the supernatural level, for she supplies man with the supernatural help he needs. No other society can supply this. That is why the Church is necessary and supernatural. For the same reason, the Church is perfect. She has an end to reach. She has the means of reaching that end. No other society could do so. No other society contributes to any insufficiency of the Church, because the Church is self-sufficient. She has her own end: the salvation of souls — eternal happiness. She has her own means: divine grace. She has her own authority: the Word of God. She has her own subjects: souls regenerated by Baptism. Her helping hand is of greatest length, because it reaches even unto eternity, equipping man with supernatural life, food, and strength, and directing man thither until he has touched the eternal shores. Civil society's aim is shorter. It supplies man with opportunities for living a good life now. In other words, it supplies him with the temporal helps he needs to live well *in time*.

An Imperfect Society

The Church, therefore, and the State are perfect societies. The family is not. The family's resources are inadequate to develop the full human personality. It cannot supply its members with all they need for a good life. The family must reach out beyond itself and ask for help. If a family does not, then the members of that family attain but a low degree of human development. They have some companionship, it is true, but insufficient to guarantee much mental development. They may provide themselves with enough to eat and drink and have sufficient clothing and shelter and with some mental and moral development, but not to an extent sufficient to perfect the human individual. Man can rise much higher than a well-fed individual. The family, therefore, is an imperfect society because it cannot fully accomplish by itself its purpose — it cannot complete the generation and proper education of offspring — unless it is helped by Church and State.

Pope Pius Writes

Pope Pius XI summed all this up in these penetrating words:

> Now there are three necessary societies, distinct from one another and yet harmoniously combined by God, into which man is born: two,

namely the family and civil societies, belong to the natural order; the third, the Church, to the supernatural order.

In the first place comes the Family, instituted directly by God for its peculiar [i.e., specific] purpose, the generation and formation of offspring; for this reason, it has priority of nature, and therefore of rights, over civil society. Nevertheless, the Family is an imperfect society, since it has not in itself all the means for its own complete development; whereas civil society is a perfect society, having in itself all the means for its specific end which is the temporal well-being of the community; and so, in this respect, that is, in view of the common good, it has preeminence over the Family, which finds its own suitable temporal perfection precisely in civil society.

The third society into which man is born when, through Baptism, he receives the Divine life of grace, is the Church, a society of the supernatural order and of universal extent; a perfect society, because it has in itself all the means required for its own end, which is the eternal salvation of mankind; hence it is supreme in its own domain.

Man's Supremacy

Pope Pius's words above strike a note which may cause some surprise. He says the family has priority of nature and therefore of rights over civil society. How can this be so, for is not the smaller ordained to the greater — the family to the State? Furthermore, if the family is granted priority of rights, does not that make the State subservient to the family, and if so, how can the civil government exact, as it necessarily must, the contribution which individuals are bound to make to the common good? But if you say the civil society cannot make such exactions, does that not amount to so thorough a denial of civil authority's rights as to cause the destruction of the State? But if the State is, as we have said repeatedly, a *necessary* society, can it be thus unceremoniously undermined? And again, if the individual is insufficient for himself, what perfection could he reach without the help of the State?

These questions do not constitute a puzzle. The key to their answer lies in an earlier chapter. The State is a *means*. Man is possessed of an ultimate end which transcends the State. Man must march on through life, day by day approaching more closely that final destiny. Society offers him its help; it gives him provisions for the journey. The help which comes to man from the State is *not* the reason for man's journey; it is not the end of the march for man. He must not be deterred by a means, no matter how noble the means;

for a means is always a *way* to the end. It is merely a direction. It is never the goal. It is movement but not rest.

But, if the State had absolute control over man, the State would then constitute man's *end*. Man's end, as we saw in the first chapter, could never be anything temporal. The State is temporal. "Society is for man," said the Holy Father, "and not man for society." Therefore, man must have rights which entitle him to help and to the freedom necessary to complete his journey without undue molestation.

Man's rights are subject to regulation, but never to abolition. It is inconceivable to think of a human being devoid of natural rights. For natural rights are rights rooted in man's nature and exhibited in his activities. A man cannot be human unless he has a human nature, but with this human nature comes his rights. They are inseparable. Human nature means human rights. Human rights mean human freedom. Human freedom is manifested in human activity. Human activity is movement toward the goal of life. Nature, rights, freedom, not only accompany man to his goal, but they are the stepping-stones to it. Man could never reach his rational nature's everlasting goal without his human capacities, human rights, human freedom.

This is precisely why man's priority of nature gives him priority of rights and makes him superior to society, though not in an absolute way. He is superior in a relative way: in relation to his final destiny and his right to work toward it.

Rights Subject to Limitation

The subjection of man, his rights, and his freedom, to society amounts to this: that by the free exercise of his personal rights, no man may deprive another of that which is his due. It is a matter of justice. Every man is headed toward the same goal. Society has the task of directing them, collectively and individually. It meets their needs; supplies opportunities for self-development; protects their rights. Now it must do this to all and to each, otherwise society would fail in distributive justice. Conflicting rights, therefore, have to be harmonized, for the common good must be sought. It is here that the individual must consent to the curtailment of his liberty *if*, in the exercise of it, he is (1) retarding the progress of the commonweal; (2) preventing the distribution of the common good (viz., the advantages of social living) from reaching other individuals with whom he is associated; or (3) unjustly hindering any one from pursuing the goal marked out for him by the Almighty. This limitation must not amount to an abolition of a man's rights; it must not be so stringent that the exercise of his rights is made impossible; it amounts merely to the easing of a tenseness in the social nervous system, so that the whole of the social body will be relaxed and better able to work more harmoniously and efficiently toward the mutual goal of the straining members. To effect this harmonization, civil society is possessed of coercive powers despite the fact of man's priority of rights. The State is a protective power. It is the very guarantee of man's liberties, when it acts with justice, that is, when it stays within the limits set down for it by God and nature.

Church Supremacy

Is there conflict between the two perfect societies which contribute to man's needs and enable him to overcome his natural insufficiencies in himself and in the family? If Church and State were *naturally* hostile, would it be possible for them to work in the same subject, as they do? If within the very character of the Church there were elements which of necessity conflicted with the character of the State, would God, the all-wise ruler of mankind, have ordained that they contribute to the perfection of the same subject? Furthermore, *can* there be conflict of rights when the two societies have their ends in entirely different orders, namely, one in the natural order and the other in the supernatural order?

Pope Leo has said:

The Almighty has appointed the charge of the human race between two powers, the ecclesiastical and the civil, the one being over divine and the other over human things. Each in its kind is supreme; each has fixed limits within which it is contained, limits which are defined by the nature and special object of the province of each, so that there is an orbit traced out within which the action of each is brought into play by its own native right. But inasmuch as each of these two powers has authority over the same subjects, and as it might come to pass that one and the same thing — related differently but still remaining one and the same thing — might belong to the jurisdiction and determination of both, therefore God, Who foresees all things, and Who is the Author of these two powers, has marked out the course of each in right correlation to the other.

How unwilling we would be to think that God who planned so harmoniously the multiple teeming activities of the universe with its many natures and forces, would in the case of His most noble creature in that universe, have made him subject to two powers between which there was inherent disharmony.

We would be most unwilling to think that the tranquil Godhead would have introduced constant strife in that part of His creation which so closely resembles His own image and likeness! As a matter of fact, human beings are most unlike God when they are most contentious. They most closely share in the divine image when they are most peaceful and harmonious.

The fact that throughout history various civil authorities have contended with the Church, so that there existed between the two powers a state of conflict, is not due to any inherent necessity for conflict in either society. It is due, as a matter of fact, primarily to the non-recognition by civil rulers of the rights of the Church. Just as with individuals, when civil authority exceeds its limits and attempts to abrogate the rights of its subjects, there is conflict and rebellion which would never have arisen had just rights been respected. So too, in the case of the Church, when rulers deny to her any rights, when rulers deny her divine mission, when rulers hamper her God-given work, then conflicts arise which would never have arisen had the just rights of the Church been recognized and respected.

But, one may ask, has the Church rights which are to be recognized by civil society? The answer is not difficult. If the Church has a goal to achieve, most certainly she has certain rights without which she cannot achieve her end. But is the Church necessary? That, too, is simple. If any other society could do the work of the Church, Christ would not have established her and sent His apostles to preach it to the world. That was a gigantic task. If there were no need for it, if another society already in existence could have done it just as well or better, then the Church would have no reason for existing, because she would have no specific purpose to fulfill.

But, has the Church a definite goal? The answer is still very simple. Yes, she has. She is a supernatural society. Civil society is natural. The family is natural. No society can dispense goods beyond its capacity. Yet supernatural goods must be dispensed, and a supernatural society alone is capable of dispensing them. Only in the Church does God, the Source of supernatural life and grace, abide. To no civil society did Christ say, "Behold I am with you all days, even to the consummation of the world" (Matt. 28:20). He said that to the Church. He gave her a mission: "Going, therefore, teach ye all nations; baptizing them in the name of the Father, and of the Son and of the Holy Ghost" (Matt. 28:19). And thus, because she has a supernatural and God-given goal, she must have rights which will enable her to pursue her way toward that goal, even as the individual, with his eternal destiny, is granted by this very fact, rights which enable him to attain that personal destiny.

State Supremacy

But are only individuals and the Church supreme? No. The family is, too, in its way. So, too, is the State. The principle is this: each of these has its own goal and so each has the right to use freely the means to it. Thus, for the State, it must effect social well-being. It must be free to do so. It must be able to use the proper means. It may force the unwilling and punish the offending subjects, all for the sake of attaining its goal. In this way, civil society is supreme; namely, in its own field, to attain its own end. Thus, it is with every society. You see, it is not *absolute* supremacy but only relative; its rights bear a relationship to its end and means as well as to the rights of other societies. A society must keep in mind its purpose and must strive for it virtuously, without, however, surpassing the limits of its authority.

No Necessary Conflict

Therefore, between the Church and the State there is no inherent conflict. God never intended you or me to be torn between two conflicting allegiances. That would be out of order in a universe of harmony. Between the two perfect societies there must exist an order, even as there is order between the body and the soul in man. In the quotation given above, Pope Leo pointed out that each of these is supreme in its own domain. Certainly, if both are *perfect* societies, it must be thus. To what purpose would a society be perfect if it were not supreme? God and nature do nothing in vain. When God gave to each society a perfect nature, He ordained each to its own sphere of activity wherein each could maintain its supremacy. Pope Leo expressed it thus: "There is an orbit traced out within which the action of each is brought into play by its own native right."

Pope Leo continues:

> The nature and scope of that connection (between the two powers) can be determined only ... by having regard to the nature of each power and by taking into account the relative excellence and nobleness of their purpose.
>
> One of the two has for its proximate and chief object the well-being of this mortal life; the other, the everlasting joys of heaven. Whatever, therefore, in things human is of a sacred character, whatever belongs either of its own nature or by reason of the end to which it is referred, to the salvation of souls, or to the worship of God, is subject to the power and judgment of the Church. Whatever is to be ranged under the civil and political order is rightly subject to the civil authority.

Christian Social Principles

Direct and Indirect Objects

The Holy Father implies that besides the proximate and chief purpose of each society, there is another purpose, indirect, as it were, and secondary. Let us investigate this point. We have noted several times before that the end of society is the life of virtue, "the good life," a better human existence. Does a civil government which strives earnestly to promote such a life contribute anything toward the future eternal well-being of its subjects? Can there be conflict between the goal of civil society and the goal of the individuals if both are straining for *the good*? "The good is what all things seek"; *all things*: man, society, the Church.

If both sun and soil work together for the good of a straining, developing seed, may we not hope for a perfect blossom, though the work of the sun differs from the work of the soil and both differ from the work of the seed? The sun could not redouble its work while the soil did nothing; nor could the soil give of its nourishment more abundantly while the sun made no contribution. Neither could the seed be unresponsive if to blossom be the goal. Each must do its work and the harmonious co-action of sun, soil, and seed produces a perfect flower.

So, too, it is with man. When the individual, civil society, and the Church all tend toward *the good* as toward their goals, certainly the harmonious co-action will produce a *good man*, a fully developed human personality. Hence we may say that for a secondary goal or purpose, the State has the eternal happiness of its citizens as an indirect goal. It amounts to this: that through providing temporal means for a better human life, a definite contribution is made toward a better future life. With the Church, it is the same. She, too, has a secondary or indirect purpose, namely, a better temporal existence, as distinct from the eternal existence which is her primary aim. When the Church, through her supernatural powers, makes a subject a better man, she is by that fact contributing to a better and happier temporal existence. Note that I do not say necessarily that it is a more abundant existence considered from the material viewpoint as more food, clothes, and a bigger, better car; but material things are the least of man's good things. A good conscience, that is, a life of grace, adds immeasurably to man's happiness in time as well as to his glory in eternity.

The Church in History

But the course of history has shown that the Church has been the source of many temporal blessings to the world. Christianity has subdued barbarous nations, changing them from savagery to civility, from superstition to true worship. She has contributed, through her children and her encouragement, to the sum total of knowledge in the world, to its philosophy, its science, its arts, and its letters. She has taught obedience to authority, the sacredness of debts, the inviolability of rights, the value of human life, and countless other benefits. Truly history shows the Church as a fond mother of the human race and a generous provider of culture and virtue.

We have traveled some distance and covered much ground in this chapter. We know, now, in general, the three necessary and primary societies and their mutual relations. We shall discuss each of these societies in particular, and thus acquire a rounder, fuller knowledge of the particular societies to which God, in His goodness, has imparted an extension of His authority over us.

Some Original Sources

Make use of these in your discussion and explanations. Try to accustom yourself to make apt quotations to substantiate your statements in discussion and debates.

1. "As one man is a part of the household, so a household is a part of the State: and the State is a perfect community. Therefore, as the good of one man is not the last end, but is ordained to the common good, so too the good of one household is ordained to the good of a single State which is a perfect community." (*Summa Theologica*, vol. 8, p. 7)

2. "The goodness of any part is considered in comparison with the whole.... Since then every man is a part of the State, it is impossible that a man be good unless he be well proportionate to the common good: nor can the whole be well consistent unless its parts be proportionate to it. Consequently the common good of the State cannot flourish, unless the citizens be virtuous, at least those whose business it is to govern." (*Summa Theologica*, vol. 8, p. 24)

3. "The common good of the realm and the particular good of the individual differ not only in respect of the *many* and the *few*, but also under a formal aspect. For the aspect of the common good differs from the aspect of the *individual* good, even as the aspect of *whole* differs from that of *part*." (*Summa Theologica*, vol. 10, p. 116)

4. "The individual good, the good of the Family and the good of the city are different ends. Wherefore there must needs be different species of prudence corresponding to these different ends, so that one is prudence simply so called which is directed to one's own good; another, domestic prudence, which is directed to the common good of the home, and a third, political prudence, which is directed to the common good of the state or kingdom." (*Summa Theologica*, vol. 10, p. 19)

5. "Coercive power is not exercised in human affairs, save by those who hold public authority: and those who have this authority are accounted the superiors of those over whom they preside whether by ordinary or by delegated authority." (*Summa Theologica*, vol. 10, p. 238)

6. "The greater power should exercise the greater coercion. Now just as a city is a perfect community, so the governor of a city has perfect coercive power: wherefore he can inflict irreparable punishments such as death and mutilation. On the other hand, the father and the master [of a slave] who preside over the family household, which is an imperfect community, have imperfect coercive power, which is exercised by inflicting lesser punishments, for instance by blows, which do not inflict irreparable harm." (*Summa Theologica*, vol. 10, p. 217)

7. "The end and object [of civil society] viz., the common welfare in the temporal order, consists in that peace and security in which families and individual citizens have the free exercise of their rights, and at the same time enjoy the greatest spiritual and temporal prosperity possible in this life, by the mutual union and coordination of the work of all.

"The function, therefore, of the civil authority residing in the State is twofold: to protect and to foster, but by no means to absorb, the Family and the individual or to substitute itself for them." (Pope Pius XI, *Christian Education of Youth*)

8. "The more closely the temporal power of a nation aligns itself with the spiritual, and the more it fosters and promotes the latter, by so much the more it contributes to the conservation of the commonwealth. For it is the aim of the ecclesiastical authority by the use of spiritual means to form good Christians in accordance with its own particular end and object; and in doing this it helps at the same time to form good citizens and prepares them to meet their obligations as members of a civil society.

"This follows of necessity because in the City of God, the Holy Roman Catholic Church, a good citizen and an upright man are absolutely one and the same thing.

"How grave, therefore, is the error of those who separate things so closely united, and who think that they can produce good citizens by ways and methods other than those which make for the formation of good Christians. For, let human prudence say what it likes and reason as it pleases, it is impossible to produce true temporal peace and tranquility by things repugnant or opposed to the peace and happiness of eternity." (Cardinal Silvio Antoniano, quoted by Pope Pius XI, *Christian Education of Youth*)

9. "Both man and civil society derive their origin from the Creator Who has mutually ordained them one to the other. Hence neither can be exempted from their correlative obligations nor deny or diminish each other's rights. The Creator Himself regulated this mutual relationship in its fundamental lines...

"The teaching of the Church maintains a constant equilibrium of truth and justice, which it vindicates in theory and applies and promotes in practice, bringing into harmony the rights and duties of all parties.

"Thus authority is reconciled with liberty, the dignity of the individual with that of the State, the human personality of the subject with the Divine delegation of the superior; and in this way a balance is struck between the due dependence and well-ordered love of a man for himself, his family and country, and his love of other families and other peoples, founded on the love of God, the Father of all, their first principle and last end.

"The Church does not separate a proper regard for temporal welfare from solicitude for the eternal." (Pope Pius XI, *Atheistic Communism*)

10. "Thus we have the Family; the society of a man's own household; a society limited indeed in numbers, but a true society, anterior to every kind of State or nation, with rights and duties of its own, totally independent of the commonwealth." (Pope Leo XIII, *The Condition of Labor*)

11. "Man cannot be exempted from his divinely-imposed obligations towards civil society and the representatives of authority have the right to coerce him when he refuses without reason to do his duty.

"Society, on the other hand, cannot defraud man of his God-given rights, the most important of which are: the right to life; to bodily integrity; to the necessary means of existence; the right to tend towards his ultimate goal in the path marked out for him by God; the right of association, and the right to possess and use property.

"Nor can society systematically void these rights by making their use impossible. It is therefore according to the dictates of reason that ultimately all material things should be ordained to man as a person, that through his mediation they may find their way to the Creator." (Pope Pius XI, *Atheistic Communism*)

Summary

1. The society of the human race may be seen as being composed of lesser units called particular societies, as parts which are contained in a whole.
2. Particular societies may be public or private. Civil society is a public society; domestic society is a private one. They are related, says St. Thomas, as houses to a city; that is, as parts to the whole.
3. Particular societies may be perpetual or temporary. A family is a perpetual society; bridge clubs are temporary.
4. The State is a public, perpetual society. The family is a private, perpetual society.
5. A *necessary* society is one whose existence is required by some law: either the law of nature, in which case it is a necessary, natural society, or by the law of God, in which case it is a necessary, supernatural society.

6. The State and the family are necessary, natural societies. The Church is a necessary, supernatural society. All three are called *primary* societies.

7. Individuals enter into civil society through the family. They are born directly into the family. They are born into the supernatural society of the Church only through Baptism.

8. These three societies are means to man's end. They all tend to lead man to "a good life," a better human life, the life of virtue.

9. The family and the State do this by providing conditions required for temporal happiness. The Church does this by supplying the supernatural help needed for eternal happiness.

10. A perfect society is self-sufficient in the sense that it has within itself the means to reach its own end. It has adequate means to do so. It does not depend upon other societies for help in its own particular work.

11. An imperfect society is not self-sufficient. It is dependent in the sense that it has not adequate means within itself to arrive at its end. It must go outside itself to receive the help necessary to complete the work it is to do.

12. The State and the Church are self-sufficient. While there is need of co-operation and recognition of mutual rights between them the State does not, indeed it cannot, call upon the spiritual resources of the Church to aid her in the promotion of temporal happiness *directly*. The Church does, however, through promoting the life of virtue, contribute *indirectly* to the goal of the State.

13. The Church neither does nor can supplement her spiritual resources from the temporal resources of the State. The two work on different planes; one works in the natural order and has natural means to its end; the other works in the supernatural order and has supernatural means to her end.

14. No natural society can replenish the spiritual treasury of the Church. This is so for several reasons: (1) Material resources cannot add to spiritual ones. The State may contribute a carload of food to starving church members but it can never augment their supply of grace. (2) The spiritual treasury of the Church is infinite and hence never needs replenishing.

15. The State and the Church, therefore, are perfect societies directed toward proximately distinct aims, the one toward temporal well-being, the other toward eternal life. They are ultimately directed toward the same end: God, since *all things* tend toward Him as toward their good.

16. The family is not a perfect society. It must draw upon the resources of both the State and the Church for the complete development of its members. It requires the services of the civil government in the natural order and the services of the Church in the supernatural order. The family is, therefore, an imperfect society.

17. The family existed in nature and in time before the State and therefore it has priority of rights over civil society. This is necessary in order that the family and its members may work out their lives in freedom, according to the plan of God for them.
18. Civil society has power to regulate, restrict, and harmonize the rights—even the basic natural rights—of man for the promotion of the true common good. The civil government is bound in justice to do nothing contrary to the good of the individual unless for a justifiable reason in harmony with the commonweal.
19. Natural rights may never be abolished by any human society. They are God-given. They are rooted in man's nature. Without them man would not be man, for he would be lacking freedom. Human authority may neither abolish these rights nor limit them so as to render the use of them impossible.
20. There is no natural conflict among the primary societies. Wherever and whenever disharmony occurs it is due to failure to recognize and respect rights. God, the Master of the universe who created everything with internal and external harmony, could not have made His most noble visible creature a subject of disharmony within himself, nor made him subject to two conflicting authorities.
21. Each of the primary societies has its specific goal. Each has the proper means to it. Each has rights demanded by its nature and the goal it must attain. Each, immediately or ultimately, directs its subjects to the selfsame goal: God Almighty. How could there be inherent conflict?
22. The primary and direct aim of civil society is better living for the multitude: unity, peace, physical necessities, opportunity for personal development. Its secondary and indirect aim is ultimately man's eternal happiness.
23. The primary and direct aim of the Church is the salvation of souls. The secondary and indirect aim is better human existence in time. There can be no inherent cross-purposes in the aims of the Church and the State.
24. The Church:
    - is concerned primarily and directly with the spiritual welfare of men and the salvation of souls
    - is concerned secondarily with man's temporal happiness since this is a means to a good life
    - is not justified in interfering in matters wholly temporal, for this is not the realm of the Church
    - does not ignore the State but promotes its well-being through fostering obedience and submission to lawful authority and the virtues proper to social living

The State:

* is concerned chiefly and directly with the material and temporal welfare of men through the promotion of the common good
* indirectly furthers man's approach to God through making him contented and happy in this life
* is not justified in interfering in matters spiritual, for this is not the realm of the State
* must not ignore the Church, but must protect and support her, and in its laws it must submit to the moral teaching of the Church

For Study and Discussion

1. Explain the difference between public and private societies. What is the difference between perpetual and temporary ones? Name a public perpetual society. Name a private perpetual one.

2. Explain what is meant by a *necessary* society. Why is the family said to be a necessary society? Why the Church? Is the State necessary?

3. What is a *natural* society? Would labor unions be a natural society? Why? Is the Church a natural society? Why?

4. Civil society is inescapable. Tell why. Is the Church inescapable? Discuss.

5. In what way are the three primary societies said to be *means* to man's last end? What does each society contribute to the individual? Will these three primary societies terminate? Discuss.

6. When is a society said to be *perfect*? Explain fully. Which of the primary societies are perfect societies? How do they differ as to their proximate goal?

7. When is a society said to be *imperfect*? Does that mean the society has no goal? Explain. Where does an imperfect society find its supplement? Which of the primary societies is imperfect?

8. Pope Pius XI wrote: "God alone is man's last end in this life and in the next." How can God be man's last end *in this life*?

9. St. Thomas wrote: "Man's need for society applies not only to the necessities of life, but also to seeking his supernatural end." If society is only a temporal association, how can it lead to man's supernatural end? Explain.

10. Reread in the text Pope Pius's words concerning the three primary societies. Tell on what basis man has priority of rights and on what basis civil society has priority of rights. Do these come into conflict? Is it necessary that they come into conflict? How can conflict be avoided? Discuss.

11. In the same quotation as referred to in no. 10, find the brief statement of the three ends of the primary societies and quote them in the words of Pope Pius.

12. What does priority of rights on the part of the family amount to? Why are the rights of the family and the individual not *absolute*? To what must all human rights in social living be related?
13. What is the difference between the State having absolute power over its subjects and having only restrictive powers over them?
14. Discuss the difference in practice between "Man is for society" and "Society is for man."
15. Explain how human freedom requires that man have natural, inalienable rights. What are the inalienable rights enumerated in the Declaration of Independence?
16. In what does the subjection of man to civil society consist?
17. Explain Pope Leo's teachings about the "fixed limits" of the two powers between which the care of the human race is divided.
18. Why is there no inherent conflict between these two powers? Discuss.
19. Can one individual be subject to more than one society? Give an illustration. Explain.
20. Why is it unthinkable that God should be the cause of conflict between Church and State? What is the real reason for the conflicts which each age has witnessed?
21. Explain both the proximate and the indirect goals of civil society. Explain both the proximate and the indirect goals of the Church. Is there conflict between the goals?
22. How can the State further man's eternal happiness? How can the Church further man's temporal well-being?

For the Advanced Reader

St. Thomas:
> *An Apology for Religious Orders*, pp. 87–91
> *Commentary on the First Book of Politics of Aristotle*, chap. 1
> *On the Governance of Rulers*, bk. 1, chap. 1
> *Summa Theologica*, Tracts on Law and Virtue, passim, vols. 8, 10

Papal Encyclicals:
> Pope Leo XIII: *Chief Duties of Christians as Citizens*
> *Civil Government*
> *Condition of Labor*
> *Evils of Modern Society*
> Pope Pius XI: *Atheistic Communism*
> *Christian Education of Youth*
> Pope Pius XII: *Unity in Opposing World Evils*

Christian Social Principles

Philosophy of the State, reprinted 1940 from 1939 proceedings, American Catholic Philosophic Association: "The Individual and the State"; "Civil Rights"

Any good book on Christian social ethics

14

The Family: Its Nature, Its Origin, Its Role

We come now to a discussion of the first of the three necessary primary societies: the family. You will recall that Pope Leo spoke of it as "the society of one's household ... anterior to every kind of state or nation ... a true society, governed by a power within itself." From this we see that it is a primary community wherein social living is first experienced; that it is older than any state; that it is directed by an authority of its own, and that it has a purpose and goal of its own.

We discussed earlier the fact that society in general — the human race as one association — consists of particular societies each with its specific purpose. There is the family; there is the State; there is the Church; there are economic groups and the like. The very fact that each particular association has a purpose which is its very own and not another's, is a justification for their several existences. Each society's purpose explains the meaning and the activities of that society. Each society's purpose entitles it to everything necessary for the fulfillment of that purpose. If one association with one specific purpose could have answered all man's needs, then one would be all that God would have ordained. God does nothing in vain, as we said before. The existence of several primary and necessary societies means there are several distinct purposes to attain, and that one society alone is not sufficient to attain them.

Since each society has its goal and the right to the use of those things required for its attainment, it follows that each society has the freedom to act in its own sphere in such a way that the purpose of its existence will be assured. It must preserve to itself its right to exist and its freedom of activity. There is, however, this restriction on its activity: that it be kept within the sphere of reason and that it be not contrary to the common good. In other words, its right is not absolute but relative.

In our discussion of the family we shall look for these things.

Definition

St. Thomas speaks of the family as a group of persons established according to nature for daily mutual help, using together the daily needs of life, living a common life in the home, eating together at the same table, sitting at the same fire. It is, indeed, "the society of man's own household." Now the family, though it is a unit, is made up of parts. It is a composite society. Within the society of the family there is the very necessary society which is called the *conjugal society*; namely, the society of husband and wife. Without it, there would be no family. It is the foundation stone of the society of the family, just as the family is the foundation stone of the society of the State. There is a second component of domestic society: the parents-children relationship. Though the family as such exists from the time of the marriage of husband and wife, it is perfected when children are born. A third element of the family which, in our times, is not generally looked upon as part of the domestic society, is the master-servant relationship. In the "society of a man's household" these three may be found. The first set of ties, the husband-wife society, must exist; the second set of ties, the parents-children bond, usually exists; the third set of ties, the master-servant tie, is by no means an essential part of family life today. When a family requires the services of others, it has obligations toward them, and it was with respect to this that St. Thomas spoke of that third relationship.

Conjugal Society

In human society, an individual man and an individual woman voluntarily consent to form a life partnership. Their consent, which expresses the free union of their wills in a permanent bond, constitutes the marriage contract. They then become husband and wife. Conjugal society is established. It is this husband-wife bond, this conjugal society or marriage, which brings into existence the society of the family. The consent of the parties establishes the contract; the contract establishes marriage; marriage establishes the family. Thus the family is said to be brought into existence through the ties of Matrimony which effect the perpetual union of a man and a woman as husband and wife.

The individual man and woman who contracted the matrimonial bond became husband and wife in conjugal society or marriage, and father and mother in domestic society or the family. In each case a new perfection was added to the parties, for the union of wills in love and helpfulness on the part of husband and wife is a greater perfection than was found in the individuals as such; and the extension of themselves and their personality in their children is a greater perfection of the father and mother than was found in the union of their wills in love and friendship as husband and wife.

Marriage

Marriage and the family have for their purpose something which no other society can effect. Therefore, as we pointed out before, this specific purpose is the sufficient reason for the existence of domestic society effected through marriage. Let us look at some of the characteristics of the marriage contract.

It is, first of all, a contract freely entered. By a contract, we mean that it is binding, as are all just, freely entered contracts. It is voluntary; that is, it is freely and deliberately entered. Coercion hinders the bond from forming, so that without free consent there is no contract. It is a permanent union, for unless it is lasting, its purposes could not be achieved. It must be a union of one man and one woman only; otherwise the required unity in domestic affairs would be lacking. Though it is a voluntarily entered union, it carries with it obligations and rights which bind the contracting parties. Though the marriage tie is freely embraced, it may not be freely broken. In this it differs from other contracts in which the parties concerned may dissolve the contracting bond. Marriage has inviolable stability. This is demanded by the very purpose of the family: the procreation and education of children and the mutual love and fidelity of husband and wife.

Aims of Marriage

Nature had a specific aim in human marriage. This aim concerns the good of the human race. Marriage was intended by nature as the means to perpetuate the race. It is through marriage and into the family circle that new members of the race enter into human societies. Human marriage has for its chief aim, therefore, the procreation of children. But nature did not intend that children merely be born. The Author of nature ordained an immortal existence for human beings, and for this destiny, each person must be prepared.

Life on earth is a time for perfecting human capacities. It is a time for developing the human personality. New members of the race, therefore, must be *educated*. They must be reared according to standards of human perfection with the aim of developing their highest faculties as well as their lowest. They require physical, intellectual, and moral education. Hence it is that not alone the generation of children, but also their education, is nature's end. This end is, as you can see, one that affects, chiefly and directly, the common good of society. It might be called the *social function* of marriage.

Primary Aims

Our discussion of aims of marriage would not be complete were we to neglect to call attention to other aims of marriage. What we have called above the *social function* of marriage, namely, the procreation and education of children, is said to be the *primary* aim of marriage. Now the primary end of anything is the foremost end. It is the principal good for which a thing exists. In this sense, then, the primary end of marriage is offspring, and this end concerns the good of the race. It is the end of the common good.

It is interesting to note St. Thomas's remark that generation alone among all the acts which are natural to man is directed toward the common good. Eating is directed primarily to the good of the individual. So, too, is sleeping. So too, other natural acts, by their very nature, are directed toward the individual or private good. Generation directly benefits the common good.

Secondary Aims

Marriage has secondary aims which concern the individual good apart from the primary aim which concerns the common good. Secondary ends are added purposes, benefits over and above the primary one. Now the secondary aims of marriage are all those benefits which accrue to the married couple personally by reason of their marriage.

It is not difficult to name a number of personal benefits which married couples derive from their marriage. Mutual help, lifelong companionship, mutual development of personality, fullness of life, strengthening of conjugal friendship, perfection of conjugal love, union of mind and will, mutual security, and a number of others might be mentioned. These added, personal benefits which come to the married couple might be summed up in the expressions, "development of personality," "perfection of conjugal love," and "mutual helpfulness and companionship."

Primary versus Secondary Ends

It is not difficult to understand, then, these differences between the primary and the secondary ends of marriage. The secondary ends might be called the truly human ends; those which belong to human marriage, that is, to the marriage of rational beings capable of knowledge and of love. The primary ends belong to man less as human and more as animal. In other words, generation is common to all animals, irrational and rational. The love, fidelity, helpfulness, companionship, personal development, and so forth, which are the secondary ends of marriage are ends possible only to rational creatures. The union of heart and will in conjugal society is possible only to creatures which possess heart and will.

Let us use an illustration to bring out the differences between these ends. Let us use the eye. The primary purpose of the eye is to see. It is the end or purpose which first arises from the very nature of the eye. Now a secondary end of the eye is the enjoyment of nature or of beauty in any visible form. This is an added advantage, a further benefit. So, too, in marriage, there are both primary and secondary ends. The primary ends, we repeat, concern the common good; the secondary ends concern the private good of the contracting parties. Ultimately, however, the secondary ends affect the common good, too, insofar as they affect the individuals who contribute to the common good.

Principal Ends

This is not a further division of ends. We will merely gather together in this section several of the most important ends, whether they be primary or secondary, and classify them as *principal* ends. Our purpose is to bring out more clearly the Catholic teaching on the ends of marriage. The principal ends of marriage are the generation of offspring, their education, and the mutual development and perfection of the personalities of husband and wife. That this mutual helpfulness is a true end of marriage we can see from the words of Holy Scripture: "Let us make him [Adam] a help like unto himself" (Gen. 2:18). This would sum up concisely the secondary aims of marriage. In the command: "Increase and multiply" (Gen. 1:28), we have an expression of the primary aim.

Of this Pope Leo XIII wrote:

If we consider the end of the Divine institution of marriage, we shall see very clearly that God intended it to be a most fruitful source of individual benefit and public welfare. Not only, in strict truth, was marriage instituted for the propagation of the human race, but also that the lives of husbands and wives might be made better and happier. This comes about in many ways: by their lightening each other's burdens through mutual help; by constant and faithful love; by having all their possessions in common; and by the heavenly grace which flows from the sacrament.

Pope Pius XI also speaks of this (my emphasis):

This mutual inward moulding of husband and wife, this determined effort to perfect each other, can in a very real sense, be said to be the chief reason and purpose of matrimony, *provided matrimony be looked at,* not in the restricted sense as instituted for the proper procreation and education of children but *in a wider sense as the blending of life as a whole and the mutual interchange and sharing thereof.*

Pope Pius XI here mentions not only the social advantages but also the personal benefits of Matrimony.

As a Sacrament

The lives of husband and wife are made better and happier by the heavenly grace *of the sacrament.* Marriage is a contract, as we have already said. It was a contract when God gave to Adam the woman Eve to be his helpmate and the mother of his children. It was ennobled later when Christ established it as a channel of divine grace flowing from the infinite treasury of the Church into the hearts of husband and wife. It still remained a contract, but one nobler in nature and richer in returns. As a contract, Matrimony is directed to the good of the offspring inasmuch as it is a permanent thing, since the proper care of children requires a long period of time to effect. As a sacrament it is directed to the good of the husband and wife in that it guarantees a flow of grace to strengthen and vivify the love, the fidelity, the helpfulness which make life "a better and happier one." By the grace of the sacrament, the contracting parties, through cooperation with it, are strengthened, sanctified, and in a manner consecrated. Through Christian marriage the contracting parties are adorned by the bond of the sacrament; they are assisted in their domestic duties and activities; in their spirit and their lives they remain the living image of that most fruitful union of Christ with the Church which is the sacred token of most perfect love.

Institution of Marriage

God is the Author of the marriage bond. God is the source of the laws which strengthen, confirm, and elevate Matrimony. The marriage bond is indissoluble; it is perpetual; it is stable. The marriage bond and the laws of marriage are beyond the power of human beings to alter or abrogate. Marriage ever remains a divine institution. The will of God has called it into being; the will of individuals may or may not embrace the state, but it cannot modify the marriage bond.

Let us repeat that last point. The will of individuals may consent to enter the state of Matrimony. The will of individuals may consent not to enter that state. In either case, the will is free to act. But, once having consented to the marriage bond, the contracting parties are bound by it. They accept the married state with its right and its obligations; they must abide by the indissolubility, the inviolability, the unity which characterize the married state. With these elements of the contract they have nothing to do but to accept them. They cannot accept one of them to the exclusion of the other two. They cannot accept one or all of them for a given time only. The nature of marriage is the work and the will of God; its laws are equally divinely made. As such they are beyond tampering by human beings, even by the contracting parties themselves. The freedom of the individual parties with regard to the married state amounts to this: they may choose to enter it or not to enter it; they may choose this individual or that individual for their life's partner. That is all. Once they have entered it, they must conform to the nature, the laws, and the characteristics of the marriage contract; they must accept them as they are, for these things lie beyond the power of human beings to touch.

Pope Pius XI, in his encyclical on *Christian Marriage*, writes:

> Although matrimony is of its very nature of divine institution, the human will, too, enters into it and performs a most noble part. For each individual marriage, inasmuch as it is a conjugal union of a particular man and woman, arises only from the free consent of each of the spouses; and this free act of the will ... is so necessary to constitute true marriage that it cannot be supplied by any human power.
>
> This freedom, however, regards only the point whether the contracting parties really wish to enter upon matrimony or to marry this particular person; but the nature of matrimony is entirely independent of the free will of man, so that if one has once contracted matrimony he is thereby subject to its divinely made laws and its essential properties.

Blessings of Marriage

Married life, in its Christian ideal, is a beautiful thing. Love is its basis. A life of virtue is its blossom. The union of Christ with His Church is its exemplar. The peopling of the earth is a primary aim. The perfection and extension of human personality is a second aim. However, married life has its difficulties. There are worries and trials and hardships in married life, even as there are in other states of life. But each state of life has its bright spots, its recompenses. So, too, with the married state. It, too, has recompenses for the difficulties of domestic society.

St. Augustine speaks of these as "the blessings of matrimony." They are offspring, conjugal faith, and the sacrament. St. Thomas speaks of them as *the goods* of marriage. These goods are attributable to man under a threefold aspect; namely, as animal, as rational, and as Christian respectively in his nature and character. Pope Leo XIII and Pope Pius XI enumerate these *goods* and explain their meaning in their respective encyclicals on *Christian Marriage*.

The first *blessing* or *good* of Matrimony is offspring. To beget and care for children is a supreme joy to parents. They see in their children the continuation of themselves. They lavish love upon them and serve them unselfishly. They delight in the doings and sayings of their children and watch tenderly their growth and development. Truly Christian parents see in their children heirs of Heaven and future companions of God and the saints. Offspring is, indeed, a blessing of Matrimony.

The second *blessing* or *good* of Matrimony is directed toward the good of the parents, namely, the faithfulness, mutual trust, and the confidence which exists between them. Where this blessing exists, marriage is characterized by that complete unity which safeguards the home. Neither husband nor wife is unfaithful, disloyal, or undutiful to the other. They are truly one as Christ is one with the Church. This blessing admits of but one wife or one husband until death claims one of the partners. This matrimonial fidelity demands that love should unite the husband and wife; that love should pervade all the duties of married life; that love should be the inspiration of the mutual help which husband and wife give to each other in all their dealings, even to the perfecting of themselves in the life of grace and virtue.

"The love of which We are speaking," says Pope Pius XI,

> is based on deep attachment of the heart which is expressed in action, since love is proved by words. This outward expression of love in the home demands not only mutual help but must go further; must have as its primary purpose that man and wife help each other day by day in forming and perfecting themselves in the interior life, so that through their partnership in life they may advance ever more and more in virtue, and above all that they may grow in true love towards God and their neighbor.

"These are the elements which compose the blessings of conjugal faith," writes this same pope,

> unity, chastity, charity, honorable, noble obedience which are at the same time an enumeration of the benefits which are bestowed on husband and wife in their married state, benefits by which the peace, the dignity and the happiness of matrimony are securely preserved and fostered. Wherefore it is not surprising that this conjugal faith has

always been counted amongst the most priceless and special blessings of matrimony.

These are the distinctly human ends of Matrimony; the ends attributed to man *as man*, that is, as rational.

The third *blessing* or *good* of Matrimony consists in the indissolubility of the bond which is derived from *the sacrament*. The grace of the sacrament gives permanence to the marriage bond so that it cannot be broken. Even before marriage was dignified by the character of a sacrament, however, it carried with it inviolable stability. The common good of society demands it. The good of the offspring demands it. God's law has ordained it. Every true marriage, even where it does not have the added dignity of the sacramental character, as among those who have not been baptized, bears the perpetual bond which God gave to it and which is not within the right of any civil power to dissolve.

> How many and how important are the benefits which flow from the indissolubility of matrimony cannot escape any one who gives even a brief consideration either to the good of the married parties and the offspring or to the welfare of human society.... In the training and education of children which must extend over a period of many years, it plays a great part, since the grave and long enduring burdens of this office are best born by the united efforts of the parents. Nor do lesser benefits accrue to human society as a whole. For experience has taught that unassailable stability in matrimony is a fruitful source of virtuous life and of habits of integrity. Where this order of things obtains, the happiness and well-being of the nation is safely guarded; what the families and individuals are, so also is the State, for a body is determined by its parts.

In these words Pope Pius XI upheld the inviolable permanence of Matrimony.

These, then, are the blessings of marriage, which is that voluntary contract of lifelong union between a man and a woman upon which the family is established. How important are those two words, "I do," which signify the union of wills effected in the marriage contract.

One cannot but see, therefore, that the ends of marriage constitute the ends of the family; that the characteristics of the marriage state are the characteristics of the family; that the naturalness and necessity of marriage are the naturalness and necessity of the family. It is not to be wondered at that the

Church has ever striven to keep intact the matrimonial bond, for its relation to the family is so close that the breakdown of the bond of marriage breaks down the unity of the family, and the breakdown of the family is the forerunner of the social decay in the State, for "as the families and individuals are, so also is the State, for it is made up of them even as a body is made up of its members."

Domestic Relations

Let us take a glimpse into the family to see therein what constitutes its order as a society. Pope Leo reminds us that, "it is a true society, governed by a power within itself, namely by the father." Now authority denotes subordination and mastery as we saw in an earlier chapter. In what does this domestic subordination consist? Who is the master? What effects for good or for bad does subordination and mastery within the domestic society have?

The family is founded upon several relationships, as we have seen. The foremost one is that of husband and wife. The husband is the head of his wife, as Christ is the head of the Church. St. Paul thus admonished his hearers twenty centuries ago. Pope Pius XI remarks: "If the man is the head, the woman is the heart, and as he occupies first place in ruling, so she may and ought to claim for herself the chief place in love." This gives us the clue to domestic relations. The father rules. His right to rule gives him the duty of providing for the necessities of the family. Authority always is invested with the task of providing as well as directing, for one cannot reach the end without use of means. So members of a family cannot attain their personal and collective happiness without the necessities of life.

The mother's role is the role of love; it expresses itself in generous service. Home would not be home without the love of a mother within it. She looks after the children and manages the domestic duties. She rules in her own sphere under the supreme rule of the father. She is second in command, and note this well: she participates in ruling as becomes her dignity as wife and mother. She has true authority over her children.

Wifely Subjection

Order is the apt arrangement of parts, arranged according to their importance. Hence in the family, the father holds supreme rule, and this includes his authority over his wife, as well as authority over the children. This subjection of wife and children to the rule of the father is not one of slave to master. Domestic society should be confirmed in love, true love, in the love that brought together an individual man and woman and made them husband and wife and perfected them by parenthood. A wife's subjection to her husband and her willing obedience to him should, therefore, flow from her love of him. It does not take away her liberty as a human being. As such, she has equal rights with her husband. It does not make her a slave obeying his every whim, particularly if it be out of reason or not in harmony with her dignity as wife and mother. It does not put the wife on the level of the children nor the servants.

As companion in his friendship, as wife in the conjugal society, as mother of the children, a good wife is a noble creature of God and worthy of every mark of respect and honor, of love and gratitude. Her subjection and obedience extend to those things which concern the care of the household and the happiness and well-being of the family. "It forbids," says Pope Pius XI, "that exaggerated liberty which cares not for the good of the Family; it forbids that in this body which is the Family, the heart be separated from the head to the great detriment of the whole body and the proximate danger of ruin."

This is truly a rational doctrine of domestic authority. It insists upon equality of rights in the essential things of marriage, because the wife as well as the husband is a rational creature destined for eternity with God. She, as well as he, is bearer of natural rights which aid her in her journey back to God.

This doctrine of authority, however, provides a certain inequality, for every society must have a head; *one* head, not two. In the matter of directing the domestic society to its proper end, the head is supreme; otherwise in matters where the father's will and the mother's came into conflict, were neither one supreme, there would be a deadlock and the little society of the home would suffer. In things pertaining to the well-being of the family, its provisions, its protection, and its ends, the wife holds second place.

Parent-Child Relations

The first and most basic set of relationships in the domestic society is that of husband and wife. The second relationship is that of parents and children. It consists of parental authority over the children and filial love, respect, and obedience toward the parents.

Parental authority has the same source as life itself: namely, it takes its origin in God. It is a right rooted in man's nature, and therefore it becomes a duty to fulfill it. Civil society cannot abolish this right. The child belongs to the father, and it is an act of grave injustice when civil society oversteps its limits and absorbs the individual without recognition of the primary rights of the family. It is through the family that a child takes its place in civil society, and not in its own right. This expresses the principle discussed before, that the family is anterior to the State both in nature and in time, and therefore it possesses rights which lie beyond the power of the State to deny or abolish.

As the subjection of the wife was rooted in her love for her husband, so should the subjection and obedience of the children be rooted more in filial love than in fear. Fear is not to be excluded, but the fear of a child for his parents should be reverential fear; the fear that hesitates to wound loving parents, not that fear which made a slave tremble before his angry master. Filial obedience is limited. It extends to those things which are not in violation of the law of God or of nature. Should parents command a sinful act, the child is obliged, not to *obey*, but to *disobey*.

Likewise, parental authority is limited. It pertains to the due education of children and the government of the home. Parents may not compel marriage. They may not forbid marriage. No undue interference may be made with regard to the children's state in life. Neither may parents compel nor forbid their children to enter religious life. Parents may counsel, admonish, plead, but not coerce. Parents have no life-and-death power over their children, nor may they load them with inhuman indignities or impose unjust burdens upon them. As childhood passes and the children become more capable of caring for themselves, parental authority should become less stringent until such time as the children assume altogether the care of themselves.

Rights and duties are correlative. We have spoken of this before. Now children have the right to proper education. This *education* includes physical support, proper mental and moral development, love, care, and guidance. This right to proper education imposes upon children the duty of obedience, gratitude, docility, and the like toward their parents. Later when parents are old and needy, children are bound to provide for their needs. This filial obligation arises from the parental right to the respect and gratitude of their children. It is a part of the virtual piety and piety belongs to the virtue of justice, inasmuch as filiality is due to parents.

Thus we have discussed some of the more important aspects of domestic society. Before we consider the discussion on the family completed, we must further show the relations which exist between the family and the State or, more accurately, the family *in* the State. In addition to this, we must explain the nature and extent of two very basic familial rights: education and private possessions. These will come in the subsequent chapters in their appropriate places.

Some Original Sources

The first of these quotations is a chapter from St. Thomas's *Summa Contra Gentiles*. It is a simple, direct statement of the characteristics of Matrimony. Use it in connection with your readings and discussions.

1. "We must observe that when a thing is directed to several ends, it needs several directors to those ends: because the end is proportionate to the agent.

"Now human generation is directed to several ends, namely,

(1) the continuation of the species, or

(2) the securing of some good of the State, such as the preservation of the people in some particular country: again

(3) it is directed to the perpetuity of the Church which is the assembly of the faithful.

"Wherefore the generation in question needs to receive its direction from various sources.

"Insofar as it is directed to the good of nature, namely, the perpetuation of the species, it is directed by nature which inclines to this end, and thus it is called an office of nature.

"Insofar as it is directed to the good of the State, it is subject to the control of the civil authority.

"But insofar as it is directed to the good of the Church, it must be subject to ecclesiastical power.

"Now those things which are dispensed by the ministers of the Church are called sacraments. Therefore matrimony, as consisting in the union of a man and woman who intend to beget and educate children for the glory of God, is a sacrament of the Church; and hence it is that the bridal pair receive a blessing from the ministers of the Church.

"And just as in the other sacraments, something spiritual is symbolized by external actions, so in this sacrament the union of husband and wife signifies the union of Christ with the Church.

"And seeing that the sacraments cause what they signify, we must believe that the sacrament of matrimony confers on those who are joined in wedlock the grace to take part in the union of Christ with His Church, since it is most necessary that they should so act as not to be separated from Christ and His Church.

"Since then the union of husband and wife signifies the union of Christ and the Church, the figure must needs correspond to the thing signified. Now the union of Christ with the Church is the unending union of one with one, for the Church is one. Nor will Christ ever be separated from His Church.

"Therefore matrimony, as a sacrament of the Church, must needs be the indissoluble union of one man with one woman: and this pertains to the mutual troth which binds husband and wife together.

"Accordingly there are three blessings attached to matrimony as a sacrament of the Church: namely, children, to be begotten and brought up to worship God; faithfulness, inasmuch as one husband is bound to one wife; and the sacrament, inasmuch as it is an indissoluble union, symbolizing the union of Christ with the Church." (*Summa Contra Gentiles*, vol. 5, chap. 78)

2. "Three things may be considered in matrimony.
   (a) First, its essence, which is a joining together, and in reference to this it is called the conjugal union;
   (b) Secondly, its cause which is the wedding, and in reference to this it is called the nuptial union;
   (c) Thirdly, the effect, which is the offspring, and in reference to this it is called matrimony." (*Summa Theologica*, vol. 19, pp. 108–109)

3. "It is unlawful to do a person a harm, except by way of punishment in the cause of justice. No man justly punishes another, except one who is subject to his jurisdiction. Therefore it is not lawful for a man to strike another unless he have some power over the one whom he strikes. Since the child is subject to the power of the parent ... a parent can lawfully strike his child, that instruction may be enforced by correction." (See also quotation no. 6, chap. 13.) (*Summa Theologica*, vol. 10, p. 217)

4. "Although the father ranks above the mother, the mother has more to do with the offspring than the father has." (*Summa Theologica*, vol. 19, p. 109)

5. "Just as the civic life denotes, not the individual act of this or that one, but the things that concern the common action of the citizens, so the conjugal life is nothing else than a particular kind of companionship pertaining to that common action (of husband and wife); wherefore as regards this same life the partnership of married persons is always indivisible." (*Summa Theologica*, vol. 19, p. 112)

6. "A son may lawfully enter religion, though his father command him to marry. Therefore he is not bound to obey him in this.... Further, if he were bound to obey, a betrothal contracted by the parents would hold good without their children's consent. But this is against the law (of a true marriage).

"Since in marriage there is a kind of perpetual service, a father cannot by his command compel his son to marry, since the latter is of free condition; but he may induce him for a reasonable cause; and thus the son will be affected by his father's command in the same way as he is affected by that cause, so that if the cause be compelling as indicating either obligation or fitness, his father's command will compel him in the same measure; otherwise he may not compel him." (*Summa Theologica*, vol. 12, pp. 136–137)

7. "The upbringing of a child requires not only the mother's care for his nourishment, but much more the care of his father as guide and guardian, and under whom he progresses in goods both internal and external.

"Hence human nature rebels against an indeterminate marriage, and demands that a man should marry a certain definite woman and should abide with her a whole lifetime.... This union is called matrimony." (*Summa Theologica*, vol. 13, p. 135)

8. "According to the Natural Law a son, before coming to the use of reason, is under his father's care. Hence it would be contrary to natural justice if a child, before coming to the use of reason, were to be taken away from its parents' custody or anything done to it against its parents' wishes." (*Summa Theologica*, vol. 9, p. 146)

9. "Man is directed to God by his reason, whereby he can know God. But a child before coming to the use of reason, in the natural order of things, is directed to God by his parents' reason, under whose care it lies by nature: and it is for them to dispose of the child in all matters relating to God." (*Summa Theologica*, vol. 9, p. 147)

10. "Let no one then be deceived by the distinction upon which some court legists have so strongly insisted, that is, the distinction by virtue of which they sever the matrimonial contract from the sacrament, with intent to hand over the contract to the power and will of the rulers of the State, while reserving questions concerning the sacrament to the Church.

"A distinction, or rather severance, of this kind cannot be approved; for it is certain that in Christian marriage the contract is inseparable from the sacrament; and that, for this reason, the contract cannot be true and legitimate without being a sacrament as well.

"For Christ Our Lord added to marriage the dignity of a sacrament; but marriage is the contract itself, whenever that contract is lawfully concluded.

"All ought to understand clearly that, if there be any union of a man and woman among the faithful of Christ which is not a sacrament, such union has not the force and nature of a proper marriage; that although contracted in accordance with the laws of the State, it cannot be more than a rite or custom introduced by the Civil Law.

"Further, the Civil Law can deal with and decide those matters alone which, in the civil order, spring from marriage, and which cannot possibly exist, as is evident, unless there be a true and lawful cause for them, that is to say, the nuptial bond." (Pope Leo XIII, *Christian Marriage*)

11. "Since the valid matrimonial consent among the faithful was constituted by Christ as a sign of grace, the sacramental nature is so intimately bound up with Christian wedlock that there can be no true marriage between baptized persons without it being by that very fact a sacrament.

"By the very fact, therefore, that the faithful with sincere mind give such consent, they open up for themselves a treasure of sacramental grace from which they draw supernatural power for the fulfilling of their rights and duties faithfully, holily, perseveringly even unto death.

"Hence this sacrament not only increases sanctifying grace ... but also adds particular gifts, dispositions, seeds of grace, by elevating and perfecting the natural powers.

"By these gifts the parties are assisted not only in understanding, but in knowing intimately, in adhering to firmly, in willing effectively, and in successfully putting into practice, those things which pertain to the marriage state, its aims and duties, giving them, in fine, right to the actual assistance of grace, whensoever they need it for fulfilling the duties of their state." (Pope Pius XI, *Christian Marriage*)

12. "It is hardly possible to describe how great are the evils that flow from divorce. Matrimonial contracts are by it made variable; mutual kindness is weakened; deplorable inducements to unfaithfulness are supplied; harm is done to the education and training of children; occasion is afforded for the breaking up of homes; the seeds of dissension are sown among families; the dignity of womanhood is lessened and brought low.

"Since, then, nothing has such power to lay waste families and destroy the mainstay of kingdoms as the corruption of morals, it is easily seen that divorces are in the highest degree hostile to the prosperity of families and States, springing as they do from the depraved morals of the people, and, as experience shows us, opening out a way to every kind of evil-doing in public alike and in private life." (Pope Leo XIII, *Christian Marriage*)

Summary

1. The family is a true society. It has an end of its own. It has activities of its own. It possesses rights which enable it to pursue its end. It is entitled to the necessary freedom to pursue its end, though limited, of course, by the common good.

2. Pope Leo called the family "the society of one's household." St. Thomas mentions three relationships which comprise a household: husband-wife ties; parents-children relationship; master-servant relations.

3. The family, though a primary unit in itself, is made up of lesser units, those relationships mentioned above. The most important of these is the husband-wife relationship which constitutes conjugal society. Without this the family would not exist.

4. Conjugal society, or marriage, brings the family into existence. It is a contract to which free consent is given. The free consent constitutes the contract and binds the parties.

5. The marriage contract differs from other contracts in that it is indissoluble. It may be freely embraced or it may be rejected as one's state of life, but if it be embraced, a lasting union of lifelong duration is effected.

6. Nature intends the perpetuation of the race. For this reason marriage and family life are necessary as it is through them that children are born. This is the primary end of marriage.

7. Individuals may have personal ends, apart from nature's intention, for embracing the marriage state. Marriage should be founded upon true love for only true love can effect a happy union of husband and wife. Personal happiness, companionship, friendship, and a common life may all be legitimate aims for embracing marriage. These, together with development of personality, constitute distinctly human ends of matrimony.

8. Individuals are not obliged to marry. Though marriage and family life be necessary for the good of the race, they are not necessary in the case of particular individuals in the race. The obligation to perpetuate itself is placed on the race but not on every individual in the race.

9. Marriage therefore has a double aim: the perpetuation of the race and fuller, happier lives of the married couples.

10. Marriage as a contract was ennobled by Christ to be a channel of divine grace. The grace of the sacrament enables the couples to live virtuously in the married state.

11. Marriage is a divine institution. The laws of marriage are divine laws. The will of God instituted marriage with its rights and obligations. The contracting parties may will to embrace it, and will to accept this or that individual as life partner. They have no jurisdiction over the nature and laws of the marriage contract. These things are beyond human control.

12. Marriage has a threefold blessing: (1) the offspring; (2) the fidelity and mutual helpfulness between husband and wife; (3) the inviolable stability or indissolubility of the sacrament.

13. These are the characteristics of Christian marriage. Added to them are the equality of husband and wife in human dignity and in the essential rights of marriage, and the supremacy of the father's rule in the conduct of the household.

14. The father is the head; the mother is the heart; the child is the object of affection and care in the domestic society.

15. Subjection to the father ought to be that of filial love and reverential fear. It does not detract from the dignity of the wife as companion and mother. It is needful for the right ordering of the household, for *one* head should rule.

16. Parents are obliged to provide their children with the necessities of life, with a good moral education, and with intellectual training at least sufficient to insure the children's future care of themselves and in keeping with their position in life.

17. Children are obliged to show reverence, respect, love, gratitude, and obedience to their parents and to provide for them in times of sickness, old age, and need.

18. The domestic society differs from civil society inasmuch as it is rooted in love, whereas civil society is founded upon law and force.

For Study and Discussion

1. What does the existence of a number of distinct and necessary societies show? How, in general, are these limited so that there is no overstepping of bounds?
2. What is the justification for the existence of the family as a distinct society? Could not the State perform the work of the domestic society? Explain.
3. Discuss the definition of the family as given by St. Thomas. Why "according to nature"? Explain: "living a common life in the home."
4. What are the lesser units which comprise the primary unit known as the family? Why is conjugal society necessary for the society of the family?
5. What establishes conjugal society? What establishes the family?
6. Explain the marriage contract: (a) as a contract; (b) as a sacrament.
7. What are the aims (ends) of marriage? What may be called nature's end? What legitimate (though secondary) ends may be personal reasons for entering the married state?
8. In what way may marriage be said to be "a most fruitful source of individual benefit and public welfare"?
9. Discuss Pope Pius's statement on the perfection of husband and wife as a chief reason of matrimony. In what sense must matrimony be viewed to make that statement true?
10. What has the human will to do with the marriage contract? What has it to do with the rights and duties of married life?
11. How can marriage claim to be a divine institution? Why are its laws and rights beyond the power of human institutions?
12. Name and explain each of the three *blessings* or *goods* of marriage.
13. What are the elements which compose the blessing of conjugal faith? Why is conjugal faith one of the most priceless blessings of matrimony?
14. In what way is marriage said to be necessary? In what way is it said to be voluntary?
15. Explain the supremacy of the father in the family: the nature of his authority, its purpose and extent.
16. Discuss wifely subordination. In what does it consist? Why does it not degrade her? Why should she be subordinate to the husband?
17. Explain: the father is the head, the mother is the heart of the domestic society.
18. Why is parental authority rooted in nature? Why may the family and not the State exercise authority over the child in the home?
19. What are the characteristics of filial love? What duties do children owe their parents?
20. What obligations have parents toward their children? What rights have parents? What limits parental authority?

21. By what virtue is the relationship of parents to children governed?
22. Why should the home and family life be a sacred thing?

For the Advanced Reader

St. Thomas:

Commentary on I Ethics
Commentary on I Politics
Summa Contra Gentiles, vol. 5, chap. 78
Summa Theologica, vol. 19, Tract on Marriage

Farrell, Walter:

A Companion to the Summa, III, chap. 17

Ostheimer, Anthony:

The Family, vol. 50, Philosophical Studies, C.U.A.

Papal Encyclicals:

Pope Leo XIII: *Christian Marriage*
The Condition of Labor
Pope Pius XI: *Christian Marriage*

15

Mutual Relations: Individual, Family, State

Is the foundation stone of civil society the individual or the family? Does the State touch directly and absorb into a collectivity the individual men and women who live under its rule? Or does the State stop before the family, respecting its oneness, and deal directly with it, and, through it, with the individuals which compose it? The answer depends on whether we see the State as a collection of individuals or a collection of families. What are the component parts of the State?

Basis of Civil Society

St. Thomas keeps calling attention to the principle that "the imperfect is ordained to the perfect"; "the part is for the sake of the whole." But what is "the imperfect" and "the part" in the case of civil society?

"As one man is a part of the household, so a household is a part of the State: and the State is a perfect community." This statement of St. Thomas gives a clue to the answer. Individuals comprise the household (the family); families comprise the State. Without the individuals, there would be no family; but on the other hand would there be individuals without the family? It would seem, then, that since individuals are required for the society of the family, and since the family is imperfect as a society, and therefore is ordained to the perfect (which is the State), both individuals and families constitute the basis or foundation of the State.

St. Thomas continues: "As the good of one man is not the last end, but is ordained to the common good; so too, the good of one household is ordained to the good of a single state which is a perfect community." Here St. Thomas states the individual must contribute to the common good inasmuch as he is part of the larger society of the State, and also that the family must contribute to the common good in which it is entitled to share.

In the case of the majority of individuals, normal life for them is living in domestic society and the contribution which they make to the common good of the family contributes its part to the common good of the whole society, since the family must direct its efforts toward the common good of the State. Individuals who have no home ties are not, by that fact, relieved of their responsibility toward the common good. They make their contribution to the well-being of the State directly, and not indirectly in part, as do the individuals who live in domestic society.

Pope Leo XIII sums up the principle by saying: "The child takes its place in civil society, not in its own right, but in its quality as a member of the family in which it is begotten." It is therefore through the family and its well-being that the individual makes the greater portion of his contribution toward the State. There are some services which are made directly from individuals to the State as in the case of military services. But for the most part it is through the family that the common good is advanced, and the strength and unity of the social whole depends upon the strength and unity of the family circle. "It is evident," says St. Thomas, "that a household is a mean between the individual and the city or kingdom, since just as the individual is part of the household, so is the household part of the city or kingdom."

We say, therefore, that neither the individual alone, nor the family alone, but both the individual and the family are to be considered as the basis of civil society. The individual, who is so inadequate for attaining his own human perfection, is perfected partly through the imperfect society of the family, and partly through the perfect society of the State. Pope Pius XI writes:

> On this point [the rearing of children] the common sense of mankind is in such complete accord, that they would be in open contradiction with it who dared maintain that the children belong to the State before they belong to the Family, and that the State has an absolute right over their education. Untenable is the reason they adduce, namely, that man is born a citizen and hence belongs primarily to the State, not bearing in mind that before being a citizen, man must exist; and that existence does not come from the State, but from the parents.

It is necessary to emphasize this point again and again in view of the totalitarian philosophy of government which is sweeping the world and which claims absolute dominion over the individual in himself and in all that he is. Let us hear St. Thomas again.

In speaking of prudence as being necessary in government, he classifies several species of prudence: reignative, or kingly prudence, directive of the laws made; domestic prudence, which guides the household, and so forth. Then he tells us that an individual directs himself to his own individual good by means of prudence commonly so called, but, on the other hand, he directs himself in relation to the common good by *political prudence* whereby he is directed in obeying his superiors.

Then St. Thomas explains the end or purpose of this political prudence. "The end of political prudence *is a good life in general* as regards the conduct of the household." The individual, therefore, in promoting the common good through obedience to his superiors, has, for his purpose, the promotion of the family. He seeks well-rounded, good, human life, *a better life,* and he finds this in the family through the promotion of the common good of the whole society of which families are the component parts.

Absorption Not an Advantage

It must always be remembered that the family is an imperfect society, that it must reach out beyond itself and its capacities in order to attain the "better life" to which it aspires. That life is found — and should be found — through the State as the perfect society. It does not mean the absorption of the family into the State. Parts are not absorbed; if so, they cease to be parts. But we have seen that the family cannot be absorbed into the State because the family has functions to perform which are proper to it; functions which no State can perform. Further, without the family, what would comprise the State? Would you say individuals? Then there would fall upon the human race a universal totalitarianism with no other destiny for the individual than loss of personality, of rights, of human happiness, and of strictly human perfection. It is to save the race from such a disastrous outcome that philosophers of keenest mind and balanced judgment have always placed the family as the *mean* between the individual and the State.

Pope Pius XI has said of this:

The end and object [of civil society], namely, the common welfare in the temporal order, consists in that peace and security in which families and individual citizens have the free exercise of their rights, and at the same time enjoy the greatest spiritual and temporal prosperity possible in this life, by the mutual union and coordination of the work of all. The function of civil authority residing in the State is twofold: to protect and to foster the Family and the individual, but by no means to absorb them or to substitute itself for them.

In summing up, let us recall that both the individual and the family constitute the basis of civil society; that the individual enters the State through the family; that the individual is obligated to the common good of the domestic society and civil society; that the family finds its perfection and that of its members through the common good of the State to which all have contributed; that the family is a *mean* between the individual and the State, and that this alone saves the individual from being absorbed by the State. The fact that the family has a purpose proper to itself and which no other society can perform is a certain natural guarantee of its complete non-absorption.

It is true that Russia, particularly, has attempted to dissolve family life and perform the functions of the domestic society on a wholesale scale, but the movement has been and ever will be doomed to failure. No public society can substitute itself for the private society of the family; no civil authority based, as it is, on power, can long substitute itself for the parental rule, based on love. It has been an experiment with sad results, and it is sadder because it is in such contradiction to the promptings of nature and the law of nature. The family is a natural society; man is inclined thereto by nature, and the promptings of nature may not long be ignored. Though rulers may attempt to abolish the family, the very need for the domestic society will be the cause of its ever-renewed vitality; it simply cannot be choked out of existence permanently, for human nature cannot be snuffed out of man's being. Man will always be human: man will always be man.

So important did the preservation of the family seem to St. Thomas that he declared that any money or goods given to keep a home intact is a far greater act of charity than giving an alms to keep an individual alive. The family must be preserved, and today the Catholic Church alone among the social institutions is engaged in battle for its preservation.

The role of the individual and the family, therefore, inasmuch as neither is self-sufficient, is one of subordination and subjection, as of the imperfect to the perfect, or as of the part to the whole. Note, "of the imperfect to the perfect," or "of the part to the whole." There is a further relationship which we might express as "of the temporal to the eternal"; a relationship which saves the "part to the whole" from being a relationship of abject slavery. We shall show how the *imperfect*, which is ordained to the end of the *perfect*, can, at the same time, be viewed as the temporal which is ordained to the eternal.

"Not in All That He is"

We noted earlier in this work that man, though he is ordained to the common good insofar as he is bound to strive for it, is not obliged to be its slave. St. Thomas assures us, and we have an inner conviction of its truthfulness, that man is not ordained to the political society according to all that he is, and has. We are convinced that we must be made for something more than temporal existence alone. There is something higher than temporal existence. "All that a man is, and can, and has, must be referred to God," says St. Thomas. In virtue of his spiritual nature, that is, his soul, he is ordained to God ultimately; to this end also is the State ordained. Man must not rest in the goods of the State; he cannot find in political society sufficient goods to make him perfectly happy. Man marches on beyond the immediate goal of the State to the ultimate goal which is God. He is a *person* endowed with immortality, with rights, with an eternal destiny. He is ordained in all that he is to God, his Creator and his only adequate end. He is ordained only in part of what he is to the body politic.

Let us understand this in the thought of St. Thomas. He discusses the relationship of parts to the whole and he shows how everything in the universe is ordained to its particular end and thus to the good of the universe and ultimately to God. Trace in the following words of St. Thomas the individual's activity, the activity of the family and of the State, and finally the onward surge of the entire universe toward its Maker.

Hierarchical Order in the Universe

St. Thomas writes: "Now if we wish to assign an end to any whole, and to the parts of that whole, we shall find, first, that each and every part exists for the sake of its proper act" (What is the proper act of the individual in society?); "Secondly, that less honourable parts exist for the more honourable" (Is private good of a temporal nature more honorable or less honorable than the common good of a temporal nature?); "Thirdly, that all parts are for the perfection of the whole, since the parts are, as it were, the material of the whole" (How do the individual and domestic society compare with the State?); "Furthermore, the whole man is on account of an extrinsic end, that end being the enjoyment of God." (Refer this to the statement that "man is not ordained to the body politic in all that he is." Is the body politic the ultimate end?)

"So, therefore, in the parts of the universe also, every creature exists for its own proper act and perfection" (Think: what is the perfection of a mineral? of a plant? of a brute animal? of man?); "the less noble for the nobler, as those creatures that are less noble than man exist for the sake of man" (May man have minerals, plants, and the brute animal for his own use and enjoyment?); "whilst each and every creature exists for the perfection of the entire universe" (Does the perfect operation of all natures contribute to the perfection of operation of the universe as a whole? Is there order, cooperation, and harmony in the universe?); "Furthermore, the entire universe, with all its parts," (living and non-living things; brute natures and rational natures,) "is ordained towards God as its end, inasmuch as it imitates, as it were, and shows forth the Divine goodness, to the glory of God." (How do non-rational natures show forth the goodness of God? How do they give glory to God? How does the sun do this? a flower? a bird? the rain?) "Reasonable creatures, however, have in some special and higher manner God as their end, since they can attain to Him by their own operations, by knowing and loving Him." (Why did God make you?) "Thus it is plain," concludes St. Thomas, "that the Divine goodness is the end [i.e., the goal] of all corporeal things."

This beautiful quotation from St. Thomas describes what we might justly call "the hierarchical order of the universe." Certainly in it we see the justification for St. Thomas's insistence that, though man is subject to the State, inasmuch as he must strive earnestly for the common good of the State of which he is a part, he nevertheless surpasses the State and transcends its authority to some degree inasmuch as he is ordained to God. Just as the individual must serve the common good of the family and civil society, so must civil society in turn serve the good of the individual and the family. The reason is clear: neither the individual nor the family finds its ultimate end in the State, nor does the State exist for itself alone but rather for those that comprise it. "The whole universe with all its parts is ordained to God as to its end."

Man Transcends Society

This, then, is the second principle governing the relations of the individual and the family to the State. Man, as a human person, transcends the State and is subject to it not absolutely, but only relatively; that is, he is the bearer of inalienable rights which he is free to exercise in the attainment of his final destiny, there being, however, this condition: that the individual not only contribute positively to the advancement of the common good, but that negatively, he refrain from injuring it. Thus, within the limits of the requirements of the common good, an individual is free to aim for and to enjoy the fullness of life to which his human nature constantly urges him.

A third principle to be used in our discussion is the priority of the family and the individual over that of the State. "The domestic household is anterior both in idea and in fact to the gathering of men into a commonwealth," says Pope Leo XIII, therefore "the former must *necessarily* have rights and duties which are prior to the latter, and *which rest most immediately on nature.*" Elsewhere in this same encyclical on *The Condition of Labor*, the Holy Father remarked: "[The family is] a true society, anterior to every kind of a State or nation, with rights and duties of its own, totally independent of the commonwealth."

Let us look into this independence of the family. When we speak thus of the independence of the family because of its priority, we include also the independence of the individuals which compose it, for a family is made up of individuals.

That the family is prior to the State *in idea*, that is, *in nature*, is immediately evident. Nature ordained that the domestic society should have care of the essentials of life, namely, the bringing into existence, the nourishing, and the upbringing of the individual members. This the State cannot perform. That the family is prior *in fact*, that is, *in time*, is also evident, as the family and larger family units, such as the clan and the tribe, existed before any civil government existed.

Neither the individual nor the family, therefore, owes to civil government its basic rights. The rights in question were inherent in the individual and the family from the very beginning of human existence. They rest, as Pope Leo said, "most immediately on nature." We cannot fail to see this if we remember that, though civil society (the State) is a natural institution as is the family, it rests immediately on the need of the family and only through that upon nature itself. It rests, therefore, less immediately on nature than does the family. This is so because nature dictates that the family should be concerned with the most elementary functions of human existence, and that the State should be to the family the *supplement to its insufficiency in attaining its proper end.*

Basic Rights Enumerated

"The Family is more sacred than the State," Pope Pius XI remarks, "and men are begotten not for earth and for time, but for heaven and eternity." It is on this basis that their natural rights are inalienable. The chief rights which we might enumerate quite generally are these: (1) the right to existence and the means thereto. This includes life, means of livelihood, and the possession and use of property; (2) Offspring: marriage, domestic life, education, possession and inheritance rights; (3) Pursuit of the proper goal of human nature: freedom of activity within the limits of the true common good, religious worship, a better life, and a life of happiness.

Pope Pius XI in his encyclical on *Atheistic Communism* enumerates them thus:

> Man has a spiritual and immortal soul. He is a person, marvelously endowed by his Creator with gifts of body and mind.... God alone is his last end in this life and the next.... In consequence he has been endowed by God with many and varied prerogatives: the right to life, to bodily integrity, to the necessary means of existence; the right to tend towards his ultimate goal in the path marked out for him by God; the right of association and the right to possess and use property.

The Declaration of Independence sums them up as life, liberty, and the pursuit of happiness. These rights are inalienable. They may not be taken from man as man, because they are *natural* rights and not *civil* rights, natural in the sense that nature bestows them on man prior to the formation of any civil society. Civil society exists to protect these rights and to harmonize the exercise of them in the multitude which is civil society.

Rights Not Absolute

These rights are not absolute in the sense that men may exercise them freely to the detriment of the common good or the good of other individuals. The possession of them is natural; the use of them is subject to limitation by the civil authority, for the sake of the true common good. Civil authority does not act contrary to the virtue of justice when it deprives a man of his life (capital punishment) for the safety and well-being of the commonwealth. Neither does civil authority act unjustly when it deprives a man of the exercise of his liberty by imprisoning him for crimes of which he has been convicted. To do this is the duty of civil authority, that the whole might not suffer from disorderly parts. "Every individual person," says St. Thomas, "is compared to the whole community as part to whole. Therefore if a man be dangerous and infectious to the community, on account of some sin, it is praiseworthy and advantageous that he be killed in order to safeguard the common good."

Let us be sure we understand this point. The right to these basic moral powers is natural; that is, it is bestowed by nature and ultimately by the Author of nature. The use of these rights is subject to authority, since man is a social being and his nature demands that he live in association with others who are equally possessed of such natural rights. Now since social life is based on the virtue of justice whereby each gives to the other what is his due, it becomes necessary that the exercise of natural rights be based on justice. A man must voluntarily withhold the exercise of a natural right if and when it comes into conflict: (1) with the common good and (2) with the equally basic rights of other individuals. An instance of this can be seen with the right to a livelihood. In the pursuit of a living, individuals are bound by justice to give to each man his due; that is, an individual may not justly deprive another of gaining an honest livelihood on the plea that the former is entitled to all that he can earn. It falls to the part of civil authority, therefore, to regulate the exercise, but not to abolish, the natural rights of individuals and families. "Society cannot defraud man of his God-given rights ... nor can society systematically void these rights by making their use impossible," says Pope Pius XI.

More Specifically Considered

"If the citizens of a State — that is to say, the Families — on entering into association and fellowship, experience at the hands of the State hindrance instead of help, and find their rights attacked instead of protected, such association were rather to be repudiated than sought after." This is found in Pope Leo's encyclical on *The Condition of Labor*.

Let us take, one by one, the more particular rights of the family and let us see how the State ought to act with reference to them. First, with respect to marriage, since the family is instituted by the consent which makes the marriage tie. Individuals are allowed to marry. The natural law gives them this right. The ends of marriage (the purposes), as we have seen, are (1) the procreation of offspring, which is a good of the race as a whole, and (2) the love, happiness, and fidelity of the contracting parties, which is a good of the individual members of the race. No human law can abolish those ends of marriage. No human law can limit those ends. In its essential nature, marriage and its purposes are beyond the arm of human law.

As regards *accidental* things connected with marriage, such as obtaining a marriage license, inheritance rights, and the like, the State has jurisdiction. In the things that truly concern the nature of marriage itself, only God and the law of nature have jurisdiction. "No Human Law," wrote Pope Leo, "can abolish the *natural* and *original* right of marriage, nor in any way limit the chief and principal purpose of marriage."

With regard to the temporal prosperity of the family, it has the right to pursue, within the limits of the common good and the law of justice, a better life, a life of greater material, intellectual, and social advantages. "It is true that a just freedom of action should be left to the individual citizen and families, but this principle is only valid as long as the common good is secured and no injustice is done," wrote Pope Leo. The family is entitled to the aid of the State if it finds itself unable to provide for its members. Since the advantage of the whole depends in goodly measure upon the good of the parts which compose it, it is to the interest of civil authority that it provide the poor and needy with what they require for a decent human existence.

"To the State," says Pope Leo,

the interests of all are equal whether high or low. The poor are members of the national community equally with the rich; they are real component parts, living parts, which make up, through the Family, the living body; and it need hardly be said that they are by far the majority. It would be irrational to neglect one portion of the citizens and to favor another; and therefore the public administration must duly and solicitously provide for the welfare and the comfort of the working people, or else that law of justice will be violated which ordains that each shall have his due.

It is therefore no more than right that the extreme needs of the poor be met from public funds and that, as far as possible, such poverty be avoided through proper legislation for the social and economic uplifting of the working classes. In this way will the State be fulfilling its purpose as laid down by Pope Pius XI:

The duty of rulers is to protect the community and its various parts; in protecting the rights of the individual they must also have special regard for the infirm and needy.... The State [however] must not absorb the individual nor the Family; both should be allowed free and untrammeled action as far as is consistent with the common good and the interests of others.

Where a family is able to provide for itself, it has the right to do so. "Man holds the right of providing for the life of his body prior to the formation of any state," wrote Pope Leo. Thus, the means to livelihood is a natural right. An individual holds the right not only to provide for his own wants but also for those of his offspring and dependents. It is a duty imposed upon him by nature that he provide all the necessities of life for those whom he has begotten. No State may abolish this primitive right of individuals and families to provide for their own material wants. This right is the basis of man's right to own and to use private possessions. A longer discussion of this important natural right will be given in a subsequent chapter.

Parental authority is a natural familial right. It is a violation of justice if the State intrudes into the home and usurps parental authority over the child. The child "is something of the father" — "the extension of his personality" — and as such it is under the father's care and government. "The Socialists," says Pope Leo, "in setting aside the parent and introducing the providence of the State, act against natural justice, and threaten the very existence of family life ... and such interference is not only unjust, but is quite certain to harass and disturb all classes of citizens and to subject them to odious and intolerable slavery."

Against this usurpation of parental rights in the upbringing of the children, Pope Pius wrote: "A conception of the State which makes the young belong to it without any exception, from the tenderest years up to adult life, can not be reconciled by a Catholic with Catholic doctrine, nor can it be reconciled with the natural rights of the Family." This right of parental authority includes, of course, the right to give the children physical, moral, intellectual, and spiritual training. Though certain forms of education may be and are reserved to the State, it is the *natural right* of families to educate their offspring as they see fit, provided, of course, as always in the case of natural rights, it be not detrimental to the *true* good of the commonwealth. A fuller discussion of the parental right to educate will come in a subsequent chapter.

A further right of the family is freedom to pursue its goal as laid down by God. This includes, besides the freedom of marriage, education, property, and others already mentioned, the right to be secure in their domestic society. It forbids the undue entrance of the State into the privacy of the home. No unlawful interference is to be tolerated; intervention, yes, if and when the rights of the individuals are being violated and justice can in no other way be secured. If the State enters to offer its services either in procuring material necessities or advancing the education of the children, its services may be accepted without fear of surrendering to the State any of the familial rights. The State must consider it its duty to give such help and services; but it must consider its duty fulfilled and withdraw when the situation has been relieved. It must then leave to the family its freedom in the pursuit of the better life. Pope Leo wrote:

If within the walls of the household there occur grave disturbances of mutual rights, the public power must interfere to force each party to give to the other what is due; for this is not to rob the citizens of their rights, but justly and properly to safeguard and strengthen them. But the rulers of the State must go no farther. Nature bids them stop there. Parental authority can neither be abolished nor absorbed by the State, for it has the same source as human life itself.

We have discussed briefly the more important of the rights of individuals and the family. Since it is only through the State, as a perfect society, that the individual and the family can procure their fullness of human living in the temporal order, they ought to give to the State all that it demands of them by way of obedience and effort in order to procure the true good and well-being of the commonwealth. Individuals and the family must never forget that it is only through the State that they can achieve their aims, for the family is an imperfect society and requires the help of the State to advance toward the goal of temporal prosperity and happiness.

The State's role is that of a director, protector, and provider. It directs all toward the commonweal. It protects the basic rights of individuals and of families. It provides opportunities for advancement and it meets the needs of the unfortunates. More detailed discussion of the aim, purposes, and work of the State will be found in the chapter devoted to that topic. Suffice it here now to say that the State's general aim is to ensure a good living to the multitude; to do its utmost to make that good living a permanent characteristic of the society; and constantly to strive to improve conditions to raise mankind ever higher toward a fullness of human living which means a decent material existence with no small measure of intellectual, moral, and spiritual development. This is the "better life": the life of virtue, the life that will bring peace and security to the society in which it is established.

Some Original Sources

Read these Thomistic and papal quotations thoughtfully. Try to make them add to your understanding of the chapter. Make reference to them in your explanations and discussions.

1. "Since men must live in a group, because they are not sufficient unto themselves to procure the necessities of life were they to remain solitary, it follows that a society

will be the more perfect the more it is sufficient unto itself to procure the necessities of life. There is, indeed, to some extent sufficiency for life in one family of one household, namely insofar as pertains to the natural acts of nourishment and the begetting of offspring and other things of this kind; ... but it exists in a city which is a perfect community, with regard to all the necessities of life." (*On the Governance of Rulers*, chap. 1)

2. "Even as part and whole are somewhat the same, so too, that which pertains to the whole, pertains somewhat to the part also: so that when the goods of the community are distributed among a number of individuals each one receives that which, in a way, is his own." (*Summa Theologica*, vol. 10, p. 159)

(N.B.: Instances could be multiplied wherein St. Thomas quotes the part-whole relationship on which is based the subordination and subjection of the lesser parts to the whole.)

3. "This is the bounden duty of rulers to the people over whom they rule: for one and all we are destined, by our birth and adoption, to enjoy, when this frail and fleeting life is ended, a supreme and final good in heaven, and to the attainment of this, every endeavor should be directed. Since, then, upon this depends the full and perfect happiness of mankind, the securing of this end should be of all imaginable interests the most urgent.

"Hence civil society, established for the common welfare, should not only safeguard the well-being of the community, but have also at heart the interests of its individual members, in such mode as not in any way to hinder, but in every manner to render as easy as may be, the possession of that highest and unchangeable good for which all should seek." (Pope Leo XIII, *Christian Constitution of States*)

4. "Family life, which is the cornerstone of all society and government, necessarily feels and experiences the salutary power of the Church, which redounds to the right ordering and preservation of every State and kingdom. For you know ... that the foundation of this society rests first of all on the indissoluble union of man and wife according to the necessity of Natural Law, and is completed in the mutual rights and duties of parents and children, masters and servants. You know also that the doctrines of Socialism strive to dissolve this union; for when the stability which is imparted to it by religious wedlock is lost, it follows that the power of the father over his own children, and the duties of the children towards their parents, must be greatly weakened." (Pope Leo XIII, Encyclical on Socialism and Communism)

5. "What has been said of the liberty of individuals is no less applicable to them when they are considered as bound together in civil society. For, what reason and the Natural Law do for individuals, that Human Law, promulgated for their good, does for the citizens of states.

"Of the laws enacted by men, some are concerned with what is good or bad by its very nature. They command men to follow after what is right and to shun what is wrong, adding at the same time a suitable sanction.

"But such laws by no means derive their origin from civil society, because just as civil society did not create human nature, so neither can it be said to be the author of the good which befits human nature, or of the evil which is contrary to it.

"Laws come before men live together in society, and have their origin in the Natural, and consequently in the Eternal Law. The precepts, therefore, of the Natural Law contained bodily in the laws of men have not merely the force of Human Law, but they possess that higher and more august sanction which belongs to the law of nature and the Eternal Law.

"And within the sphere of this kind of laws, the duty of the civil legislator is mainly to keep the community in obedience by the adoption of a common discipline and by putting restraint upon refractory and viciously inclined men, so that, deterred from evil, they may turn to what is good, or at any rate, may avoid causing trouble and disturbance to the State.

"Now there are other enactments of the civil authority, which do not follow directly, but rather remotely, from the Natural Law and which decide many points which the law of nature treats only in a general and indefinite way.... It is in the formulation of these particular rules of life ... that Human Law properly so-called, consists, binding all citizens to work together for the attainment of the common end proposed to the community, and forbidding them to depart from this end; and the same law, insofar as it is in conformity with the dictates of nature, leads to what is good and deters from what is evil.

"From this it is manifest that the Eternal Law of God is the sole standard and rule of human liberty, not only in each individual man, but also in the community and civil society which men constitute when united.

"Therefore the true liberty of human society does not consist in every man doing what he pleases, for this would simply end in turmoil and confusion and bring on the overthrow of the State; but rather [it consists] in this, that through the injunctions of the Civil Law, all may more easily conform to the prescriptions of the Eternal Law.

"Likewise the liberty of those who are in authority does not consist in the power to lay unreasonable and capricious commands upon their subjects which would equally be criminal and would lead to the ruin of the commonwealth; but the binding force of human laws is in this, that they are to be regarded as applications of the Eternal Law and incapable of sanctioning anything which is not contained in the Eternal Law, as in the principle of all law....

"Therefore the nature of human liberty, however it be considered, whether in individuals or in society, whether in those who command or in those who obey, supposes the necessity of obedience to some supreme and Eternal Law which is no other than the authority of God, commanding good and forbidding evil.

"And so far from this most just authority of God over men diminishing or even destroying their liberty, it protects and perfects it; for this real perfection of all creatures is found in the attainment of their respective final end. But the supreme end to which human liberty must ever aspire is God." (Pope Leo XIII, *Human Liberty*)

Summary

1. The individual and the family constitute the basis or foundation of civil society. The individual enters into the State through the family into which he is born.

2. The individual contributes to the common good of the domestic society as well as to the common good of civil society. His greatest contribution to the civil society is made indirectly through his contribution to the domestic society.

3. Individuals who do not live in a family pay their social dues directly to the commonwealth. Individuals who live in family life pay *some* of their social dues directly to the commonwealth as military services and the like; other dues, indirectly, through the family.

4. The child belongs to the family. The State has no absolute rights over the child. Parental authority is a right of nature and the natural law.

5. Neither the individual nor the family may be absorbed by the State. The family has its own special purpose which no other society can perform. It has its end, and the means to its fulfillment at least in an imperfect way. The State's help is supplementary to the insufficiency of the family. The goal of the State is the common good of the families that it comprises.

6. The State is to safeguard the natural rights of individuals and the family. It must protect them. It must foster their well-being. It may neither absorb them nor substitute itself for the family.

7. Any attempt to break up the family as a natural society causes great havoc on the individuals who suffer from it. However, the family is a natural society: it is prompted by nature and so it can never be abolished from human living. It may be, and often is, weakened. When this occurs, the social life of the whole civil community is always weakened, because as the family is, so is the State.

8. Because of their insufficiency, individuals and the family require the help of the State. They are therefore in subjection to it. The basis of this subjection is the subordination of the "imperfect" to the "perfect" or the "part" to the "whole."

9. Man's ultimate destiny transcends the immediate end of the State which is common temporal happiness. Therefore individuals and the family are

not wholly subordinated to the State in all their being, but only in what pertains to the common temporal happiness of the social order.

10. Man, like all of the universe, including societies such as the family and the State, is ordained to God, the Supreme Ruler of the world. Man, therefore, transcends the State in the pursuit of his personal destiny. His activities, however, must not detract from the common good. As a citizen, he is subject to civil authority in what pertains to his temporal welfare and the true common good of the State.

11. As an immortal soul possessed of a divinely given destiny, man is free to pursue this end. In this case, the private good of the individual is of a supernatural order and transcends the common good of the temporal order. For instance, a man ought not to lose his soul for the sake of enriching the common treasury of the State. Neither ought a man to desist from worshiping God because civil authorities declare it, arbitrarily, to be opposed to the common good of the State (which, of course, cannot be conceded!).

12. Individuals and the family immediately rest on nature. Civil society is a natural institution, too, but it depends upon the need of the family, immediately. It is derived from the natural law only through the family, inasmuch as the family is insufficient to provide all the necessities for a good life.

13. The family is prior to the State in nature and in establishment. It possesses rights prior to the formation of any State. Such rights are outside the power of human law to abolish.

14. Civil authority, since it was instituted to provide means for the life of virtue, has the right and the duty to regulate the exercise of natural rights so as to bring them into conformity with the common striving of all the individuals and families that compose the State.

15. This limitation of the exercise of natural rights does not, and must not, amount to abolition.

16. Certain natural rights of individuals and the family are:
    1. the right to existence and the means thereto—livelihood, life, property
    2. the right to offspring and their rearing—marriage rights and education
    3. the right to pursue their goal as marked out by God—freedom of worship, liberty to exercise their rights, and so forth

17. The family has the right to receive help from the State when it is impoverished and unable to meet its ordinary needs.

18. The State may intervene to see that all members of the household give to others within the household that which is their due. The State's entrance into familial matters is strictly restricted to doing only what must be done

to ensure justice. Beyond that it cannot go. The family is equally a natural institution with rights and authority of its own.

19. The State should promote the common good, protect the basic natural rights of its citizens (individuals and families), and supplement the imperfect society of the family by helping it to meet its needs and to live "the better life."

For Study and Discussion

1. In what way can it be said that neither the individual alone nor the family alone, but that both constitute the foundation of civil society?

2. Discuss: "As one man is a part of the household, so a household is a part of the State: and the State is a perfect community." Why is that last comment made: namely, "the State is a perfect community"?

3. Are individuals who do not live in domestic society released from any obligation to serve the common good? In what way do members within the domestic circle serve the common good?

4. In what way is a household the mean between the individual and the State? Which in the order of nature is a newborn child's first claim: "son" or "citizen"? Explain.

5. What, in the words of Pope Pius XI, is the twofold function of civil authority residing in the State? What two actions are forbidden to the State, as mentioned by the same Holy Father in the same place?

6. On what basis can giving money to keep a home intact be considered a greater act of charity than almsgiving to save an individual life? Discuss this point.

7. Explain: "Man is not ordained to the body politic according to all that he is and has." Discuss this point.

8. Discuss St. Thomas's explanation of the hierarchy of nature and natural aims. To what does the universe as a whole naturally tend?

9. Explain: "The entire universe, with all its parts, is ordained towards God as its end." Discuss the various natures and show how each tends toward God.

10. How does man tend toward God? Is this *natural* to man? Is man superior to other visible creatures in his knowledge of God? Explain. Why does St. Thomas say, "reasonable creatures have, in some special and higher manner, God as their end"?

11. Name two principles discussed in this chapter that govern the relations of the individual and the family toward the State. How do you account for man's subordination and subjection? How do you account for his transcendence?

12. Discuss the priority of the family and the individual over the State. What consequences follow from that priority?

13. Explain: "The rights and duties of the Family rest more immediately on nature."

14. What arguments can you advance for the non-abolition of the natural rights of the family and the individual?

15. Why would justice be violated if the natural rights of the family and the individual were abolished by the State?

16. In what ways should the family be considered an independent society inasmuch as it is not a self-sufficient society?

17. Indicate the fallacy underlying this statement: an imperfect society such as the family is, ought to be *totally dependent* upon the State which is a perfect society.

18. What is Pope Pius's enumeration of the chief natural rights of man? How does the Declaration of Independence list them?

19. What is wrong with this statement: "Man's basic natural rights are absolutely independent of any civil authority"? Explain. What is the correct statement?

20. Explain how and why the common good is the standard of judging the extent of the exercise of natural rights. What virtue is involved? Upon what virtues is social life based? Explain.

21. Discuss the family-State relations with respect to marriage and domestic society. Include parental authority and means of livelihood.

22. Discuss the limits which restrict the State's entrance into the family circle. Explain "nature bids them stop there."

23. What, in general terms, is the work of the State with respect to the family and the individuals?

For the Advanced Reader

St. Thomas:

Summa Theologica, vol. 8, Tract on Law

vol. 10, On Justice and Its Parts

vol. 12, On Various Virtues: piety, obedience, etc.

Farrell, Walter:

A Companion to the Summa, III, subjection; right; rights of man; obedience; justice, etc.

Ostheimer, Anthony:

The Family, vol. 50, Philosophical Studies, C.U.A. chaps. 5–7

Papal Encyclicals:

Pope Leo XIII: *Chief Duties of Christians as Citizens*
Christian Constitution of States
Civil Government
The Condition of Labor
Human Liberty
Socialism and Communism

Pope Pius XI: *Atheistic Communism*
Christian Education of Youth
The Reconstruction of the Social Order

Pope Pius XII: *Unity in Opposing World Evils*

Any good book on Christian social ethics

16

The Christian State

We have discussed the nature of the family and its relations to the State. There still remain for discussion in connection with the family, the very basic rights of education and private property. However, since these touch so intimately upon the rights of the State, it is deemed preferable to delay a discussion of them until we have considered in greater detail than we have heretofore, the nature and function of the State.

The State Natural

We have gained no slight knowledge of the State thus far in our considerations on society in general and on the particular primary societies which are necessary for man. Now the State is *natural* inasmuch as man's social nature requires help beyond that which the family can provide for it. This insufficiency of the family can be met only outside the family. It is met in the association of families known as the State. Were the family a perfect society instead of an imperfect one, then the State would not necessarily be called into existence. Authority there would have to be, but it is not quite accurate to associate authority with the State as if they were strictly synonymous. That they are generally so associated is true. Authority is the ruling portion of the social multitude; the State, however, strictly speaking, is the multitude — ruling and ruled — which associates because it finds in association a more perfect way of living the better human life.

The factors which make the State necessary, therefore, are these: (1) man's individual insufficiency, plus the insufficiency of the family to provide all the means necessary to man's final end; (2) man's natural inclination to social living whereby his needs can be adequately met. Of this Pope Leo says: "Man's natural instinct moves him to live in civil society, for he cannot, if dwelling apart, provide himself with the necessary requirements of life, nor procure the means of developing his mental and moral faculties. Hence it is ordained by God that man should lead his life, be it family, social, or civil, with his fellowmen amongst whom his several wants can be adequately supplied."

By way of passing, it is interesting to note St. Thomas's attitude toward solitary living. He says: "A man may lead a solitary life for two motives. One is because he is unable, as it were, to bear with human fellowship on account of his uncouthness of mind; and this is beast-like. The other is with a view to adhering wholly to divine things; and this is superhuman. Hence Aristotle says that he who associates not with others is either a beast or a god, i.e., a godly man."

We have seen in an earlier chapter that the State is a perfect society. The reasons were there given. In brief, they are: (1) The State has a specific end and purpose; (2) it is possessed of the means of attaining that end. It is in this latter sufficiency that the perfection of the State consists. We have seen its relation to the individual and the family, and the role, in general, which it plays in their strictly human development. Our chief concern in this chapter, therefore, is a discussion of the rule of the State over its subjects. It will have to do more specifically with the functions of the State, that is, of the rulers of the State, rather than with the essential nature of the State.

Now in speaking of the State, Pope Leo said: "By the State we here understand not the particular form of government which prevails in this or that nation, but the State as rightly understood; that is to say, any government conformable in its institutions to right reason and the Natural Law, and to those dictates of the Divine Wisdom which we have propounded in the Encyclical on the *Christian Constitution of States*."

Our chapter, now, becomes still more limited. It will be restricted to a discussion of a *Christian* State; that is, to a State founded upon Christian principles of man and of society. It precludes, therefore, a discussion of any theory of civil government which rejects the authority of God and attempts to distort the nature of man so as to limit him to finite, material, earthly existence only.

What Form Is Best?

Our century marks a terrific struggle between conflicting theories of political government. Will democracy survive? Will totalitarianism gain the ascendency over twentieth-century humanity? Those are questions which only time can settle. However, there are principles which can be laid down concerning the best form of government. A government cannot be "the best form" unless it adequately considers the needs of those over whom authority is exercised, and acts in accord with them. Now needs cannot be determined unless one has a clear understanding of the *nature* of the one in whom the needs are found. Animals need food; man needs food, but the two needs are not of equal importance. A man has a greater title to food than a beast. Man's life is more precious. He is a more noble creature. His need for food is more urgent than a beast's. In fact, man has a *right* to food, but a beast has not — not even a right to life has a beast. If otherwise, why is it proper and according to God's design that man may kill beasts for his food whereby he preserves his life?

Hence needs must be considered in relation to the nature of the one who needs, and so, unless the nature of man is understood, unless his origin and destiny are taken into consideration, it is futile to speak of meeting his needs, for they would not be known. And unless a government does meet man's needs, it cannot be "the best form" of government.

Democracy

The democratic form of government can be traced very far back into history. It has not, however, been the *only* form of government. St. Thomas mentions several forms which can lead men to their final happiness. The American ideal is the democratic form of government — popular government. We have pointed out that the Church is not committed to any one form of government rather than to another. We shall enumerate in this chapter the principles which underlie "the best form" and which can be applied to any age and condition of men.

In the United States the Constitution provides for a representative form of government. Perhaps Abraham Lincoln best expressed it as government "of the people, for the people, and by the people." This is the essence of popular government. It is the American ideal. It is held by us to give the fullest possible freedom to individuals to pursue happiness in conformity with mutual rights and duties. For Americans brought up in the tradition of democratic government, with the Declaration of Independence and the Constitution of the United States among their most widely quoted literature, the democratic ideal of government is the only ideal form. The reader will derive enlightenment and profit from reading Mortimer Adler's article, "In Terms of What Moral Principles Is Democracy the Best Form of Government?"

The word *democracy* in its root meaning implies popular government and connotes the preservation and inviolability of personal liberty and natural rights. However, in some quarters the term has received much abuse. Under the shadow of its name are found groups radically opposed to one another and to the principles of true democracy. It has even been known that anti-American groups have made use of the term to deceive the unwary and to carry on subversive activities destined to undermine that true concept of democracy for which the Declaration of Independence and the United States Constitution stand — the genuine "government of the people, for the people, and by the people" which is the ideal and the basis of American culture.

It ought to be remembered that, because certain democratic states have fallen before totalitarian powers, the latter need not, of necessity, be the sole remaining type of government possible to the world at large, should all or most democracies fail. For the basic principles of genuine democracy — recognition and acknowledgment of God and of man's relation to God — will always survive among right-thinking men. Perverted forms of democracy may fall through godlessness; true democracies may temporarily cease to function through the action of hostile systems, but ultimately democratic principles will reassert themselves on earth in keeping with man's innate desire for personal happiness. The reader will spend his time profitably if he studies Adler's arguments in favor of a democratic form of government as the best form. The reader will likewise profit from a study of Fr. Farrell's analysis of the threats to representative government in the article, "The Fate of Representative Governments."

Let us give our attention now to Pope Leo's discussion of the basic principles which underlie "the best form" of government.

Fundamental Principles

The "best form" of government must be judged from its principles. It is from these that a government's activities arise. If the principles of government are based (1) on the nature of man with a recognition of his having a destiny beyond that of material well-being in time; (2) on the necessary means to procuring the welfare of the social whole and all its parts (individuals and families); and (3) if it involves no injustice, whether of the individual subjects or of the Church, then such government may be considered "the best form."

Pope Leo discussed this in his encyclicals whenever the occasion offered. In the encyclical *Civil Government* he says:

> With regard to forms of government, there is no reason why the Church should not approve of the ruling power being held either by one man or by more than one, with this condition, however, that the administration be just and that it tend to the common good. Hence, so long as justice is respected, the people are not prevented from choosing for themselves

that form of government which best suits their own needs or the institutions and customs of their nation and tradition.

Again in the encyclical, *The Christian Constitution of States*, he writes:

No one of several forms of government is in itself condemned, inasmuch as none of them contains anything contrary to Catholic doctrine, and all of them are capable, if wisely and justly managed, of insuring the welfare of the State. Neither is it blameworthy in itself, in any manner, for the people to have a share, greater or less, in the government; for at certain times, and under certain laws, such participation may not only be of benefit to the citizens, but may even be of obligation.

In still another encyclical, *Human Liberty*, he states:

It is not of itself wrong to prefer a democratic form of government if only the Catholic doctrine be maintained as to the origin and exercise of power. Of the various forms of government, the Church does not reject any that are fitted to procure the welfare of the subjects; she wishes only this — which nature itself requires — that they should be constituted without involving wrong to any one, and especially without violating the rights of the Church.

Thus we may sum up three fundamental characteristics which must mark good government: it must (1) be in conformity with the eternal and natural laws; (2) insure the common good; (3) involve no injustice. It is evident therefore, that that form of government is best at any given period of human history which meets adequately the needs of human nature and entails no injustice to any legitimate institution, such as the family and the Church, or to individuals.

Whence Is Power?

Obviously all power originates in the Supreme Ruler of the universe. But what are the channels through which this power flows to human authority?

We said that good government must be in conformity with the eternal and natural laws. Without this bedrock of law, no human law can have more force than physical coercion. Moral persuasion is rooted in spirituality, not in physical mightiness. Hence only when authority is recognized as originating in God, can it have an adequate basis for obligation. One man's wish is as good as another's, so far as man to man is concerned. But when one man (or a group of men) exercises the ruling power and has authority conferred on him by God, then obedience can be exacted. In that case obedience is rendered, not as to man, but as to God.

A question which might now profitably claim our attention is how God's authority is conferred on man in a civil society where the people participate in the governing powers. Let us remember that the multitude (the community ruled) designates the ruler, as we in the United States do by election. Not only is the ruler designated, but the manner of exercising the rulership is determined by the people, as the Constitution of the United States illustrates.

One possible channel by which authority is conferred might be said to flow directly from God to the ruler whom the people designate. The people indicate (by election or otherwise) him whom they desire as their ruler. They consent to his rule. God then confers authority directly upon him. This is one possible channel. There is, however, a second possible flow of God's authority from Himself to the human ruler. We might consider this as a flow of authority from God to the people and thence, through their action, to the ruler whom they designate. In either case, the actual *conferring of authority* is the action of God. Only God can share His right to rule. In the people resides the power to designate their ruler and the mode of his ruling. Government that is legitimately established must derive its power from the consent of the governed. This does away with the usurpation of public power by one individual (or group) who might claim for himself a divine right to rule. Remember neither God nor nature directly designates the ruler. A ruler depends *for his authority to exercise governmental power* on God whose rulership he shares; and for his being chosen to rule, on the people who have designated him and have consented to his governing.

Pope Leo XIII, in speaking of authority in the encyclical *Civil Government*, says:

> Man, when excited by pride, has often striven to cast aside the reins of authority, yet never has he been able to arrive at the state of obeying no one. In every association and community of men, necessity itself compels that some should hold preeminence, lest society, being deprived of a prince or head by which it is ruled, should lose its unity and be prevented from attaining the end for which it was created and instituted.... Not a few men of more recent times ... hold that all power comes from the people; so that those who exercise it in the State do so, not as their own, but as delegated to them by the people, hence they

hold that, by this fact, it can be revoked by the will of the very people by whom it was delegated. But from these principles Catholics dissent, for they affirm that the right to rule is from God as from a natural and necessary principle.

"It is of importance, however," continues Pope Leo,

to remark in this place, that those who rule in the State, may in certain cases, be chosen by the will and decision of the multitude without opposition to the Catholic doctrine. By this choice of the people, *the ruler is designated, but the rights of ruling are not thereby conferred.* Nor is the authority conferred on the delegate [by the people], but rather the person by whom it is to be exercised is determined upon [by the people].

We might indicate the difference between the Catholic view and the opposing view by indicating the words *delegate* and *designate*. Authority is *delegated* by God to man. The people *designate* the man to rule. This is the Catholic doctrine. Note: the people *designate* the ruler; God *delegates* His authority. The other view holds that the *people delegate* the authority. This attributes to the people a power that is beyond their ability to exercise.

Pope Leo repeatedly makes the assertion that all authority is from God, and he states that political power will have the force, dignity, and firmness required by the safety of the commonwealth and the common good of the citizens, only when it is understood to have emanated from God as from its most sacred source.

Duties of the State

We have discussed the duties of the State in general, showing it to be the promotion of the common good and the individual good. Concretely, how is this accomplished? The duties of the State can be viewed under several aspects.

First, its duties toward God. The State is a moral person and as such is obligated to a recognition of God, to obedience to His laws, to the rendering of gratitude, worship, and honor to Him. Furthermore, as an institution ordained by God for the good of His rational creatures, the State owes to God the recognition of His rulership over the world and the State's participation in His supreme rule. Again, the State must not only acknowledge God and His right to its service and worship, but the State must care for religion. It must favor it, protect it, foster it, shield it, and do nothing to undermine the Church, religion, or morality among its subjects. It must recognize that religion is the link which binds man and society to God, and that without religion, neither man nor society can do the will of God.

Second, its duties toward the Church. The State must recognize that the Church is a society of divine origin and supernatural necessity; that she has for her aim a purpose impossible for any other institution to achieve; that she is a perfect society, capable of fulfilling her mission. It must acknowledge that the authority of the Church is the most exalted of all authority, and that because of the nobility of her end, she is in no way inferior to the civil power nor dependent upon it.

Third, its duties toward the common good. In this regard civil authority is obligated to pursue the welfare of the social whole and the welfare of the individuals who comprise it and who make their contribution to the commonwealth. The laws that it frames must conduce to the good of the community, and not to the personal gain of the ruler or of a few members of the society. Concerning this Pope Leo writes:

> Rulers should anxiously safeguard the community and all its individual members — the community, because the preservation of the community is so emphatically the business of the Supreme Power that the safety of the commonwealth is not only the first law, but is a government's whole reason of existence. The ruler should safeguard the individuals because ... the object of the administration of the State should be not the advantage of the ruler but the benefit of those over whom he rules.

The goal of the common good, toward which the State is obliged to tend, demands that the State do nothing to harm the virtue of its people. It must lead all to "a better human life," and this life, as St. Thomas says, is the life of virtue, the life of peace. Therefore, it would be contrary to the purpose of the State if it were to do anything that would discourage virtuous living or make the people less good.

Fourth, its duties toward its subjects, that is, the family. These we have already discussed in our chapter on the family. We shall sum them up here in the words of Pope Pius XI in his encyclical on *Christian Marriage*. He says:

> Every effort must be made that ... in the State such economic and social methods should be adopted as will enable every head of a family to earn as much as, according to his station in life, is necessary for himself, his wife, and for the rearing of his children.... Provision must be made, also, in the case of those who are not self-supporting, for joint aid by

private or public guilds.... When such means do not fulfill the needs, particularly of a larger or poorer family, Christian charity absolutely demands that those things which are lacking to the needy should be provided.... If, for this purpose, private resources do not suffice, it is the duty of the public authority to supply for the insufficient forces of individual effort, particularly in a matter which is of such importance to the commonweal, touching, as it does, the maintenance of the Family and married people.

If families, particularly those in which there are many children, have not suitable dwellings; if the husband cannot find employment and means of livelihood; if the necessities of life cannot be purchased except at exorbitant prices; if even the mother of the family, to the great harm of the home, is compelled to go forth and seek a living by her own labor; if she, in the labors of childbirth, is deprived of proper food, medicine and the assistance of a skilled physician, it is patent to all to what an extent married people may lose heart, and how home life and the observance of God's commands are rendered difficult for them; indeed, it is obvious how great a peril can arise to the public security and to the welfare and very life of civil society itself when such men are reduced to that condition of desperation that, having nothing which they fear to lose, they are emboldened to hope for chance advantage from the upheaval of the State and of established order.

Wherefore those who have the care of the State and of the public good cannot neglect the needs of married people and their families, without bringing great harm upon the State and on the common welfare. Hence, in making the laws and in disposing of public funds, they must do their utmost to relieve the needs of the poor, considering such a task as one of the most important of their administrative duties.

Thus Pope Pius explains with great clarity the duty of the State with regard to the family. The excerpt is worthy of close reading.

Fifth, its duties toward particular groups among its subjects. Included in this group are property owners, wage earners, the poor, the weak, working men's associations, and private enterprises.

(a) Since care of offspring is a dictate of natural reason, it belongs to the head of the family to effect this. For this reason, private ownership is a right, not only of individuals, but all the more is it a right of fathers who must provide the necessities of life for their families. Since the proper care of offspring is primarily the work of the family, and since the welfare of the family is the concern of the State, it is to the advantage of the State to promote private ownership which tends to establish the family in a certain measure of economic security. Through private property the family justly strives to better its condition; the father, should he die, finds in property a means of continuing his care of the family, for he can transmit it to his children by inheritance. The State must safeguard private property by legal enactment, for, in the words of Pope Leo: "neither justice nor the common good allows anyone to seize that which belongs to another, or, under the pretext of futile and ridiculous equality, to lay hands on other people's fortunes." The State must see in the working man's little estate the fruit of his toil; it is his wages in another form, and just as it is unjust to seize his wage or to tax him exorbitantly, so is it unjust for the State to seize or to permit others to seize, unjustly, the private possessions of anyone.

"The right to possess private property is from nature, not from man; and the State has only the right to regulate its use in the interests of the public good, but by no means to abolish it altogether. The State is, therefore, unjust and cruel, if, in the name of taxation, it deprives the private owner of more than is just." This is found in the encyclical on *The Condition of Labor*.

(b) Wage earners, who contribute to the wealth of the State by their labors, are entitled to the protection of the State and the promotion of their well-being. The richer population have many ways of protecting themselves. They are less in need of the help of the State. Wage earners frequently have no resources of their own to fall back upon, and this fact, together with their contribution to the wealth of the State, entitle them to be specially cared for and protected by the State.

Whatever shall be conducive to the well-being of the laborers, whatever shall make their life more tolerable, whatever may be done to house them properly, to provide them with sufficient and decent clothing, to give them the necessities of life and some recreation — these ought to be the object of the State's attention. Distributive justice demands that the members of the social order receive their just dues at the hands of those who rule. The wage earner is entitled to this justice inasmuch as he contributes so largely to the advantage of the community. It is not only a matter of justice for the State thus to act toward this portion of the population, but it is a matter of securing its own advantages, for, as the families are, so is the State. A more prosperous State, therefore, is found where the wage earners, on whom the State so largely depends, are given sufficient means to raise them above the miseries of extreme poverty.

It is part of the duty of the State to provide laws which protect the rights of the working man. Hours and conditions of labor, minimum wage, compensation laws, and the like should be enacted. They should assist in overcoming, in whatever way is in accord with the rights of all concerned and with the common good, the causes which lead to conflict between employers and employees. In thus protecting the laborers' rights, the State lessens the possibility of strikes which bring havoc on the working man, the family, trade, the prosperity of the State, property, public peace, and security. Of this Pope Leo writes in the encyclical on *The Condition of Labor*:

> When working-people have recourse to a strike, it is frequently because the hours of labor are too long, or the work too hard, or because they consider their wages insufficient. The grave inconvenience of this not uncommon occurrence should be obviated by public remedial measures; for such paralysis of labor not only affects the masters and their working-people, but is extremely injurious to trade, and to the general interests of the public. Moreover, on such occasions, violence and disorder are generally not far off, and thus it frequently happens that the public peace is threatened. The laws should be beforehand, and prevent these troubles from arising; they should lend their influence and authority to the removal in good time of the causes which lead to conflicts between masters and those whom they employ.

(c) The poor constitute another group of citizens. These have a special claim to attention. It is a mark of good human law that the burdens be laid equally on all. This equality is not the equality of one-for-one, but equality based on ability. It is a proportional equality. Take, for instance, the matter of taxation. A one-for-one equality would not be just. The poor are not able to pay equally with the rich. The State must so distribute the burden that the richer citizens will bear a more proportional share in view of their better condition.

As for supplying help to the family when it is poor, we have indicated the extent of that aid when we quoted Pope Pius a few pages previous to this one. Again in his encyclical on *Atheistic Communism* he says:

> It must be the special care of the State to create those material conditions of life without which an orderly society cannot exist. The State must take every measure necessary to supply employment, particularly for the heads of families and for the young. To achieve this end demanded by the pressing needs of the common welfare, the wealthy classes must

be induced to assume those burdens without which human society cannot be saved nor they themselves remain secure. However, measures taken by the State with this end in view ought to be of such a nature that they will really affect those who actually possess more than their share of capital resources, and who continue to accumulate them to the grievous detriment of others.

It belongs to the duty of the ruler to benefit every order of the State. Amongst these, the poorer classes should receive special consideration, as we said before, and this without arousing envy or exposing itself to the charges of either favoritism or undue interference. For the more that is done to alleviate the sufferings of the poor and the working people by the laws of the land, the less need will there be to establish particular means, such as organized relief, to meet their necessities.

(d) The weaker members of the social order are entitled to consideration. Chief among these, are the incurably sick, the insane, the sick-poor, and the dependent aged. Others are women and children, particularly those whose lot is cast in the labor markets.

For the first group, the State provides maintenance in its institutions which are operated from public funds. For the second group, labor laws are enacted forbidding certain types, hours, and conditions of employment for women and children. "It is wrong to abuse the tender years of children or the weakness of women," writes Pope Pius; and Pope Leo remarks: "Work which is suitable for a strong man cannot reasonably be required from a woman or a child."

It falls to the duty of the State to save laborers from the cruelty of speculators in labor, who use human beings as mere instruments for making money. This shall be discussed in detail later. Our chief concern at this point is to lay down the principles whereby the State is obliged, by virtue of its mission, to protect the weak. Women and children, especially when they are in the grasp of labor speculators, require help from the State for the protection of their rights. Of woman and child labor, Pope Leo, in the encyclical on *The Condition of Labor*, writes:

> In regard to children, great care should be taken not to place them in workshops and factories until their bodies and minds are sufficiently mature. For just as rough weather destroys the buds of spring, so too-early an experience of life's hard work blights the young promise of a child's powers and makes any real education impossible.
>
> Women, again, are not suited to certain trades; for a woman is by nature fitted for home work, and it is that which is best adapted at once

to preserve her modesty and to promote the good bringing up of children and the well-being of the Family.

In all matters the help of the State is not only desirable but needful, for it is the duty of the State to promote the common good. The limits of the State's actions, however, are determined by the nature of the occasion which calls for the interference of the law. The general principle is that by which its entrance into the family circle is limited: nature bids them stop when they have justly safeguarded rights and achieved harmony. "The law must not undertake more," says Pope Leo, "than is required for the remedy of the evil or the removal of the danger."

(e) In addition to property owners, wage earners, the poor, and the weak, other particular groups within the circle of civil society are entitled to recognition, respect, and freedom of operation within their sphere. These are private associations, the chief of which is the working men's organizations. Because private societies are formed in response to man's social instincts, they are natural societies, but not in the complete sense of the word *natural* as we have used it throughout this book. They are natural because they respond to nature's inclinations, but they are not natural in the sense that they are necessary to human nature. Civil society is rooted more deeply in nature than working men's associations are, and whereas civil society has for its aim the common good, working men's associations and other lesser societies have a private aim, namely, the private good of the associates. But as societies they must be recognized by the State.

Working men's organizations, provided they do not endanger the common good or the private morality of the associates, have the right to adopt rules and organizations which are best for the attainment of their aims: the betterment of the working classes. The State must realize that such organizations contribute mightily to the common advantage of civil society, on condition, of course, that they conform to the standards of the common good. For this reason the State must not unduly interfere with their activities nor attempt to absorb them. It should leave to the working men's organizations the settlement of business entailed in the nature of their purpose. The role of the State should be one of directing, watching, encouraging, and restraining as circumstances suggest or necessity demands. It has the right to intervene in these smaller societies, just as it may properly intervene in the larger and necessary societies, when justice or the common good requires such action.

Such, then, are the duties of the State. Later we shall have to touch upon some of them again when we discuss the relations which would exist between the Church and the State and when we discuss man in economic society. For the present, let this suffice.

We might sum up this chapter on the State and its work by quoting again the words of Pope Leo in his encyclical on *The Condition of Labor*:

> Whenever the general interest or any particular class suffers, or is threatened with evils which can in no other way be met, the public authority must step in to meet them. Now among the interests of the public, as of private individuals, are these:
>
> That peace and good order should be maintained; that family life should be carried on in accordance with God's laws and those of nature; that religion should be reverenced and obeyed; that a high standard of morality should prevail in public and private life; that the sanctity of justice should be respected, and that no one should injure another with impunity; that the members of the commonwealth should grow up to man's estate strong and robust, and capable, if need be, of guarding and defending their country.
>
> If by a strike, or other combination of workmen, there should be imminent danger of disturbance to the public peace; or if circumstances were such that among the laboring population the ties of family life were relaxed; if religion were found to suffer through the workmen not having time and opportunity to practice it; if in workshops and factories there were dangers to morals through the mixing of the sexes or from any occasion of evil; or if employers laid burdens upon the workmen which were unjust, or degraded them with conditions that were repugnant to their dignity as human beings; finally, if health were endangered by excessive labor, or by work unsuited to sex or age — in these cases there can be no question that, within certain limits, it would be right to call in the help and authority of the law. The limits must be determined by the nature of the occasion which calls for the law's interference — the principle being this, that the law must not undertake more, nor go farther, than is required for the remedy of the evil or the removal of the danger.

Such is the Christian State. The benefits to be derived from it are manifold. Human and divine things are given their proper places; rights and duties are upheld and respected; individuals, families, and the commonwealth itself prosper; and civil rulers bear in mind that God is the paramount Ruler of the world, and they pattern their rule after His, ruling with even-handed justice, tempered with a father's kindness. Thus civil society, along with all other creatures of God, tend earnestly toward Him who is their last end — God, the True and Supreme Ruler of the universe.

Some Original Sources

Use these in your readings, explanations, and discussions.

1. "Nature, or rather God, Who is the Author of nature, wills that man should live in a civil society; and this is clearly shown both by the faculty of language, the greatest medium of intercourse, and by numerous innate desires of the mind, and the many necessary and important things, which men isolated cannot procure, but which they can procure when associated with others in a society.

"But now, a society can not exist or can it be conceived in which there is no one to govern the wills of individuals, so as to make, as it were, one will out of many, and to impel them rightly and orderly to the common good. Hence,

"God has willed that in civil society there should be some to rule the multitude. And this also is a powerful argument, that those by whose authority the State is administered must be able so to compel the citizens to obedience that it is clearly a sin in the latter not to obey.

"But no man has in himself or of himself the power of constraining the free will of others by bonds of authority of this kind. For this power resides solely in God, the Creator and Legislator of all things; hence it is necessary that those who exercise it should do so as having received it from God....

"Those who believe civil society has arisen from the free consent of men, and who seek the origin of its authority from the same source, say that each individual has given up something of his right, and that voluntarily every person has put himself into the power of the one man in whom the whole of those rights has been centered.

"But it is a great error not to see that men ... have been created without their own free will for a natural community of life. It is plain, moreover, that the agreement which they allege is openly a falsehood and a fiction, and that it has no authority to confer on political power such great force, dignity, and firmness as the safety of the State and the common good of the citizens require.

"Then only will the government have all those ornaments and guarantees when it is understood to emanate from God as its august and most sacred source." (Pope Leo XIII, *Civil Government*)

2. "The State, constituted as it is, is clearly bound to act up to the manifold and weighty duties linking it to God by the public profession of religion. Nature and

reason which command every individual devoutly to worship God in holiness, because we belong to Him and must return to Him since from Him we came, bind also the civil community by a like law.

"For men living together in society are under the power of God no less than individuals are, and society, not less than individuals, owes gratitude to God Who gave it being and maintains it, and Whose everbounteous goodness enriches it with countless blessings.

"Since, then, no one is allowed to be remiss in the service due to God, and since the chief duty of all men is to cling to religion in both its teaching and practice ... it is a public crime to act as though there were no God.

"So too is it a sin in the State not to have care for religion, as a something beyond its scope, or as of no practical benefit; or out of many forms of religion to adopt that one which chimes in with the fancy, for we are bound absolutely to worship God in that way which He has shown to be His will." (Pope Leo XIII, *Christian Constitution of States*)

3. "In the Christian organization of the State there is nothing that can be thought to infringe upon the dignity of rulers, and nothing unbecoming them.... Without doubt in the constitution of the State such as we have described, divine and human things are equitably shared; the rights of citizens assured to them and fenced round by Divine, by Natural, and by Human Law; the duties incumbent on each one being wisely marked out, and their fulfillment fittingly ensured.

"Furthermore, domestic society acquires that firmness and solidity so needful to it, from the holiness of marriage, one and indissoluble, wherein the rights and duties of husband and wife are controlled with wise justice and equity; due honor is assured to the woman; the authority of the husband is conformed to the pattern afforded by the authority of God; the power of the father is tempered by a due regard for the dignity of the mother and her offspring; and the best possible provision is made for the guardianship, welfare, and education of the children.

"In political affairs and in all matters civil, the laws aim at securing the common good, and are not framed according to the delusive caprices and opinions of the mass of the people, but by truth and by justice; the ruling powers are invested with a sacredness more than human, and are withheld from deviating from the path of duty and from overstepping the bounds of rightful authority; and the obedience of the citizens is rendered with a feeling of honor and dignity, since obedience is not the servitude of man to man, but submission to the Will of God, exercising His sovereignty through the medium of men.

"Now this being recognized as undeniable, it is felt that the high office of rulers should be held in respect; that public authority should be constantly and faithfully obeyed; that no act of sedition should be committed; and that the civic order of the commonwealth should be maintained as sacred.

"So, also, as to the duties of each one towards his fellowmen, mutual forbearance, kindliness, generosity, are placed in the ascendant; the man who is at once a citizen and a Christian is not drawn aside by conflicting obligations; and lastly, the abundant benefits with which the Christian religion, of its very nature, endows even the mortal life of man, are acquired for the community and civil society.

"And this to such an extent that it may be said in sober truth: 'The condition of the commonwealth depends on religion with which God is worshipped: and between one and the other there exists an intimate and abiding connection.'" (Pope Leo, *Christian Constitution of States*)

Summary

1. The State is a perfect, natural, necessary society. It meets the insufficiency of the family group by supplying opportunities for procuring the necessities of a good human life.
2. By the State we understand any form of government which is conformable in its institutions to right reason and the natural law, and ultimately to the eternal law of God, so that in all its acts it will conform to the order and harmony existing in God's creative plan.
3. The fundamental principles upon which the "best form" of government rests are these: (a) the recognition of human personality and dignity as possessing a divine origin and destiny, and fortified by sacred rights and obligations in the pursuit of its goal; (b) the necessary means and the good will to strive earnestly for the common good of its citizens, both individuals and families; (c) true justice in all its enactments toward all.
4. The Church is in no way opposed to a democratic form of government any more than it is opposed to any form of government which is based upon justice, solicitude for the commonweal, and the Christian view of human nature.
5. All power has its origin in God. Rulers receive from God their authority to govern. The people ruled may designate the one who is to be their ruler and the mode of his ruling, but they cannot give, of themselves, what they have not; namely, God's authority.
6. Whether God confers His authority directly upon the ruler whom the people have designated or to whose rule they consent, or whether the delegated authority passes through the people to the ruler, is open to question. Both views may be legitimately held, provided only that it be borne in mind that it is God who *confers the authority*, for He alone and in His own right, is the fullness of authority and the sole source of it among civil rulers.
7. In general the duties of the State concern themselves with the advancement of the common good of civil society and all its parts. In particular,

rulers have duties toward (a) God; (b) the Church; (c) the commonweal; (d) its subjects: individuals and families; (e) particular groups among the subjects.

8. Among the individuals and particular groups in civil society, the State has duties toward: (a) property owners; (b) wage earners; (c) the poor; (d) weak members; (e) lesser private societies; for example, working men's organizations.

9. The foremost character of the Christian State is that it should reflect God's own power and care over the human race. Rulers must keep God as their model and exemplar.

10. Rulers must not legislate or administer the goods of the State for personal profit but for the common welfare. To provide for the poor and the needy is not to administer public goods unjustly, for this portion of the population is deserving of special consideration that the common good may not suffer from the misery of its members.

11. A government must acknowledge its dependence upon God. It must make open profession of faith in God. It must promote and encourage religion. It must not do anything that will harm the virtuous behavior of its people. It must foster whatever will develop the virtues which are necessary for successful human living — the life of virtue, the life of peace.

12. The virtues which the State should strive to promote are justice, truthfulness, obedience, reverence for authority, generosity, charity, and fidelity.

13. The State may supplement, from the common good of the civil society, the efforts of the family to live a decent human life, but the State may in no way absorb the individuals or the family.

14. The State is a creature of God. It is not an end in itself. It is ordained (a) to the common good directly, and (b) to the final good of the individuals and families and (c) it is ordained to God ultimately, as all else in creation, as to its last end.

For Study and Discussion

1. Explain the need for the State.
2. How is the State a *natural, necessary* society?
3. Upon what grounds may the State be called a *perfect* society? Explain its end and means.
4. By the term *State* are we to understand a particular form of government such as a democracy, a monarchy, or any other mode of government? Explain.
5. What is the distinction implied in the terms: a *State* and a *Christian State*? To a discussion of which of these terms is this chapter devoted?

6. Explain what qualifications a State should have to be called "the best form" of government.
7. Why must man's whole nature—physical, intellectual, moral, and spiritual—be taken into consideration in any discussion of a good government?
8. Explain and discuss the three fundamental principles underlying a good form of civil government.
9. Tell whether the Church approves of government by the people. Quote Pope Leo. Explain the meaning of the quotation given.
10. In the quotation taken from the encyclical on *Civil Government* find two conditions which Pope Leo mentions as being necessary for the proper basis of a government chosen by the people.
11. In the quotation taken from the encyclical on *The Christian Constitution of States*, which of the above conditions are repeated? Is any additional condition laid down?
12. In the quotation taken from the encyclical the *Nature of Human Liberty*, is there any further condition laid down? Enumerate directly from the three sources the principles which underlie a good form of government.
13. Explain: the source of all authority is God.
14. Does authority originate in the people? Discuss.
15. In what two ways is it possible that God confers His authority on human rulers? What part is played by the people who are ruled?
16. Explain the difference between "designating the ruler" and "conferring authority." Discuss this.
17. Why does Pope Leo say that Catholics dissent from the opinion of those who hold that "all power comes from the people"?
18. What difference, in principle, is there between those who say "all power is from the people" and Pope Leo's own words: "The ruler is designated [by the will and decision of the multitude] but the rights of ruling are not thereby conferred"? Explain the difference.
19. Discuss the duty of the State toward God and religion.
20. What, in general, should be the attitude of the State toward the Church?
21. What is the obligation of the State toward the common good?
22. Discuss singly the duties of the State toward its subjects: (a) the family; (b) property owners; (c) wage earners; (d) the poor; (e) the weak and unfortunate; (f) child and woman labor; (g) private societies such as working men's organizations.
23. Discuss paragraph by paragraph Pope Leo's words which sum up the chapter on the role of the State in human society.
24. What limits are set on the intervention of the State into affairs pertaining to the well-being of its subjects?

Christian Social Principles

For the Advanced Reader

St. Thomas:
On the Governance of Rulers, bk. 1

Sheen, Fulton J.:
Whence Come Wars, chap. 4

Papal Encyclicals:
Pope Leo XIII: *Chief Duties of Christians as Citizens*
Christian Constitution of States
Civil Government
The Condition of Labor
Human Liberty
Pope Pius XI: *Atheistic Communism*
Christian Marriage
The Reconstruction of the Social Order
Pope Pius XII: *Unity in Opposing World Evils*

Philosophy of the State, reprinted 1940 from the 1939 proceedings, American Catholic Philosophical Association:
"The Democratic State"
"In Terms of What Moral Principles Is Democracy the Best Government?"
"The Metaphysical Basis of Political Action"
Proceedings, American Catholic Philosophical Association, 1938: "The Derivation of Political Authority"

The Thomist: "The Fate of Representative Government," vol. 2, no. 2, April 1940

Any good book on Christian social ethics

17

The Church: Her Proper Sphere; Catholic Action

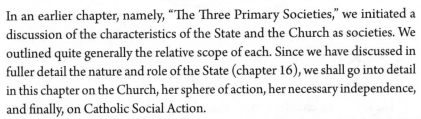

In an earlier chapter, namely, "The Three Primary Societies," we initiated a discussion of the characteristics of the State and the Church as societies. We outlined quite generally the relative scope of each. Since we have discussed in fuller detail the nature and role of the State (chapter 16), we shall go into detail in this chapter on the Church, her sphere of action, her necessary independence, and finally, on Catholic Social Action.

Recall the words of Pope Leo in his famous encyclical on *The Christian Constitution of States*: "The Almighty has appointed the charge of the human race between two powers, the ecclesiastical and the civil, the one being set over divine and the other over human things."

Here we find man having at his service two perfect societies, each of divine appointment. Each derives its authority, as well as its nature, ultimately from God. The Church was commanded by divine positive law: "The only-begotten Son of God established on earth a society which is called the Church, and to it He handed over the exalted and divine office which He had received from His Father, to be continued through the ages to come," writes Pope Leo in the same encyclical as mentioned above. So, too, has the State its origin in God, not indeed by divine positive law, but by natural law, which is, as we learned, derived from the eternal law. The State is divinely appointed because it is founded upon man's nature which was created and equipped by God. "Man's natural instinct [i.e., human reason] moves him to live in civil society, for he cannot, if dwelling apart, provide himself with the necessary requirements of life, nor procure means of developing his mental and moral faculties. Hence it is *divinely ordained* that he should lead his life ... with his fellowmen."

Now inasmuch as God is the God of truth and of peace and of harmony, it cannot be conceived of as possible that these two divinely ordained societies should be in contradiction. "The divine right which is of grace does not destroy the human right which is of reason," declares St. Thomas. And so we shall try to discover here the spheres of action within which each society properly functions according to God's creative plan. "God," remarks Pope Leo, "who foresees all things, and who is the Author of these two powers, has marked out the course of each in right correlation to the other."

A Perfect Society

In the first place, the Church is a perfect society. Her authority is from God as we said above; she possesses a particular purpose, namely, the salvation of souls and the securing of our happiness in Heaven; she has all the means necessary to attain that end, including authority which has the right to legislate, enforce, and judge. She has, in other words, legislative, executive, and judiciary powers. She is the divinely established society for effecting man's eternal salvation, and as such, she must necessarily be unhampered in her work in time or in place. She requires, through her very nature and purpose, independence of other societies.

The following characteristics, therefore, might be said to belong to the Church: (a) integrity, or wholeness as a distinct and perfect society in her own right; (b) priority in certain things over the civil society because of the excellence of her nature and purpose; (c) independence of the State because of her universal mission through divine commission; (d) authority to act without hindrance according as she thinks best, in those things which pertain to her end and means. Let us sum up these in the words of Pope Leo in *The Christian Constitution of States*:

"As Jesus Christ came into the world that men might have life and have it more abundantly, so also has the Church for its aim and end the eternal salvation of souls, and hence it is so constituted as to open wide its arms to all mankind, unhampered by any limit of either time or place" (her purpose — a supernatural end).

"Over this mighty multitude God has Himself set rulers with power to govern; and He has willed that one should be the head of all, and the chief and unerring teacher of truth, to whom He has given the keys of the kingdom of heaven" (divine authorization to supremacy in her own sphere under the pope).

"This society is made up of men, just as civil society is, and yet is supernatural and spiritual, on account of the end for which it was founded, and of the means by which it aims at attaining that end" (the supernatural character of her end and means).

"Hence it is distinguished and differs from civil society, and, what is of highest moment, it is a society chartered as of right divine, perfect in its nature and in its title, to possess in itself and by itself, through the will and loving kindness of its Founder, all needful provision for its maintenance and action" (distinct from civil society and self-sufficing in her own sphere).

"And just as the end at which the Church aims is by far the noblest of ends, so is its authority the most exalted of all authority, nor can it be looked upon as inferior to the civil power, or in any manner dependent upon it" (independent of civil power — has supreme authority).

"In very truth, Jesus Christ gave to His Apostles unrestrained authority in regard to things sacred, together with the genuine and most true power of *making laws*, as also with the twofold right of *judging* and *punishing* which flow from that power" (legislative, judiciary, and executive powers).

"Now this authority, perfect in itself, and plainly meant to be unfettered, ... the Church has never ceased to claim for herself and openly to exercise." (The claim to the free exercise of her authority is a matter of history.)

"Hence it is the Church, and not the State, that is to be man's guide to Heaven. It is to the Church that God has assigned the charge of seeing to, and legislating for, all that concerns religion; of teaching all nations; of spreading the Christian faith as widely as possible; in short, of administering freely and without hindrance, in accordance with her own judgment, all matters that fall within its competence" (supernatural end and means beyond the scope of temporal powers).

Church Independent

This last paragraph recalls to our minds that prior to the time of Christ, among practically all peoples of the world, the Jews alone excepted, worship was a function of State administration. Though it is not impossible for human reason, unaided by the certainty of divine revelation, to come to a recognition of a supernatural end for man and the need of a supernatural society to attain that end, such a conclusion seems not to have been reached. The State dominated the religious beliefs and practices of the people. Religion was made a political function and the rulers were its official interpreters. The political well-being of the society was superior to its spiritual well-being, and the ruler directed his subjects alike in temporal and in spiritual matters.

We said that human reason, unaided, might have attained to a knowledge of a distinct society required to direct man's spiritual activities, but history shows that only among the Jews was religion not subordinated to politics.

Even when the Jews were under Roman control, they observed the more important of their religious functions and considered them free from the Roman jurisdiction. You will recall that Pontius Pilate, when confronted by the Jews desirous of convicting Jesus, yielded to the cry: "We have a law and according to that law He ought to die because He blasphemed God" (see John 19:7). You will recall, too, that throughout the history of the Jewish people, God gave them distinct laws governing their sacrifices and religious rites, so that it was not strange, when the time came for God to establish a distinct society which should have as its primary purpose the eternal salvation of souls, that He should send His only-begotten Son to the Jewish race and found on certain of its members that perfect society of which we are speaking.

With the spread of Christianity the Church began her struggle with civil powers for the necessary independence which her nature, purpose, and means required. The Middle Ages witnessed a well-ordered Christian social order wherein Church and State functioned harmoniously in a deeply Christian social whole. Later, however, the Protestant Revolt brought in its retinue a spirit of individualism in religion, which, through generations of steadily growing force, developed into the economic and social Liberalism of later centuries and dealt the death blow to an integrated social order based on Christian justice, charity, and brotherly love. The totalitarian reaction to the individualistic philosophy is equally destructive of any effective Church-State integration, which integration is both desirable and necessary in the social order.

The Church and State

Now this doctrine of the independence and supremacy of the Church *in her own sphere* does not in any way detract from the supremacy of the State in *its* sphere. We recognize in the State a divinely ordained society; a perfect society; one that has its natural and immediate goal, and carries with it the authority from God to exercise legislative, judiciary, and executive powers to attain its end. We must emphasize this point, however: that one has for its *natural* and *immediate* goal the salvation of souls, and the other has the temporal welfare as its end. Both, however, exercise their jurisdiction over the same subjects — human beings, and because this is so, God has marked out the right domain of each, for, says Pope Leo:

> Were this not so, deplorable contentions and conflicts would often arise, and not infrequently men, like travelers at the meeting of two roads, would hesitate in anxiety and doubt, not knowing what course to follow.

Two powers would be commanding contrary things, and it would be a dereliction of duty to disobey either of the two. But it would be most repugnant to deem thus of the wisdom and goodness of God.

Despite the varieties of natures in the physical universe, there is order and harmony. Yet each nature is fulfilling its specific goal, and it might at first seem that conflicts would naturally arise therein. But this is not so. From the very fact that God created each of the various natures as distinct from every other nature, it was needful that He set before each an immediate goal that is distinct from the goal of every other nature. It is the perfect coordination of strivings among the various natures that accounts for the harmonious action of the physical universe. A flower could not do the work of a bird, nor could a bird perfect its nature by acting as a plant. If the natures and their operations were unstable, in what a universe man would find himself! As a matter of fact, each nature acts according to its specific laws of operation, and so harmony is in the whole.

Let us apply this to the activities of the Church and the State. Each has its own role, one that only it can perform, and each has the means of doing its work. The Church could not lead men to temporal well-being, because the Church works with spiritual powers, whereas temporal well-being is material. Neither could the State lead men to the life of divine grace, for grace is a supernatural gift of God directed to man through supernatural channels, and the State is not a supernatural society. Therefore, as do natures in the physical universe, the Church and the State should work together harmoniously, each giving to the common subject of their direction, the contribution which each is so aptly fitted to give. Thus, in the words of Pope Leo:

> Whatever in things human is of a sacred character, whatever belongs (1) either of its own nature (such as grace and the sacraments), or (2) by reason of the end to which it is referred (as moral implications in human affairs), to the salvation of souls or to the worship of God, is subject to the power and judgment of the Church. Whatever is to be ranged under the civil and political order (as the details of just government) is rightly subject to the civil authority. Jesus Christ has Himself given command that what is Caesar's is to be rendered to Caesar, and that what belongs to God is to be rendered to God.

Harmonious cooperation and coordination between the two societies flourished in the ages of faith when all men recognized God as the source of all authority, and saw in human legislation the expression of the divine will made known to man through lawfully constituted authority to which God gave the right to exercise power over other human beings. This desirable interaction weakens and is lost in proportion as men and nations refuse to recognize God as the Supreme Ruler of the universe and the Source of all law and authority, and to set themselves up as the end and object of government.

Indirect End of the Church

Does "each in its own domain" mean that the Church confers no benefits upon civil society and that the State confers no benefits upon religion? That is far from the truth. For if the Church perfects man, making him truly a man in all his actions, do not these actions include also his social relations? Therefore, the more Christian a man, the less prone he is to disturb the harmony of the social body. And likewise, if the State places at man's disposal, as the object of his efforts, the attainment of a decent living according to human standards, then man will not be so harassed by the worries of gaining a temporal livelihood that he will fail to recognize the gracious bounty and goodness of God and render to God his grateful services. Pope Leo remarks:

> The Catholic Church, that imperishable handiwork of our all-merciful God, has for her immediate and natural purpose saving souls and securing our happiness in heaven. Yet in regard to things temporal she is the source of benefits as manifold and great as if the chief end of her existence were to ensure the prospering of our earthly life. And in truth, wherever the Church has set her foot, she has straightway changed the face of things, and has attempered the moral tone of the people with a new civilization, and with virtues before unknown. All nations which have yielded to her sway have become eminent for their culture, their sense of justice, and the glory of their high deeds.

Thus, we can say with truth that the immediate and primary end of the Church is the salvation of souls, and the indirect and secondary end is temporal advancement.

Indirect End of the State

If it can be said of the Church that her labors rebound to the good of the citizens so as to benefit the State, so can it be said of the truly Christian State that it contributes to the good of the individual in such a way as to promote his eternal salvation. Thus the direct and immediate end of the State is temporal well-being, and the indirect and secondary end is the eternal happiness of its subjects. But that secondary end pertains to religion and to the supernatural. Therefore, the State must not be unconcerned about the progress of religion, but it must do everything in its power to foster and promote it in addition to making a public profession of faith in God and in worshiping Him publicly. Pope Leo says:

> Since no one is allowed to be remiss in the service due to God, and since the chief duty of all men is to cling to religion in both its teaching and practice ... it is a public crime to act as though there were no God. So, too, is it a sin in the State not to have care for religion, as a something beyond its scope, or as of no practical benefit.... All who rule, therefore, should hold in honor the holy Name of God, and one of their chief duties must be to favor religion, to protect it, to shield it under the credit and sanction of the laws, and neither to organize nor enact any measures that may compromise its safety. This is the bounden duty of rulers to the people over whom they rule: for one and all we are destined by our birth and adoption, to enjoy, when this frail and fleeting life is ended, a supreme and final good in heaven, and to the attainment of this, every endeavor should be directed. Since then upon this depends the full and perfect happiness of mankind, the securing of this end should be of all imaginable interests the most urgent.

A Just Subordination

When two societies govern a common subject (somewhat comparable to father and mother governing the same children in the household) one of the two societies must be the ultimate one in its authority. As father and mother in the home are equal in the dignity of their human person and natural rights, but unequal in respect to their authority, so the Church and the State are equally distinct and perfect societies, possessed of specific end and means, but there must be some kind of inequality in respect to the authority possessed by each. The Church, by reason of the more exalted dignity of her end and means, claims for herself the more exalted authority, and this not only in respect to her end and means, but also to her direct institution by God Himself. The supremacy of the Church's authority implies, therefore, subordination of the State to the authority of the Church in those matters which pertain to definite moral issues, for of morality and religion the Church is the custodian. "The Church of Christ," says Pope Leo, "is the true and sole teacher of virtue and guardian of morals. She it is who preserves in their purity the principles from which duties flow."

We learned in an earlier chapter that order meant the proper arrangement of parts according to their importance, contribution, and the like. So now, the supremacy of the Church and the subordination of the State in moral issues implies a like ordering of parts. The supremacy of the Church is claimed for her in certain matters because of the end or purpose to which she is devoted: namely, the eternal salvation of souls. Now in comparison with this, the temporal welfare is less important. Man's body has a limited earthly existence; man's soul is immortal and thus has an unending existence. Man's eternal goal is more important than man's temporal goal, and so that society which has the eternal happiness as her end is more important than that one which has temporal happiness for its end. To deny this principle is to make man live primarily for temporal happiness to the probable loss of eternal happiness, and thus man's nature would be frustrated in its purpose: the attainment of perfect happiness. Nature is subordinated to grace, but not destroyed by it. Temporal things are subordinated to eternal things, but not condemned by them.

> To wish the Church to be subject to the civil power in the exercise of her duty is a great folly and a sheer injustice. Wherever this is the case, order is disturbed, for things natural are put above things supernatural; the many benefits which the Church, if free to act, would confer on society are either prevented or at least lessened in number; and a way is prepared for enmities and contentions between the two powers; with how evil results to both, the issue of events has taught us only too frequently.

The Lay State

The Holy Father here laments the ever-increasing denial of the Church supremacy, which denial has been spreading over ever greater numbers of people in the last few centuries. That civilization is not in the least better, but rather the worse for the denial of divine authority, is evident in the social vices which are breaking down the unity of the social organization of the race today. The *lay* State, completely cut off from the authority of the Church, attempts to find a new basis for its government. Refusing to mount to the realm of the divine for its right to rule, it bases itself on human authority alone with such results to stability and real human progress as occasion deep regret and great fear in the minds of the thoughtful. For human authority must, if it fulfills its purpose, be more stable than the changing will of the people. A human basis of sovereignty constitutes a perpetual threat to the peace and security of the State, inasmuch as seditions are possible at any time, since princes are considered delegates of the people and enjoying only the sovereignty conferred upon them by the people and at any time revoked by them. Public peace and the life of virtue, therefore, are in the power of the wills of the majority rather than in the custody and protection of the rulers who derive their authority from God and are accountable to Him for the character of their rule.

"If those who are in authority," writes Pope Leo, "rule unjustly, if they govern overbearingly or arrogantly, and if their measures prove hurtful to the people, they must remember that the Almighty will one day bring them to account, the more strictly in proportion to the sacredness of their office and the preeminence of their dignity."

The *lay* State constitutes one of the most serious problems confronting the Church today, for nations more and more are cutting themselves off from divine authority and drifting about no longer anchored to the eternal and natural laws. To what extent the Church may face subjection in the future is not known, of course, but that it is a serious problem is not to be doubted. However, as in times past, when the welfare of the Church seemed to be most hazardous, the Divine Spirit who remains with it "to the consummation of the world" (Matt. 28:20) will infuse into her new life, new energy, new spirit to meet the trials which beset her. So we hope for the future, relying not on the mightiness of nations nor the force of any physical power within the Church, to protect her in her rightful claims, but rather upon "the Spirit [which] breatheth where he will" (John 3:8) and which will abide with her forever, guiding her in holiness and in truth.

Let us repeat: the loss of the sense of true values, of morality, of justice and its accompanying virtues, of charity, and of peace can be traced to the *lay* State which, by its surrender of divine authority, has lost the only anchor hold of its stability, and the true purpose of its existence: namely, to lead men, through temporal well-being, to eternal happiness.

Claim to Enter Economic Spheres

It remains now to consider the role of the Church in the political and economic spheres. The Church claims for herself, by virtue of her supreme authority, the right to enter into all and any phase of human life when a question of morality is concerned. Insisting as she does on the primacy of the spiritual over the temporal, she insists upon the transcendence of the moral law and holds that any law not in harmony with the natural law — and so with the eternal law — is not a just law. Because of the dignity of the human person and the sacredness of human liberty, the Church claims for herself the right to pass judgments on the morality of acts of individuals and of moral persons such as the State, economic groups, and the like.

This must not be considered as undue interference in a realm not her own, but rather as the fulfillment of her duty as the custodian of morals. For laws have more than a political and economic character; they have moral implications as well, and the realm of morality is precisely the sphere of the Church. Pope Pius writes: "The deposit of truth entrusted to Us by God, and Our weighty office of propagating, interpreting and urging in season and out of season the entire Moral Law, demand that both social and economic questions be brought within our supreme jurisdiction, *insofar as they refer to moral issues.*"

In Moral Issues

It will be well to point out again the restrictive clause in the Holy Father's statement: "insofar as they refer to moral issues." Without this limitation, the State would be justified in complaining of undue interference. The limitation set by the Church upon her entrance into the political and economic spheres, constitutes the protection of the State. It also shows the Church takes recognition of the State's right to supremacy in the matters which concern its end and the means thereto. Pope Pius, writing of this limitation, says:

> It is not of course, the office of the Church to lead men to transient and perishable happiness only, but to that which is eternal. Indeed [and here he quotes Pope Leo], "the Church believes that it would be wrong for her to interfere without just cause in such earthly concerns"; but she can never relinquish her God-given task of interposing her authority, not indeed in technical matters for which she has neither the equipment nor the mission, but in all those that have a bearing on moral conduct.
>
> For though economic science and moral discipline are guided each by its own principles in its own sphere, it is false that the two orders are so distinct and alien that the former in no way depends on the latter. The so-called laws of economics, derived from the nature of earthly goods and from the qualities of the human body and soul, determine what aims are unattainable or attainable in economic matters and what means are thereby necessary, while reason itself clearly deduces from the nature of things and from the individual and social character of man, what is the end and object of the whole economic order assigned by God the Creator.

Note this point: it is within the sphere of the Church to lay down the moral principles which should guide social and economic groups in their natural activities. It is *not* the role of the Church to reduce these principles to detailed application in given situations. That is the work of the leaders of the social and economic groups. They work out the details of their problems according to the immediate necessities of the times. This is their sphere. They deal with "the technical matters" for which the Church has "neither the equipment nor the mission." They act upon the findings of their respective sciences, but always must their laws and the application of their laws be in conformity with the moral law. Not only does the Church claim the right to lay down the moral principles according to which social and economic groups must be guided, but she claims as a necessary complement of this first right, a second one: namely, to pronounce on the morality of the end and means of social and economic laws and their application. And these claims the Church makes in virtue of her divine commission to lead souls to Heaven. "If the Moral Law be faithfully obeyed," says Pope Leo, "the result will be that particular economic aims, whether of society as a body or of individuals, will be intimately linked with the universal purposefulness in the world order and as a consequence we shall be led by progressive stages to the final end of all, God Himself, our highest and lasting good."

Certainly, there is in this doctrine no violation of justice, no insufferable indignity imposed on the State, no attempt at absolute subordination of it to the Church. What could be fairer than that each be granted power within its own realm, whether it be the temporal or the eternal, with this restriction only, that the eternal be not subordinated to the temporal, but contrariwise, the temporal to the eternal as the less noble to the more noble, as the less dignified to the supreme, the means as to the end.

Particular applications of the Church's concern in the morality of human life will be noted when discussions of "Man in Economic Society" will occupy our attention in part 4.

Catholic Social Action

When a society endures, as has the Church, throughout so many centuries, it finds itself faced with particular problems at particular times. It sees the rise and fall of empires; various philosophies of life and of government come into being and pass away defeated; it meets with tyrants and lives on despite their despotism and persecution; it comes to grips with heresies within its fold and mourns the schismatics who leave its maternal bosom. In some centuries it blossoms in glorious works, in others, it is crimsoned by the blood of its children; at times it meets with false accusations and refutes them by its very life and works, at other times the enemy seems about to crush the very life out of it but it revives and continues to exist as they go down in annihilation.

A human institution could not stand all this, but the Church is not human, though her subjects are all human. The constant flow of divinity into the Church keeps her pulsating despite numerous obstacles, any one of which could wipe a human society off the face of the earth. The Church is divinely ordained and with the constant breath of the Spirit upon her, she meets each new obstacle and each new century with the proper weapons of defense; proper, not because of her human choice of them, but because of the inspirations of the Holy Ghost who enlightens and sanctifies her in holiness and truth.

Our present century is no exception to this reaction of the Church. The subtleties of false philosophies, the evils of immorality, and the grossness of amorality must be met and defeated in order that souls may be saved. Hence the Spirit of Truth has raised up in the Church, more plentifully than ever before, zealous, enlightened, genuinely Christian lay apostles who assist in the spread of Christ's Kingdom on the face of the earth. These have come to be known as *Catholic Actionists*.

Nature of Catholic Action

Catholic Action is not synonymous with "the action of Catholics," whether that be good action or not. Catholic Action is a corporate activity — the activity of a body — of lay Catholics who operate under the direction of the hierarchy for the extension of Christ upon earth. As a body of lay Catholics, it includes men and women, the married and the single. Its essential requisite is that it be in subordination to the hierarchy. To the hierarchy was given the commission to teach and to preach; it belongs to the lay apostles only by their participation in the work of the hierarchy, that is, only insofar as they are under the direction and control of the hierarchy. The purpose of Catholic Action is identical with the purpose of the Church. It aims to bring society more and more into contact with the supernatural life of divine grace which is the only source of supernatural life to the soul. It is strictly the supernaturalness of its end and means which prevents Catholic Action from ever identifying itself with party politics or becoming confused with mere materialistic benevolence. Let us repeat: its aim is the aim of the Church; namely, the increase of supernatural life throughout the social order. Its interests are the higher interests, and though it crosses the paths of political and economic activities, it never comes to rest therein. These latter activities seek temporal prosperity and peaceful social life, whereas Catholic Action, being essentially religious, seeks prosperity and happy earthly existence from a higher motive: that is, as a means to the complete fulfillment of man's destiny as a child of God.

Subordination is necessary. So is organization. The chief reason for subordination is that moral issues are at stake. Reasons for organization are evident. Without organization, there is little accomplished. There can be no solidarity of organization without a competent head, even as there can be no unification of effort or effectual action. It is only by keeping in actual and close contact with the Church that Catholic Action can be effective. Otherwise the soul of the apostolate would be missing, for where the Church is, there is Christ. No one can hope to restore all things *in* Christ and *to* Christ if they reject the aid of the head of Christ, His vicar.

Because the sphere of morality is the realm of the Church, and because to the hierarchy is addressed Christ's command to teach, it is not surprising to learn that from the hierarchy alone — under the pope — comes the mandate to establish Catholic Action organizations. The pastor automatically becomes an official only after the organization has been so instituted by the bishop. He becomes the vicar of the bishop in parochial units. This is the fundamental note of Catholic Action, namely, to be linked up with and subordinated to constituted authority.

Field of Action

The threefold field of Catholic Action can briefly be enumerated thus: piety, study, action. First there is personal piety to be acquired. This includes the development of the life of prayer in the individual Catholic Actionist, the example of a good life, impregnated with piety, justice, charity, and all virtues. It includes, too, the proper formation of one's conscience, the development of an acute sense of right and wrong in the various phases of private and public life. This field of Catholic Action — personal piety — is the seed time. The harvesting comes later. Before the harvest time there must be a period of development, a growing to maturity. The *growing time* is the second field, that of study.

The study phase of Catholic Action includes securing a profound grasp of the things of faith and of Catholic teaching. It should equip the Catholic Actionist with a defense of the dogmas of the faith, an understanding of Catholic social philosophy in its principles as well as in its application to the social life of the family and of civil society. This field of Catholic Action is the indoctrination phase and its needs are best met through study circles and discussion clubs under authorized and competent auspices. When personal piety has taken deep root, and study has sharpened the mind and equipped it with the necessary knowledge, the "action" proper commences.

Action begins in one's immediate circle, by word and example, shedding the glow of a good life and the truths of an enlightened mind upon those within the circle. Then its influence becomes extended through discussions of social, economic, and religious questions with any and all with whom the Catholic Actionist comes in contact. The outward expansion of the inner spirituality and intellectual knowledge continues until it envelops homes, workshops, business, politics, recreation centers, and the like. It consists also in the creation of good public opinion through purity of life and the application of Christian social principles to everyday living; it includes, therefore, the consistent application of catholicity to any and every undertaking of the Catholic Actionist. This is to spread the Kingdom of Christ; this is to restore Christ to society and society to Christ.

Catholic Action organizations are not labor unions, political party affiliates, or any such groups. They are a training school for laymen and laywomen who are in the heat of political and industrial and professional and governmental life. As training schools, Catholic Action organizations give their members a thorough religious and moral training so that, as individuals, they may spread abroad the influence of their knowledge and example in the various walks of life: in business, in politics, in labor organizations, in government circles, and everywhere, with this crowning final aim: to restore all things in Christ!

"Catholic Action," writes Pope Plus, "should be the universal and harmonious action of all Catholics without exception of age or sex, of social condition, of culture, or of national and political tendencies."

Every practical Catholic should strive to become and pride himself on being a practical Catholic Actionist, for the aim of Catholic Action is the aim of the Catholic Church, the salvation of souls, the spread of Christ's Kingdom.

Some Original Sources

St. Thomas, in making comments on the meaning of the words *holy Catholic Church*, says:

1. "As in a man there is one soul and one body, yet a diversity of members, so the Catholic Church is one body and has different members.

"The soul which quickens this body is the Holy Ghost; and that is why, after faith in the Holy Ghost, we are required to have faith in the Catholic Church, as the Creed itself makes clear.

"He who says *Church* says *Congregation*; and he who says *Holy Church* says *Congregation of the Faithful*, and he who says *Christian Man* says *Member of that Church*.

"The Church is one, and this unity of the Church is grounded in three elements. It is grounded:

(a) First, in the oneness of faith; for all Christians belonging to the body of the Church believe in the same reality.

(b) Second, this unity comes from the oneness of hope, for all are rooted in the same hope of attaining to eternal life.

(c) Thirdly, there is the oneness in love, for all are joined unto the love of God, and to one another in the love of one another.

"The Church of Christ is holy ... with a holiness which is grounded in three things:

(a) First, in this, that the faithful have been washed in the Blood of Christ,

(b) Second, in that spiritual anointing which they have received and whereby they have been sanctified ... which anointing is the grace of the Holy Ghost, and

(c) Thirdly, in the fact that the Trinity dwells in her.

"Furthermore, the Church is Catholic, that is, Universal.

(a) First, in virtue of her spatial or geographic catholicity, which springs from her diffusion through the whole world, then

(b) Second, from the catholicity which she has by inclusion of all kinds and conditions of men of which none is left without; and

(c) Thirdly, she is universal in time ... enduring from Abel till the end of the world, after which she shall continue to endure in heaven.

"Lastly, the Church is indestructible ... having

(a) First, Christ for her chief foundation, and

(b) Second, the Apostles and their doctrine, and that is why she is called Apostolic." (Translated by M.J. Congar, O.P., in *Thomist*, vol. 1, no. 3, October 1939: "The Idea of the Church in Saint Thomas Aquinas")

Hear the masterly words of Pope Leo on the Church-State relations:

2. "We must go more deeply into the nature of the Church, as being not a mere chance union of Christians, but as a society divinely constituted and wonderfully organized, having as its direct object to bestow peace and holiness on the soul; and since for this end it alone by divine gift possesses the necessary means, it has fixed laws, fixed functions, and in the direction of Christian peoples follows a method most consonant with its nature.

"But the course of its government is difficult and but seldom runs with smoothness. The Church is the mistress of nations scattered over the whole earth, differing in race and customs, whose duty it is, living each in its own state under its own laws, to submit both to civil and ecclesiastical power. And these duties are incumbent on the same persons, and not at odds with each other, nor are they confused, as we have said, for the former [i.e., civil power] promotes the prosperity of the State, the latter [i.e., ecclesiastical power] the common good of the Church, and both are for the perfection of man.

"And with this definition of mutual rights and functions, it is quite clear that rulers of states should be free to guide their affairs and this not only without the opposition, but with the assistance of the Church; for since she above all things teaches the practice of piety, which is justice toward God, in the same way she urges men to act with justice toward their rulers. However the ecclesiastical power has this far nobler aim—to rule the minds of men by having regard 'to the Kingdom of God and His justice,' and it is entirely devoted to this object.

"Moreover it cannot without rashness be doubted that the direction of souls has been given to the Church alone, so that in this matter political power has no right to interfere; for not to Caesar, but to Peter, did Jesus Christ entrust the keys of the kingdom of heaven. And with this doctrine on political and religious affairs there are bound up matters of considerable importance, on which We would not here be silent.

"From all political societies the Christian Church differs widely. If upon its face there rests the likeness and shadow of a kingdom, it has in truth an origin, a motive, an essence very remote from the kingdoms of this world.

"It is fitting that the Church should live and protect herself by institutions and laws that are in harmony with her nature. And since her society is not only perfect, but is also placed above every human society, she, in the fulfillment of her right and her office, firmly refuses to side with any parties, and to worship before the fleeting and changeable politics of the civil order.

"And in like manner, while being the guardian of her rights and most careful against encroachment, the Church has no care what form of government exists in a state or by what customs the civil order of Christian nations is directed. Of the various kinds of government there is none of which she disapproves, so long as religion and moral discipline live untouched....

"In truth, both Church and State have each an individual domain; therefore in fulfilling their separate duties neither is subject to the other, within the limits fixed by their boundary lines. From this, nevertheless, it follows that they are by no means things with separate and distinct aims, much less that they are in mutual opposition.

"Indeed, nature not only gave us existence, but bade us dwell together; hence a man has a right to demand of a state at peace with itself—which is the immediate object of the civil bond—that it should be a benefactor to him, and, much more, that it should give efficient means for enforcing purity of morals, which consists only in the knowledge and exercise of virtue.

"At the same time a man desires, as is right, to find assistance in the Church towards winning the perfect gift of a perfect piety, which consists in the knowledge and practice of true religion, the mother of all virtues, since by referring man to God, she fulfills and compasses them all.

"In establishing and approving institutions and laws, man's moral and religious character should be regarded, and his perfection sought after in due order; nor should anything be commanded or forbidden unless on the ground of benefit to the civil society and in accordance with religion.

"For this reason the Church cannot but concern herself about the laws formulated in states, not for their connection with the government, but because they sometimes encroach on the right of the Church by passing their due bounds.

"Nay, it is a duty assigned by God to the Church to resist, if, at any time, the State harms religion, and it is a duty to strive that the teachings of the Gospel shall influence the laws and institutions of peoples.

"And since the welfare of the State is peculiarly dependent on the direction of its governor, the Church cannot give either patronage or favor to the men at whose hands she knows only oppression; to those who in the broad day refuse to respect her rights, and who strive to tear asunder civil and sacred polity, bound together as they are in their very essence." (Pope Leo XIII, *Chief Duties of Christians as Citizens*)

The following excerpts all deal with Catholic Action, and are by Pope Pius XI.

3. "We extend Our paternal invitation to Our beloved sons among the laity who are doing battle in the ranks of Catholic Action.... Catholic Action, is, in effect, a social apostolate also, inasmuch as its object is to spread the Kingdom of Jesus Christ not only among individuals, but also in families and in society.

"It must, therefore, make it a chief aim to train its members with special care and to prepare them to fight the battles of the Lord. This task of formation, now more urgent and indispensable than ever, which must always precede direct action in the field, will assuredly be served by study-circles, conference, lecture courses, and the various other activities undertaken with a view to making known the Christian solution of the social problem.

4. "The militant leaders of Catholic Action, thus properly prepared and armed, will be the first and immediate apostles of their fellow workmen. They will be an invaluable aid to the priest in carrying the torch of truth and in relieving grave spiritual and material suffering, in many sectors where inveterate anti-clerical prejudice or deplorable religious indifferences have proved a constant obstacle to the pastoral activity of God's ministers.

"In this way they will collaborate, under the direction of especially qualified priests, in that work of spiritual aid to the laboring classes on which We set so much store, because it is the means best calculated to save these, Our beloved children, from the snares of Communism.

5. "In addition to this individual apostolate which, however useful and effica-cious, often goes unheralded, Catholic Action must organize propaganda on a

large scale to disseminate knowledge of the fundamental principles on which, according to the Pontifical documents [viz., the encyclicals] a Christian social order must be built.

6. "Here we should like to address a particularly affectionate word to Our Catholic workingmen, young and old. They have been given, perhaps as a reward for their often heroic fidelity in these trying days, a noble and an arduous mission. Under the guidance of their bishops and priests, they are to bring back to the Church and to God those immense multitudes of their brother-workmen who, because they were not understood or treated with the respect to which they were entitled, in bitterness have strayed far from God.

"Let Catholic workmen show these wandering brethren by word and example that the Church is a tender mother to all those who labor and suffer, and that she has never failed, and never will fail, in her sacred duty of protecting her children." (*Atheistic Communism*)

Summary

1. Almighty God has ordained two perfect societies to serve man: namely, the State which has for its primary purpose the common temporal welfare of its citizens, and the Church which has for her primary purpose the salvation of souls — the common eternal happiness of her children.

2. Each is a perfect society, having authority from God, and entitled to the three functions of government: legislative, executive, and judicial.

3. It is repugnant to think that the eternal wisdom of God which ordained so harmoniously the action of things in the physical universe should have left man a prey to indecision and doubt regarding the societies which are to direct him. To avoid any such confusion God has marked out the limits of each of these societies.

4. In things purely temporal, the State has supreme authority. In things purely spiritual, the Church has supreme authority. Because of the dignity of the end and the means thereto, the Church is a more noble society and her authority is the more exalted one.

5. For this reason the Church claims for herself independence from civil powers and authority to act without hindrance according as she thinks best, in those things which pertain to her end and means.

6. Ecclesiastical authority is distinct from political authority. It was to establish a distinct society to direct man toward his supernatural end that God sent His only-begotten Son to establish the Church.

7. The autonomy and the influence of the Church are subject to variation through the favorable or the hostile attitude of men and civil society. In the Middle Ages a truly Christian social order functioned and the Church

was indeed the leader of men in their efforts to acquire complete human development.

8. With the rise of individualism and the awakening of nations to self-consciousness the brotherhood of all mankind was forgotten and social unity began to disintegrate. Today we are witnessing the logical results of the breakdown of the truly Christian social order.

9. Because the Church and the State deal with the same subject, they cannot run in isolated grooves, unmindful one of the other. The Church indirectly advances the common well-being of the State and the State indirectly advances the common well-being of the Church. The whole human person of man is developed along all lines and this includes the spiritual as well as the material, the eternal as well as the temporal.

10. The State is bound to recognize God, His authority, His Church, and to revere His holy name. It must also favor religion, protect and shield it, and do nothing contrary to its advance and good.

11. It is not an unjust subordination (that is, slavery) to which the Church would relegate the State when she insists upon supremacy. It merely "orders" the temporal for the sake of the eternal; the material for the good of the spiritual; the natural for the supernatural; the less noble for the more noble. It recognizes in the State a perfect society, God-appointed, possessed of its particular end and means, and with divine authority to function and to preserve itself in existence. By claiming superiority, the Church does so because of her commission to lead souls to Heaven which is a higher commission than to lead souls to temporal happiness.

12. The State is supreme in its own domain; the Church is supreme in her own domain. When there is conflict between claims (no *natural* conflicts but only *provoked* ones really exist) the Church claims priority of authority.

13. The *lay* State cuts loose from the moral authority of the Church. It establishes its right to rule, not in divine authority, but in the authority of the people. It is therefore characterized by instability, for the will of a multitude or the will of an individual is subject to change, often and inconsistently. A *lay* State is prey to seditions, insecurity, and the like. It is not a desirable mode of civil society. He who cuts himself off from the Church as the custodian and teacher of the moral law, cuts himself off from God. With God gone, what purpose does there remain?

14. The Church claims the right to enter into the fields of economic and political activity "in so far as they refer to moral issues." This does not overstep the boundaries of the authority of the Church.

15. The work of the hierarchy of the Church is effectively carried out through cooperation of zealous Christian laymen and laywomen who (1) live truly

Christian lives; (2) study the Christian social, political, and economic doctrines, and the moral law as it applies to the former; (3) spread, by word and example, the essence of the Church's teachings in whatsoever sphere of life they are in.

16. Catholic Action may be defined as "A lay apostolate in subordination to the hierarchy for the extension of Christ's Kingdom." It is a training school in militant catholicity and it means "the fighting of the battles of the Lord" in economic, professional, political, governmental, and domestic circles.

17. Its threefold field of action is personal piety, study, and action.

18. Its platform may be summed up thus:

(a) belief in Christian social, economic, political principles;

(b) application of them to the social order as a whole;

(c) creation of good public opinion for the Church and her doctrines;

(d) a constant application of catholicity to all duties of life;

(e) restoration of Christ to society and of society to Christ.

For Study and Discussion

1. Exclusive of the family, are two powers sufficient to manage essential human affairs? Discuss.

2. Draw up a comparison between the Church and the State with respect to these things: origin; perfection as a society; primary end; means to primary end; dignity by nature, office, and goal; supremacy of authority; legitimate domain.

3. What characteristics might be said to belong to the Church as a society directive of human activities? Discuss the characteristics.

4. Why should the Church be "unhampered by any limit of either time or place"? Discuss.

5. If the Church is made up of men, as is civil society, why can the Church be said to be *supernatural* whereas we call civil society *natural*?

6. Discuss the nature and the operation of the legislative, the judiciary, and the executive powers of the Church; of the State. Why are these threefold powers needed?

7. Explain how man's religious direction was an aspect of political authority before the establishment of the Church of Christ. In what nation was there an exception to political dominance over religion?

8. Why was it natural (to our way of thinking) that Christ should have become a Jew when He assumed our nature? Show from the Gospel account of our Lord's trial that the Jews still held to the independence of religious laws from political authority—even of Roman authority—of which they were then conquered and unwilling subjects.

9. Discuss the importance of the words "each in its own sphere" when used of the function of the Church and the State.
10. Explain Pope Leo's words: "Whatever in things human is of a sacred character," and so forth.
11. Why must integration of some kind exist between Church and State? What is the *lay* State? Why does it constitute a grave problem for the Church?
12. Does the Church confer any benefits upon civil society? Discuss.
13. Is the State obliged to public acknowledgment of God and to acts of public worship? Explain.
14. What are the duties of the State with regard to religion?
15. Explain in what the supremacy of the Church and the due subordination of the State consist.
16. Why is it injustice to wish the Church to be subject to civil power in the exercise of her duty?
17. Under what restrictions, imposed by herself, does the Church claim the right to enter the field of politics, government, economics, and the like? What is the twofold character of the action of the Church in this regard?
18. Why does the Church "believe it would be wrong for her to interfere without just cause in earthly concerns"?
19. What is the nature of Catholic Social Action? What are its essential characteristics? What is its threefold field?
20. Why must Catholic Actionists be subordinated to the hierarchy? Why must there be organization?
21. In what does the *piety* consist? the *study*? the *action*? How can you share in the activity of Catholic Action?
22. How are the principles of the Church gotten across to the masses? Why should you lead a truly Christian life in private and in public?
23. How can the aim of Catholic Action be said to be the aim of the Catholic Church?
24. Explain the meaning of: "To restore Christ to society and society to Christ."

For the Advanced Reader

St. Thomas:
> *Summa Theologica*, vol. 8, the Old Law, its moral, ceremonial, and judicial precepts, pp. 84–279

Farrell, Walter:
> *A Companion to the Summa*, II, chap. 19

Sheen, Fulton J.:
> *Whence Come Wars*, chaps. 4–5

Christian Social Principles

Papal Encyclicals:

    Pope Leo XIII: *The Chief Duties of Christians as Citizens*

                       The Christian Constitution of States

                       Christian Popular Action

                       Civil Government

                       The Condition of Labor

                       Evils of Society

                       Socialism and Communism

    Pope Pius XI: *The Reconstruction of the Social Order*

    Pope Pius XII: *Unity in Opposing World Evils*

Philosophy of the State, reprinted 1940 from 1939 proceedings of the American Catholic Philosophical Association, "The Church and State," pp. 94–103

The Thomist: "The Idea of the Church in Saint Thomas Aquinas," pp. 331–359, vol. 1, no. 3, Oct. 1939

18

Education: A Social Activity

We have deferred until this point a discussion of education. The reason can be given best in the words of Pope Pius XI: "Education is essentially a social, and not a mere individual activity." It was deemed advisable therefore to defer its discussion until the nature of the three primary societies and their functions had been adequately presented. That being completed in the last chapter, we present in this one the nature, rights, subject, and ends of Christian education.

Inasmuch as it is a social activity it belongs, therefore, to society to educate. But to which society? That question is an important one and it is becoming more and more discussed and disputed in proportion as totalitarian philosophies of political government are tending toward establishment in the modern world.

To Whom Does It Belong?

Is education the concern of the State? It might seem so, since the immature child citizen of today becomes the mature adult citizen of a later day. But that looks at only one aspect — the social. Is education the concern of the family? Well, certainly the child belongs to the family, for it is begotten by its parents, is born into a family, and finds its first needs met in the family circle. But one cannot linger wholly on that view, for it concerns the individual view and the view of an imperfect society which is not sufficient to give to the offspring all that full human development requires. Then, is education the concern of the Church? She would seem to have a strong case in her favor, since the ultimate goal of humanity is a supernatural one and the Church supplies the means thereto. But to look only at that view is to see only a partial aspect of man, for man is body and soul and he makes his way to God through temporal existence, and of temporal matters as such the Church is not the director.

Again we shall let Pope Pius speak: "Education, which is concerned with man as a whole, individually and socially, in the order of nature and in the order of grace, necessarily belongs to all these three societies, *in due proportion*, corresponding, according to the disposition of Divine Providence, to the coordination of their respective end."

This is a revealing statement! The three societies into which man is born are responsible for his education. They are responsible, moreover, as a matter of *necessity*; that is, education *must* belong to the three societies. It follows, then, that each society has the right to contribute to the education of the young, and if it has the right, it has the duty to do so. But since not any one of these societies of itself has the sole right, each must acknowledge itself bound to respect the rights of the other societies. Pope Pius's statement, however, contains another element for thoughtful consideration. He says, "in due proportion." That means, of course, there exists a certain relationship among the educative agencies — a *due* relationship, one regulated by the virtue of justice. The question remains, then, how is this relationship determined? What is *due proportion* between the rights of the family, the State, and the Church in the matter of education?

The answer is given by the Holy Father. He says, in effect, that the due proportion is that which corresponds to what God planned when He appointed to each of these societies a specific end to which it must strive. The three ends of the three societies, being distinct one from the other, must harmoniously combine in order to effect the final end of the individual being educated: namely, eternal beatitude.

We must remember that if all three societies were of the same nature, the limiting of their respective rights in the matter of education would be more difficult than it is. However, not all three are natural societies. The Church is a supernatural society and hence as the imperfect is ordained to the perfect, and as the natural is ordained to the supernatural, so education (not of this or that individual but education in general) belongs preeminently to the Church.

By Divine Command

Pope Pius lays down this principle and he bases it upon two titles or claims. He says: "First of all education belongs pre-eminently to the Church by reason of a double title in the *supernatural* order, conferred exclusively upon her by God Himself; *absolutely superior therefore to any other title in the natural order.*" The titles of the family and of the State are titles in the *natural* order, it is well to recall. Because the Church's title exists in the supernatural order, she can claim that absolute superiority over any claim in the natural order. The twofold title upon which the Church bases her claims to preeminence in the matter of education as such, are these:

First: Because of the mission of the Church. Christ our Lord, the Divine Founder of the Church, expressly authorized His Church to teach all nations. The Church possesses the truth — the whole truth — the divine truth. It is this divine truth which she is commissioned to teach, the truths of religion and of morality. So important did Christ hold this duty, that He conferred infallibility upon His Church at the same time that He imposed on her the duty to teach His doctrine. "All power is given to me in heaven and in earth. Going therefore, teach ye all nations; baptizing them in the name of the Father, and of the Son, and of the Holy Ghost. Teaching them to observe all things whatsoever I have commanded you: and behold I am with you all days, even to the consummation of the world" (Matt. 28:18–20). Sublime words! A magnificent commission! A divine certitude!

Secondly: Because of her supernatural motherhood. The Church claims preeminence in the field of education because she "mothers" souls in the supernatural life, and the fullness of supernatural life is the ultimate goal which God has set for man. Hence the Church claims superiority for her right.

These two claims constitute the Church the mistress of men, with the inviolable right to teach matters of faith and morals unmolested by any human power whatsoever. This independence of the Church pertains to her magisterial mission both in its *origin* and in its *exercise*, inasmuch as it was from God she received her mission, and from God she received the truths which were to be taught. In other words, the Church does not accept her office as teacher from any human authority; neither does she accept the truths which she teaches from any human authority. God is the origin and God's truth is the material of the Church's office as educator and mistress of mankind. Hence she claims independence of any human authority.

Furthermore, not only does the Church demand independence because of the supernatural character of her goal, her divine commission, and the divine truth which she teaches, but she demands independence also in regard to the means necessary and proper to the attainment of that end. One of the chief means with which we are familiar in this country, is the system of parochial schools wherein the young are trained in their religious and moral duties, as well as in intellectual knowledge and their civil duties.

God is truth. He is perfect truth. He is infinite, unlimited truth. He is the fullness of truth. All finite truths are partial truths of the Infinite Truth.

Truth is one. Hence the truths of mathematics, of science, of the arts, are all aspects of that truth which is God. And since it is the mission of the Church to propagate divine truth, the Church claims an independent right to make use of all kinds of human learning and instruction which is the common heritage of individuals and of society. The schools operated under the patronage of the Church claim the right to teach secular branches of learning as well as religious and moral truths. In virtue of her mission and her end, the Church claims also the right to pronounce on what in secular branches is *truth* and what is not; on what is conducive to a Christian education and what is harmful to it. "This must be so," remarks Pope Pius XI, "because (1) the Church as a perfect society has an independent right to the means conducive to its end, and (2) because every form of instruction, no less than every human action, has a necessary connection with man's last end, and therefore cannot be withdrawn from the dictates of the Divine law, of which the Church is infallible guardian, interpreter, and teacher."

We may conclude, therefore, that the Church has the full right to make use of and promote letters, science, and art if and when she finds it necessary or even helpful to the Christian education of the young and to the salvation of souls. All branches of learning are subject to her watchful solicitude and supervision, even physical education, for this, as other branches, may prove detrimental to the salvation of souls or to the formation of a Christian character.

The supervision of the Church includes her right and duty to watch over the entire education of her children whether they be in institutions conducted by the Church or in other institutions, public or private. This solicitude does not extend merely to religious instruction but it is concerned with all types of instruction for the reasons stated above. This right of the Church to watch over the entire education of her children in all institutions extends to all branches of learning, with this limitation: namely, *insofar as religion and morality are concerned*. We have met that statement before. We noted in the previous chapter that the Church claims the right to intervene in all political, civic, and economic matters insofar as religion and morality are concerned. We have given the reason several times: the Church is the custodian, guardian, and interpreter of morality and of religion. This is the basis of her claim. It is the limit, likewise, of the extent of her intervention.

Extent of Her Mission

Christ said, "Teach ye all nations" (Matt. 28:19). That expresses the extent of the Church's mission: the extension of Christ *on earth*. It embraces every nation without exception and since the command is a divine command, there is no power on earth that may lawfully oppose the Church or stand in her way. Foremost does her mission extend to those within the fold. For centuries she has conducted schools where every kind of real learning has been taught. For centuries she has fostered and promoted the sciences, art, architecture, literature, philosophy, and letters. Her mission extends, however, beyond the confines of the fold and embraces all those who are called to be children of God. Her interests lie, in other words, not merely in the converted, but in those not yet converted — the convertible — who, by reason of their human nature, are destined to eternal salvation. That is why the Church will be found in all climes and countries; why the Holy Sacrifice of the Mass is continuously offered throughout the twenty-four hours of the day; why the blood of her martyrs fertilizes all continents, and why the crosses on her chapels pierce the skies in every locality under the sun.

No Conflict of Rights

An unbiased mind finds wonderful harmony in the "due proportion" which exists among the three primary societies in the matter of education. Primarily the principle is this: that the right of the Church is a supernatural right, whereas the rights of the family and of the State are natural rights. In no way does the supernatural weaken the natural for both proceed from the God who is the cause of both orders. The supernatural elevates and perfects the natural, and when the Church concerns herself in the matter of education concretely with this or that particular child or man or woman, it is to elevate and to perfect the endeavors of the family and of the State on behalf of that individual. Our discussion thus far has not dealt, as you must have noticed, with the concrete application of the Church's mission to individuals. It concerned itself wholly in treating of the right of the Church to educate generally, that is, to give to any and every individual and nation a participation in her deposit of divine truths. It has not descended from the general to the particular; it treated merely of the magisterial office of the Church rather than with the detailed application of her educative system to this or that particular child.

The Family's Right

Here we step down from the level of the supernatural to that of the natural. The right of the family to educate is based immediately on nature and the law of nature, though ultimately, of course, it has its source in God who is the Author of nature and the foundation of the law of nature. God communicates to the family, in the natural order, fertility and authority. In other words, He gives to the family as basic natural rights the right to offspring and the right to govern the domestic society. But the generation of offspring imposes the duty of caring for them until such time as they can adequately care for themselves. Furthermore, the *care* must include more than physical care; it must be care that is directed to the welfare of the mind, the will, and the heart; it must include the whole child, body and soul, the order of nature and the order of grace. But this *care* is education, for the subject of education is, in the words of Pope Pius XI: "man whole and entire, soul united to body in unity of nature, with all his faculties natural and supernatural, such as right reason and Revelation show him to be."

The right of the family extends, in each individual family, to the education of its own children. This is particularizing the term *education* — in using it of the Church we used it in a universal way: *all nations*, hence to every individual nation and to every individual subject of all nations. The Church's mission is universal — the family's limited each to its own few members.

St. Thomas tells us: "The father is the principle of generation, of education, of discipline and whatever pertains to the perfection of human life." The statement means, of course, that the father (as head of the family) is the source, not only of the life, but also of the education of the offspring.

Now that we are down on the natural level, we will find that the right of the family in the matter of education has priority over the right of the State. The family is closer to nature and the natural law. The family arises directly from the needs of nature; the State arises indirectly, that is, it arises through the family because of the needs of the family. Therefore the family's more immediate contact with nature gives to the family priority of rights. The State still maintains its role: that of supplementing the endeavors of the family, and in education, as in livelihood and other aspects of family life, the State supplements, but must not abolish, the family's initial efforts.

The Right Inviolable

Pope Pius XI writes: "The Family holds directly from the Creator the mission, and hence the right, to educate the offspring, a right inalienable because inseparably joined to the strict obligation, a right anterior to any right whatever of civil society and of the State, and therefore inviolable on the part of any power on earth."

Note, the right of the family is "inviolable on the part of any power on earth." That includes, of course, any human authority such as civil authority in general, federal, State, or local, or particular authorities as school boards, principals, teachers, and the like. This right of the family continues until such time as the child can care for itself. If the child is physically or mentally unable to assume charge of itself, the duty remains on the parents throughout life. We are dealing now not only with the right of the family in general, but also with the right of particular parents to educate their particular children. Mr. and Mrs. Smith have the right to educate the little Smiths until such time as the young ones are capable of caring for themselves. This right is inviolable because it is a basic natural right. This right is anterior to any right of the State inasmuch as the child belongs to the father and is, as it were, the extension of the father's personality.

In condemning the opinion that the child belongs to the State because it is destined for citizenship in the State, Pope Pius XI declares:

> On the point of the parental right to educate the common sense of mankind is in such complete accord that they would be in open contradiction with it who dared maintain that the children belong to the State *before they belong to the Family*, and that the State has an absolute right over their education. Untenable is the reason they adduce, namely, that man is born a citizen and hence belongs primarily to the State, not bearing in mind that before being a citizen man must exist; and existence does not come from the State, but from the parents, [and here he quotes Pope Leo XIII] and they [the children] enter into and become part of civil society not directly by themselves, but through the Family in which they were born; and therefore, the father's power is of such a nature that it cannot be destroyed or absorbed by the State for it has the same origin as human life itself.

Parental Right Not Absolute

The absoluteness and relativeness of rights is beginning to have a familiar sound, for we have spoken of them in other parts of this work. Even inviolable rights are not absolute rights. For instance, the family has the inviolable right to educate its offspring, but this right is limited, it is relative, bounded by the rights of others. If a family were to rear its children with a hatred of the State and of lawfully constituted authority, in contempt for its laws and with hostility toward its rulers, the family would be violating the right of the State to maintain itself in peace, to preserve itself in existence, and to receive the due subjection, obedience, and loyalty of its subjects. The parental right to educate, *primary, direct,* and *inviolable* as it is, is limited by the rights of the other societies, maintaining, of course, the due proportion discussed earlier in this chapter. Hence we say the family rights are relative, since they bear a relation to others' rights and duties; therefore, they are not absolute and despotic.

That the right of the family to educate is a natural right, was upheld by the Supreme Court of the United States in 1925. The State of Oregon had attempted to set a uniform standard of education by forcing its children to receive instruction exclusively in the public schools. The struggle between the litigants was long and bitter. Finally the Supreme Court reviewed the case and issued the decision, quoted here in part:

"The fundamental theory of liberty upon which all governments in this Union repose, excludes any general power of the State to standardize its children by forcing them to accept instruction from public teachers only. *The child is not the mere creature of the State.* Those who nurture him and direct his destiny have the right, coupled with the high duty, to recognize and prepare him for additional duties." Needless to say, this decision ended the controversy. The natural rights of the family were upheld.

Church-Family Relations

The Church is the supernatural mother and foremost teacher of mankind. She generates, nurtures, and educates souls in the divine life of grace. She operates on the supernatural level, in obedience to the expressed command of Christ, her Founder, to "teach ye all nations" (Matt. 28:19). In a remarkably similar manner, though on the natural plane, the family is the natural mother and primary teacher of its offspring. The family generates, nurtures, and educates its children in the whole life of human perfection, physical, intellectual, moral, and spiritual. The family, too, proceeds from God though through the natural law and not by direct command as the Church proceeds. Is not the similarity of origin and office, though they be on distinct levels, the explanation of the lack of discord which should exist between the two societies?

As a matter of fact, there has been no discord to any extent existing between the Church and the family in the matter of education. That the State has violated family rights not infrequently, the course of history shows us. Even today under totalitarian regimes, the State is attempting to usurp the familial rights and to take the child at a tender age from the bosom of the family and to train it exclusively for State purposes. We noted previously the warning issued by Pope Leo XIII: "The Socialists and Communists, in setting aside the parent and introducing the providence of the State, act against natural justice, and threaten the very existence of family life." There will have to be an intelligent struggle on the part of the family to maintain its natural rights, or else the long arm of totalitarianism will sweep them away and reverse the order of things in society, making man exist for society instead of society for man.

Now the family has never felt the need of defending itself against the Church in the matter of education, for the family has ever found in the Church the champion of its natural rights, its defender and protector. Pope Pius XI notes that from the earliest days of Christianity down to present times, the family has confided to the Church a major share in the training of its offspring, knowing well that the Church will never deceive it, nor betray the confidence reposed in it by the family.

The Church, as you know, is the foremost teacher of *all mankind*. The family is the first teacher of the particular individuals within the domestic circle. Now since the family is an imperfect society requiring outside help in the complete performance of its purpose, it is natural that it turn first to the Church in the matter of education. In virtue of being the universal teacher, the Church may be called upon to be the particular teacher; because the Church is all mankind's teacher by divine authority, she may be this particular individual's teacher through the delegated authority of the family. It corresponds to the application of a general law to a particular case. It could not be the other way around. If, for instance, Christ commissioned the Church to teach only Jews, or only Asiatics, the Church could not, by that authority, claim to be the universal teacher of mankind. The particular cannot be made to fit the general. But since, in virtue of Christ's command, the Church is to "teach all nations" (see Matt. 28:19), she may therefore justly claim the right to teach this or that nation, this or that individual. And in this matter, the State may not deny the claim.

Therefore, when a given family or a number of families reach the point where they are unable sufficiently to educate their children in moral and spiritual truths, it or they are justified in calling upon the Church to assist them in this matter. The Church is free to answer the call. She is free to give her assistance. She is free to erect schools for this purpose. She is free to teach secular knowledge as well as moral and religious knowledge if she deems that procedure useful and necessary to her purpose. More simply, the Church may conduct schools in which all secular branches of learning are taught in addition to moral and religious truths. The teaching power of the Church is not, and must not, be restricted to the conducting of the familiar "Sunday School," that is, of religious instruction classes.

In discussing the two facts mentioned above, namely, the willingness of parents to call upon the Church and the eagerness of the Church to offer her assistance to the family, Pope Pius remarks (my emphasis):

> We have two facts of supreme importance to note: (1) the Church placing at the disposal of families her office of teacher and educator, and (2) the families eager to profit by the offer, and entrusting their children to the Church in hundreds and thousands. These two facts recall and proclaim a striking truth of the greatest significance in the moral and social order. They declare that *the mission of education regards before all, above all, primarily the Church and the Family, and this by Natural and Divine Law, and that therefore it cannot be slighted, cannot be evaded, cannot be supplanted.*

The Right of the State

Thus far we have discussed the supernatural right of the Church in the matter of education. Only the Church holds this *supernatural* right, and because it is supernatural, and because it was given expressly by Christ Himself, it is inviolable and prior to any right in the *natural* order. The family has a *natural* right, derived from the natural law, and therefore God-given; and because the family is prior to any form of civil society, the right of the family is anterior to any right of civil society. The family's right to educate may therefore be said to be natural, direct, primary, and inviolable, though not absolute. This seems to exhaust all rights. Is the State therefore to be excluded from the field of education? By no means.

Because the Church and the family hold priority of rights in the matter of education, it must not be believed that any damage accrues to the true and just rights of the State. God is the God of harmony and order. All the universe is striving for the common good of the universe, and this harmony is maintained despite the fact that each nature is independently striving to attain its specific end. So, too, in the case of the Church, the family, and the State. Each has a specific end, and yet, ultimately, the end of all is the good of the individual man and woman and child. There can be no discordant note, therefore, if end and means are duly considered and the work and rights of each society understood in its relative importance to other societies and to the whole of society to which each particular society is as a part to a whole.

Just as God, through the mouth of Jesus Christ, is the direct source of the rights of the Church, and God, through the natural law, is the direct source of the rights of the family, so, too, through the natural law and the needs of the family (hence less directly derived than the right of the family) God is the source of the right of the State in the matter of education. The basis of the claim of the State does not rest on supernatural motherhood (as does the Church's right) nor on natural parenthood (as does the family's right), but on the authority it has to promote the common good. This authority is traceable to the natural law as we said repeatedly before, but it is traceable less immediately, since it is traced first to the insufficiency of the family and from that to the natural law. It is expected, therefore, that the right of the State in the matter of education is less fundamental than that of the family or the Church, and that it is restricted to those things only which pertain to the *common good of society*, for that alone is the precise purpose of the existence of the State.

Therefore it is easy to be seen that in those things in which the individual transcends civil society, the State has no authority to legislate in matters of education. An example of this is the free exercise of religion. In his religious beliefs and practices, the individual is superior to the State, for such things pertain to the final destiny of man which is superior to the common temporal welfare of the State. Now if the individual is free to believe and free to practice his religious beliefs without undue interference on the part of the State, it follows that the State can in no way make laws regarding the religious education or the moral education of its subjects, other than those which are destined to foster religion and promote morality. It cannot legislate that its subjects be educated according to this or that particular religious sect or that they be educated in no religious or moral beliefs. Religion is a matter of individual conscience, and before the child comes of age, his religious and moral education rests with the family and with the Church to which the family has delegated the task. Regarding this right of the family Pope Pius writes:

> This duty on the part of the parents continues up to the time when the child is in a position to provide for itself.... The wisdom of the Church in this matter is expressed with precision and clearness in the Codex of Canon Law: "Parents are under a grave obligation to see to the religious and moral education of their children, as well as to their physical and civic training, as far as they can, and moreover to provide for their temporal well-being." ... So jealous is the Church of the family's inviolable natural right to educate the children, that she never consents, except under peculiar circumstances and with special cautions, to baptize the children of infidels, or provide for their education against the will of the

parents, till such time as the children can choose for themselves and freely embrace the Faith.

The right of the State, therefore, bears a connection with the common good of civil society, and since this relation differs from the relation of education with the family and the State, it follows that education does not pertain to the State in the same way that it does to the Church and the family. The precise end and object of the State is the life of peace and security, by means of which individuals and families can exercise their divinely bestowed natural rights, while at the same time enjoying the greatest spiritual and temporal prosperity possible in this life. This end of the State is involved in the expression *the common good*. The right of the State in the matter of education is measured by the common good. That is the primary principle to bear in mind when considering the State and education. How does the State go about meeting this condition?

"To Protect, to Foster, to Preserve"

The authority of the State includes legislative powers, powers of enforcement, and powers of judgment. In the Supreme Court decision in the so-called "Oregon School Law" case, we have an instance of the exercise of the judiciary powers of the State in the realm of education. Now in the exercise of its legislative powers on behalf of education the State must protect the prior rights of the family and of the Church. The State exists for the protection of basic rights and the free exercise of them by the possessors of those rights; hence it must safeguard the family and the Church in the functioning of the basic right to educate. An instance of this protection of the family and Church rights is seen in the recently adopted *released time* laws in the various states, according to which children attending public schools are released from school during regular hours that they may attend special classes for religious instruction.

In some instances the individual needs protection. It might seem strange to say that a child needs to be protected against his parents, but such a contingency does at times exist. Parents can be either morally or physically unqualified to educate their children. Since the right to educate is not a despotic right, even though it be inviolable, the State may remove a child from his parents and take upon itself (in State institutions) or delegate to others (foster parents and Church-conducted institutions) the promotion of the child's education. This may happen if the parents are convicted of (1) neglect, (2) incapacity, or (3) misconduct. When the State thus intervenes and "protects" the individual against harm through parental disqualifications, it in no way substitutes itself for the family so as to acquire the family's inviolable right; the State merely makes up the deficiencies, hence if and when the parents again qualify, the child must again be placed under the parental care.

The natural rights of the child and of the family, and the supernatural rights of the Church must receive adequate and due consideration on the part of the State authorities when they remove a child from the company of his parents. An instance of this is seen in the case of providing homes in private families for children who are wards of the State. The Catholic child is entitled to being placed with Catholic foster parents, that his faith may not be lost through lack of opportunity to learn it and to practice it. The same is true with State wards who receive institutional care. They are entitled to receive adequate religious and moral instructions and to the free exercise of their religious beliefs. To guarantee this, the Church has sponsored thousands of institutions where her children (young and old), who are unable to provide for themselves, are not deprived of their rightful spiritual and moral heritage.

Pope Pius XI sums this up by saying: "In general, it is the right and duty of the State to protect, according to the rules of right reason and faith, the moral and religious education of youth, by removing public impediments that stand in the way."

In addition to the protection of their prior rights possessed by the family, the Church, and the individual, the State must foster their efforts to procure a good education for the young. It has the duty to remove any public impediments which stand in the way, as we said above. It should encourage and assist the initiative and the activity of the Church and of the family. It should do this, not under compulsion, but freely of its own accord, knowing well that the efforts of these two societies bring untold benefits upon the State and greatly promote and enhance the common good.

When the efforts of the Church and of the family fall short of what is necessary, the State should supplement their work. We have an instance of this in the recently passed laws providing free transportation for Catholic school children, and in some states of the United States, the purchase of books out of state funds. All these things have a bearing on the common good, the peace, and the security of the commonwealth, and hence the State has the right, which involves also the duty, to have a care for such things. Pope Pius XI writes: "The State should supplement the work of the Church and the Family whenever this falls short of what is necessary, even by means of its own schools and institutions. For the State more than any other society is provided with the means put at its disposal for the needs of all, *and it is only right that it use these means to the advantage of those who have contributed them.*"

The right of the State goes beyond the protection and the fostering of others' rights, however. It may take measures to ensure its own safety through a proper civic and political education. No one can deny that physical, intellectual, political, civic, and moral training is conducive to the common good, to the safety of the commonwealth. Now as this is precisely the end of the State, the State has the right and the power to effect such education of its children. Its right is not absolute, however, but like all rights, it is limited by the rights of others. Hence in pursuing a program of physical, intellectual, moral, civic, and political education, the State may not violate the rights of the family and the Church. There is no natural hostility among them because all three societies tend by divine authority toward the perfection of the individual. If, however, any one of these societies swerves from its true end and the proper means thereto, there is bound to be conflict as there would be in the physical order if the heavenly bodies swerved from their appointed courses.

Provided, therefore, the Church is able to supply adequate intellectual, physical, civic, and political training in addition to the moral and spiritual education to which it has primary rights, no State can legitimately deny to Catholic schools the right to function along all those lines. A law such as the one proposed by the state of Oregon, in which that state claimed for itself a monopoly in the field of education, is unjust and unlawful. Families may not legitimately be forced to make use of government schools through either physical coercion or moral sanctions, if such schools are contrary to their consciences or opposed to their lawful desires.

On the other hand, since the State is responsible for the right administration of public affairs and for the protection of the peace of the commonwealth, it may reserve for itself the right to train its citizens along certain lines. It may, for instance, for the sake of safeguarding peace, establish and direct special schools intended to prepare for certain civic duties, especially for military training, provided in all that it does, the State does not transgress any of the rights of the Church and the family. It would not be lawful, because it would be in violation of the rights of the Church and the family, if a State were to take very young children from their parents and train them wholly in the service of the State without regard for religious and moral training, or in any kind of religious and moral training contrary to the wishes of the parents. Such a State would err on two scores: the child belongs to the family, primarily, and is under the power and care of his parents, hence the State may not assume such total control over it; secondarily, every human being, by reason of his nature and destiny, is entitled to a religious and a moral training and of this he may not lawfully be deprived.

The State may claim, then, the right to reserve to itself certain forms of civic and military training so long as it be not in violation of the rights of others: namely, of the family, the Church, and the individual. Pope Pius XI mentions this in his encyclical on *The Christian Education of Youth*. He says:

> In these days there is spreading a spirit of nationalism which is false and exaggerated, as well as dangerous to true peace and prosperity. Under its influence various excesses are committed in giving a military turn to the so-called physical training of boys (sometimes even of girls, contrary to the very instincts of human nature); or again in usurping unreasonably on Sunday, the time which should be devoted to religious duties and to family life at home.

The right of the State to give a civic education may extend to adults as well as to the young; to the less thoroughly educated as well as to those of higher education; to the various branches of secular learning which will encourage upright, virtuous living. It may include education in good citizenship, in letters, in arts, in sciences, in business, and professional training, and in whatever will encourage the good of the individual and the commonwealth and will lead to the suppression of what is evil. Pope Pius remarks: "This civic education, so wide and varied in itself as to include almost every activity of the State intended for the public good, ought also to be regulated by the norms of rectitude, and therefore cannot conflict with the doctrines of the Church which is the Divinely appointed teacher of these norms."

"To Church and State, in Different Ways"

In quoting from Pope Leo concerning the government of the human race and how it is divided between two authorities, the ecclesiastical and the civil, we noted this sentence: "As the same subjects are under the two authorities, it may happen that the same matter, though from a different point of view, may come under the competence and jurisdiction of each of them." Education is an instance of this "same matter" over which each is entitled to exercise jurisdiction. Pope Leo went farther, declaring that, what in human affairs is sacred or has reference to the salvation of souls, is subject to the Church; and that whatever is comprised in the civil and political order, is subject to the State. We saw in this chapter that education pertains, not only to the salvation of souls (and hence is subject to the Church), but it pertains also to the common good of society (and hence is subject to the State).

The principles enumerated by Pope Leo are important: (1) sacred things are under the power of the Church; (2) civil things are under the power of the State. They who refuse to recognize these principles, or who refuse to apply them to education, thereby deny that Christ established His Church for the salvation of souls. They are saying, in effect, that the civil authorities have jurisdiction over things sacred; or else they reduce sacred things from the supernatural plane to the level of the natural, and hence deny the need of any supernatural institution. On the other hand the application of these basic principles to the realm of education brings great advantages to the social order by reason of the kind of citizen it forms. St. Augustine and early apologists, as Tertullian, challenged the enemies of the Church in words such as these, and we might repeat them from the house tops today:

> Let those who declare the teaching of Christ to be opposed to the welfare of the State, furnish us with an army of soldiers such as Christ says soldiers ought to be; let them give us subjects, husbands, wives, parents, children, masters, servants, kings, judges, taxpayers and tax-gatherers who live up to the teachings of Christ; and then let them dare assert that Christian doctrine is harmful to the State. Rather let them not hesitate one moment to acclaim that doctrine, rightly observed, the greatest safeguard of the State. (Tertullian)

The work of the Church in promoting secular learning, as well as religious and moral, does not in any way interfere with the rights of the State or with its regulations. The Church is willing to keep up the standards of her schools in conformity with the legitimate and just demands made upon her by the State. She is willing to abide by certain standards of teaching. She is willing to meet justifiable State requirements in the matter of teacher training; in the equipment of libraries, gymnasiums, laboratories, and the like. She is willing to abide by State regulations concerning the number of school days per year, the number of hours per day, credit values, and details of administration such as roll books, transfer records, marking systems, and the like. She does not hold her right to be an absolute one, but relative to the rights of others, even though it be on a higher plane and therefore inviolable by any human power, on earth.

Hence the right to educate belongs to the Church and the State in different ways. To the one, directly by the expressed command of God, and on the supernatural plane; to the other, indirectly through the insufficiency of the family to attain its own end adequately, and hence on the natural plane. We shall close this question of the right of education on the natural plane by these words of Pope Pius XI in *Christian Marriage*:

> The blessing of offspring is not completed by the mere begetting of children, but something else must be added; namely, the proper education of them.... Now it is certain that both by the law of nature and of God this right and duty of educating their offspring *belongs in the first place to those who began the work of nature by giving them birth*, and they are indeed forbidden to leave unfinished this work and so expose it to certain ruin.

Among the natural societies, therefore, the family holds first place in the matter of educating the children. In virtue of her divine commission the Church is the teacher of all mankind, and hence when a family finds itself unable to provide any longer for the proper spiritual and moral education of its offspring, it is entitled to the services of the Church; when it finds itself unable to provide for the civic and political and economic or other training of its offspring, it is entitled to the services of the State.

In neither case does a family hand over its primary, natural, direct right to educate the children which belong to it. It rests with the parents to direct it within their capacities; beyond their capacities, they are supplemented by the Church and the State, each in its respective field. The Church, being the teacher of mankind generally, is teacher also of this or that child individually, according as the family of which the child is a member solicits or makes use of the services of the Church. The family is supplemented, too, by the State, inasmuch as the aim of the State is the peace and security of the commonwealth, and for this, certain types of education must be insured. "Christian parents must understand," writes Pope Pius XI, "that they are destined not only to propagate and preserve the human race on earth, indeed not only to educate any kind of worshippers of the true God, but children who are to become members of the Church of Christ, to raise up fellow-citizens of the Saints, and members of God's household, that the worshippers of God and Our Saviour may daily increase."

The Subject of Education

We have confined our discussion, thus far, chiefly to understanding the nature and extent of the rights of the respective primary societies in the matter of education. We shall have a few points to make concerning the one being educated. Pope Pius makes the discussion of this easy, for he tells us very plainly that it is the whole man who is being educated: the body, the soul, the mind, and the will. Unless all the natural and supernatural faculties are developed according to their respective possibilities, and developed in conjunction one with the other, and in the fullest possible measure of perfection, then education has failed.

Let us cite an example in the order of nature. A tree normally should develop roots, trunk, bark, branches, leaves, flowers, and fruit as well as "feed lines" for the flow of sap within the tree. Now if a tree, to which these functions are natural, should develop only roots and trunk, but nothing else, it would be a "freak" tree; an unnatural development; a matter for curiosity, perhaps, but certainly not of profit or advantage to itself or to anything else. Its nature has been frustrated; its capacities have been unfulfilled; its attainments negligible; its goal unreached. Unless an enterprising promoter sees a possibility of making money on it by establishing a "sideshow" feature, the tree is good for nothing but to be cut down and cast into the fire.

Now suppose a mother attempted to nourish only one side of her child's body (if that could be done) and permitted the other side to atrophy: she would have a monstrosity, rather than a human being. Nothing is really developed unless it is fully developed; nothing really fulfills its purpose unless it fulfills its whole purpose; nothing is really perfected unless all its parts are perfected. So it is with education.

Unless the whole man, body, soul, mind, and will, are developed according to their respective natures and in the fullest possible measure in any given individual, then that individual is not a perfect specimen of an educated man. Parts of his being are atrophied, because he is under-developed in some of his faculties. He is a kind of monstrosity because his powers have not kept pace one with the other; either he is overdeveloped physically to the exclusion of mental, moral, and religious training, or, as is often the case in modern education outside the Church-directed education, he is developed in body and mind, but not in soul and will. He is a tree that is all bark and branches, but he cannot bear flowers or fruit because the inner development necessary to put forth good works and a life of virtue has been neglected altogether, or only very weakly begun and encouraged. Its growth is not virile enough to produce the expected fruits. Such an individual has been frustrated in his nature, his capacities, his fruits. The soul of true education is moral and spiritual education. Otherwise an individual is a physically strong, walking encyclopedia but not a worshiper of God nor a doer of good deeds.

A true education must correct the evil inclinations resulting from Original Sin; it must direct, and encourage, and regulate tendencies toward the true and the good; it must enlighten the mind and strengthen the will, and all this can be done in no other way than by an education which gives a due place to the religious and moral training of its subjects. Pope Pius XI writes:

> Disorderly inclinations must be corrected, good tendencies encouraged and regulated from tender childhood, and above all the mind must be enlightened and the will strengthened by supernatural truth and by the means of grace, without which it is impossible to control evil impulses, impossible to attain to the full and complete perfection of education intended by the Church, which Christ has endowed so richly with Divine doctrine and with the Sacraments, the efficacious means of grace.

The End of Christian Education

Every society has its proper end and object. Every distinctly human action, likewise, has its proper end and object. Thus, to eat has for its end the physical well-being of the body; to study has as its end the intellectual perfection of the mind. Education, too, has its end and object. It is a glorious end; one surpassing man's unaided powers, for the proper and immediate end of Christian education to make human individuals Christ-like. Pope Pius XI expresses it thus: "The proper and immediate end of Christian education is to cooperate with Divine grace in forming the true and perfect Christian, that is, *to form Christ Himself in those regenerated by Baptism.*" It is to make individuals live a supernatural life in Christ and to display it in all their actions. This does not mean that the true Christian renounces the activities of this life and goes into a kind of spiritual coma from which he does not emerge. It means, that as before, he is active in the daily affairs of human life, but he attacks them in a different way; he uses different principles to guide him; he has different values by which to judge them. A true Christian does not cramp his natural faculties; rather he develops them and perfects them by bringing them into harmony with his spiritual faculties, and thus he is more fully a man. He ennobles what is merely natural in his life and he secures for his life new strength in temporal matters as well as in eternal things. His individual and familial, his physical and intellectual, his social and economic life are all elevated, regulated, and perfected by the overflowing of his supernatural life, for the supernatural elevates and perfects the natural, and grace does not destroy but sublimates nature.

"The true Christian [who is the] product of Christian education," says Pope Pius XI, "is the supernatural man who thinks, judges, and acts constantly and consistently in accordance with right reason, illumined by the supernatural light of the example and teaching of Christ; he is *the true and finished man of character.*"

The formation of the true Christian man of character is the primary end of Christian education. The secondary end is the formation of useful citizens. The "true and finished man of character," he who images Christ and acts as Christ acted, makes a better citizen than one less virtuous. You will recall that St. Thomas remarked that the goal of human law was not to enforce all virtue but those virtues, at least, which pertained to the welfare of the social order. If the social virtues are the minimum requirements for good social living, how much more will he contribute to the social order who conforms himself to Christ, for he will take as his motive power the words of Christ, "Render therefore to Caesar the things that are Caesar's" (Matt. 22:21), and in this good citizenship consists. This is the legal justice of which St. Thomas speaks when he says that general justice directs the individual in his relations toward the common good; and this general justice which prompts an individual to give to society what is its due, is legal justice.

History Justifies the Church's Existence

History has proved that Christianity and its institutions have brought immense advantages to civil society. Pope Pius XI, near the conclusion of his encyclical, says:

> The Saints have ever been, are, and ever will be the greatest benefactors of society, and perfect models for every class and profession, for every state and condition of life, from the simple and uncultured peasant to the master of sciences and letters, from the humble artisan to the commander of armies, from the father of a family to the ruler of peoples and nations, from simple maidens and matrons of the domestic hearth to queens and empresses. What shall we say of the immense work which has been accomplished even for the temporal well-being of men by missionaries of the gospel, who have brought and still bring to barbarous tribes the benefits of civilization together with the light of the Faith? What of the founders of so many social and charitable institutions, of the vast numbers of saintly educators, men and women, who have perpetuated and multiplied their life work by leaving after them prolific institutions of Christian education, in aid of families and for the inestimable advantage of nations?

Beyond doubt, Christian education has been the most potent single factor in the civilization and progress of nations. When Christian education is denied to the people of a country, they eventually degenerate into beings more beastlike than human, for physical development displaces the spiritual development which is Christ-likeness, and when a man is less than perfectly a man, less than the bearer of Christ in his person and his deeds, he is to be feared more than savage beasts and the most devastating pestilence.

In closing his masterly encyclical on *The Christian Education of Youth* (which this chapter summarized for you), Pope Pius XI prays:

> Let us raise our hands and our hearts in supplication to heaven, to the Shepherd and Bishop of our Souls, to the Divine King who gives laws to rulers, that in His almighty power He may cause these splendid fruits of Christian education [namely, the Christian character and the useful citizen] to be gathered in ever greater abundance in the whole world for the lasting benefit of individuals and of nations.

Read this beautiful encyclical in its entirety someday.

Some Original Sources

Incorporate these sources into your discussions and explanations. They will add weight to what you say. Read them carefully.

In discussing the question whether or not children of unbelievers ought to be baptized against their parents' wishes, St. Thomas sets down two reasons against it. They are pertinent in the light of what we have discussed in this chapter.

1. "It seems hazardous to repeat the assertion that the children of unbelievers should be baptized against their parents' wishes, in contradiction to the Church's custom observed hitherto. There are two reasons for this:

   (1) One is on account of the danger to faith. For children baptized before coming to the use of reason, afterwards when they come to perfect age, might easily be persuaded by their parents to renounce what they had unknowingly embraced; and this would be detrimental to the faith.

   (2) The other reason is that it is against natural justice. For the child is by nature part of its father: thus, at first, it is not distinct from its parents as to its body ... and later on before it has the use of its free will, it is enfolded in the care of its parents ... for so long as man has not the use of reason, he differs not from an irrational animal;

"So that, even as an ox or a horse belongs to someone who, according to the civil law, can use them when he likes, as his own instrument, so, according to the Natural Law, a son, before coming to the use of reason, is under his father's care.

"Hence it would be contrary to natural justice if a child, before coming to the use of reason, were to be taken away from its parents' custody, or anything done to it against its parents' wish.

"As soon, however, as it begins to have the use of its free-will, it begins to belong to itself, and is able to look after itself in matters concerning the Divine or the Natural Law, and then it should be induced, not by compulsion, but by persuasion, to embrace the faith:

"It can then consent to the Faith and be baptized, even against its parents' wish; but not before it comes to the use of reason. Hence it is said of the children of the fathers of old that they were saved in the faith of their parents; whereby we are given to understand that it is the parents' duty to look after the salvation of their children, especially before they come to the use of reason.

"In the marriage bond, both husband and wife have the use of the free-will, and each can assent to the faith without the other's consent. But this does not apply to a child before it comes to the use of reason: yet the comparison holds good after the child has come to the use of reason, if it is willing to be converted." (*Summa Theologica*, vol. 9, pp. 145–146)

Listen to what Pope Pius XI has to say along similar lines:

2. "History bears witness how, particularly in modern times, the State has violated and does violate rights conferred by God on the Family. At the same time it shows magnificently how the Church has ever protected and defended these rights, a fact proved by the special confidence which parents have in Catholic schools. As We pointed out recently in Our letter to the Cardinal Secretary of State:

> The Family has instinctively understood this to be so, and from the earliest days of Christianity down to our own times, fathers and mothers, even those of little or no faith, have been sending or bringing their children to places of education under the direction of the Church.

"It is parental instinct, given by God, that thus turns with confidence to the Church, certain of finding in her the protection of family rights, thereby illustrating that harmony with which God has ordered all things.

"The Church is indeed conscious of her Divine mission to all mankind, and of the obligation which all men have to practice the one true religion; and therefore she never tires of defending her right, and of reminding parents of their duty, to have all Catholic-born children baptized and brought up as Christians.

"On the other hand so jealous is she of the Family's inviolable natural right to educate the children, that she never consents, save under peculiar circumstances and with special cautions, to baptize the children of infidels, or provide for their education against the will of the parents, till such time as the children can choose for themselves and freely embrace the Faith." (*The Christian Education of Youth*)

All the following excerpts are taken from the same encyclical.

3. "By nature parents have a right to the training of their children, but with this added duty, that the education and instruction of the child be in accord with the end for which, by God's blessing, it was begotten.

"Therefore it is the duty of parents to make every effort to prevent any invasion of their rights in this matter, and to make absolutely sure that the education of their children remain under their own control in keeping with their Christian duty, and above all, to refuse to send them to those schools in which there is danger of imbibing the deadly poison of impiety.

4. "It is as important to make no mistake in education, as it is to make no mistake in the pursuit of the last end, with which the whole work of education is intimately and necessarily connected. In fact, since education consists essentially in preparing man for what he must be and for what he must do here below, in order to attain the sublime end for which he was created, it is clear that there can be no true education which is not wholly directed to man's last end, and that, in the present order of Providence, since God has revealed Himself in the Person of His only begotten Son ... there can be no ideally perfect education which is not Christian education.

5. "Let it be loudly proclaimed and well understood and recognized by all, that Catholics no matter what their nationality, in agitating for Catholic schools for their children, are not mixing in party politics, but are engaged in a religious enterprise demanded by conscience.

"They do not intend to separate their children either from the body of the nation or its spirit, but to educate them in a perfect manner, most conducive to the prosperity of the nation.

"Indeed, a good Catholic, precisely because of his Catholic principles, makes the better citizen, attached to his country, and loyally submissive to constituted civil authority in every legitimate form of government."

Summary

1. Education is said to be a social activity. This is naturally so, since man is a social being, hence his education contributes to or detracts from the common good of society. If man were an isolated individual, his rearing would be an individual activity.
2. Education belongs to the three primary societies into which man is born: The family, the State, the Church.

3. Education pertains to each society not with equal rights but *in due proportion* corresponding to the end of each society.

4. Pope Pius says that education belongs to the three of them of *necessity*. No one society could adequately train the whole man, for each has an end and means proper to itself and distinct from every other society.

5. The three societies can and ought to coordinate their efforts and thus easily and naturally effect the education of the whole man in all his faculties of body and soul.

6. The Church has her commission to teach all nations. This came to the Church directly from her Founder, Jesus Christ. It applies to every nation and the right thus given to the Church applies to each particular nation and to the individuals which comprise it.

7. The Church has a twofold claim to education: (1) the divine commission; (2) her supernatural motherhood, giving life and nourishment to souls through grace. Only the Church can do this. The Church is on the supernatural level, therefore, and prior in rights to any society on the natural level.

8. The Church demands independence of any civil power in her mission of teaching. She does not derive the right from human authority but from God; therefore she is directly responsible to God.

9. The Church claims the right to make use of any and all secular knowledge which may help her advance the cause of Christian education. She claims this in virtue of the fact that she is the deposit of truth—of all truth—and that she leads souls to Eternal Truth of which partial truths of earthly knowledge constitute limited aspects.

10. As moral teacher and guardian of truth and morality, the Church claims the right to supervise all branches of learning inasmuch as they involve matters of faith and morals and may prove detrimental to the good of souls for the formation of a true Christian character.

11. The extent of the mission of the Church is universal in time and place.

12. There is no natural conflict of rights in the matter of education among the various societies. The Church's right rests on a level above and beyond that of the family and the State, because of the supernatural character of the Church, her end, and the means.

13. On the natural level, the rights of the family are prior to those of the State. The family is more directly founded on the natural law, which commands that a father provide for his offspring.

14. The right of the family in the matter of education is primary, direct, natural, and inalienable. It is inviolable on the part of any power on earth.

15. The family's *care* for the offspring extends to more than physical well-being. Inasmuch as the family is an imperfect society, it requires outside help.

In this way, the family finds in the Church and the State the supplement to its limited resources.

16. The family, without handing over its primary, natural right, accepts the ready services of the Church and of the State to complete the thorough education of the children. Here the Church, as a supernatural society, is supreme in matters of faith and morals. The State, as a natural society, is supreme in matters pertaining wholly to the common good.

17. In virtue of its universal mission as teacher of mankind, the Church has full right to respond to the wishes of any and every family which is unable to give sufficient spiritual and moral help to the children.

18. The family has the duty of developing its children not only physically, but spiritually and morally as well, but there comes a time in the upbringing of the child when the family is inadequate to fill these moral and spiritual needs. For instance, the family cannot give the divine grace of Baptism; it cannot remove sins; it cannot supply the Bread of Life which is Holy Communion; it cannot, as a rule, give adequate instruction in matters of doctrine and good morals. For these the Church has been established and it is perfectly justified in contributing its services to each and every family which stands in need of them.

19. So, too, there comes a time when the State is needed to contribute to the upbringing of the children. The family finds itself unable to continue the work alone. Ordinarily, instruction in human knowledge is one specific piece of work for which the family calls upon the services of the State. Where children attend Catholic schools, however, this service is there rendered to the family in addition to instruction in spirituality and morality. Certain features of civic training there are which only the State can give adequately, and it has full right to do so. Its commission is from God, too, and comes to the State through the natural law and the family's need.

20. The work of the State in the matter of education may be summed up in three words: to protect, to foster, to reserve. It must protect the prior rights of the family and the Church; it must foster the efforts of the family and the Church; it may reserve to itself certain forms of education conducive to the common good.

21. The subject of education is the "whole man"; that is, the body, soul, mind, and will. Less than that, education is not truly education.

22. The end of education is the formation of the perfect Christian and the useful citizen: *the true man of character.*

For Study and Discussion

1. Discuss the reasons why education is "a social activity" rather than an individual activity.

2. Explain in what way education concerns the family; the State; the Church. Discuss these points in detail.

3. What do the words "in due proportion" imply when used of the rights of the three primary societies in the work of education?

4. What are the two titles to which the Church lays claim in her right to educate? Discuss each one of these claims. Is it justifiable?

5. Why does the Church demand independence of any human power in the matter of education? In what two ways does she demand independence?

6. Give a brief talk or write a paper on "The Divine Commission of the Church to Teach and How She Has Fulfilled It."

7. What is the attitude of the Church toward secular knowledge? Discuss this in detail. Does she scorn it? Explain. Does she claim the right to supervise it? Discuss. Does she use it? Explain. How does the Church look upon the truths of human knowledge?

8. Why is the Church's mission worldwide? Upon what does she base her claim to teach this or that individual child or group of children?

9. In accepting the services of the Church in the matter of education, does the family give up its natural, primary right to care for its offspring? Explain.

10. Why is there no natural, inherent conflict of rights between the family, the Church, and the State in the matter of education? How do you account for the controversy between the State and the Church which marks the course of history?

11. Explain the nature and derivation of the right of the family in the matter of education.

12. What is the difference between an absolute and despotic right and a relative right in the matter of education? What kind of right has the family? the State? the Church? Explain.

13. Explain: "The child is not the mere creature of the State."

14. Explain the cooperation between the family and the Church in education. Why does the family need outside help?

15. Why must the jurisdiction of the Church in education extend beyond the familiar "Sunday School"?

16. Explain the nature and derivation of the right of the State in the matter of education.

17. What is the limit of the right of the State in education? What relation does this bear to the end and the means of the State?

18. Why may the State not demand religious instruction according to this or that particular sect? Discuss.
19. Does the Church recognize the right of the family as being inviolable? Quote Pope Pius XI.
20. Summarize the three aspects of the right of the State in the matter of education.
21. Why is the right to educate different in the Church and in the State? Discuss the reason for the difference.
22. Why is a better Christian more likely to be a better citizen? What contribution have saints made to civilization and the progress of their civil societies?
23. Explain why a person receiving a so-called "fine" education in the human sciences but in no other branch of knowledge (such as moral and spiritual and religious learning) is not completely "a man."
24. What is implied in the expression *completely educated*?
25. What is the subject of Christian education?
26. Explain the purpose of Christian education. Does "Christian education" imply a stunted intellect? Explain.
27. How does Pope Pius XI describe the true Christian? Quote Pope Pius.
28. Show how history justifies the existence of the Church and her eminent rights in education.
29. Why should Catholic children attend Catholic schools?

For the Advanced Reader

St. Thomas:
> *Summa Contra Gentiles*, vol. 1, chaps. 1–8, on truth and faith
> *Summa Theologica*, vol. 9, pp. 3–147, on faith and unbelief

Farrell, Walter:
> *A Companion to the Summa*, III, chaps. 1–2

Papal Encyclicals:
> Pope Leo XIII: *Christian Constitution of States*
> *Christian Marriage*
> *Human Liberty*
> Pope Pius XI: *Christian Education of Youth*

Proceedings of the American Catholic Philosophical Association, 1937: "The Essential Features of the Philosophy of Education of Saint Thomas," pp. 22–37

19

Non-Christian Philosophies of Society

It seems advisable at this point in *Christian Social Principles* to devote a chapter to the discussion of several philosophies of society which are based on non-Christian principles. Two distinct philosophies will receive attention. They are selected because they are extreme views, at opposite poles. They are at variance one with the other, and both are at variance with the Christian concept. One is the Liberalistic view of society and the other is the Socialistic view. Of the latter, Communism is one of its forms.

By Excess and Defect

Certainly you have all heard the expression "too much of a good thing." When a little brother or sister begs pennies too often, it becomes "too much of a good thing." When chores around the house are unfairly distributed among the several children, to the overburdened one the demand made on his services becomes "too much of a good thing." In other words, a good thing has been run to excess, and it thereby ceases to be *good*. An excess of anything no longer is good.

Very much in the same way, Liberalism and Communism are each "too much of a good thing." Each philosophy of society started off with at least some truth, but each has ceased to remain true because it has been pushed to excess or left to fail by defect. Each of these philosophies of society has distorted a portion of the truth, has abandoned the fullness of truth, and each becomes a social monstrosity.

The Part and the Whole

Recall for a moment St. Thomas's view of society. The individual is ordained to the common good of society, and the common good of society has, as its end, the perfection of the individual. Individual well-being results from socially controlled action bounded by the limits of law and reason. The individual is ordained to, as well as limited by, the common good of the social whole. The common good is ordained to, as well as limited by, the final goal of the individual. Both society and the individual possess rights in virtue of their own nature and end. Both likewise bear duties in virtue of the nature and end of the other. Here neither the individual nor the whole society has *absolute* rights. All rights are relative. This view of society and the individual is the *mean*, the middle position. It does not glorify the individual by clothing it with divine prerogatives of self-sufficiency. Neither does it deify society by legitimatizing despotism. The social philosophies of Liberalism and Communism swing respectively to opposite extremes from the Christian concept.

The Absolute "I"

The philosophy of Liberalism concentrates on the importance of the individual person. It forgets that man is also a social being. It glorifies the "I" and forgets the "we." Pope Leo XIII nicely sums up its principal tenets in his famous encyclical *Christian Constitution of States*. He shows the havoc that is wrought by it. For Liberalism, in declaring the individual politically, economically, and religiously free from authority, would isolate him from his true atmosphere, namely, the social order, and neither the individual nor society can thrive under those conditions. You will see at once how far this theory departs from the Thomistic concept. St. Thomas conceived so close a bond between the individual and society that he could explain it best by calling it a relationship of "the part to the whole." Now the "part" is in the whole, and the "whole" is comprised of the parts. However, under Liberalism, the individual is isolated from the whole. Rights are said to be absolute. Man is gloriously free, they say, to pursue his goal unhampered by anyone, by anything. He is a law unto himself.

The reasoning of Liberalistic philosophy runs like this: all men are alike by race and by nature, and so they are equal in the control of their life. So far, that is good thinking. It conforms to Christian standards provided, of course, that the expression *control of their life* means, "the right to pursue the goal of their nature as ordained by God." However, if *control of their life* means that each individual is absolute master of himself, then the thinking breaks down. No man is absolute master of himself. Only God can claim perfect self-possession. God is man's absolute master, and duly constituted authority is man's relative master, because it has the source of its power in God. The Christian concept certainly does not accept man's absolute mastery over himself, his thinking, his acting. All thinking and acting are referable to man's last end which is God.

This necessitates standards of judgment, norms of conduct; it necessitates, in other words, *law*.

"No Law above the Individual"

Liberalism rejects law. What need is there for law, it argues, when each man is a law unto himself? Since equality of nature makes all men equal, who has the right to rule another? It answers that no one has such rights. Under Liberalism there is no lawful authority with its roots sunk in the Godhead. No authority, therefore, which obliges. The result is that man is told he is free, absolutely his own master. The State has no positive right to rule and direct. Its only "authority" is of a negative type. Like a policeman, it walks the beat and quells disturbances. It has no "right" to remove the cause of the disturbance; that would be to dominate, and, according to the Liberalists, no man has that right. Hence those who rule merely "run the business" of government, but they are not considered to be possessed of any *right* to rule. For under Liberalism, government is only the will of the people, and "the people," being under no power other than itself, is alone the ruler. The people hold themselves alone to be the source of authority, of power, of government. Anything is said to be right if it accords with the will of the people, and wrong if it does not accord with it. The authority of God is ignored as if no God existed. Pope Leo says of it: "Thus, as is evident, a State becomes nothing but a multitude, which is its own master and ruler. And since the populace is declared to contain within itself the springhead of all rights and of all power, it follows that the State does not consider itself bound by any kind of duty towards God." This is Liberalism as we see it applied to politics and government.

Liberalism in Religion

Liberalism, carried into the realm of religion, is free-thinking, individualism, interpret-the-Bible-as-you-please thinking, or don't interpret the Bible at all, if *that* pleases you. Just do as you please. It means license instead of morality. It begins with a false type of freedom and ends with abject slavery: slavery to passions, to vices, to human weaknesses, to self. And when one looks no higher than self, no farther than his own interests, his own pleasures, his own gains, he is indeed shortsighted even unto blindness. "Do-as-you-please" is its catchword and, by the hidden force within the practice of this philosophy, it is at the same time Liberalism's condemnation.

In the realm of economics, Liberalistic philosophy has become known to history in virtue of its *laissez-faire* theory of economics. "Hands off! Business is business," cries the Liberalistic economist. "There is no morality in economics. Anything is right. As in the realm of government, so in the realm of economics, there is independent morality. Every man is a law unto himself." *Right* becomes for the Liberalist whatever is useful or good. *Wrong* is what opposes his wishes or is of no use to him. Hence a flow of vices corrupts economic regimes possessed or tainted by Liberalism. Greed, avarice, injustice, unlimited competition, and the like characterize their economic transactions. *Liberty* for them is the right to be self-seeking. "Get everything you can," they say in effect, "or else you are stupid. Never mind about the rights of the others. It's up to them to look out for themselves." And so under the Liberalistic-economic regime, liberty meant wealth for those who could get it. It meant inhuman spoliation, injustice, poverty, and misery for the weaker ones who couldn't so readily assert their "liberty." The world became divided into the "Haves" and the "Have-nots." The former were "free" because they were strong; the latter became "unfree" for the simple reason that they were weak.

Pope Leo's Condemnation

Pope Leo XIII condemned this false notion of liberty in his encyclical *Human Liberty*. He says:

Many there are who follow in the footsteps of Lucifer and adopt as their own his rebellious cry, "I will not serve." Consequently for true liberty they substitute what is sheer and most foolish license. Such, for instance, are the men belonging to that widely spread and powerful organization who usurp the name of liberty and style themselves *Liberals....* What *Naturalists* aim at in philosophy, that the supporters of *Liberalism ...* are attempting in the domain of morality and politics.... These followers of Liberalism deny the existence of any Divine authority to which obedience is due, and proclaim that every man is the law unto himself. From this arises that ethical system which they style *independent* morality, and which, under the guise of liberty, exonerates man from any obedience to the commands of God, and substitutes a boundless license.... When once man is firmly persuaded that he is subject to no one, it follows that the efficient cause of the unity of civil society is to be sought simply in the free will of individuals; that the authority in the State is then taken to come from the people only; and that, just as every man's individual reason is his only rule of life, so the collective reason of the community should be the supreme guide in the management of all public affairs.

Read again "Some Original Sources," numbers 9, 10, 11, and 12 of chapter 8.

The "I" Defeated

The evil of Liberalism can be summed up by saying it glorifies the individual to the exclusion of the common good. It is this glorification of the individual to the exclusion of the common good that makes Liberalism a one-sided philosophy of life. It is true that the individual, in some respects, is superior to the common good. However this transcendence of the individual over society is never an absolute transcendence; it is always relative. It is in the absoluteness of the Liberalistic view that the first grave error is made. This is so because it follows as a consequence from the absolute supremacy of the individual, that God's authority and divine law are denied. The overweening importance of the individual under Liberalism becomes "too much of a good thing"; that is, it goes to excess, and Liberalism goes down in defeat as a true philosophy of life, as its offspring, Communism, rises up to consume it.

The Absolute "We"

Liberalism sinned by excess and by defect inasmuch as the importance of the individual exceeded all bounds while God and His authority were ignored. The result was that the common good likewise was ignored and morality denied. Communism turns this order upside down. The individual is ignored; the common good is exalted. Thus, Communism, too, sins by defect and excess. The common good displaces God, the Author of all good. Divine law and Christian morality are no longer the standards of right and wrong.

Under Communism, man is stripped of his liberty. He is robbed of his human personality. There is no such thing as distributive justice, for an individual, they say, has no rights in his relations to the collectivity. The individual lives and labors for the social whole. The "We" completely absorbs the "I" and man becomes a mere cog wheel in the Communist social order. Spiritual things are denied. Man lives for time, for earth, for material advancement, but not for God and eternal happiness. There is nothing sacred or spiritual in human life. There is only the material: the body, the strength of the body, material wealth, physical greatness, tyrannous force and power, but no moral obligation, no spirituality, no God. Every man and all men are ordained to the good of the collectivity. The "group" must prosper. The "group" must continue when the individual has worn out and died in making his contribution to it. The collective good is the "be-all" and "end-all" of the individual's existence. Authority, divine and parental, is nonexistent. What Communists call authority is derived from the community as its first and only source. And this authority is absolute. It dominates. The individual is wholly suppressed; wholly annihilated as a person; definitely less than a man in effect.

Under Communism, there are rights, but they are all on the side of the group. There are duties, but they are all found in the suppressed individual. There are laws, but they are based on human force. There is a god, but it is written with a small *g*. It is the god of mammon and iniquity. The individual is gone; only the group is left. There is no room for persons in the group; no room for beings of a rational nature and freedom of choice; no room for divine goals and natural rights. There is place only for group activity, group purposes, group attainments. Communism is like a nursemaid who dominates over her charges; who dictates to them what is to be done in each and every circumstance of life. It is not the policeman of Liberalism, who quells riots resulting from license. Communism is a jailor who dictates thoughts, words, and movements to his prisoners in an oppressing and destructive regime.

Hence Communism, like Liberalism, is "too much of a good thing." Christian philosophy not only recognizes the advantages of the common good as the aim of society, but it holds that the individuals are morally obliged to contribute to it. Communism, on the other hand, does not use moral persuasion but physical force in attaining the common good. This is done with absolute disregard for the welfare of the individual and his personal, natural, final goal. Communism is therefore an extreme philosophy. It has tried to make a *single truth* (the common welfare) the *whole* truth. It has, by that excess, lost the truth.

Communism is a degenerate form of Socialism, and for its rise, declares Pope Pius XI, Liberalism prepared the way. Communist propaganda has appealed to a despondent working class because it promised them a remedy from the destitution into which Economic Liberalism cast them. A despondent working class, propertyless and abused, is told that in Communism it will find the utopia of a classless society, absolute equality, and an abundance of material things. We shall see what the *utopia* of Communism really can offer the working man.

"Fraternity," Says the Church

Let us say, first, that the Church noted the abuses of Liberalism and condemned them. She witnessed with sorrow to what abuses the glorification of the individual led. She saw an oppressed working class. She saw a wealthy class, limited in numbers, increasing their wealth and, through the increased wealth, wielding greatly augmented power. The Church has never ceased to cry out against the evils of Liberalism and to declare that its so-called liberty was not genuine but spurious liberty, leading to lawlessness and license. However, the Church will not accept Communism as the remedy. For centuries — in fact, throughout her lifetime — has the Church advocated fraternity as the basic principle of a just social order. "You are all brothers in Christ," she said to the world. "Brotherly love must direct society. It must curb selfishness, injustice, intolerance." But Communism says, "Let us all be absolutely equal; that will solve the problem." But crying "equality" won't make men absolutely equal any more than crying "liberty" made all men free.

Communism's "Great Ideal"

The great ideal of Communism is the classless class. In this condition of things, there will be no need for the State. Now we have seen that the Christian concept of the State holds that the individual and the family constitute its foundation. Since there is to be no State in Communism's classless society, then the individual and domestic society must be done away with. Now this does not mean "killed" (though in Russia millions have been killed in the initial steps of this Communistic venture). It means that the dignity of human personality and the nature and role of the family are denied. What Communism has done, or is trying to do, to the individual, we have noted above. It has depersonalized him, or at least it has tried to do so. It has made him utterly and absolutely subordinate, in all that he is and has, to the powers that are above him. This, as we saw, is slavery. St. Thomas reminds us that man is not subject to the body politic in all that he is and has.

Now religion holds out to man the hope of eternal happiness. It teaches man that there is a God above the universe to whom individuals and society are subject. It teaches a man that there is equality only in nature and origin and destiny but not in the possession of earthly goods. Hence it teaches man to consider the spiritual more important than the material. Therefore, because of its teachings, religion must be done away with in the Communist social order. God must be exiled from society and banished from the heart of the individual. So Communism tells the people: "Religion is an opiate. It kills your sense of the truth. It slows down your faculties so that your judgments are not sound. You never saw God, how can you believe what you have never seen? There is no hereafter; no future happiness. Only this life counts! Religion and the ministers of religion are your greatest enemies. Down with religion!"

With the individual bound to the collectivity, with religion and supernatural things cried down, and God banished from man's thoughts and hopes,

Communism next attacks the family. "There is nothing sacred about marriage," it tells the people.

> There is no God, so you cannot say God instituted marriage, or gave it grace or its laws and obligations. From society come the laws and obligations of marriage. Divorce is not an evil. How can it be? There is no matrimonial bond which binds perpetually. Marriage is a free contract, and you are free to break the contract if you choose. Nay, society may demand that you break it, if it be deemed good for the social order. Society instituted the family. Society instituted marriage. Offspring is solely for the good of society!

These are Communism's ideas.

From our careful study of the preceding chapters, we are able to judge correctly in the light of Christian principles each of these false statements. The author feels that these arguments of the Communists for a purely artificial and civil concept of marriage have already been answered in this work. The exposition of the Christian doctrine is their answer. It is believed, too, that the student can detect the unsound thinking underlying the principle that man is for society. Hence we will pass on to the Communists' method of breaking down the family.

Free divorce is legalized. At the mere whim of one of the parties the marriage tie is dissolved, frequently without more than mere notification to the other party. The children become wards of the government or are left to wander the streets, homeless. Marriage becomes only a means for increasing the number of children given over to the custody of the government, and since the government assumes the unnatural role of rearing the children, family life is unnecessary.

The mother, therefore, is not needed in the home. She is therefore withdrawn from her womanly occupation for which she has been fitted by nature and thrust into public life and collective production under the same conditions as the men. She, too, becomes a unit in collective production, of importance only because she hands over to the collectivity the care of her children and takes her place in the ranks of material producers. Education then becomes the work of the community rather than the family. The child belongs to the collectivity and it must be reared according to the ideas and ideals of the group. It must be taught to hate religion, to deny the spiritual, to view marriage as a civil institution, the family as unnecessary, the role of the individual to be of use to the collectivity for group purposes alone. The child must be taught that material well-being is the sole end of existence and that at death the individual goes down into oblivion. He must be told that only in time is there life, and the individual's greatest glory lies in what he contributes to the collectivity here and now, without thought of any such thing as natural rights to this or that higher goal or future destiny.

The evils of this philosophy of life can scarcely be comprehended. Applied to any one family, the results are appalling. Applied to a quarter of the world's population, one's breath is taken away at the thought of the consequences to the race. Applied beyond the quarter to the half of humanity, and what hope in human living remains? And yet the precise purpose of Communistic endeavors is to spread this satanic doctrine *throughout the world!*

Communism Needs No State

We have seen Communism's designs on the individual, on God and religion, and on the family. What does it hope to accomplish with regard to the State? Recall, first, that in the Christian concept of the social order, the State is a society of divine origin insofar as man cannot live alone if he would meet his needs adequately. His nature necessitates social living. This includes family life in which he receives existence and the things necessary to meet the first needs of his human nature. But familial resources are limited, hence the family reaches out to the larger society of the State in which its temporal wants are adequately met. The State is founded on the needs of man's nature, and hence can be traced, through the family, to the law of nature, and from thence to the eternal law of God. The State is therefore a divinely appointed society, necessary and natural to man.

But since Communism denies the Christian concept of man, it denies, as a logical consequence, his needs. According to Communism, man doesn't need a divine destiny because his origin was not divine. He doesn't need family life because he is destined for the collectivity. He doesn't need natural rights because he doesn't exist for a personal goal. He doesn't need God and religion because they do not exist. He has been duped — there is only material progress as a reality. He doesn't need the State, because there is no family in the true sense of the word. The State, therefore, like the family, the individual, religion, and God must be abolished. The whole social order must be overthrown and an entirely new order initiated. But, we ask, what of man's nature? Can that be discarded, too, and a new nature given to future men? And if so, by whom? Now God is the Author of man's nature. It was He who gave man his divine origin and destiny, his social nature, his natural, inalienable, inviolable rights, his consequent obligations, the family, the State, human authority, law, and government. Is Communism going to turn creator and produce a new type of men? Impossible! Never so long as God makes men and breathes into them an immortal soul with all that that means, can Communism succeed in its experiment. All things are made for a purpose, and to misuse the thing is to defeat the purpose; to distort the purpose is to wreck the thing. Unless Communism, therefore, creates a new type of nature (*which it is unable to do*) it will fail to achieve its goal. It will have wrecked humanity in attempting a job with an instrument (man) unsuited to the purpose (a classless, propertyless society) for which it was being used.

Pope Pius XI writes: "Communism is a system full of errors and sophisms. It is in opposition both to reason and to Divine Revelation. It subverts the social order, because it means the destruction of its foundations; because it ignores the true origin and purpose of the State; because it denies the rights, dignity and liberty of human personality."

Overthrow of the State

Communistic writings have outlined the procedure for this vast undertaking sponsored by the party. To effect the goal of absolute equality, society must be leveled off. There must be no one wealthier, more powerful economically, more influential politically, than any other. Therefore private possessions, the Capitalistic system, and the State must all go. We shall treat of the first two in part 4, reserving for now the explanation of the method by which the Communists hope to abolish the State.

The State, claims Communism, has no other end than exploitation, that is, the selfish or unfair use of things for one's advantage, for what one gets out of them. Now let us remark here that exploitation is a base end. It is, for instance, to simulate friendship for this or that person because of the shows and dinners one gets out of it. It is to "treat" a classmate in order to copy his homework or notebook. Exploitation is base, very selfish, unfair.

This is the charge that Communism levels against the State. Communism says, in effect, that the State exploits the working man by permitting the capitalist to receive the profit on his productions. Communism says, again, that the State is guilty too, because it protects the exploiters of the workman, it shields those who rob workmen of the profit on production. The only thing to do about the State, therefore, is to abolish it, for its only end is exploitation.

With that conclusion reached, and with the dissemination of this principle to the working classes everywhere, the actual overthrow will, they say, commence. It is to be a violent one, for it must overthrow the whole existing social order. It must be by means of revolution and bloodshed for the "exploiters" will resist their overthrow. They will not accept it mildly; it must be imposed upon them. The "exploited" must pull down the "exploiter" from the higher levels of wealth, power, and influence which they have attained. Then, when all are leveled off, when society is a single classless class, there will be no further need for the State. In a classless society there are no exploiters who need the protection of the State. The need for the State will no longer be felt. It will have no reason for existence. It will be put out of existence — overthrown.

How long the process will take, Communists cannot predict. It is twenty-four years since the Red Revolution of October 1917, in Russia and in that time, despite the deliberate destruction of millions of lives, *even economic equality has not been attained*. But the revolution will continue, they insist, until their aim is won. Russia, Mexico, Spain have all felt the revolution sponsored by Communism. Since those horrible days, history has not advanced far enough to give an accurate picture or to reveal the true results.

An official Communistic document, *The Communistic Manifesto*, indicates that a constitutional method of effecting a reform is not acceptable to the party. From that document we quote:

> The Communists everywhere support every revolutionary movement against the existing social and political order of things.... Communists disdain to conceal their views and aims. They openly declare that their ends can be attained only by the forcible overthrow of existing conditions. Let the ruling classes tremble at the Communist revolution. The proletarians [working classes] have nothing to lose but their chains. They have the world to win.

Briefly, the procedure is planned in this way: By revolution the working classes (the proletarians) hope to seize the Capitalistic state (the bourgeois state). They hope to paralyze its activity. They aim then to set up a dictatorship of the workers (the proletarian dictatorship or state). The process is not completed at that. *No state* must be allowed to survive, not even the proletarian state. That state is a necessary halfway measure to keep down the defeated bourgeois state which will try to regain its power. It is the duty of the proletarian dictatorship to see to it that the destruction of the Capitalistic state is final and absolute. The proletarians must seize the State power and the means of production. It must use the powers and the machinery of the State to turn over to the workers the total means of production. The government of persons then becomes the administration of things. No government will be necessary because all are equal. There will be no ruler and ruled. The only thing necessary will be the administration of the wealth of the collectivity.

Let us remark here that the administration of the goods of the collectivity requires a body of administrators even as in the State the governing of persons requires a body of governors. Now if there are to be no classes, if all are to be absolutely equal, who will constitute the body of administrators? Dr. Sheen aptly remarks that the whole scheme merely substitutes the privilege of power under Communism for the privilege of wealth under Capitalism. The distinction between the "privileged" and the "unprivileged" still remains. Only the title has been changed. *Wealth* becomes *power*. Pope Leo XIII remarked:

> No matter what changes may be made in forms of government, there will always be differences and inequalities of condition in the State; society cannot exist or be conceived without them. Some there must be who dedicate themselves to the work of the commonwealth, who make the laws, who administer justice, whose advice and authority govern the nation in times of peace, and defend it in war. Such men clearly occupy the foremost place in the State, and should be held in the foremost estimation, for their work touches most nearly and effectively the general interests of the community. Those who labor at a trade or calling do not promote the general welfare in such a fashion as this; but they do in the most important way benefit the nation, though less directly.

To return now to the Communist program: after the State with its machinery has been seized, a new type of State will arise temporarily in order to cut loose the working men from their exploiters and to establish the true Communist social order which is a classless class. Then, when that final step has been reached, the intermediate state, the proletarian dictatorship, will wither away. Stalin, in writing of this period of the dictatorship of the proletariat, says:

> There are three fundamental aspects of the dictatorship of the proletariat: (1) The utilization of the power of the proletariat for the suppression of the exploiters, for the defense of the country, for the consolidation of the ties with the proletarians of other lands, and for the development and the victory of the revolution in all countries; (2) the utilization of the power of the proletariat in order to detach the toiling and exploited masses once and for all from the bourgeoisie, to consolidate the alliance

of the proletariat with these masses, to enlist these masses in the work of socialist construction, and to assure the state leadership of these masses by the proletariat; (3) the utilization of the power of the proletariat for the organization of socialism, for the abolition of classes, for the transition to a society without classes, to a society without a state.

Equality under Communism

This, then, is the Communist program as it affects the State. Naturally we find its starting principle in opposition to the Christian concept of the State. The State, in God's plan, is for a good purpose. It is a means and not an end. It makes a definite contribution to the complete development of the human personality, and as such it is necessary in human association. *It must not be allowed to be seized and overthrown! A* classless society is an impossibility among human beings, and even in its starting principle, Communism is doomed to failure. Listen to Pope Leo XIII in his encyclical on *The Condition of Labor:*

> Let it be laid down, in the first place, that humanity must remain as it is. It is impossible to reduce human society to a level. The Socialists may do their utmost, but all striving against nature is vain. There naturally exists among mankind innumerable differences of the most important kind; people differ in capability, in diligence, in health, and in strength; and unequal fortune is a necessary result of inequality in condition. Such inequality is far from being disadvantageous either to individuals or to the community; social and public life can go on only by the help of various kinds of capacity and the playing of many parts, and each man, as a rule, chooses the part which particularly suits his case.... If any there are who hold out to a hardpressed people freedom from pain and trouble, undisturbed repose and constant enjoyment — they cheat the people and impose upon them, and their lying promises will only make the evil worse than before.

The Communists are a degenerate offspring of Socialists.

Pope Leo said, as quoted above: "There naturally exist among mankind innumerable differences of the most important kind." Let us see in what ways equality cannot be effected. Is there equality of physical powers among individuals? of health? of strength? of stature? of capacity? Equality of physique can be ruled out at once. Is there equality of mind? Is there a universal intelligence level? Is there equality of mental attainments? power of judgment? clarity of ideas? Ordinary experience declares that there is not, and the words of Pope Leo quoted above lend certitude to our experience. Is there equality of willpower? Is there equality of virtue? Is there equality of supernatural life in souls? The closest we can come to equality in human beings is in man as man. That is, each man is possessed of a human nature, created by God, destined for God, the bearer of rights and having a morally free will. In the whole of his humanity every man is a man; in his individual capacities he differs from every other man.

Let us go outside of man and look for equality in the things of man. Can there be equality of returns made for labor? Can there be equality of incomes? "Equality of incomes" renders the question more difficult to answer, because it means more than pecuniary returns. Real income includes more than the material. It includes the pleasures derived from the labor. For instance, a boy who likes the work may spend a whole holiday clerking in a store for two dollars. A boy who dislikes the work and who derives displeasure from it would not be satisfied even if he were paid five dollars for the same work. Real income, therefore, includes the satisfaction one derives. The states of mind add to or detract from the income. Now to try to attain equality of returns on labor, one would have to include the pleasure or the pain, the peace of mind or the anxiety, which accompany a task. But these things cannot be measured in terms of money or material goods, which is the ordinary medium of payment for services rendered.

Apart from states of mind and feeling, can there be equality of condition of labor: environment, skill, hours, fatigue, and the like? We know that there cannot be. Surely there is a great difference between working in a coal mine and working in a pleasant office. Between opportunities in laboring there can be no equality, either. Nature, for instance, provides some with soil more fertile than others, hence one farmer has a better "opportunity" than another. We agree with Pope Leo and Christian philosophy that inequalities of all kinds exist by the very nature of things, and the ideal of establishing a classless class is impossible of attainment. The ideal is based on several erroneous suppositions: (1) that equality of rewards can be measured; (2) assuming that they could be measured, that equal distribution could be made to each according to their contribution and their needs; (3) that, even if equal distribution of equal rewards could be made, everyone would be satisfied that the whole process really was just and each had received equal returns.

Neither social, economic, nor political equality can be established no matter how the Communists might struggle to achieve it. All struggle against nature is in vain.

Thus we have viewed Communism as it is seen in its effects upon the individual, the family, and the State. These phases of Communism rightly belong in our discussion of man in society. Other aspects of Communism, namely, the two sharpest weapons it uses, will be discussed in part 4. Those two weapons are the fomenting of class hatred and the abolition of property rights.

Pope Pius XI writes:

> We do not think it necessary to warn upright and faithful children of the Church against the impious and nefarious character of Communism. But We cannot contemplate without sorrow the heedlessness of those who seem to make light of these imminent dangers and with stolid indifference allow the propagation far and wide of those doctrines which seek by violence and bloodshed the destruction of all society. Even more severely must be condemned the foolhardiness of those who neglect to remove or modify such conditions as exasperate the minds of the people, and so prepare the way for the overthrow and ruin of the social order.... No one can be at the same time a sincere Catholic and a true Socialist. (Encyclical on *The Condition of Labor*)

Totalitarian Philosophies

A brief discussion of totalitarianism will help to clarify our thoughts as to the likenesses between Communism which aims to overthrow the State; and Nazism and Fascism which grant the State supreme domination. We shall see why the term *totalitarian* can be predicated for all three forms.

Mussolini is reputed as being the first to use the term *totalitarian*. In a now-famous article explaining the Fascist doctrine and movement, he wrote: "For the Fascist, everything is in the State, and outside of the State nothing legal or spiritual can exist or be of any value. Thus is Fascism said to be *totalitarian*." In this sense, too, is Nazism totalitarian.

The chief tenets of totalitarianism are these: (1) Individual rights and liberties are destroyed. (2) The ruling power is supreme and unlimited in its functioning. (3) There is only one political party tolerated. ("All the others are in jail," remarked one Russian labor journal. We might add, "or in concentration camps, or perhaps even purged out of existence!") (4) The doctrines of *the Party* are given expression through what we might designate as a *party religion*, which disseminates the views and acts as some kind of "authority" for the policies of the party. (5) Nothing outside of the State, without direct reference to the State, has foundation or worth. But since God is "outside the State" and divinely granted rights are "outside the State" according to Christian philosophy, God and inalienable rights become meaningless in a totalitarian regime. "Everything is in the State" means just that for the advocates of the system: authority arises with the State and party; rights are State-granted and, by that fact, State-revoked arbitrarily. No freedom of speech and of press, of religion and education are recognized by the State, hence they are neither "legal nor sacred." The family has State purposes to perform. Any purposes of family and marriage life apart from State purposes, cannot "be of any value." (6) The individual is completely the instrument of the State and the State powers are limited by nothing; they are claimed to be absolute. Religion, the family, and the individual must give way before State-conducted education. Family rights and Church rights in education simply are nonexistent; the State or party is the only educator. (7) Law becomes, not an effective direction to man's goal and a protection of natural rights, but a means to the concentration of immense power: a means to effect and control party purposes. Law has no religious and ethical basis because religion and God are nonexistent in totalitarian philosophies, for the State or party is the ultimate end of man's existence.

These are the chief features of totalitarian regimes. Note that we used the expression repeatedly "the State or party." In a longer discussion of totalitarianism this could receive more detailed attention. Let it suffice here to indicate that *totalitarianism* assumes various forms. If it had one and only one form, then we would not distinguish between Fascism and Nazism and Communism as we do. In Italy, the State is the *total*; and this stands for the nation. In Germany, the *total* is the *party* which dominates the State machinery, namely, the National Socialist Party, and this stands for the *race*. In Russia, the *total* is the party effecting the Communist reform, and this stands for a classless society. We have shown above that the proletarian state is merely an intermediate state destined to wither away when the classless class will have been established. It is not strictly the Communist concept therefore to designate the State as the total in Communistic society. Their substitute for the State is the collectivity — the group. This, therefore, constitutes the Communists' *total*.

There is this in common among the three major totalitarian systems today: the individual is absorbed by the "State," be that the nation, race, or class. The family's purpose is reduced to nation, race, or class purposes. The political religion dictates the policies and directs the activities of the "total." No higher authority than human authority is admitted or deemed even admissible. No religious or moral basis, but only utility — usefulness to party purposes — is the foundation of law and order.

Our Holy Father, Pope Pius XII, writing his encyclical *Unity in Opposing World Evils*, pointed out two grave enemies of peace. The first is the forgetfulness of that law of human solidarity and charity which is dictated and imposed by our common origin and by the equality of rational nature in all men. The second is the divorce of civil authority from every kind of dependence upon the Supreme Being and from every restraint of a higher law derived from God. Then Pope Pius XII shows the effect of this second evil. He says:

> Once the authority of God and the sway of His law are denied in this way, the civil authority as an inevitable result tends to attribute to itself that absolute autonomy which belongs exclusively to the Supreme Maker. It puts itself in the place of the Almighty and elevates the State or group into the last end of life, the supreme criterion of the moral and juridical order, and therefore forbids every appeal to the principles of natural reason and of the Christian conscience.... Where the dependence of human right upon the Divine is denied, where appeal is made only to some insecure idea of a merely human authority, and an autonomy is claimed which rests only upon a utilitarian morality, there Human Law itself justly forfeits in its more weighty application the moral force which is the essential condition for its acknowledgment and also for its demand of sacrifices.

In closing this chapter let us recall that the Christian concept of society says, "Society is for man." The totalitarian concept turns it about: "Man is for society." And by the transposition of those two terms, *man* and *society*, complete chaos characterizes both man and society.

Some Original Sources

Make use of these quotations in your discussions and readings. The first four are all taken from Pope Leo's encyclical on *Human Liberty.*

1. "To reject the supreme authority of God and to cast off all obedience to Him in public matters or even in private and domestic affairs, is the greatest perversion of liberty and the worst kind of Liberalism."

2. "On the one hand the followers of Liberalism demand for themselves and for the State a license which opens the way to every perversity of opinion; and on the other, they hamper the Church in divers ways restricting her liberty within narrowest limits, although from her teaching not only is there nothing to be feared, but in every respect very much to be gained."

Christian Social Principles

3. "Liberalists, who make the State absolute and omnipotent, and proclaim that man should live altogether independently of God, do not admit the liberty of which we speak [namely, true liberty of conscience] which goes hand in hand with virtue and religion; hence whatever is done for its preservation is considered to be an injury and an offense against the State."

4. "We must now consider briefly liberty of speech and liberty of the press. It is hardly necessary to say that there can be no such right as this, *if it be not used in moderation*, and if it pass beyond the bounds and ends of all true liberty.

"For right is a moral power which it would be absurd to suppose that nature has accorded indifferently to truth and falsehood, to justice and injustice.

"Men have a right freely and prudently to propagate throughout the State what things soever are true and honorable, so that as many as possible may possess them. But lying opinions, than which no mental plague is greater, and vices which corrupt the heart and moral life, should be diligently repressed by public authority lest they insidiously work the ruin of the State. The excesses of an unbridled intellect, which unfailingly end in the oppression of the untutored multitude, are no less rightly controlled by the authority of the law than are the injuries inflicted by violence upon the weak....

"If unbridled license of speech and of writing be granted to all, nothing will remain sacred and inviolate; even the highest and truest mandates of nature, justly held to be the common and noblest heritage of the human race, will not be spared.

"Thus truth being gradually obscured by darkness, pernicious and manifold error will easily prevail. Thus, too, license will gain what liberty loses; for liberty will ever be more free and secure, in proportion as license is kept in fuller restraint.

"In regard, however, to any matters of opinion which God leaves to man's free discussion, full liberty of thought and of speech is naturally within the right of every one; for such liberty never leads men to suppress the truth, but often to discover it and to make it known."

The following are all from the encyclical of Pope Pius XI on *Atheistic Communism*.

5. "In such a doctrine [materialistic] there is no room for the idea of God; there is no difference between matter and spirit, between soul and body; there is neither survival of the soul after death nor any hope in a future life....

"Communism strips man of his liberty, robs human personality of all dignity, and removes all the moral restraints that check the eruptions of blind impulse.

"There is no recognition of any right of the individual in his relations to the collectivity; no natural right is accorded to the human personality, which is a mere cog-wheel in the Communist system.

"In man's relations with other individuals, Communists hold the principle of absolute equality, rejecting all hierarchy and divinely-constituted authority, including the authority of parents. What men call authority and subordination is derived from the community as its first and only font.

"Nor is the individual granted any property rights over material goods or the means of production, for inasmuch as these are the source of further wealth, their possession would give one man power over another. Precisely on this score, all forms of private property must be eradicated, for they are at the origin of all economic enslavement.

"Refusing to human life any sacred or spiritual character, such a doctrine logically makes of marriage and the Family a purely artificial and civil institution.... There exists no matrimonial bond of a juridico-moral nature that is not subject to the whim of the individual or of the collectivity. Naturally, therefore, the notion of an indissoluble marriage-tie is scouted.

"Communism is particularly characterized by the rejection of any link that binds woman to the family and the home, and her emancipation is proclaimed as a basic principle. She is withdrawn from the Family and the care of her children, to be thrust, instead, into public life and collective production under the same condition as man. The care of the home and children then devolves upon the collectivity.

"Finally, the right of education is denied to parents, for it is conceived as the exclusive prerogative of the community, in whose name and by whose mandate alone parents may exercise this right."

Perhaps a few Communistic sources will not be out of order.

1. "The bourgeois State does not wither away according to Engels but is put an end to by the proletariat in the course of the revolution. What withers away after the revolution is the proletariat state or semi-state." (Lenin, *State and Revolution*)

2. "The proletarian revolution signifies the forcible invasion of the proletariat into the domain of property relationships of bourgeois society; the expropriation of the exploiting classes, and the transference of power to a class that aims at the radical reconstruction of the economic foundations of society and the abolition of all exploitation of man by man....

"The characteristic feature of the transition period as a whole is the ruthless suppression of the resistance of the exploiters.... The bourgeoisie can be oppressed only by the stern violence of the proletariat. The conquest of power by the proletariat is the violent overthrow of bourgeois power, the destruction of the capitalistic state apparatus (bourgeois armies, police, bureaucratic hierarchy, the judiciary, parliaments) and substituting in its place new organs of proletarian power to serve primarily as instruments for the suppression of the exploiters.

"The victorious proletariat utilizes the conquest of power as a lever of economic revolution; i.e., the revolutionary transformation of the property relations of capitalization into the relationships of the Socialists' mode of production. The starting point of this great economic revolution is the expropriation of the landlord and capitalist, i.e., the conversion of the monopolistic property of the bourgeoisie into the property of the proletariat state." (All taken from *A Program of Communism*)

3. "The revolution does not simply 'happen'; it must be made. This does not mean that the Communist party 'makes' the revolution. The Socialist revolution is carried out by the great masses of toilers. The Communist party, as the vanguard of the most conscious toilers, acts as their organizer and their guide." (Browder, *What Is Communism?*)

4. "We say that our morality is wholly subordinated to the interests of the class-struggle of the proletariat. We deduce our morality from the facts and needs of the class-struggle of the proletariat.... That is why we say that a morality taken from outside of human society does not exist for us; it is a fraud. For us morality is subordinated to the interests of the proletarian class-struggle." (Lenin, *Religion*)

5. "In what sense do we deny ethics, morals? In the sense in which they are preached by the bourgeoisie, which deduces these morals from God's commandments. Of course, we say that we do not believe in God. We know perfectly well that the clergy, the landlords, and the bourgeoisie all claimed to speak in the name of God, in order to protect their own interests as exploiters. We deny all morality taken from superhuman or non-class conceptions. We say that this is a deception, a swindle, a befogging of the minds of the workers and peasants in the interests of the landlords and capitalists." (Lenin, *Religion*[1])

In addition to others, which will be given later, we give now several excerpts from Pope Pius on *Liberalism* (individualism). He says:

1. "You know, Venerable Brethren and Beloved Children, you know full well the admirable teaching which has made the encyclical on *The Condition of Labor* forever memorable. In this document the Supreme Shepherd, grieving for 'the misery and wretchedness pressing unjustly' on such a large proportion of mankind, boldly took in his own hands the cause of workingmen, 'surrendered, isolated and helpless, to the hardheartedness of employers and the greed of unchecked competition.' He sought help neither from Liberalism nor Socialism. The former had already shown its utter impotence to find a right solution of the social question, while the latter would have exposed human society to still graver dangers by offering a remedy much more disastrous than the evil it designs to cure.

2. "With regard to the civil power, Leo XIII boldly passed beyond the restrictions imposed by Liberalism, and fearlessly proclaimed the doctrine that the civil power is more than the mere guardian of law and order, and that it must strive with all

---

[1] Quoted by Charles J. McFadden, *The Philosophy of Communism* (New York: Benziger Brothers, 1939).

zeal 'to make sure that the laws and institutions, the general character and administration of the commonwealth, should be such as of themselves to realize public well-being and private prosperity.'

3. "The encyclical on *The Condition of Labor*, completely overthrew those tottering tenets of Liberalism which has long hampered effective interference by the government. It prevailed upon the peoples themselves to develop their social policy more intensely and on truer lines, and encouraged the elite among Catholics to give such efficacious help and assistance to rulers of the state that in legislative assemblies they were not infrequently the foremost advocates of the new policy. Furthermore, not a few recent laws dealing with social questions were originally proposed to the suffrages of the people's representatives by ecclesiastics thoroughly imbued with Leo's teaching, who afterwards with watchful care promoted and fostered their execution."

In speaking of Pope Leo's plea for organization of workers, employers, Pope Pius says:

4. "Among these societies Leo attributed prime importance to societies consisting either of workingmen alone, or of workingmen and employers together. He devotes much space to describing and commending these societies and expounds with remarkable prudence their nature, reason and opportunities, their rights, duties and laws.

"The lesson was well timed. For at that period rulers of not a few nations were deeply infected with Liberalism and regarded such unions of workingmen with disfavor, if not with open hostility. While readily recognizing and patronizing similar corporations amongst other classes, with criminal injustice they denied the innate right of forming associations to those who needed them most for self-protection against oppression by the more powerful."

Summary

1. There is some truth underlying both Liberalism and Communism. For instance, it is perfectly true that the individual is possessed of inalienable rights and in this he transcends society (Liberalism's principle). On the other hand, it is true, too, that society has rights which the individual is bound to respect and to subject himself (Communism's principle). They are each *partial aspects*. The partial aspects *cannot be divorced* one from the other without forfeiting truth. Liberalism and Communism are one-sided because they admit one aspect only and deny the other. They carry the one admitted principle to excess until it ceases to be a *good*.

2. Liberalism makes the individual politically, economically, and religiously free from authority. It isolates the individual from society and makes each one a law unto himself.

3. Liberalism scorns the idea of an authority beyond the individual. No one has the right to rule another for all are equally free. There is really no *right*

to rule, they say, and those who run the government merely "run the business" without positive right to rule and sanctions to enforce government.

4. Government is merely the will of the people, according to Liberalistic political theory. Authority, it claims, is resident in the people. It has no origin in the Almighty Being, and no religious or moral sanctions.

5. Liberalists misuse the word *liberty*, for what they advocate as freedom of thought and action is a false concept and it degenerates into license.

6. Greed, avarice, unlimited free competition, domination of the masses, and violation of rights mark Liberalistic society.

7. Communism is the offspring of Liberalism, declared Pope Pius XI. Where the latter extolled the individual to the exclusion of the group, the former absorbs the individual for the sake of the group.

8. Communism is a materialistic philosophy of society and life. There is nothing supernatural, spiritual, sacred in life. Everything is for the good of the collectivity.

9. Under Communism, the collectivity is possessed of all the rights; the individual is burdened with all the duties.

10. Neither the "liberty" of Liberalism nor the "equality" of Communism can be the keynote of the social order. Only fraternity—recognition of the brotherhood of humanity in the common sonship of the almighty Father—can effect the harmony required for successful social living.

11. The "great ideal" of Communism is the classless class. All society is to be leveled until one is equal to every other in the collectivity. It is an ideal impossible of accomplishment, for society cannot exist or be conceived without inequalities—that is, without hierarchy or levels.

12. With the complete absorption of the individual into the Communistic society, the family naturally disappears. It has no purpose other than to supply new citizens to the nation, new soldiers to the army, new workers in production.

13. Divorce is not only permitted but fostered. The matrimonial ties are not founded on principles of religion or morality; hence they are made subject only to the whim of the contracting parties and to the authority claimed by the group.

14. Mothers are sent to work among the ranks of producers of material things. The collectivity assumes control of the education of the children.

15. With no God, no soul, no free will, no individual personal rights, and no family purposes beyond group purposes, Communism has surrendered the only firm foundations of the State.

16. The aims of Communism extend to the abolition of the State. It plans a worldwide revolution of the workers against the capitalists—the proletariat against the bourgeoisie.

17. With the overthrow of the bourgeois society, the proletariat aim to set up the temporary state known as the *dictatorship of the proletariat.* Its purpose is to complete the destruction of the bourgeoisie. Its duration is indefinite. It will last until the bourgeois class no longer exists. So plans Communism.

18. With the total destruction of the bourgeois society, the Communistic society is ready to function. The proletariat dictatorship will then wither away. It will have fulfilled its purpose. It must cease, because it, too, is a kind of domination of group against group. In the ideal Communistic society there are to be no such inequalities. So speaks Communism.

19. Instead of government of persons, there will be only administration of things. But this, *we claim,* is only a transfer of privilege: namely, from that of wealth to that of power. There will still be inequalities, because there will be those who administer public benefits and those to whom they are administered. What is to prevent injustice in the distribution?

20. Inequalities will always exist in human society, says Pope Leo. That is due to the very nature of things. Society cannot be conceived without them.

21. Totalitarian governments or *movements* such as those in Germany and Italy absorb the individual and set up society as the goal of man just as thoroughly as does the Communistic society.

22. Totalitarian philosophies place the origin and functioning of government, of the individual, and of the family within the State or party. All natural rights are denied. Rights, they hold, arise only within the State or party and can, by that very fact, be denied arbitrarily by the State or party.

23. "For the Fascist, everything is in the State, and outside of the State nothing legal or spiritual can exist, or be of any value. Thus is Fascism said to be totalitarian." (Mussolini)

24. Totalitarian regimes are characterized by the following features: no individual rights and liberties; ruling power concentrated and supreme; only one political party; a *party religion* which directs and authorizes all party activities; the individual the instrument of the State or party; law a means to control and enforce; no religious or moral basis for anything; no freedom of speech, press, worship, and so forth.

25. Fascism, Nazism, and Communism are all totalitarian. Fascism preaches supremacy of the *nation;* Nazism, the *race;* Communism the *classless society.*

For Study and Discussion

1. Liberalism is a one-sided aspect of human association. Explain why. What partial truth underlies Liberalistic philosophy? Why is Liberalism a pernicious doctrine?

2. Communism is a one-sided aspect of human associations. Explain why. What partial truth underlies Communistic society? Why is Communism a pernicious doctrine?

3. How do Liberalism and Communism each fall into defect in their views? How do they err by excess?

4. Sum up briefly the Christian view which is the mean between the extremes of Liberalism and Communism.

5. "Each individual is a law unto himself." Explain this. Whose doctrine is it? How would you answer it?

6. Explain: "Communism impoverishes human personality by inverting the terms of the relation of man to society." Prove the truth of the statement.

7. What foundation have law and authority in Liberalism and Communism?

8. What is the attitude of each toward religion, God, and morality?

9. Name two striking likenesses between the two philosophies. Name two striking differences between them.

10. What right to rule does Liberalism allow? What right to rule does Communism allow? Where does authority reside according to each?

11. What are the effects of a Liberalistic philosophy when it is applied to religion? to economics?

12. Why is Liberalism's "liberty" a false liberty?

13. Without religion and a moral law, upon what does Liberalism base its notion of right and wrong? How stable is this notion? What effect does it have upon the social order?

14. Sum up Pope Leo's condemnation of Liberalism as quoted from his encyclical on *Human Liberty*.

15. Explain why "no one can be at the same time a sincere Catholic and a true Socialist."

16. Discuss the use of the following words in this chapter: *liberty, equality, fraternity*.

17. How does this principle of St. Thomas apply to Communism: "Man is not subject to the State in all that he is and has."

18. Explain: "Religion is the opium of the people." (Communism)

19. What is the effect of Communistic doctrines on the individual? on the family?

20. Discuss the aims of Communism concerning the revolution; the proletarian dictatorship; the classless class; the fate of the State.

21. What substitute does Communism advocate in place of constitutional reform of the present social order? What do you think of their substitute?

22. What will be the threefold task of the proletariat state or dictatorship? Why must that, too, eventually cease?

23. What grievance has Communism against the present social order and social institutions, especially the State? Who are the exploited? the exploiters?
24. Who are the bourgeoisie? the proletarians?
25. According to the Communist program, what will substitute for the government of persons?
26. Explain the privilege of wealth; the privilege of power; the administration of things.
27. Discuss the impossibility of equality in human society. Quote Pope Leo. Explain the hierarchy of contributions which he mentions. Find the two long excerpts from his *Labor* encyclical and compare them.
28. Discuss the chief tenets of totalitarian philosophy of government.
29. Discuss the variety of expressions of totalitarianism as it is found among the three nations of Italy, Germany, and Russia.

For the Advanced Reader

St. Thomas:
> *Commentary on Second Book of Politics*, chap. 2, lesson 4. (A criticism of Communism from a thirteenth-century philosopher!)

Belloc, Hilaire:
> *The Servile State*

Berdyaev, N.:
> *The Bourgeois Mind*

Lasky:
> *Communism*

McFadden, Charles J.:
> *The Philosophy of Communism*

Tawney:
> *The Protestant Ethic* (for his views on equality)

Papal Encyclicals:
> Pope Leo XIII: *Christian Constitution of States*
> *The Condition of Labor*
> *Human Liberty*
> Pope Pius XI: *The Reconstruction of the Social Order*
> Pope Pius XII: *Unity in Opposing World Evils*

Philosophy of the State, reprinted 1940 from 1939 proceedings of the American Catholic Philosophical Association "The Totalitarian State," pp. 50–65

Man in Society

Human society comprises the human race. Every human being is a member of the society of the human race. There are lesser social units, particular societies, to which men belong. Some of the lesser associations among human beings are necessary for full human development. Some human associations are not so necessary. Among the necessary societies are the family, the State, and the Church. These are primary societies. They are *necessary* societies because they are required by some law. The natural law is the basis of the family and the State. These two societies, therefore, are natural societies, as well as being primary and necessary. God's eternal law whereby He directs all mankind to its goal, and His providence whereby He directs each individual in its multiple activities, is the basis of the supernatural society of the Church. God sent His only-begotten Son to redeem mankind. It is through the Church and the sacraments, chiefly, that the effects of the redemption are applied to individual men.

Society is the means to man's end. The family makes its contribution to this. The State contributes. The Church contributes. All three are necessary. Each has its domain marked out for it by the Almighty. The family, in itself and its resources, is insufficient to attain the true purpose of familial society. It is incomplete as to the means, though its goal is uniquely its own. The family is thus said to be an imperfect society. Its imperfection is due to its insufficiency of means to attain its end. Both the State and the Church come to the assistance of the family and complete its efforts. The State and the Church are perfect societies because they are self-sufficient insofar as they have the means to attain their own ends, respectively. The goal of the Church is the salvation of souls. The end of the State is the common temporal happiness. Ultimately, God, and the possession of God by individual men, is the final end of all creation.

The family, even though an imperfect society, is prior in nature and in time to the State. It possesses in its own right, therefore, priority of natural rights over the State. The natural rights of the family and its individual members are inalienable because they are God-given. They are inviolable by any power on earth.

The family is constituted by marriage. The marriage contract is indissoluble, and in this it differs from other contracts freely entered. Marriage has as its primary natural aim the perpetuation of the race. Nature intends the preservation of the race through the generation of offspring. Without conflicting with this aim, individuals have secondary motives such as personal happiness, community of life, friendship, companionship, and the like.

Christ ennobled the marriage contract by elevating it to the supernatural level. He made it a channel of supernatural life through the grace of the sacrament. Marriage is blessed with a triple good: offspring, mutual fidelity, and inviolable stability. The indissoluble union of one man with one woman is symbolized by the union of Christ and the Church.

The exercise of natural rights by the family is subject to the common good. The family may do nothing in violation of the common good, otherwise it would defeat the very channel through which its own temporal well-being flows. The limitation of the exercise of natural rights, however, must not become abolition of natural rights. The State may not absorb the family or the individual. Both must be allowed free and untrammeled action insofar as no violation of justice toward other families, other individuals, or the common good is incurred.

Though the State and the Church have fixed limits within which lie the spheres of their activities, they are not mutually excluded one from the other. The harmonious cooperation between them results in untold blessings to the State and to the family and to the individual. Because of her mission and her commission, the Church claims the right to be independent of civil authority in matters purely spiritual. For the same reasons, the Church claims the right to lay down the moral principles which should guide human actions in the realms of politics, of economics, and the like. The Church holds herself the foremost teacher of mankind, since Christ commissioned her to "teach all nations" (see Matt. 28:19). She claims the right, therefore, to conduct schools wherein religion and morality are consistently taught. And since she is the deposit of truth, she claims the right to teach all truth — and this includes secular knowledge as well as religious and moral.

The Christian idea of the State holds that all authority, hence civil authority, is derived from God. For this reason the State must acknowledge its dependence upon God. It must have care for religion and morality, and publicly offer worship to God. It must consider itself a creature of God and, in His divinely established plan of creation, it is a means to man's ultimate end, but it is not an end in itself. Its purpose is to promote the common temporal happiness that through its means man may attain his ultimate end which is personal, unending happiness in the possession of the supreme good — union with God.

Non-Christian philosophies of man and society distort the true view of man and society. Either man is made an end in himself and a law unto himself, or society is made man's ultimate end and the source of human rights. Thus the transcendence of man over society is denied and with this denial comes the denial of his divine goal and even the denial of his divine origin. But neither man nor society can long act as though there were no God. God's providence overtakes them and shows to men and to nations their dependence upon Him and the futility of striving against nature and nature's God.

Part 4

Man in Economic Society

20

Man the Worker

Throughout the three previous parts of *Christian Social Principles* we have discussed man, his nature, his social environment, his personal and social rights and duties. We come now, in part 4, to another distinctly human activity: namely, labor.

Labor Distinctly Human

Perhaps you have thought that labor originated as God's punishment upon our first parents. "In the sweat of thy face shalt thou eat bread" (Gen. 3:19). If you have thought this to be the origin of manual labor, you have been mistaken. St. Thomas assures us that man has a *natural inclination* to manual labor. (St. Thomas called all corporal labor *manual.*)

> Manual labor is directed to four things. First and principally to obtain food.... Secondly, it is directed to the removal of idleness whence arise many evils.... Thirdly, it is directed to the curbing of concupiscence, inasmuch as it is a means of afflicting the body. Fourthly, it is directed to almsgiving. It must be observed that under manual labor are comprised all those human occupations whereby man can lawfully gain a livelihood, whether by using his hands, his feet, or his tongue. For watchmen, couriers, and such like who live by their labor, are understood to live by their handiwork.

Quoting Holy Scripture, he reminds us that "man is born to labor as the bird to fly" (see Job 5:7). Now the bird, by its very nature, flies. It would be a very imperfect bird if it had no aptitude for flying. Indeed we could scarcely call it a bird. So man, primarily by his nature rather than by his sin, is ordained to work. Labor is distinctly a human activity. To say it is "distinctly a human activity" means that the term *labor* cannot properly be used of God or of non-human creatures. Let us see why this is so.

Labor is activity. Some activities begin inside the agent and remain inside, producing their effects within him. A thought, for instance, is an activity that begins inside and remains inside. A decision of the will is another activity wholly inside the agent. Labor is not that kind of activity. It is that kind of activity which begins inside and ends outside the one laboring. Its beginning is within the agent; its effect is produced outside. For example, suppose I conceive the notion of making fudge. My will decides that to make fudge is very desirable. Directed by the intellect to do so, the will chooses to take the steps necessary to make the fudge. This activity so far is all within me. So with a deliberate will I begin to act outside of me. I start to work on the ingredients. I meet certain difficulties and overcome some amount of resistance. As a result, I change the materials. I give them a new form; I produce the effect of my activity — fudge. Thus I have worked. I have done a truly rational thing. I have used the powers of my soul and of my body and have produced an effect. I have, to say it quite simply, *labored*.

Now God does not labor in the strict sense of the word. Properly speaking, God did not labor when He produced the world. In the first place, He created the world out of nothing. In the second place, He met with no resistance; He encountered no difficulties. When we speak of the universe as "God's work," it is not in the strict sense of the word that we use *work*. We use *work* in this sense: namely, that God has a purpose and the will and the power to make the universe. At the expression of His will, *Lux fiat*, the universe began to exist. In that way, God is said to *work* and so to be the exemplar of man's work. Man imitates God in these actions, inasmuch as man conceives a purpose for acting, chooses to take the means necessary, and has the power to produce the effect. But man has preexisting materials upon which to expend his energies, whereas God had none nor needed none.

We have said that labor is distinctly a human power. Therefore neither do subhuman creatures labor in the strict sense of the word. Though a beaver, for instance, might act "for a purpose," it certainly is not a *known* purpose to the beaver. God knows the purpose, but the beaver cannot know it. The latter acts wholly through instinct which impels it to fulfill God's purpose without knowing the purpose or the reason. With man it is otherwise. Man knows the purpose of what he does. He wills the means to attain it. He overcomes the difficulties involved. He effects the end through an expenditure of his personal energy. The effect he produces is both known and desired by him.

In the exercise of his faculties, both spiritual and corporal, man has the opportunity of perfecting himself. This is to labor.

Labor Natural and Necessary

We said man's labor is natural. St. Thomas writes: "The Natural Law holds that man lives by his labor . . . and this right is bestowed on man by his Creator." You will recall the statement made in discussing man's need for society. We said God gave to animals food ready-prepared, thick hides and hair for covering, sharp teeth and claws for protection, speed in motion for ready flight. Man is not so provided. However, God gave man reason and hands by means of which he could provide the necessities of life for himself. It is this combination of reason and hands that makes labor possible. Reason is needed to recognize the purpose. Hands are needed to effect the purpose. Now man had both reason and hands before Original Sin. Hence from the very beginning man was equipped by nature for labor. After the Fall, man still had reason and hands. Man was always man. Before the Fall, labor brought enjoyment to Adam and Eve. After the Fall, labor became an absolute necessity for the race as well as a means of atonement for sin.

Pope Leo XIII, in his encyclical on *The Condition of Labor*, remarks: "As regards bodily labor, even had man never fallen from the state of innocence, he would not have been wholly unoccupied; but that which would then have been his free choice, his delight, became afterwards compulsory, and the painful expiation of his sin."

Man must labor to supply at least his physical wants. It is by the expenditure of his physical and mental energy that he can obtain what is necessary for complete living. Let us attempt to formulate a definition of labor. In general we might say that it is the application of effort to the gifts of nature for attaining the things necessary for life's purposes. Here are several more specific definitions given of it. The first one, by Pope Leo XIII says: "To labor is to exert one's self for the sake of procuring what is necessary for the purposes of life, and most of all for self-preservation." In another part of the same encyclical (*The Condition of Labor*) he stresses the fact that what is needed for the preservation of life and for life's well-being cannot be procured from the earth unless man first cultivates it, lavishes his care upon it, and spends the energy of his mind and the strength of his body in procuring it. All this is labor, and it is a natural right inasmuch as man has the right to life and to the things necessary for the attainment of life. But since labor is necessary for procuring nature's gifts, the right of labor is rooted in the natural law.

Pope Pius XI, in speaking of capital and labor, says:

Universal experience teaches us that no nation has ever yet risen from want and poverty to a better and loftier station without the unremitting toil of all its citizens, both employers and employed. But it is no less self-evident that these ceaseless labors would have remained ineffective, indeed could never have been attempted, had not God, the Creator of all things, in His goodness, bestowed, in the first instance, the wealth and resources of nature, its treasures and its powers. For what else is work but the application of one's forces of soul and body to these gifts of nature for the development of one's powers by their means?

Our conclusion then, is this: labor is natural to man and it is necessary to him as well. It is also a distinctly human activity. Let us discuss man's efforts to exercise this natural right. Let us look at him in the realm of economics.

Laissez-Faire versus Economic Dictatorship

It does not seem advisable in a work of this kind to go into an historical study of man's labor from the earliest days of recorded history to the present time. We shall confine our discussion to present economic conditions. You will recall that unlimited competition marked the Liberalistic economic order. The *laissez-faire* or "hands-off" policy gave rise to a minority which was possessed of great wealth and a majority which was possessed of nothing. With an increase of wealth went an increase of power over workmen and of control of production. The right to life and to the means of sustaining life became increasingly more difficult for the worker. It caused a decided rift in the economic order so that the terms *capital* and *labor* have become almost synonymous with opposing armies facing each other with unmasked hostility.

It is precisely this antagonism which Communists take as their starting point. They purpose to sharpen class hatreds as a means to the proletarian revolution. Pope Leo insists that this hostility between the classes is not natural; on the contrary, so unnatural is it, that it upsets the equilibrium of the body politic, for each class requires the other. Labor cannot exist without capital nor can capital exist without labor. The working man needs the means of production, namely, the material and the machines. He needs also the directive agency which effects the goal of production and the distribution of the product. On the other hand, capital needs the working man. It needs the exercise of labor's skill and the employment of labor's strength in tilling the soil, in operating factories, in trading, and in all enterprises of modern economic life. "Indeed," remarks Pope Leo, "their cooperation in this respect is so important that it may be truly said that it is only by the labor of the working man that States grow rich."

Twofold Aspect of Labor

The interdependence of capital and labor, and the relation they bear to the prosperity of the State, call our attention to the dual character of labor. Labor is *personal* and labor is *social*. The personal element of labor can be seen, first, in man. It consists in the "application of one's forces of body and soul." It is the expenditure of the laborer's personal strength. It is a gradual surrender of his life to effect the fruits of labor. Indeed, a workman who spends eight or more hours per day in a factory knows that his labor is personal. Again this personal element of labor can be seen in the thing produced by labor. Pope Leo speaks of man's leaving "the impress of his personality" on the thing produced. In claiming for man the right not only to the use of the land but to the land itself, Pope Leo says: "The soil which is tilled and cultivated with toil and skill utterly changes its condition. It was wild before; it is now fruitful. It was barren, and now it brings forth an abundance. That which has thus altered and improved it [namely man's labor] becomes so truly part of the land as to be in a great measure indistinguishably inseparable from it." The tiller of the soil has put something of himself into the land and he can never completely regain it. So, too, with labor of all kinds. It is truly personal, both on account of the effect on the laborer, and the effect on the thing "worked."

But labor is social, too. This cannot — it must not — be overlooked. Man is a social being. His labor is social as well as personal. His rights and duties are social as well as personal. To say that man's labor is social is to recognize the truth that "it is by the labor of the working man that the State grows rich." The great inventors of all times — from the inventor of the wheel and the discoverer of fire down to modern inventors of the radio and television — have all given the fruits of their labor to others. If Edison had kept exclusively for personal use his numerous inventions, and Alexander Bell had retained the telephone for personal use only, and Field had retained exclusive rights to the ocean cable, if these, we repeat, had not shared their findings, what advance would the world have made? Of what benefit to society would have been their inventions?

Now in the realm of labor in general, rather than in the field of particular inventors, the social aspect of labor is equally important. No civilized country today retains to any degree the factory-in-the-home kind of production.

Production has become socialized. Have you seen the one who made your shoes? who spun the cloth you wear? who sowed and harvested the wheat in your bread? who cared for the cattle which produced milk and meat for your food? No, you have not, for labor has become increasingly social with the advent of large-scale production. It is not primarily individual as in earlier times when each family supplied its own needs. Now, under modern methods, and because of the social contribution the laborer makes, he is entitled to more than mere existence. He must have sufficient means to rear, in decent comfort, the future generation of workers. This is a very great contribution, over and above his labor, which the laborer gives to society.

In decrying the opinion that class is naturally hostile to class and that the rich and poor are intended by nature to live at war with one another, Pope Leo explains the organic unity which should characterize economic endeavors. He likens the efforts of capital and the efforts of labor to the various parts of the body. Each part has its particular task, yet it contributes to the good of the whole inasmuch as it does its own work well. The eye is for seeing, and the ear for hearing, and the feet for walking, and the lungs for breathing, and this is without loss of symmetry in the whole body. So, too, in the economic realm, each "part" has its particular task. There are those who supply the means of production; others who supply the brainpower; still others who supply the physical exertion. These three, distinct as to function, should nevertheless combine to effect harmonious co-action in the body politic, especially in the economic order.

This should not result in discord. Rather the striving of all parts should be characterized by an organic symmetry. The Holy Father writes:

> Just as the symmetry of the human body is the result of the disposition of the members of the body, so, in a State, it is ordained by nature that these two classes [capital and labor] should exist in harmony and agreement, and should, as it were, fit into one another, so as to maintain the equilibrium of the body politic.... Mutual agreement results in pleasantness and good order; perpetual conflict necessarily produces confusion and outrage.

Pope Pius XI takes up the same theme. Stressing the fact that labor has a social as well as an individual (personal) aspect to be considered, he says (my emphasis): "Unless human society forms a truly social and organic body; unless labor be protected in the social and juridical [i.e., governmental] order; unless the various forms of human endeavor dependent one upon the other are united in mutual harmony and mutual support; *unless, above all, brains, capital and labor combine together for common effort,* man's toil cannot produce due fruit."

Before discussing antagonism between capital and labor, let us make sure that we understand the meaning of the second term, namely, of capital.

What Is Capital?

In the time of St. Thomas (the thirteenth century) the term capital was unknown among the people. They spoke of their *goods* and their *possessions.* To the people of that time, money was considered only a means of exchange. They did not think of it as being *productive.* For us today, the term capital implies that money is productive. Capital is wealth, and wealth is devoted to the creation of new wealth. We think of property and of capital in the same terms, because we view money, not alone in itself, but in its substitutes and derivatives; that is, in notes, in mortgages, in possessions of any kind, particularly in *the means of production*: that is, in land, in shops, in machines, and the like. In other words, capital is the accumulation of economic goods used to promote the production of other goods.

Capitalism, therefore, is the system which promotes the production of wealth through wealth. The production, distribution, and exchange of goods is systematized and is effected through the cooperation of those who supply the wealth, those who supply the labor, and those who supply the direction or the management and the distribution of the products.

When one speaks of *capital and labor* he means (and it is so understood generally) the two groups which effect the production of wealth. *Capital* is used for *Capitalism* and *labor* for *laborers,* so that the conflict spoken of by the Holy Fathers means a conflict between *persons.* The distinction is important, because only *persons* are moral beings; only persons know and will right or wrong. If one were to conceive of the conflict as being between the money and machines on the one hand, and the abstract physical exertion on the other, it would not be viewing a moral issue.

It must be remembered that Communism and Catholicism are in agreement in this: that there exist class differences; that injustice characterizes the system; that a remedy ought to be applied as quickly and efficiently as possible. But Communism and Catholicism are not in agreement beyond this. Communism holds that the differences are necessary ones. Catholicism denies their necessity and their naturalness. Communism declares the system to be wholly unjust and therefore to be overthrown. Catholicism denies inherent injustice and shows that the system is not unjust in its nature, but that injustices have sprung up in the practice. Communism aims to abolish the classes. Catholicism aims to abolish the conflict. Communism offers as the remedy, the abolition of the Capitalist system and therefore of private possessions; Catholicism preaches the abolition of the injustices, the return to morality, and the inviolability of private property. Communism denies that any morality is involved in the issue. Catholicism claims the basic issue is a moral and religious one because it concerns human personality and dignity and the exercise of the virtue of justice. Communism declares that the first step in the abolition of the system is to stir up class hatred to such a pitch that revolution ensues, property is seized, and capitalists are obliterated. Catholicism insists upon a reconciliation of the classes, the wider distribution of property, and a bond of union being formed between those who possess the wealth and those who render it increasingly productive.

Economic Dictatorship

Pope Pius XI characterized the present century economic situation as "hard, cruel, and relentless in a ghastly measure." He points (1) to "the vast difference between the few who hold excessive wealth and the many who live in destitution"; (2) to the "small number of very rich men who have been able to lay upon the masses of the poor a yoke little better than slavery itself"; (3) to the economic dictatorship arising from the fact that: "in our days not alone is wealth accumulated, but immense power and despotic economic domination is concentrated in the hands of a few and those few frequently not the owners, but only the trustees and directors of invested funds, who administer them at their good pleasure"; (4) to its cause: "This accumulation of power, the characteristic note of the modern economic order, is a *natural* result of limitless free competition which permits the survival of those only who are the strongest, which often means those who fight most relentlessly, who pay least heed to the dictates of conscience" (my emphasis); and (5) to its remedy in general terms: "A just share only of the fruits of production should be permitted to accumulate in the hands of the wealthy, and that an ample sufficiency be supplied to the working men ... that by thrift they may increase their possessions."

Possessed versus Unpossessed Wealth

Capital and labor need one another. That is a basic principle. Pope Pius expresses it thus: "Unless a man apply his labor to his own property, an alliance must be formed between *his toil* and his neighbor's property, for each is helpless without the other." It is very false to hold, as the Communists do, that the full result of labor belongs to the workers. They hold that it is by labor alone that capital becomes fruitful; hence labor has the right to all the returns. Marx's theory supposes that the capital one works upon is unpossessed by anyone. That is false. Money, money substitutes, land, shops, machines, raw products, and so forth are *capital*; but they are possessed.

When Robinson Crusoe was shipwrecked on an uninhabited island, the "wealth" of the island was unpossessed. There were no human beings on the island with a just claim to the resources of the island. Robinson Crusoe, therefore, was justified in using trees for a shelter, animals for food and clothing, and any other things with which he supplied his needs from the island's wealth. The justification rests upon the fact that the goods were unpossessed. But the wealth upon which the laborer works is not unpossessed. Either it is his own possession, in which case he has the right to the returns on it; or it is the possession of another, in which case, in the words of Pope Pius XI, he must, "form an alliance between his toil and his neighbor's property."

Against the Communistic theory of labor returns, Pope Pius writes: "It is entirely false to ascribe the results of their combined efforts to either party alone; and it is flagrantly unjust that either should deny the efficacy of the other and seize all the profits."

Capital Claims All

Over a long period of years capitalists claimed all the products and profits. They left to the laborer the barest minimum necessary to repair his strength. They paid wages which permitted only the most meagre existence for the parents and children. This is a violation of justice. Human beings are not to be used merely as instruments for money making. They have a dignity that is theirs by reason of their nature and their labor. Human labor is dignified in virtue of the example of Christ who, being the Son of God, chose to become a carpenter and to be esteemed as the Son of a carpenter. From this we learn that man's true dignity lies, not in his wealth, but in his virtue. It has been no uncommon violation of the laborers' rights to grind down men's bodies and stupefy their minds by excessive amounts and intolerable conditions of labor.

Labor Claims All

Equally unjust is the doctrine advanced by the laboring man, namely, that all products and profits, excepting those required to repair and replace invested capital, belong by every right to the working man. This is utterly false. Wage earners are not entitled to all the fruits of production inasmuch as they worked on their neighbor's property. An equitable share must be given to each class, not a one-for-one distribution, but rather to each what is *due* to it in the light of the common good.

Pope Pius XI writes: "Entirely false is the principle, widely propagated today that the worth of labor and therefore the equitable return to be made for it, should equal the worth of its net result. Thus the right to the full product of his toil is claimed for the wage earner. How erroneous this is appears from what We have written concerning capital and labor."

To determine what is a due share, and to bring the distribution of wealth into conformity with the common good and social justice, is not at all easy. Pope Leo writes,

> It is not easy to define the relative rights and the mutual duties of the wealthy and of the poor, of capital and of labor. And the danger lies in this, that crafty agitators constantly make use of these disputes to pervert men's judgments and to stir up the people to sedition.
>
> But all agree, and there can be no question whatever, that some remedy must be found, and quickly found, for the misery and wretchedness which press so heavily at this moment on the large majority of the very poor.
>
> The ancient workmen's Guilds were destroyed in the last century and no other organization took their place. Public institutions and the laws have repudiated the ancient religion.
>
> Hence it has come to pass that the workingmen have been given over, isolated and defenseless, to the callousness of employers and the greed of unrestrained competition. The evil has been increased by rapacious usury ... which is practiced by avaricious and grasping men.
>
> And to this must be added the custom of working by contract, and the concentration of so many branches of trade in the hands of a few individuals, so that a small number of very rich men have been able to lay upon the masses of the poor a yoke little better than slavery itself.

This statement of Pope Leo in the encyclical on *The Condition of the Working Classes* gives a true picture of that domination in economic affairs which has been termed *economic dictatorship*.

"Not Vicious of Its Very Nature"

The Capitalistic system comprises the *means* of production and the *agents* of production: namely, capital and labor. This system, even though in its present practice it be dominated by greed and avarice and injustice, is not to be condemned *as a system*, but only in its practices. The system is capable of producing the good of individuals and of the common good if it be rightly administered, that is, according to the norms of justice. For just as in human nature there is a hierarchy of capacities which is found naturally in civil society, so in the economic realm there is also a hierarchy of contributions with the resultant inequality of position and its consequent subordination and mastery which inevitably attends inequality in fortunes and in position. Hence the Capitalistic system, simply because it is based on classes, is not, by that fact, to be condemned, for it is not, *in itself*, vicious. Its practices become vicious when the due order of parts is upset, when failure to respect justice enters into the system, when its activity departs from the norms of religion and of morality.

The first step, therefore, in the breakup of this economic dictatorship, is to unite the classes. "Unite," we say, not "equalize." Society cannot be conceived of or exist without inequalities, Pope Leo reminds us. An alliance between capital and labor will effect a cure. Perhaps it will not be the whole cure, but assuredly it will be some portion of the only cure, for mutual agreement results in pleasantness and good order. A recognition of the dignity of human labor will lend its help. The poor will learn that there is no disgrace in poverty, that there is nothing to be ashamed of in seeking one's bread by labor. They will hold before their eyes the example of Christ in the workshop of Nazareth and appreciate the new dignity which came to the working man by Christ's labor.

The rich will remember that Christ loves the poor; that Christ Himself was poor; that He associated with the poor. They will realize that it is through the bounty and goodness of God that the earth has great resources stored away for the use of man. Reflecting thus, the rich will see in themselves the stewards of God in the dispensation of nature's wealth. This reflection will keep down the pride of the rich. It will incline them to generosity. It will make them see in the poor their brothers in Christ, and hold out their hands to the poor in friendly accord. But this requires the teachings of religion. It requires the practice of the virtues of justice and of charity, of humility and of benevolence. It requires a strong faith in God and a recognition of His Mystical Body. But these things cannot be had by those who deny God, nor by those who arrogate to themselves all rights, nor by those who despise the poor and the laboring man. So that, ultimately, the alliance which ought to be effected between the rich and the poor, between capital and labor, must be rooted in religion and morality.

Pope Leo writes:

> If Christian precepts prevail, the two classes will not only be united in
> the bonds of friendship, but also in those of brotherly love. For they will
> understand and feel that all men are the children of the common father,
> that is, of God; that all have the same end, which is God Himself, Who
> alone can make either men or angels absolutely and perfectly happy;
> that all and each are redeemed by Jesus Christ, and raised to the dignity
> of children of God, and thus are united in brotherly ties both with each
> other and with Jesus Christ; that the blessings of nature and the gifts
> of grace belong in common to the whole human race, and that, to all,
> except to those who are unworthy, is promised the inheritance of the
> Kingdom of Heaven.

Some Original Sources

The basis of the statement that only man labors but not the lower creatures is found
in St. Thomas's discussion of how things tend toward an end. One might object to
the statement that "the beaver does not labor," but perhaps the following will clarify
the point. It is true that all things act for an end, even the water flowing downstream.
The point is, the end is not known by beings lower than man, and hence they *are
directed* rather than that they *direct* their actions.

St. Thomas speaks of the classes of finite beings which "act for a purpose" but
the term cannot be used in the same sense of all of them. He writes:

1. "A thing tends to an end by its action or movement in two ways:
   (a) First, as a thing, moving itself to the end—as man;
   (b) Secondly, as a thing moved by another to the end, as an arrow tends to
       a determinate end through being moved by the archer, who directs his
       action to the end.

"Therefore those things that are possessed of reason, move themselves to an
end, because they have dominion over their actions, through their free will which
is the faculty of will and reason." (Man belongs to this class of things.)

"But those things that lack reason tend to an end, by natural inclination, as being moved by another and not by themselves; since they do not know the nature
of an end as such, and consequently cannot ordain anything to an end, but can
be ordained to an end only by another." (This applies to any subhuman creature.)

"Consequently it is proper to the rational nature to tend to an end as directing
and leading itself to the end; whereas it is proper to the irrational nature to tend

to an end, as directed or led by another, whether it know the end, as do irrational animals, or do not know it, as is the case of those things which are altogether void of knowledge." (*Summa Theologica*, vol. 6, pp. 4–5)

Concerning the nature of work itself, namely, that it is activity or operation, St. Thomas says this:

2. "It is impossible to know a thing perfectly unless we know its activities: since from the manner and kind of its operations, we judge the measure and quality of its power; while the power of a thing demonstrates its nature: because a thing has naturally an aptitude for work according as it actually has such and such a nature."

(Man has reason and hands by which and with which he works. His works show forth his rational nature because he can judge present and past and make provisions for the future.)

St. Thomas continues:

"Now the activity of a thing is twofold: one that stays in the very worker and is a perfection of the worker himself, such as to sense, [hear, smell, taste, etc.] to understand, and to will;

"[There is] another that passes into an outward thing, and is a perfection of the thing that has been made by the labor, such as to heat, to cut, to build.…

"Now both of these two kinds of activity belong to God: the former, in that He understands, wills, rejoices, and loves; the latter, in that He brings forth things into being, preserves them, and rules them.

"Since, however, the former operation is a perfection of the one who performs them, while the latter operation [which passes out into the thing made] is a perfection of the thing made, and since the agent is naturally prior to the thing made and is its cause, it follows that the first of the above mentioned operations is the reason of the second one, and it naturally precedes it, as a cause precedes its effect."

(Reason and will precede and are the reason of the exterior activities which are properly called *work*; hence work is that activity which produces an effect in a thing, by an agent that can know and will to produce the effect.)

"This is clearly seen in human affairs: for the thought and the will of the craftsman is the origin and reason of the work of building.

"Accordingly the first of the two operations [that which remains wholly within] which perfects the doer, claims for itself the name of *operation* or *action*, while the second, as being a perfection of the thing which is made, takes the name of *work*; wherefore those things which a craftsman brings into being by an action of this kind are said to be his handiwork." (*Summa Contra Gentiles*, vol. 2; pp. 1–2)

3. "Manual labor is … a precept of the Natural Law.

"Now the very constitution of our bodies teaches us that nature intends us to labor. We are not provided with raiment, as other animals are furnished with hides. Neither has nature given us weapons, like the horns which she has bestowed on cattle; nor the claws wherewith lions defend themselves. Nor is any food, except milk, supplied naturally to us.

"In place of the gifts bestowed upon other animals, man is endowed with reason which teaches him to supply his needs, and with hands, wherewith he can carry out the dictates of reason.

"As the precepts of the Natural Law regard all men without distinction, the law of manual labor does not apply more to religious than to others." (St. Thomas was defending religious against the charges of those who said that religious *must* devote their lives to manual labor.)

"Nevertheless, it is not true, that all men are bound to work with their hands. There are certain laws of nature, which, in their observance, are of profit to none except to him who obeys them. Such is the law obliging man to eat. These laws must be obeyed by every individual man.

"Other Natural Laws, for example, that of generation of offspring, regard not only the man who obeys them, but are advantageous to the whole human race. It is not necessary that all these laws should be obeyed by every individual; for no single man is competent to perform all the activities which are needed for the continuation of the human race.

"One individual would not suffice for the different works of reproduction, of invention, of architecture, of agriculture, and for the other functions which must be exercised for the continuance of the human race. To supply the needs common to all mankind, one individual must assist another; just as, in the body, one limb is subserved by another.

"Hence we see that no man is bound to any particular work, unless necessity obliges him to it, and unless no one else will accomplish it for him.... With regard, therefore, to manual labor, I maintain that it is not incumbent upon anyone unless he be in want of something which must be produced by such labor, and which he cannot, without sin, [as by theft] procure from any other man.

"Nor can it be proved that anyone, be he layman or religious, is bound to manual labor, except to save himself from death by starvation, or to avoid a sinful manner of gaining a livelihood." (*An Apology for Religious Orders*, pp. 157–159)

4. "Manual labor is directed to four things:
   (a) First and principally to obtain food.
   (b) Secondly, it is directed to the removal of idleness whence arise many evils.
   (c) Thirdly, it is directed to the curbing of concupiscence; inasmuch as it is a means of afflicting the body;
   (d) Fourthly, it is directed to almsgiving.

"It must be observed that under manual labor are comprised all those human occupations whereby man can lawfully gain a livelihood, whether by using his hands, his feet, or his tongue. For watchmen, couriers, and such like who live by their labor, are understood to live by their handiwork." (*Summa Theologica*, vol. 4, pp. 240–242)

From Pope Leo XIII, on *The Condition of Labor*, we have:

5. "Towards the close of the nineteenth century the new economic methods and the new development of industry had sprung into being in almost all civilized nations, and had made such headway that human society appeared more and more divided into two classes.

"The first, small in numbers, enjoyed practically all the comforts so plentifully applied by modern invention. The second class, comprising the immense multitude of workingmen, was made up of those who, oppressed by dire poverty, struggled in vain to escape from the straits which encompassed them.

"This state of things was quite satisfactory to the wealthy, who looked upon it as the consequence of inevitable and natural economic laws, and who, therefore, were content to abandon to charity alone the full care of relieving the unfortunate, as though it were the task of charity to make amends for the open violation of justice, a violation not merely tolerated, but sanctioned at times by legislators.

"On the other hand, the working classes, victims of these harsh conditions, submitted to them with extreme reluctance and became more and more unwilling to bear the galling yoke. Some, carried away by the heat of evil counsels, went so far as to seek the disruption of the whole social fabric. Others, whom a solid Christian training restrained from such misguided excesses, convinced themselves nevertheless that there was much in all this that needed a radical and speedy reform."

6. "Capital was long able to appropriate to itself excessive advantages; it claimed all the products and profits and left to the laborer the barest minimum necessary to repair his strength and to ensure the continuation of his class. For by an inexorable economic law, it was held, all accumulation of riches must fall to the share of the wealthy, while the workingman must remain perpetually in indigence or reduced to the minimum needed for existence....

"The cause of the harassed workingman was espoused by the 'intellectuals,' as they are called, who set up in opposition to this fictitious law, another equally false moral principle: that all products and profits, excepting those required to repair and replace invested capital, belong by every right to the workingman. This error, more subtle than that of the Socialists who hold that all means of production should be transferred to the State (or, as they say, socialized), is for that reason more dangerous and apt to deceive the unwary. It is an alluring poison, consumed with avidity by many not deceived by open Socialism."

7. "Now not every kind of distribution of wealth and property amongst men is such that it can at all, and still less can adequately, attain the end intended by God. Wealth,

therefore, which is constantly being augmented by social and economic progress, must be so distributed amongst the various individuals and classes of society that the common good of all be thereby promoted. In other words, the good of the whole community must be safeguarded. By these principles of social justice one class is forbidden to exclude the other from a share in the profits.

"This sacred law is violated by an irresponsible wealthy class who, in the excess of their good fortune, deem it a just state of things that they should receive everything and the laborer nothing; it is violated also by a property-less wage-earning class who demand for themselves all the fruits of production, as being the work of their hands.

"Such men vehemently incensed against the violation of justice by capitalists, go too far in vindicating the one right of which they are conscious; they attack and seek to abolish all forms of ownerships and all profits not obtained by labor, whatever be their nature or significance in human society, for the sole reason that they are not acquired by toil."

8. "When work-people have recourse to a strike, it is frequently because the hours of labor are too long, or the work too hard, or because they consider their wages insufficient. The grave inconvenience of this not uncommon occurrence should be obviated by public remedial measures; for such paralysis of labor not only affects the masters and their work-people, but is extremely injurious to trade, and to the general interests of the public; moreover, on such occasions, violence and disorder are generally not far off, and thus it frequently happens that the public peace is threatened.

"The laws should be beforehand, and prevent these troubles from arising; they should lend their influence and authority to the removal in good time of the causes which lead to conflicts between masters and those whom they employ.

"But if the owners of property must be made secure, the workman, too, has property and possessions in which he must be protected; and, first of all, there are his spiritual and mental interests.

"Life on earth, however good and desirable in itself, is not the final purpose for which man is created; it is only the way and the means of that attainment of truth, and that practice of goodness in which the full life of the soul consists.

"It is the soul which is made after the image and likeness of God; it is in the soul that Sovereignty resides, in virtue of which man is commanded to rule the creatures below him, and to use all the earth and ocean for his profit and advantage. In this respect all men are equal; there is no difference between rich and poor, master and servant, ruler and ruled, for the same is Lord over all.

"No man may outrage with impunity that human dignity which God himself treats with reverence, nor stand in the way of that higher life which is the preparation for the eternal life of Heaven. Nay, more; a man has here no power over himself.

"To consent to any treatment which is calculated to defeat the end and purpose of his being is beyond his right; he cannot give up his soul to servitude; for it is not man's own rights which are here in question, but the rights of God, most sacred and inviolable.

"From this follows the obligation of the cessation of work and labor on Sundays and certain festivals. This rest from labor is not to be understood as mere idleness; much less must it be an occasion of spending money and a vicious excess, as many would desire it to be; but it should be rest from labor consecrated by religion.

"Repose united with religious observance disposes man to forget for a while the business of this daily life, and to turn his thoughts to heavenly things and to worship which he so strictly owes to the Eternal Deity. It is this, above all, which is the reason and motive for the Sunday rest; a rest sanctioned by God's great law of the ancient covenant, 'Remember thou keep holy the Sabbath day,'

"And taught to the world by His own mysterious 'rest' after the creation of man; 'He rested on the seventh day from all His work which He had done.'" (*The Condition of Labor*)

9. "Society today still remains in a strained and therefore unstable state, being founded on classes with contradictory interests and hence opposed to each other, and consequently prone to enmity and strife. Labor, indeed, is not a mere chattel, since the human dignity of the workingman must be recognized in it, and consequently it cannot be bought and sold like any piece of merchandise." (Pope Pius XI, *The Reconstruction of the Social Order*)

Summary

1. Man has a natural inclination to labor. "Man is born to labour and the bird to fly" (Job 5:7). Labor was meant to develop man's faculties.
2. Man would have labored even if Original Sin had not afflicted the race. Labor would have been man's delight and a sweet occupation of time had he remained innocent.
3. Labor, after man's fall, became compulsory. It became, too, a means of expiation for his sins. St. Thomas says it is a means of chastising and subduing the body.
4. Labor is a human activity; it is distinctly a human activity because it calls into exercise the intellect and the will of man.
5. Labor cannot properly be said of God nor of subhuman living things. God does not labor to effect His works. He does not have to overcome any difficulty in getting things done. God's nature is too perfect for labor; subhuman beings are too imperfect.
6. Man meets with difficulty in performing tasks. It is the exertion plus overcoming the difficulty that makes work what it is. It requires the previous exercise of the intellect and the will. (See no. 3, "Some Original Sources.")

7. Subhuman living things exert themselves and overcome difficulties, but it is not properly *labor* because they are not directed by their own, but by God's reason in the exercise.

8. God gave man "reason and hands" to obtain a livelihood and preserve his life. Lower creatures are more immediately equipped by nature with the means of obtaining the things they need. Reason and hands make work possible.

9. "To labor is to exert one's self for the sake of procuring what is necessary for the purpose of life, and most of all for self-preservation." (Pope Leo)

10. Labor is a natural right of man because it is chiefly by labor that a man keeps alive and maintains a decent human living. No one therefore may justly interfere with a man's right to labor for himself and his family.

11. Labor has a twofold aspect: it is personal (individual) and social. It is personal in the expenditure of one's strength and in the change wrought on the thing produced. It is social inasmuch as by labor the State is enriched and the common good made more secure. It is social, too, inasmuch as there is large-scale production in which any one worker rarely produces a complete article or produces anything for his personal use.

12. The terms capital and labor as we use them today are class names standing for capitalists and laborers.

13. *Capital*, in the second sense in which we use it, means *wealth*. When we think of the word in this sense we think of it as wealth that is productive of other wealth. *Wealth* might be money or money substitutes: notes, drafts, mortgages, bonds, or property, particularly *means of production* such as land and machinery.

14. Capitalism is the system which promotes the production of wealth through the use of wealth.

15. A vast accumulation of wealth in the hands of a few, the result of free competition (Liberalistic philosophy), has resulted in a concentration of power. This leaves the working man helpless in the hands of "economic dictators." "Unbridled ambition has succeeded the desire for gain," writes Pope Pius. "Free competition is dead; economic dictatorship has taken its place."

16. Communistic theories conflict with the Christian philosophy of society. The Communists aim to abolish the classes. Catholicity aims to abolish the conflict.

17. Communistic theories demand full returns for the laborer with no profits for the owner. They assume that wealth is unpossessed as were the natural resources on the island on which Robinson Crusoe lived.

18. Wealth is not unpossessed. It has legitimate owners with legitimate claims to their wealth. At times so-called "claims" are not just claims. A just claim must be within the limits set by the virtue of justice.

19. Both capital and labor are unjust in their claims when either demands the full returns on the product without consideration for the other. Neither capital nor labor could work without the other, so that between them a just alliance must be formed and the due returns to each must be determined.

20. Capitalism is not evil in its nature. It has been and is evil in some of its practices. It can be a just system of production if the principle be borne in mind that labor must be directed "for the good of all and the good of each."

21. The first step in effecting a reform in the present undesirable conditions of economic affairs is to *unite* capital and labor and not to create a worse situation by causing the overthrow of the class which supplies the means of production.

22. The aim of Communism is to overthrow the Capitalistic regime and to set up a government of the workers for an indefinite period of time to ensure the complete overthrow of the capitalistic class. Pope Leo insists that society cannot exist nor can it be conceived without classes.

23. Pope Leo insists that a wholehearted return to religion and morality will unite the classes, for each will see in the other a brother in Christ Jesus.

For Study and Discussion

1. In what way can we say that *labor* is natural to man? Is it not a punishment due to Original Sin? Explain. Does the natural law dictate that a man should work? Discuss.

2. Why is labor "distinctly a human activity"? Why is God not a "laborer"? Why is the beaver not a laborer? Why do we say, and what is the meaning of, the expression that God is man's exemplar in labor?

3. What is meant by *to labor*? What benefits accrue to man from his labor?

4. In what ways do laborers need the capitalists? Is conflict between these two classes natural? Is it necessary? In what way can it become a very probable reaction?

5. Discuss the twofold aspect of labor.

6. The individual and social character of labor is taken from the individual and social character of the laborer. Explain.

7. Discuss the effects on the equilibrium of the body politic when dissensions arise between capital and labor.

8. What is to be understood by the following terms: capital, means of production, money substitutes, wealth, capital, and labor?

9. What is the policy of the Communists toward the classes in society, particularly toward capital and labor? What is Pope Leo's answer to this attitude?

10. Discuss the differences between the Catholic and the Communist doctrines concerning the conflict between the classes.
11. What is meant by *economic dictatorship*? Discuss the statement: "Free competition is dead; economic dictatorship has taken its place." (Pope Pius XI)
12. What is the difference between possessed and unpossessed wealth? Discuss.
13. What unjust claims do capital and labor not infrequently make?
14. Discuss the nature of the Capitalistic system. Is it evil of itself?
15. Discuss each of these as a remedy for the present economic disorder: (1) make the classes more hateful; (2) make the classes more brotherly.
16. How can religion and morality benefit the economic order? Why must the change take place primarily in man's hearts and only secondarily outside of man?

For the Advanced Reader

St. Thomas:
   An Apology for Religious Orders, pp. 144–167
   Summa Contra Gentiles, bk. 3, chap. 134
   Summa Theologica, vol. 14, pp. 238–245
Farrell, Walter:
   A Companion to the Summa, III, chap. 20

Kileen, Sylvester:
   The Philosophy of Labor according to Saint Thomas Aquinas, vol. 49, *Philosophical Studies*, C.U.A.

Papal Encyclicals:
   Pope Leo XIII: *The Condition of Labor*
   Pope Pius XI: *The Reconstruction of the Social Order*

21

Man the Wage Earner

We have given, in chapter 20, the answer to Communism's avowed purpose to excite class hatred and revolution. The remedy will be not in wiping out the classes but in ending the conflict. Classes *naturally* exist; conflicts *unnaturally* exist. The human person never thrives, man's personality never fully develops in unnatural situations. It could not, for instance, endure a classless class should Communistic society be forcefully imposed upon the human race. Neither does human personality develop to any degree worthy of its dignity and heritage in the unnatural atmosphere of strife and class hatreds. In man, as in the universe at large, perfection is attained by harmonious coordination of parts. Within himself, within his family life, within the State, within the economic realm, man must have peace as the basis of progress. Reconciliation of the classes, based on religious and moral principles, therefore, constitutes one of the several noble aims for bringing symmetry into the social program.

Uplifting of the Working Classes

A second aim lies in a more equitable distribution of wealth. It means, simply, to give to the working man more possessions for a better life. The Communist program would dispossess everybody of private possessions. The papal program for the reconstruction of society calls for a wider distribution of possessions. The difference between the two programs is the difference between *no* private property and *more* private property. Pope Pius XI suggests the means. He suggests making the wage earners sharers in some way in (1) the ownership, or (2) the management, or (3) the profits of the same business.

Let us start with the third of these: namely, with sharing in the profits. This opens up two big questions for discussion. They are the question of wages and the question of private property. They accord with the second aim we have set down for a solution of the economic disorders. That second aim is a wider distribution of wealth. Now one way in which wealth is distributed is through wages. A higher wage, therefore, means a wider distribution. Pope Leo reminds us that a laboring man's little estate is his wage in another form. The wider distribution of wealth, therefore, through higher wages, is seen to result logically in a wider ownership of property. This aim, as we said, is in opposition to the second avowed aim of Communism: to dispossess everybody — to abolish private property. This is opposed to the papal plan for uplifting the working classes. "Our first and most fundamental principle when we undertake to alleviate the condition of the masses, must be the inviolability of private property," writes Pope Leo.

Though the working classes of today are less universally impoverished than they were in the days of Pope Leo (he wrote his famous *Labor* encyclical in 1891), there are still too many laboring men who merely exist, propertyless, and depressed in the extreme. Expressed in Pope Pius's words, the program for uplifting them is simply this:

> Every effort must be made that, at least in the future, a just share only of the fruits of production be permitted to accumulate in the hands of the wealthy, and that an ample sufficiency be supplied to the workingmen. The purpose is not that these become slack at their work, for man is born to labor as the bird to fly, but that by thrift they may increase their possessions, and by the prudent management of the same they may be enabled to bear the family burden with greater ease and security, being freed from that hand-to-mouth uncertainty which is the lot of the proletarian. Thus they will not only be in a position to support life's changing fortunes, but will also have the reassuring confidence that when their lives are ended, some little provision will remain for those whom they leave behind them.

A simple program it is, based on justice and well suited to bring peace and tranquility to human society. Note how carefully the steps are outlined: (1) a just share in profits for owners, (2) ample sufficiency for workers, (3) increased possessions for the masses, (4) greater security in family life, (5) inheritance to children. This will uplift the proletariat. This will secure the foundations of society. This is the rational and just program to oppose to the Communistic threat of universal dispossession.

Right to a Just Wage

The basis of man's right to a just wage is his daily recurring needs. These are supplied, generally speaking, from nature's storehouse, from "the inexhaustible fertility of the earth." Pope Leo writes: "There is no one who does not live on what the land brings forth. Those who do not possess the soil, contribute their labor; so that it may be truly said that all human subsistence is derived either from labor on one's own land, or from some laborious industry which is paid either in the produce of the land itself or in that which is exchanged for what the land brings forth." Man's right to self-preservation entitles him to make use of the fruits of the earth. As Pope Leo remarks, not everyone tills the soil and takes nature's gifts directly from nature. Under the modern economic setup, the majority of people receive nature's goods indirectly, through the medium, that is, of others. Yet in the final issue, in no way other than through nature are man's daily needs supplied. The poor have no way of obtaining these supplies than by their labor, hence in exchange for their labor they are entitled to a sufficiency of this life's goods — an "ample sufficiency," says Pope Pius, enough to live in "decent comfort."

This is the general basis for man's right to a decent living wage. If man has the *right* to it, others have *duty* with respect to it. They must not prevent man's attainment of a decent living. They must not withhold or interfere with his receiving a just wage in exchange for his labor. They must not, that is, interfere with his right to the proper means necessary to obtain it. This includes the duty of employers to provide opportunities for work for those who are willing and able to work. The duty to give workmen a just wage, and the principles governing wages, now claim our attention.

Are Wage Contracts Just?

A wage contract consists, simply, in a free agreement between the employer and the worker. The agreement covers time, type of work, quality, quantity, and remuneration, generally. "Those who hold that the wage-contract is essentially unjust ... are certainly in error," writes Pope Pius. Note his words: *essentially* unjust. That, of course, means unjust in its very nature. Hence to the question "Are wage-contracts unjust?" the answer is, "No, the wage contract is not unjust in its very nature. There are, however, grave threats to justice possible in the system." There are those who hold that a "free contract" is a "free contract," and that when an employer bargains with a worker, he is bound to the terms of the agreement only, and his only obligation rests in fulfilling those terms. Outside of meeting the terms of the agreement, the employer, it is claimed, has no moral obligation. That means the employer is not morally obliged to make a morally just bargain. His bargain can be as unjust as his rapacious nature suggests, but no moral blame can be imputed to him because he made a "free contract." It is a matter of whether we should see morality in the terms of agreement or morality only in *keeping* the terms agreed upon.

Under the free contract principle, an employer might agree to pay an adult male laborer twenty-five cents a day for picking berries. Forced to work or to starve, the laborer agrees. At the close of the day the employer pays the quarter. He has kept his bargain. In his opinion he has committed no moral injustice despite the inhuman wage. Pope Leo says; "Now if we were to consider labor merely so far as it is *personal,* doubtless it would be within the workman's rights to accept any rate of wages whatever." Pope Leo's words imply that we must not consider labor as being "merely personal," because he says, "if ... it would be." The reason for a laborer's right to accept any rate of wage is this, that just as he is free to work or not to work, so is he free to accept this or that remuneration for his labor, or, for that matter, he might be willing to accept none at all. All that is within the rights of the laborer, and the employer who bargains thus with a laborer would not be morally wrong *if* ...

Labor More Than Personal

On the word *if* hangs the key to the solution: "if labor were *merely personal.*" But labor is not. Labor is *necessary* as well as personal. It is the necessity of labor for the procuring of life's ever-recurring needs that keeps the "free contract" theory from being wholly just. The fact that labor is necessary makes all the difference between a morally good and a morally bad agreement between employers and workers. To preserve life is the bounden duty of each and all. For the poor, the means of preserving life is by their labor. Their labor, therefore, should make returns sufficient to meet life's needs, and to meet them adequately, decently.

It follows, therefore, that an employer who would bargain to pay an adult male laborer twenty-five cents a day for berry picking would not be striking a morally just bargain. There would be injustice *in the terms* of the agreement. The individual laborer, finding himself at the mercy of the greater economic strength of the employer, and having to choose between hunger and an unjust bargain, was forced into making the agreement. He was forced, please note, not physically on the part of the employer, perhaps, but physically at least, from the needs of his body for food and raiment. Because of the necessity of his labor to meet life's needs, the bargain made was not morally just.

Employers Have a Moral Obligation

Such an agreement as that just given in our supposition is morally unjust. This view does not deny the right to make free contracts. It states explicitly that the free contracts must be governed by what is a morally just remuneration considering man's need, the dignity of human labor, and the fundamental right to the preservation of his life. Pope Leo writes:

> Let it be granted that, as a rule, workman and employer should make free agreements, and in particular, should *freely agree as to wages*; nevertheless, there is a dictate of nature more imperious and more ancient than any bargain between a man and man, that the remuneration must be enough to support the wage earner in reasonable and frugal comfort.
>
> If through necessity or fear of a worse evil, the workman accepts harder conditions because an employer or contractor will give him no better, he is the victim *of force and injustice*.

What Is a Just Wage?

The arguments contained in the last few paragraphs were based on the *personal* and the *necessary* aspects of labor (to use the terms of Pope Leo). We had suggested in the chapter "Man the Worker" Pope Pius's terms: *personal* and *social*. Are these terms used in the same sense by the two popes? The use of the term *personal* by each has the same meaning, namely, individual. In this sense *personal* (individual) stands opposed to *social*. Pope Leo means *social*, but he does not use that term when he writes that "it is only by the labor of the working man that States grow rich." This is truly the *social* aspect of labor; it is thus that the two popes understood it.

The term *necessary* is used merely as a characteristic of *personal* labor. If one were to think of the different features of personal labor, for instance, one might mention that individual labor is *natural*, is *necessary*, is *morally just*, is *inviolable in its rightful claims*, and so forth. It is as one of the characteristics of *personal* labor that the term *necessary* is used. We say, therefore, that labor is either individual or social. Each of these aspects has definite characteristics, of which *necessary* is a characteristic of the individual aspect of labor. This will clear up the use of various terms in the language of the two popes.

Now in general, a just wage is one which allows ample present sufficiency and adequate future security. It should meet all the necessary household needs, it should allow for sufficient nourishment, decent housing, adequate and suitable clothing, a moderate amount of recreation (fun, vacations, hobbies), a schooling in keeping with one's station in life, old age security, the acquisition of a modest fortune (money, money substitutes, real estate), and for emergencies: sickness, accident, hospitalization, and others. "If a working man's wages be sufficient to enable him to maintain himself, his wife, and his children in reasonable comfort, he will not find it difficult, if he is a sensible man, to study economy; and he will not fail, by cutting down expenses, to put by a little property; nature and reason would urge him to do this."

The First Principle

It is from a consideration of the individual and the social aspects of labor that the principles governing the regulation of wages can be deduced. The first principle we have already suggested: namely, that the wage must be sufficient for the worker and his family — "to maintain himself, his wife and his children in *reasonable comfort*," says Pope Leo. But, you say, suppose a man is not married. Is he entitled to a wage sufficient for family support? The answer is yes. A man's wage must meet that standard. The reasons are not hard to find. It encourages young men to marry. It gives them an opportunity to provide for the first needs of married life; namely, to provide a home and furnish it. If a "family wage" were not paid to adult males, what provision could they make for successful happy married life? A second reason is the care of dependents which often fall upon unmarried men. Frequently it is aged parents who need to be supported. At other times it is orphaned children of one's brothers and sisters. It may be that an unmarried man assists in the education of his nieces and nephews when the family's income is insufficient to meet the demand. A day laborer's wage does not provide college educations for his children, and yet not infrequently children of such working men have a decided aptitude for certain professions which can be reached only through a college diploma. An unmarried uncle not infrequently contributes to this worthy cause. There is, however, an economically more important reason.

The further reason why unmarried men should receive an equal wage with married men is to avoid putting married men out of work. This would result from a low wage being paid to unmarried men. In his encyclical on the *Reconstruction of the Social Order* Pope Pius gives a word of praise to those systems which give an increased wage in view of increased family burdens and which make a special provision for special needs. That is not the general case, however, unless we limit it to the special provision for special needs made in the case of sick benefits, hospitalization, accident compensation, and the like.

On the whole, therefore, it is socially more just that every adult male laborer receive a "family wage" — a *decent family wage*. With women, this is not so necessary. The general principle governing the wage of a working woman is sufficient for individual decent support. It is quite generally agreed, however, that equal wages for equal work whether for men or women should be the rule in order to avoid the evil of unfair competition which would result in injury to the families and the common good. The word decent is always to be stressed, whether the consideration be of the family wage of a man or the individual wage of a woman.

In laying down this principle of a sufficient-for-family-needs wage, Pope Pius says that the family income ought not to be augmented by the work of the wife or young children in industrial plants — in ordinary industry as we know it. He agrees that a helping hand should be given to the father, by both the mother and the children in lesser ways: that is, in the care of one's shop, and, in rural districts, in the many chores that must be done.

> Intolerable, and to be opposed with all our strength, is the abuse whereby mothers of families, because of the insufficiency of the father's salary, are forced to engage in gainful occupations outside the domestic walls, to the neglect of their own proper care and duties, particularly the education of their children. Every effort must therefore be made that fathers of families receive a wage sufficient to meet adequately ordinary domestic needs.

The Second Principle

In determining a just wage, due consideration must be had for the owner of the business. He, too, is entitled to a just remuneration for his labor and on his investment. It is unfair to demand so high a wage as to deprive the owner of a decent just living wage for himself, his wife, and his children. If the laborer is entitled to this, so, of necessity and in justice, is he whose capital and skill make possible the employment of labor. It is an act of injustice to cause the ruin of the business through failure to compromise in the matter of a just return for labor and invested capital. The distress and misery following the closing of a business, is, for a sensible person, sufficient argument against perpetrating that act of injustice.

Inside Causes of Low Profits

Now small profits, which result in a low wage for workers, may be brought about (1) through the fault of the owner of the business or those to whom he has entrusted it, or (2) through outside influences over which he has little or no immediate control. "Little or no immediate control" merely suggests that the case is not hopeless, but that the owner of the business must have recourse to some authority such as that of the State, so that through legislative enactments, a remedy may be effected.

A business might be doing poorly through bad management. Perhaps the owner or manager is at fault. Perhaps it is lack of keen business ability; perhaps lack of cooperation and organization. Whatever be the cause, poor management is not a just reason for reducing wages even though the profits be slight. The remedy, of course, is to increase the profits through better management. This, in turn, makes possible a better wage.

Secondly, want of enterprise may be a cause for low returns. Initiative is lacking. One may not be energetic in seeing fine opportunities or courageous in running reasonable risks. Over-caution, fear, or indifference might prevent business deals which would redound to the true and just advantage of the business. The workers suffer from this. Lower returns in profits mean lower returns for their labor. This want of enterprise is not a just reason for reducing wages. The remedy, of course, is to cultivate the qualities and put into practice the things necessary for energetic, honest, upright conduct of the business.

Thirdly, the use of out-of-date methods and procedures is sometimes a cause for low profits. Inefficiency in the equipment or in the help, or perhaps insufficient modern timesaving devices, or any such things which consume money unnecessarily, would fall under the heading of "out-of-date methods." This is not an adequate justification for reducing wages. The remedy is obvious.

Outside Causes of Low Profits

There are reasons for small returns in business due to causes that are beyond the control of the owner. The first of these causes may be that he is loaded with unjust burdens which he cannot meet without diminishing his profits to a considerable extent — to so great an extent, in fact, that he finds himself confronted with the necessity of cutting wages. Unjust burdens might be exorbitant rents, excessive taxation, usurious rates on moneylending, high tariffs, and the like.

A second cause is that of unfair, unbridled competition. In this situation, the owner must cut his prices so low that there is little or no profit; in fact, he is running at a loss, and meeting his obligations out of reserve resources which soon are exhausted. At times competitors with immense reserve resources, aiming at monopoly, drive the smaller business out of competition by driving it out of business.

These causes are beyond the control of the owner. The remedy may sometimes be found in calling upon the civil authorities, either by legislation or by some legitimate mode of intervention, to remove the obstacles to the true progress of the business. Employers and employed should also unite in their efforts and plans to overcome the obstacles and they should be guided by public authority in its wise measures to aid business. The guiding spirit of employer-employee efforts should be one of Christian harmony and mutual understanding, without bitterness, without unjust blame.

Those who are responsible for the causes beyond the control of the owner of the business are guilty of great wrong. They deprive the worker of a just wage. They interfere, through selfishness and greed, with the acquisition of a decent living wage. They prevent his acquiring the needs necessary to sustain life at a human level. They force the worker unwillingly to accept lower terms than he is entitled to, considering his needs, his nature, and the necessity and dignity of his labor. The rich must religiously refrain from cutting wages by force, by fraud, or by usurious dealing, because wages are a poor man's only means of livelihood, and they are the more sacred in proportion to their scantiness.

The Third Principle

Principles one and two had reference primarily to the individual character of labor. The rights of the working man were protected by that particular justice which St. Thomas calls commutative justice. You will recall that this type of justice regulates the relations of individuals within the community: man to man, buyer to seller, employer to worker, master to servant, teacher to pupil, and the like relationships. The third principle, however, is guided by social justice, which is the species of justice that moves men to act for the common good. This principle declares that in regulating wages, a consideration must be had for the economic welfare of the whole people.

It advances the economic good of the commonwealth to have an increased number of property holders. Therefore, in the regulation of wages, some consideration should be given to making the wage adequate enough to enable the wage earner to invest in property of some form. Pope Pius XI writes that it is conducive to the common good that wage-earners of all kinds (manual laborers properly so called, as well as salaried workers, i.e., clerks and office help) "should be enabled, by economizing that portion of their wage which remains after necessary expenses have been met, to attain to the possession of a certain modest fortune."

The economic welfare of the whole people is improved when opportunity for work is provided for those who are willing and able to work. Now wages have a great deal to do with opportunities for work. If the scale of wages is too high, or if it is too low, there will be unemployment. Now unemployment brings in its wake much misery, many temptations, and loss of economic independence to the laborer. It ruins the prosperity of the nation. It endangers public peace, which is the tranquility of order in public affairs. The principle, therefore, demands that lowering or raising wages be done, not with a view to private good, but to the public good. Economists should study the question carefully. They should see the effects of proposed wage scales in relation to the good of the people at large, to the national prosperity, and to the virtue and well-being of the individual.

Production today is large-scale production. Machines and inventions have made possible the production of immense quantities of things for which a market must be found. Now if the wage-earners (we use this word wage to designate "wages" and "low salaries") receive no more than is necessary for the mere necessities of life, they will have only a limited purchasing power. They will be unable to buy the immense quantities of goods produced and put on the market. The demand for goods will be limited. Purchases will be comparatively few. The market will be overstocked. Factories will cease to produce. The production-purchase cycle will be so slowed down that factories will close and workers will be thrown out of work. A siege of "unemployment pestilence" strikes the industry, or what is worse, the whole economic realm. Its social consequences are many and serious. Obviously, a remedy would be in setting a kind of necessary and strict proportion between the amount of goods produced and the amount of purchasing power of the wage-earners. Lack of proportion between these two results in unemployment.

People earning high salaries are in the minority. By far the vast majority receive low wages. Those who earn much have great purchasing power, but they are far fewer in numbers than those who earn but little. Those with money in abundance cannot purchase all the goods produced because they are relatively few in number. Unemployment results as in the case first mentioned. It shows that a wider distribution of the profits should be made. More people should be given greater purchasing power. It does not mend matters to give increased purchasing power to a minority, no matter how much money they may have to spend. It is only when more power is in the hands of the masses that the markets can be sold out, and room made for new goods. Then the wheels of industry will keep turning. The more they turn, the more money flows to the wage-earner. The more he earns, the more he is able to spend. The more he spends, the more industry produces.

The wage scale should consider, therefore, the economic good of the whole people, and it does so when it guarantees a constant flow of production through increased purchasing power of the masses. Pope Pius IX, in indicating ways in which the common good can be advanced through a well-regulated wage scale, says: "We have shown how conducive it is to the common good that wage earners of all kinds be enabled by economizing ... to attain to the possession of a modest fortune." This is the first way in which we considered the application of principle three. Then he says: "Opportunities for work should be provided for those who are willing and able to work." That is the second means of applying principle three. A third means: "All are aware," he says, "that a scale of wages too low, no less than a scale excessively high, causes unemployment." He gives a fourth means of seeking the common good in wage regulation. He says: "A reasonable relationship between different wages here enters into consideration." He means, of course, the minority with great purchasing power and the majority with little purchasing power, which, as we have shown, tends to unemployment.

Fifthly, the Holy Father says there must be also, "a reasonable relationship between the prices obtained for the products of the various economic groups." Let us take the case of farmers. The returns on their labor are known to be generally very low. Their purchasing power is very limited. They are often unable to make many purchases from industries producing farm implements, tools, wire, and the like. They have no money. The cost of such things is comparatively much higher than the returns received by the farmer. There is little or no equality or proportion between the prices of farm products and those of manufactured products. If a greater equality existed between the price received by the farmer for his goods and the price he is asked to pay for the goods he must buy, there would be a more constant exchange of goods among the various economic groups.

When harmonious proportion is kept between wages (purchasing power) and production, the various economic groups will be acting in conjunction one with the other, and will effect, in the social economic order, a single organism tending steadily toward a common end. "For," says Pope Pius XI,

> then only will the economic and social organism be soundly established
> and attain its end, when it secures for all and each those goods which the
> wealth and resources of nature, technical achievement, and the social
> organization of economic affairs can give. These goods should be sufficient to supply all needs and an honest livelihood, and to uplift men
> to that higher level of prosperity and culture which, provided it be used
> with prudence, is not only no hindrance, but is of singular help to virtue.

How Effected?

How can the two ideals laid down — namely, the just distribution of property and the just wage scale, be effected? When we consider that Liberalism and its free competition theory brought about class hatred and the vices of greed, usury, avarice, and wholesale injustice into the heart of society, we can understand at once that a reformation must be effected. But what is to be reformed? The whole social order. How is it to be reformed? Through a correction of morals. Pope Pius speaks of it as a "renovation of morals," and Pope Leo called it "a return to Christian life and Christian institutions." It requires the restoration of true guiding principles. One does not reach his destination when he is misdirected. The only proper guides to a Christian social order are the virtues of social justice and social charity.

Moral Renovation

"When we speak of the reform of the social order," writes Pope Pius XI, "it is principally the State we have in mind." The Holy Father does not mean to give to economic groups loose reins to continue their free competition and their economic supremacy. He means, however, that it is within the province of the State to protect the working man from "the cruelty of grasping speculators who use human beings as mere instruments for making money." We have previously spoken of the State's right to intervene, remembering, always, that it has certain limits within which it must ever remain.

> If employers laid burdens upon the workmen which were unjust, or which degraded them with conditions that were repugnant to their dignity as human beings ... there can be no question that, within certain limits, it would be right to call in the help and authority of the law. The limits must be determined by the nature of the occasion which calls for the law's interference — the principle being this, that the law must not undertake more, nor go farther, than is required for the remedy of the evil or the removal of the danger.

Again and again in the papal encyclicals the rights of the laborer are upheld. "Those who are badly off have no resources of their own to fall back upon, and must chiefly rely upon the assistance of the State. And it is for this reason that the wage earners, who are undoubtedly among the weak and necessitous, should be specially cared for and protected by the commonwealth."

The reform of the social order in its social and economic principles and practices must be borne, therefore, by the State through its legislative powers and its legitimate authority. It holds these in virtue of its end which is the promotion of the general welfare.

The second means, the correction of morals, falls to religious and moral institutions for the guiding norms and to all individuals for personal application. Now morality is the special domain of the Church. She demands the right, in virtue of the deposit of truth entrusted to her by God and her mission to propagate, interpret, and to promote the observance of the moral law. Now since the moral law must be applied to problems in the social and economic realm, the Church insists, and justly so, that social and economic problems be subject to her jurisdiction insofar as they refer to moral principles.

We said in the preceding paragraph that the correction of morals falls to the work of the Church *for the guiding norms*. Obviously, the Church cannot whitewash men's souls as a painter can whitewash a cellar. The individual men must *will* to have their souls cleansed of their sins. The work of soul-cleansing is the work of the individual. No power in Heaven or on earth can cleanse the soul of an unwilling man. Note that only one thief on Calvary became converted, and we can be sure that, if the obstinate one had opened his heart, as did the "good" thief, to the flood of graces God sent to its door, he, too, would have heard the words, "This day thou shalt be with me in paradise" (Luke 23:43).

The work of the Church is to supply the norms of right morality to social and economic groups. She alone can tell them clearly and concisely what their duties are. She alone can tell them how they ought to fulfill them. She alone can indicate clearly what consequences follow upon faithfulness to duty and what disaster trails in the steps of unrighteousness. Beyond the sphere of religion and morality the Church does not go either with individuals or with groups. For this reason the State, the employers, the wealthy, the workers, the managers, and the promoters of economic life must all cooperate with the Church. They must reduce moral and religious truths to practice. To all of these belong the task of renovating morals and reconstructing the social order according to the true guiding norms indicated by the Church. We repeat: the other agents must cooperate with the Church. Their striving will be in vain, warns Pope Leo, if they leave out the Church by neglecting her teachings.

What the Church Does

We said the work of the Church was to judge of the morality of economic and social activity. She supplied the basic principles of right and wrong whereby man's actions, individually and collectively, might be brought into conformity with the law of God and the natural law. That is the general duty of the Church.

However, in her teachings she reaches to particular instances of right human behavior. She proclaims the gospel of Christ which says, "Love your enemies; do good to them that hate you" (Matt. 5:44). Constant fidelity to these teachings of Christ in her own actions as well as constancy in urging them upon her children does much to make the conflict between classes less bitter, if it does not end it altogether.

Through her schools and literature, in her discussion clubs and lecture series, she enlightens the mind and directs the life and conduct of her children. She is lovingly solicitous for all mankind, and zealously tries to make all hearts willing to be formed and guided in their life and occupations by the commandments of God and the teachings of Jesus Christ. She establishes institutions which have as their aim the uplifting of the working classes. She strives to enlist the service of all ranks in discussing and recognizing mutual rights and duties and in rendering justice toward the claims of all. She holds out to the poor the hope of a future life, and thus makes them the more satisfied to bear patiently the hardships of this life and to receive injustice without bitterness and hatred. She does all in her power to bind classes in friendliness and good understanding. She teaches obedience to authority, respect for the State, the justice of fulfilling obligations toward everyone, and the dignity of human labor.

In clear, sharp terms Pope Leo sums up the efficacy of the Church in preventing strife between social and economic groups. He says:

> There is nothing more powerful than religion (of which the Church is the interpreter and guardian) in drawing rich and poor together, by reminding each class of its duties to the other, and especially of the duties of justice. Thus, religion teaches the laboring man and the workman to carry out honestly and well all equitable agreements freely made; never to injure capital nor to outrage the person of an employer; never to employ violence in representing his own cause, nor to engage in riot and disorder; and to have nothing to do with men of evil principles, who work upon the people with artful promises, and raise foolish hopes which usually end in disaster and in repentance when it is too late.
>
> Religion teaches the rich man and the employer that their workmen are not their slaves; they must respect in every man his dignity as a man and as a Christian; that labor is nothing to be ashamed of, if we listen to right reason and to Christian philosophy, but is an honorable employment, enabling a man to sustain his life in an upright and

creditable way, and that it is shameful and inhuman to treat men like chattels to make money by, or to look upon them merely as so much muscle or physical power.

Thus again, religion teaches that, as among the workmen's concerns are religion herself, and things spiritual and mental, the employer is bound to see that he has time for the duties of piety; that he be not exposed to corrupting influences and dangerous occasions; and that he be not led away to neglect his home and family or to squander his wages.

Then again the employer must never tax his workmen beyond their strength, nor employ them in work unsuited to their sex or age. His great and principal obligation is to give to every one that which is just ... but rich men and masters should remember this — that to exercise pressure for the sake of gain, upon the indigent and destitute and to make one's profit out of the need of another, is condemned by all laws, human and divine. To defraud any one of wages that are his due is a crime which cries to the avenging anger of Heaven.

Finally, the rich man must religiously refrain from cutting down the workman's earnings, either by force, fraud, or by usurious dealing; and with the more reason because the poor man is weak and unprotected, and because his slender means should be sacred in proportion to their scantiness.

Were these precepts carefully obeyed and followed, would not strife die out and cease?

These are magnificent words, a memorial to the great Pope Leo XIII, the "Pope of the Workingman." What an *apologia* for the Church and a justification of her claims to direct man's strivings insofar as they refer to moral issues!

Certainly we are prompted to say, with Pope Leo, and without hesitation or doubt, that "all the striving of men will be vain if they leave out the Church."

Some Original Sources

We could quote passages at length from Pope Leo and Pope Pius on the matter of justice to the working classes. We shall have to limit the number and extent of them, however. Here is what Pope Leo says about the question:

1. "If we turn to things exterior and corporal [he had already discussed religion and morality], the first concern of all is to save the poor workers from the cruelty of grasping speculators, who use human beings as mere instruments for making money.

Christian Social Principles

"It is neither justice nor humanity so to grind men down with excessive labor as to stupefy their minds and wear out their bodies. Man's powers, like his general nature, are limited, and beyond these limits he cannot go.

"His strength is developed and increased by use and exercise, but only on condition of due intermission and proper rest. Daily labor, therefore, must be so regulated that it may not be protracted during longer hours than strength admits.

"How many and how long the intervals of rest should be, will depend upon the nature of the work, on circumstances of time and place, and on the health and strength of the workman.

"Those who labor in mines and quarries, and who work within the bowels of the earth, should have shorter hours in proportion as their labor is more severe and more trying to health.

"Then again, the season of the year must be taken into account; for not infrequently a kind of labor is easy at one time which at another is intolerable or very difficult.

"Finally work which is suitable for a strong man cannot reasonably be required from a woman or a child. . . .

"As a general principle, it ought to be laid down, that a workman ought to have leisure and rest in proportion to the wear and tear on his strength; for the waste of strength must be repaired by the cessation of work.

"In all agreements between masters and workmen, there is always the condition, expressed or understood, that there be allowed proper rest for soul and body. To agree in any other sense would be against what is right and just; for it can never be right or just to require on the one side, or to promise on the other, the giving up of those duties which a man owes to his God and to himself.

"We now approach a subject of very great importance and one on which, if extremes are to be avoided, right ideas are absolutely necessary.

"Wages, we are told, are fixed by free consent; and therefore, the employer, when he pays what was agreed upon, has done his part, and is not called upon for anything further. The only way, it is said, in which injustice could happen, would be if the master refused to pay the whole of the wages, or the workman would not complete the work undertaken; when this happens the State should intervene, to see that each obtains his own, but not under any other circumstances.

"This mode of reasoning is by no means convincing to a fair-minded man, for there are important considerations which it leaves out of view altogether.

"To labor is to exert one's self for the sake of procuring what is necessary for the purposes of life, and most of all for self-preservation. Therefore, a man's labor has two notes or characters.

"First of all, it is personal; for the exertion of individual power belongs to the individual who puts it forth, employing this power for that personal profit for which it was given.

"Secondly, man's labor is necessary; for without the results of labor a man cannot live; and self-conservation is a law of nature, which it is wrong to disobey.

"Now if we were to consider labor merely so far as it is *personal*, doubtless it would be within the workman's rights to accept any rate of wages whatever; for in the same way as he is free to work or not, so he is free to accept a small remuneration or even none at all.

"But this is mere abstract supposition; the labor of the working man is not only his personal attribute, but it is *necessary*, and this makes all the difference.

"The preservation of life is the bounden duty of each and all, and to fail therein is a crime. It follows that each one has a right to procure what is required in order to live; and the poor can procure it in no other way than by work and wages.

"Let it be granted, then, that, as a rule, workman and employer should make free agreements, and in particular should freely agree as to wages; nevertheless, there is a dictate of nature more imperious and more ancient than any bargain between man and man, that the remuneration must be enough to support the wage earner in reasonable and frugal comfort.

"If, through necessity or fear of a worse evil, the workman accepts harder conditions because an employer or contractor will give him no better, he is the victim of force and injustice." (Pope Leo, *The Condition of Labor*)

2. "Clearly charity cannot take the place of justice unfairly withheld. But even though a state of things be pictured in which every man receives at last all that is his due, a wide field will nevertheless remain open for charity.

"For justice alone, even though most faithfully observed, can remove indeed the cause of social strife, but can never bring about a union of hearts and minds. Yet this union, binding men together, is the main principle of stability in all institutions, no matter how perfect they may seem, which aim at establishing social peace and promoting mutual aid.

"In its absence, as repeated experience proves, the wisest regulations come to nothing. Then only will it be possible to unite all in harmonious striving for the common good, when all sections of society have the intimate conviction that they are members of a single family and children of the same Heavenly Father, and further, that they are 'one body in Christ and every one members one of another.'

"Then the rich and others in power will change their former negligence of their poorer brethren into solicitous and effective regard; will listen with kindly feeling to their just complaints, and will readily forgive them the faults and mistakes they possibly make.

"Workingmen too will lay aside all feelings of hatred or envy, which the instigators of social strife arouse so skillfully. Not only will they cease to feel weary of the position assigned them by divine Providence in human society; they will become proud of it, well aware that every man by doing his duty is working usefully and honorably for the common good, and is following in the footsteps of Him, Who, being in the form of God, chose to become a carpenter among men, and to be known as the Son of a carpenter." (Pope Pius, *The Reconstruction of the Social Order*)

3. "The wage earner is not to receive as alms what is his due in justice. And let no one attempt with trifling charitable donations to exempt himself from the great duties imposed by justice. Both justice and charity often dictate obligations touching on the same subject matter, but under different aspects; and the very dignity of the working man makes him justly and acutely sensitive to the duties of others in his regard." (Pope Pius, *Atheistic Communism*)

Summary

1. The first aim of any group attempting to reconstruct the social order should be the elimination, not of the *classes*, but of the *conflict* between the classes.
2. A second aim in attempting social reconstruction should be the uplifting of the working population. This means to give them an opportunity to live a better life; a decent human life, with the supply of their daily necessities and provision for future needs.
3. A step in this direction of improving the masses is to give to all willing and able workers a decent family wage. The wage should provide a *decent living*, one of "decent comfort," of "frugal comfort," to use the terms of Pope Leo.
4. The wage must be not only one for decent living, but decent living for the family, not merely for the individual wage earner.
5. A simple program laid down by Pope Pius gives these norms or standards for judging the distribution of profits between workers and employers: (a) a just share in profits for the owner; (b) ample sufficiency for the worker; (c) increased possessions for the masses; (d) greater security in family life through decent living, security in old age, through savings; (e) inheritance to children to carry on after death of the wage earner.
6. Man's right to a just wage is based on his nature. Nature requires man to preserve his life. To do this he must have a certain kind and amount of necessities. These are procured either through personal labor or the returns from his labor. Man, therefore, has the right to sufficient returns on his labor to provide him with what he needs.
7. Wage contracts are just, provided in their terms they do not degrade the worker or take advantage of his weakness against his will.
8. In making agreements, it must be borne in mind that man's labor has a twofold aspect: personal and necessary. As personal, a man may accept any wage whatsoever he pleases, or even none at all, if he wishes. But

insofar as labor is necessary, a man is entitled to a sufficient wage, a just wage which will meet his requirements, and those of his dependents.

9. Employers have a moral obligation to see to it that their workers are paid a decent wage in accord with the need man has to obtain his necessities through his labor.

10. In settling the question as to what a just wage is, three principles are to be considered: (a) it must be sufficient to provide a laborer and his family with the things necessary to have decent comfort; (b) the state of the business must be considered; namely whether the employer is able, without loss of his own livelihood, to pay the wage, and secondly, whether his inability (if such there be) to pay a decent wage is due to: first, his own fault or secondly, to a cause outside of himself; (c) the effect of wages on the common good must be considered in determining a wage scale.

11. If an employer is unable to pay a decent wage through no fault of his own, that is not a sufficient reason for cutting the wage or giving an inadequate one. The evil must be overcome. The employers and the employees ought to combine to discuss the case and to suggest a remedy.

12. If the inability to pay a just wage is caused by influences over which an employer has no control, the employer and employees should again discuss the question and call in the help of civil government to obtain justice from those who are withholding it.

13. The common good is a decided factor in the settling of a wage scale. Sufficient wages should be allowed to enable the workers to save and to purchase property. Providing opportunities for work for those who are able and willing to work is a second means of promoting the common good through wages. Wages too high or too low cause unemployment and the consequent distress among peoples is a decided means of retrogression from the common good.

14. The State helps in this by legislation, by protection of the rights of the laborer and the employer, by maintaining the conditions suitable for prosperous industrial enterprises, and the like.

15. The Church contributes in her basic religious and moral principles which she impresses on the hearts and minds of all her children. She proclaims a doctrine of love and not of hate.

16. The Church demands the right to come forward with the moral principles which should be operative in economic affairs inasmuch as she is the teacher of all nations; she is the deposit of all truth; she is the guardian of all moral standards.

17. The Church claims her right in virtue of God's command to lead all souls to eternal happiness. She claims the right to enter and she at the same time limits her rights in these words: "insofar as they refer to moral issues."

Christian Social Principles

For Study and Discussion

1. Discuss the need of bettering the condition of the working class.
2. Explain: Classes naturally exist but conflict unnaturally exists.
3. Which aim is more likely to satisfy the worker: the *no possessions* of Communism, or the *more possessions* of Christian social philosophy?
4. Explain how a wider distribution of wealth is effected through wages.
5. What is considered a just family wage? Do you think a single man is entitled to a family wage? Discuss.
6. What effects would follow upon the married men and their families if the unmarried men worked for a wage approximately half that of the married men. What effects would follow upon the unmarried men and their possible future families?
7. Is the purpose of giving more wages to the worker that he might become lazy? Explain the meaning: Man is born to labor as the bird to fly.
8. Why should a just wage include sufficient means to set aside some savings?
9. Discuss: Increased wages for the worker will effect greater security in family life.
10. Upon what right can men claim a decent living wage? Would it not be enough to pay them sufficient wages to keep them alive?
11. Discuss the possibility of immorality in wage contracts. What is the evil of the "free contract" theory?
12. Discuss the twofold aspect of man's labor and of the wage which is due to him in virtue of this dual character of his labor.
13. We said that man's labor is personal and social. His education is a matter of personal and social development. His wage is viewed as personal and social. Why must man in all his aspects be viewed in this dual way?
14. Explain each of the three principles which govern the regulation of a just wage scale.
15. Explain the difference between "inside causes" and "outside causes" which effect the ability of an employer to pay a just wage.
16. How is the common good affected by the wage scale?
17. Why is moral renovation necessary in effecting a better social order?
18. What help does religion give in the economic realm?
19. Discuss the right of the Church to enter the social-economic field.

For the Advanced Reader

Papal Encyclicals:
Pope Leo XIII: *The Condition of Labor*
Pope Pius XI: *The Reconstruction of the Social Order*

Any good book on social ethics and on Christian principles of economics

22

Man the Property Owner

Pope Leo declared that the first and most fundamental principle for the alleviation of the masses must be the *inviolability* of private property. Paraphrasing this, we might say that the basic Communistic principle is the *abolition* of private property. Note the complete opposition between the two fundamental principles: *inviolability versus abolition*. A discussion of private property at this point of *Christian Social Principles* flows quite naturally from the discussions in the chapters on man the worker and man the wage earner. The basis of the right to labor and to a just wage is man's need of the things necessary for self-preservation. Now the right to possess has this same foundation. Man has the right to possess because he has to preserve his life.

Ownership versus Property

These two terms are frequently used synonymously. But they are not synonyms. *Property* is objective. It is the thing possessed. *Property* is the thinker's thought, the architect's blueprint, the master's symphony, the author's book, the farmer's plow, a person's clothes, a man's house. *Ownership* is the moral right to have and to use one's property; that is, to have and to use one's thoughts, blueprint, book, plow, clothes, house, and the like. *Ownership* is the bond which links the owner to the thing owned. It is an invisible link. It is a moral force. It is a binding power. *Ownership* means dominion. *Property* is the thing over which one dominates.

Dominion of God and of Man

Now God has complete mastery over the world. He created it, and so His dominion over it, by the fact of creatorship, is absolute. Man shares to some extent in God's dominion over the earth. Man's dominion is not the absolute dominion of the Maker, but the limited dominion of the rational creature. It is the dominion of *use*. God owns the universe. Man is allowed the use of it. There is a vast difference in the two types of dominion. God's mastery is absolute, perfect, complete. It applies to all nature and to every nature. It applies to the *direction* and the *disposition* of every creature, living and non-living. Man's dominion over the earth, on the other hand, consists in a common natural right of all mankind to the *use of the earth* and the *use of its fruits*.

Common versus Private Property

You will note in the last sentence the words "*a common natural right* of all mankind." First, the right is *common*. God has given the earth to the use and enjoyment of the entire human race. Man has the right to use it because it is necessary for the sustenance of his life. St. Thomas tells us that it is because God ordained some things for the sustenance of human life that man has natural dominion over other creatures. We might question why it is *man* who has this natural dominion. Why is it not a being stronger than man, the lion, for instance? The answer can be given in one word: *person*. Of all the creatures of God that are found in the universe, only man is a *person*. And it is only intellectual beings who have the right to property. Intellectual beings have a dignity that is not found among lower creatures. Lower beings do not bear the close resemblance to God that man bears to Him. Man is like unto God in the higher part of his nature; namely, in his soul. But that soul is immortal, and hence it is destined for an end beyond the end of lesser creatures. Therefore lesser creatures are ordained to the end of man; they are meant to supply the needs of man's body and to better his condition. Hence man has dominion over them.

The primary dominion granted by God to mankind is *common*: all the universe for the use of all the human race. Common property differs, therefore, from private property. Private property means "this thing" for the sole use of "this person": John's hat for the sole use of John; Peter's dinner for the exclusive use of Peter. In this sense of *private* property, ownership means not merely the right to use the fruits of the earth, as a whole, but the right to use a definite portion of them to the exclusion of anyone else. That is important. It means, first, that a definite portion of the fruits of the earth may be claimed by a particular person. Mr. Brown may claim the house and lot at 58 Webster Avenue. He not only may claim that particular portion of the earth, but secondly, he may claim it to the exclusion of everyone else. No one may own that property while Mr. Brown's claim to it is valid. No one may use it against Mr. Brown's will so long as he retains his rightful claim to it. Should Mr. Brown return from a summer vacation to find that a stranger had moved into it during his absence, he is rightly indignant in his protest and in his insistence that the other move out. He may even call upon legitimate civil authority to uphold his claim and to force the other party to go.

There are, therefore, two kinds of ownership to keep distinguished in our minds and discussions: first, common ownership by the race of the earth and the fruits of the earth; second, private ownership by particular individuals of a portion of the earth and its fruits. Now the right to possess in common, which all mankind has, does not in any way withhold from individuals the right to possess certain definite portions of it as their own to the exclusion of everybody else. It requires, however, that the claims of individuals to particular portions of the earth and its goods be justified, that is, that they do not rob another of what is his due. Pope Leo writes:

> To say that God has given the earth to the use and enjoyment of the universal human race is not to deny that there can be private property. For God has granted the earth to mankind in general; not in the sense that all without distinction can deal with it as they please, but rather that no part of it has been assigned to any one in particular, and that the limits of private possession have been left to be fixed by man's own industry and the laws of individual peoples.

How individuals, without violating justice, obtain portions of the earth for exclusive use, will be discussed later. Our immediate concern is to investigate the foundation of man's right. We will see how *natural* it is, and upon what law it is founded.

Basis of Ownership

Some of man's rights spring very directly from his nature, and hence they are very close to the natural law. Some are less close, because less intimately bound up with the needs of his nature. Perhaps you recall that the family is more directly connected with the nature of man than the State. That is the reason why the family has priority of rights over the State in those things which concern the family's end and means. Man needs the family for his very existence and sustenance. He needs the State only to complete the insufficiency of the family's ability to provide for him adequately.

Now the right of ownership is not a primary principle of the natural law. It is a conclusion we reach upon reflection and reasoning. We reflect that man must sustain his life; that to do so he needs things daily because his needs recur daily. Our reason leads us to conclude that he has the right to have, regularly, the things which fill his needs. He has the right to have certain things for himself; things which no one may justly deny him, because he has *need* of them. This entitles him, in a general way in common with all other members of the race, to a share in the earth and its fruits. In the words of Pope Leo, we express it thus: "Nature owes to man a storehouse that shall never fail, the daily supply of his daily wants."

Therefore, the law upon which ownership is founded is the natural law. It is not rooted in the primary principles of the natural moral law, but in its more particular, less vague conclusions. *If* human life must be preserved, and *if* a man must provide for his offspring, *then* it follows that he has the right *to have* what is needful for these. But since his wants recur daily, "nature owes him a storehouse *that shall never* fail"; that is, man has a perpetual right to the necessary things; therefore he is entitled to *permanent possessions*.

Only human beings have this right to permanency. It expresses the dignity of the human person, its reflection of God's intelligence, its participation in the eternity of the Blessed Trinity, because it is on account of man's rational nature that he possesses this inviolable right. Only a rational nature can direct itself to its end. Only such a nature can provide for future needs intelligently with an understanding of the relationship between present goods and future requirements. Pope Leo does not hesitate to say that the brute has no such right to the fruits of the earth. A dog doesn't own his bone as a man does his dinner. A dog hasn't a right to a collar, a blanket, and a dog house as a man has to his clothes and his home. Nature provided the brute with the necessities of life quite near at hand, so near, in fact, that a dog always is provided with covering, whereas man has to use his head and his hands (in some way or other) to procure it for himself. The food of animals is ready-prepared, but not so with man's. The instincts of animals can attain their purpose by things which are close at hand because beyond their surroundings the brute cannot go. This is necessarily so, because brutes are moved by their senses alone, and they can know and crave only sense-goods. But with man it is different. Pope Leo writes:

> Man possesses, on the one hand, the full perfection of animal nature, and therefore he enjoys, at least as much as the rest of the animal race, the fruition of the things of the body. But animality, however perfect, is far from being the whole of humanity, and is indeed humanity's humble handmaid, made to serve and obey. It is the mind or the reason which is the chief thing in us who are human beings; *it is this* which makes a

human being human, and distinguishes him essentially and completely from the brute. And on this account — namely, that man alone among animals possesses reason — it must be within his right to have things not merely for temporary and momentary use, as other living beings have them, but *in stable and permanent possession.* He must have not only things which perish in the using, but also those which, though used, remain for use in the future.

Here is the right to permanent things as well as to temporary things; the right to productive as well as to consumptive possessions, for "things which perish in the using" are consumptive goods. They are used up. They no longer exist after they are used. Food, gasoline, clothing, and such things "perish in the use" and require replenishing regularly. However, things which "remain for use in the future" do not perish. They constantly furnish one's requirements; they keep one supplied over long periods of time, as do one's house, one's farm, one's factory, one's shop, and tools and equipment of any kind. Man has the right to this latter type of property as much as to the former type: to those which perish and to those who continue their usefulness.

You can see how this conclusion — namely, that man needs permanent possessions — is several steps away from the very first principles that one must do good and avoid evil. The need of permanent possessions is, nevertheless, connected with that primary principle, because if a man had not the necessities of life, he could not support life either in himself or in his dependents. In that case, he could not "do good"; that is, he could not do what nature prompts him to do — to care for his offspring, and sustain life. He would be doing evil, which is precisely what nature prompts him to avoid, for he would be permitting his offspring and himself to remain unnourished and uncared for and thus he would be endangering or killing life rather than sustaining it.

We say, therefore, that the right to possess things, and to possess them permanently (which means to have a permanent right to things), is rooted in the natural law through conclusions drawn from the primary and secondary principles. This, however, does not suffice for the right to *private* possessions.

Basis of Private Possessions

The natural law does not demand that possessions be privately held. Neither does it forbid private possessions. Man's reason, however, determines that to own goods privately is the best solution of the social problem, when judged in the light of human nature as human nature is. Now human nature *as it is* (since the Fall of our first parents) is inclined to selfishness, greed, injustice, and the like. Some individuals become more and more greedy with the acquisition and accumulation of goods. You've heard of misers, surely! Individuals of that type tend to acquire everything they can regardless of the needs of others. However, social life demands that there be harmony and peace, whereas greed and self-ishness disturb the social order. Now if possessions were held in common, so that everything was for everybody, there would be disorder, waste, confusion, neglect, dissatisfaction, unrest, and unhappiness. It is the very purpose of civil society to keep these vices out of the social organism. Reflecting that man's needs entitle him to the use of certain goods, and reflecting, further, that in the use of them there must be no harm done to the social body, human reason reaches the conclusion that goods ought to be held in private for the best interests of all and of each.

Pope Leo takes cognizance of this basis of private property in the encyclical on *The Condition of Labor*. He says:

The common opinion of mankind, little affected by the few dissentients who have maintained the opposite view, has found in the study of nature, and in the law of nature herself, the foundation of the division of property, and has consecrated by the practice of all ages the principle of private ownership, as being preeminently in conformity with human nature and as conducing in the most unmistakable manner to the peace and tranquility of human life.

The same principle is confirmed and enforced by the Civil Laws — laws which, as long as they are just — derive their binding force from the law of nature. The authority of the Divine Law adds its sanction, forbidding us in the gravest terms even to covet that which is another's.

Certain portions of goods should belong to certain individuals, not arbitrarily distributed, but obtained through effort — through labor or the fruits of labor, and in this way establishing a just claim to that particular portion of goods.

St. Thomas shows how the right to private possession is not found directly in the natural law but only as conclusions from it in conjunction with human reason and the common law of the nations (*jus gentium*). He writes:

Community of goods is ascribed to the Natural Law, not that the Natural Law dictates that all things should be possessed in common, and that nothing should be possessed as one's own: but because the division of possessions is not according to the Natural Law but rather arose from human agreement which belongs to Positive Law. Hence the ownership of possessions [in private] is not contrary to the Natural Law, but an addition to it which was devised by human reason.

St. Thomas wrote this explanation in answer to an objection which stated that private possessions were unlawful inasmuch as the natural law called for community of goods. But St. Thomas would not allow that objection to stand. He denied that the natural law called for possessions in common. He said the only way in which one could say that of the natural law is this: that the natural law did not mention division of goods, that is, it did not mention *private possessions*. He said, in effect, that because the natural law did not mention private possessions, this is not sufficient reason for saying that the natural law held private possessions to be unlawful. Then he went on to show how the right to private possessions is a matter of human reflection (upon natural inclinations) *and* a common verdict of the nations (human agreement). Read the exact words of St. Thomas again.

If you will read the section of chapter 7 which speaks of the *jus gentium*, you will review the statement made there. It said that the right to own possessions in private is said to belong to that "law of the nations" inasmuch as it is derived as a conclusion from a determination of the natural law viewed in connection with a universal fact: namely man's inclinations to selfishness and greed make possessions in common not a satisfactory method of meeting the needs of life and preserving unity and peace in a social organism. Pope Pius XI writes: "Now the Natural Law, or rather, God's will manifested by it, demands that right order be observed in the application of natural resources to human needs; and this order consists in everything having its proper owner." This is the foundation upon which rests the right to *private* possessions.

St. Thomas gives three arguments as to why possessions held privately are more conducive to peaceful living than common possessions. He says (my emphasis):

> Two things are fitting to man in respect *to* exterior things. One is *the power to procure and dispense them*, and in this regard it is lawful for a man to possess property [as his own]. Moreover this is necessary to human life for three reasons.
>
> First, because every man is more careful to procure what is [needful] for himself alone, than that which is common to many or to all:

since each one would shirk the labor and leave to another that which concerns the community as happens where there is a great number of servants.

St. Thomas understands human nature! Pope Leo wrote: "Men always work harder and more readily when they work on that which is their own." Soviet Russia found that out after a few years of collectivization!

St. Thomas continues: "Secondly, because human affairs are conducted in more orderly fashion if each man is charged with taking care of some particular thing himself, whereas there would be confusion if everyone had to look after any one thing indeterminately."

Imagine the confusion in New York City if everyone had to look after the cleaning of the streets — with no particular group responsible for that particular task! Suppose *everyone*, and that means without any special assignment to anyone, had to answer fire alarms to save the "common" property — how many buildings would burn to the ground?

"Thirdly," continues St. Thomas, "because a more peaceful state is ensured to man if each one is contented with his own. Hence it is to be observed that quarrels arise more frequently where there is no division of the things possessed."

That is why there are tickets issued for definite places at a ball game! That is why property is marked off and fences enclose particular portions of land. That is why buying and selling are modern standard means of transferring goods and why goods are "willed" to particular persons at death rather than left in common to any and all.

"The second thing that is fitting to man with regard to external things," says St. Thomas, "is their *use*. In this respect man ought to possess external things, not as his own, but as common, so that he is ready to communicate them to others in their need."

The Earth or Only the Fruits

Before we discuss this second thing that is fitting to man, we shall determine whether men are entitled to the use only of the earth or to particular portions of the earth as well. The point is important because it reveals the distinction between the right to *productive* private possessions and *consumptive* private possessions. It amounts to this: does a man own his farmland, or does he own only the produce of it? Can he claim only the heads of cabbage which grew in his garden, or can he claim the soil in which the cabbage grew? That might seem a silly question, but it is one much discussed in certain circles today. May a man own a factory and machines which produce goods? Communism answers no, that is "exploiting", that is, taking unfair advantage of the men who run the machines, for laborers receive merely a wage, whereas the "exploiter" (I am speaking in the language of Communism now) receives profits unjustly gained through the labor of workmen. Communism forgets, you see, that capital is entitled to a just return on machinery, investment, management of the business, and the like.

To answer the question whether men may own the land or only the fruits of it, we shall go to Pope Leo's encyclical on *The Condition of Labor*. He argues first from man's nature, saying that by his powers of reasoning, by his ability to see the present and the future, and by the fact that he is free master of his actions, he is able to foresee future needs and to provide for them in advance. You will agree that, necessary as this is in the life of the unattached individual who lives apart from the domestic circle, it is even more necessary in the case of a father of a family who must provide, by the very dictates of nature, not only for himself and his wife but for his offspring as well. "Hence," concludes Pope Leo, "man not only can possess the fruits of the earth, but also the earth itself; for of the products of the earth he can make provisions for the future. Man's needs do not die out but recur; satisfied today, they demand new supplies tomorrow."

Now what applies to the ownership of land, applies, too, to any type of productive private property. Man has the right to it. Of the *use* of the property we shall speak in detail subsequently.

Extent of Ownership

Particular persons may own particular portions of this earth's goods solely and exclusively as their own. This right to own goods means to exercise domination over them. St. Thomas speaks of it as the right to *procure* and to *dispense*. More simply, we might say that ownership is the right to *have*, to *use*, and to *dispose* of things as one's own. These three expressions mean that an owner has the right to use his property himself for his own gain; he may transfer it to another freely as a donation, or by contract, as by a sale. He may transfer the use of it, as when he rents a house to another, or he may transfer the fruits of it, as when he sells the produce which his machines or his farm have given him; he may will it to another through testament, as when a father wills his property to his wife and children; or he may exchange his property, as when one "turns in" a machine for a later model.

Just Claims to Property

The extent of ownership, discussed in the preceding section, indicates several rightful titles or claims to ownership. One may claim the sole right to something, as — let us say, to a house, either because he bought it, or because it was given to him, or because he exchanged something of his own for it, or because it had been willed to him. Perhaps he built it himself. Industry (one's own labor) is a very common claim to ownership. There is another title or claim to rightful possession of a thing which moralists call *occupation*. Occupation implies that a person has taken hold of something which belonged to no one — which was utterly unclaimed. Pope Pius XI writes that no wrong is done to any man "by the occupation of goods unclaimed and which belong to nobody."

Let us consider industry as a title of ownership. Recall the Homestead Act of 1862. The government declared itself willing to give 160 acres of land free to anyone who would live on it and till it for a period of five years. A necessary condition of the bargain was that the land was to be cultivated. At the end of the five years the government declared it would be willing to grant a legal title to the occupant provided he could show that the land had been improved.

The justification for such a claim lies in this: that the one who had tilled the soil for five years had put so much of himself into the soil that it is himself in some inexpressible way. He had impressed his personality upon it. Pope Leo says (my emphasis): "When a man spends the *industry* of his mind and the *strength* of his body in procuring the fruits of nature, *by that act* he makes his own that portion of nature's field which he cultivates — that portion on which he leaves the impress of his own personality; and it cannot but be just that he should possess that portion as his own, and should have a right to keep it without molestation."

Labor may be expended on the property of another. Do Pope Leo's words imply that a man may claim the property in this case because of the exercise of his industry upon it? No, they do not. Pope Pius XI wrote of this point and he says: "The only form of labor which gives the workingman a title to its fruits is that which a man exercises *as his own master*, and by which some new form or new value is produced." What an important statement! First, the man must exercise his industry *as his own master*. Now if a man lends his services to another, that is, if he hires himself to another, he is not his own master in respect to the work he is doing. He cannot therefore justly claim the fruits of his labor. A plumber who comes into your home to fix a leaking pipe cannot claim the pipe as his own because of his labor on it. "Unless a man apply his labor to his own property," writes Pope Pius XI, "an alliance must be formed between his toil and his neighbor's property." The "alliance" is a contract. The laborer will receive money, goods, or some other remuneration for his labor. He has no just claim to the goods upon which he worked.

An instance of *occupation* as a just title of ownership will be readily understood if we speak of the early westward movement in American history. The land, before the government had acquired, by purchase and acquisition, a right to it from coast to coast, belonged to nobody. It was unclaimed land. It was vacant. One acquired a just claim to it by "laying hold" of it with the intention of making it one's own. This differs from the instance of land being given away through the Homestead Act, for by 1862 the government had acquired a right to all the land from coast to coast. Occupation of land as a just title was common in the days of the forty-niners. You recall how they staked off their claims wherever and whenever they had reason to believe that gold was in the streams of the land.

When local civil authorities grant hunting licenses in proper seasons, then the hunter has a just claim on the basis of *occupation* when he shoots down a deer. So, too, with those who fish. Occupation as a title to possession is limited.

Wages as Possessions

Are wages to be considered as possessions? May a laborer convert his wages into personal possessions? May he convert his wages into property in the sense of real estate? The answer is a triple yes. The usual reason why a man hires out his labor is to obtain remuneration which he intends to convert into the necessities of life. Therefore, whether we consider the wage itself or the things procured through the wage, the laborer has a just claim to either form of the remuneration. Not only is it permitted to convert one's wage into real estate, but it is a desirable thing to do. It is one of the forms of property urged by the Holy Fathers when they speak of a wider distribution of property. Having purchased the real estate, the owner may dispose of it as he pleases. The right of ownership includes the procuring and the disposing of the thing owned. For this reason, the Socialists' and Communists' abolition of private property is an injustice, for property is merely the laborer's wage in another form, and the title to it is as sacred as the title to the wage itself.

Pope Leo writes:

It is surely undeniable that when a man engages in remunerative labor, the very reason and motive of his work is to obtain property, and to hold it as his own private possession. If one man hires out to another his strength or his industry, he does this for the purpose of receiving in return what is necessary for food and living; he thereby expressly proposes to acquire a full and real right, not only to the remuneration but also to the disposal of that remuneration as he pleases.

Thus, if he lives sparingly, saves money, and invests his savings for greater security in land, the land in such case is only his wages in another form; and consequently, a working man's little estate thus purchased should be as completely at his own disposal as the wages he receives for his labor.

Aspects of Property

In discussing man's labor, we said it must be viewed under two aspects: namely, individual and social. Later we saw that man's wages must be viewed under these same two aspects of individual and social. It will not surprise us, therefore, to know that in viewing man's property rights we must view them under the same dual aspects. Man's rights to possessions are individual or personal, and social inasmuch as they affect the common good. In other words, St. Thomas says man should consider his possessions as his "to have privately" and "to use publicly."

"Having privately" sends our thoughts right back to the basis of man's right to possess as we saw it drawn from the primary and secondary precepts of the natural law. Man has the individual right *to have*. The right is inalienable. It is based on nature and nature is prior to the State. "For every man has by nature the right to possess property as his own," says Pope Leo. Again, "Man's natural right of possessing [property] and transmitting property by inheritance must remain intact and cannot be taken away from man by the State."

These statements concern man's right to have property. His right to use property is a different matter. We can make the distinction clear in a simple illustration. I have the right to possess a load of bricks. I may not use those bricks to break your windows. "The right of property must be distinguished from its use," wrote Pope Pius XI. "It follows from the two-fold character of ownership, which we have termed individual and social, that men take into account in this matter not only their own advantage but also the common good. To define in detail these duties, when the need occurs and when the Natural Law does not do so, is the function of the government." Prior to that, Pope Leo had said: "The limits of private possession have been left to be fixed by man's own industry and the laws of individual peoples." This is merely to say that civil authority has the right to regulate the use of one's possessions insofar as the exercise of the right of ownership conflicts with the rights of others, in which case it disturbs the internal harmony and indirectly affects the common good, or insofar as the exercise of the right conflicts with the common good directly. The use of one's possessions must always be in accord with the demands of commutative justice and social justice. The right is inalienable. The use is controllable.

From the fact that property has a social aspect as well as an individual one, it is not difficult to see that it must never become injurious to the common good; that it is not created for privileged classes, but, in accord with the papal program for social reconstruction, it should be more widely distributed among the masses. As a human institution, it is capable of developing man's personality. It encourages man's artistic, productive, and inventive powers; it is capable of encouraging liberality and of crushing greed and avarice; it creates a sense of security and peace in the commonwealth. It induces man to virtuous living through easing the mind of anxieties about the present and the future, thus leaving it free to think of the Source of their good fortune and to thank God most abundantly for it.

Disposition of One's Property

We spoke of this when discussing almsgiving. We shall review it very briefly here. (1) One is not obliged to give of his possessions if they are needful for the necessities of life, that is, for the *absolute necessities*, without which life could not be sustained. (2) One is not required to give from that which is necessary to the maintenance of his station in life. The maintenance of one's station is considered as *relative necessity*. Justice obliges in neither case, ordinarily. One is obliged, however, to give out of one's superfluous goods, to those who are in need of help. Justice obliges this in the face of extreme necessity; ordinarily charity counsels this almsgiving. "It is an effect of love that men give their own goods to others," writes St. Thomas. Read Original Source 1 in connection with this.

Answer to Communism and Liberalism

Communism's fundamental principle is the abolition of private property. The Christian fundamental principle is the wider distribution of property. Having given the whole view of property according to Christian principles, little needs to be said for the Communistic view. It stands refuted.

In the case of Liberalism, that philosophy of life consistently ignored the social aspect of man and life — whereas in the Communistic philosophy, the individual aspect of man and life is ignored. Therefore in the matter of private possessions, Liberalistic philosophy views man's rights as absolute, while Communism denies the right completely. The position of the Church makes man's right inalienable in its nature and subject to regulation in its use; that makes the right bear the characteristics of a *relative* right; it must be exercised in view of the common good.

Where Liberalism claimed for the individual the absolute domination of God over things; Communism appropriates the absolute domination of God to the collectivity, denying any domination to the individual. The Church sees God as the sole Ruler and Master, exercising supreme domination over the entire universe of things and persons; it sees the individual, made in the image of God, exercising domination over the use of things which conduce to his final end: the acquisition of an everlasting possession — of God.

We have completed now the discussion of the second major point laid down by Pope Pius XI for the reconstruction of the social order. The first point called for a reconciliation of the classes (chapter 20). The second point called for a wider distribution of wealth. This we discussed under the two headings of a just family wage (chapter 21) and the right to private possessions (chapter 22). The third point remains to be discussed, namely, effecting a bond of union between capital and labor. That will constitute the subject of chapter 23.

Some Original Sources

In speaking of almsgiving out of one's possessions, St. Thomas writes:

1. "A thing is necessary in two ways:

"First, because without it something is impossible, and it is altogether wrong to give alms out of what is necessary to us in this sense....

"Secondly, a thing is said to be necessary, if a man cannot without it live in keeping with his social station, as regards either himself or those of whom he has charge.

"The *necessary* considered in this second place is not an invariable quantity, for one might add much more to a man's property, and yet not go beyond what he needs in this way, or one might take touch from him, and he would still have sufficient for the decencies of life in keeping with his own position.

"Accordingly it is good to give alms of this kind of *necessary*; and it is a matter not of precept but of counsel. Yet it would be inordinate to deprive oneself of one's own, in order to give to others to such an extent that the residue would be insufficient for one to live in keeping with one's station and the ordinary occurrences of life: for no man ought to live unbecomingly.

"There are, however, three exceptions to the above rule:

"First, when a man changes his state of life, for instance, by entering religion, for then he gives away all his possessions for Christ's sake, and does the deed of perfection by transferring himself to another state.

"Secondly, when that which he deprives himself of, though it be required for the decencies of life, can nevertheless easily be recovered, so that he does not suffer extreme inconvenience.

"Thirdly, when he is in presence of extreme indigence in an individual, or great need on the part of the commonweal. For in such cases it would seem praiseworthy to forego the requirements of one's station, in order to provide for a greater need." (*Summa Theologica*, vol. 9, p. 420)

2. "The temporal goods which God grants us, are ours as to the ownership, but as to the use of them, they belong not to us alone but also to such others as we are able to succour out of what we have over and above our needs." (*Summa Theologica*, vol. 9, p. 418)

3. "Since it is not possible for one individual to relieve the needs of all, we are not bound to relieve all who are in need, but only those who could not be succoured if we did not succour them.... Accordingly we are bound to give alms of our surplus, as also to give alms to one whose need is extreme: otherwise almsgiving, like any other greater good, is a matter of counsel." (*Summa Theologica*, vol. 9, p. 418)

4. "All things are common property in a case of extreme necessity. Hence one who is in such dire straits may take another's goods in order to succor himself, if he can find no one who is willing to give him something." (*Summa Theologica*, vol. 9, p. 424)

5. "Man's supreme good must consist in obtaining something better than man. But man is better than wealth: since it is something directed to man's use. Therefore not in wealth does man's supreme good consist.

"Man's supreme good is not subject to chance. For things that happen by chance, escape the forethought of reason: whereas man has to attain his own end by means of his reason. But chance occupies the greater place in the attaining of wealth. Therefore human happiness consists not in wealth." (*Summa Contra Gentiles*, vol. 3, chap. 30)

In the following, you will detect the point made in the chapter, namely, that for St. Thomas, wealth was a medium of exchange, but not a means of producing new wealth. He says:

6. "Wealth is two fold, viz., natural and artificial. Natural wealth is that which serves man as a remedy for his natural wants: such as food, drink, clothing, cars, dwellings,

and such like, while artificial wealth is that which is not a direct help to nature, as money, but is invented by the art of man, for the convenience of exchange, and as a measure of things saleable....

"Artificial wealth is not sought except for the sake of natural wealth; since man would not seek it except because, by its means, he procures for himself the necessaries of life....

"All material things obey money, so far as the multitude of fools is concerned, who know no other than material goods, which can be obtained for money. But we should take our estimation of human goods not from the foolish but from the wise." (*Summa Theologica*, vol. 6, p. 18)

7. "External things can be considered in two ways:

"Firstly, as regards their nature, and this is not subject to the power of man, but only to the power of God Whose mere will all things obey.

"Secondly, as regards their use, and in this way, man has a natural dominion over external things, because, by his reason and will, he is able to use them for his own profit as they were made on his account: for the imperfect is always for the sake of the perfect.

"It is by this argument that Aristotle proves that the possession of external things is natural to man. Moreover, this natural dominion of man over other creatures, which is fitting to man in respect of his reason wherein God's image resided, is shown forth in man's creation by the words: Let us make man to Our image and likeness: and let him have dominion over the fishes of the sea....

"God has dominion over all things: and He, according to His providence, directed certain things to the sustenance of man's body. For this reason man has a natural dominion over things as regards the power to make use of them.

"The rich man is reproved for deeming external things to belong to him principally, as though he had not received them from another, namely from God." (*Summa Theologica*, vol. 10, p. 222)

See also the long quotation on man's dominion over external things incorporated in this chapter.

Here is how St. Thomas explains the extent of private ownership:

8. "We say in the first place that he who is owner of a thing is also owner of the use of that thing.

"We say secondly that the real owner of a thing may transfer it to another gratis, or for a consideration, or in exchange for another thing.

"Thirdly, we say that the owner can transfer the use and the fruit of his property.

"Fourthly, we say also that as the real owner of a thing, he can give or sell the property of the thing, or the fruit and use of the thing for all time, so he can also give or sell it for a fixed and particular time." (*Smaller Works*, no. 66, chap. 9)

9. "Things possessed are truly subjected to the power of private persons. Therefore, by their own authority they can communicate these things to each other, for instance, by buying, selling, giving or any other such ways." (*Summa Theologica*, vol. 8, p. 257)

10. "It follows from the twofold character of ownership, which we have termed individual and social, that men must take into account in this matter not only their own advantage but also the common good. To define in detail these duties, when the need occurs and when the Natural Law does not do so, is the function of the government. Provided that the Natural and Divine Law be observed, the public authority, in view of the common good, may specify more accurately what is licit and what is illicit for property owners *in the use of their possessions*....

"Whenever civil authority adjusts ownership to meet the needs of the public good it acts not as an enemy, but as the friend of private owners; for thus it effectively prevents the possessions of private property, intended by Nature's Author in His Wisdom for the sustaining of human life, from creating intolerable burdens and so rushing to its own destruction. It does not therefore abolish, but protects private ownership, and, far from weakening the right of private property, it gives it new strength." (Pope Pius XI, *The Reconstruction of the Social Order*, my emphasis)

11. "The original acquisition of property takes place by first occupation and by industry. This is the universal teaching of tradition and the doctrine of Pope Leo, despite unreasonable assertions to the contrary, and no wrong is done to any man by the occupation of goods unclaimed and which belong to nobody.

"The only form of labor, however, which gives the workingman a title to its fruits, is that which a man exercises as his own master, and by which some new form or new value is produced.

"Altogether different is the labor one man hires out to another and which is expended on the property of another.... Unless a man apply his labor to his own property, an alliance must be formed between his toil and his neighbor's property for each is helpless without the other.

"It is therefore entirely false to ascribe the results of their combined efforts to either party alone; and it is flagrantly unjust that either should deny the efficacy of the other and seize all the profits." (Pope Pius XI, *The Reconstruction of the Social Order*)

Pope Leo's encyclical on *The Condition of Labor* is well worth reading in its entirety for the doctrine on private possessions. From it we have the following excerpts:

12. "Those whom fortune favors are warned that freedom from sorrow and abundance of earthly riches are no guarantee of that beatitude that should never end, but rather the contrary; and that a most strict account must be given to the Supreme Judge for all that we possess.

"The chiefest and most excellent rule for the right use of money is one which the heathen philosophers indicated, but which the Church traced out clearly, and has not only made known to men's minds, but has impressed upon their lives. It rests on the principle that it is one thing to have a right to the possession of money, and another to have a right to use money as one pleases.

"Private ownership, as we have seen, is the natural right of man; and to exercise that right, especially as members of society, is not only lawful but absolutely necessary. 'It is lawful,' says Saint Thomas of Aquin, 'for a man to hold private property; and it is also necessary for the carrying on of human life.'

"But if the question be asked, How must one's possessions be used? the Church replies without hesitation in the words of the same holy Doctor: 'Man should not consider his outward possessions as his own, but as common to all, so as to share them without difficulty when others are in need.'

"True, no one is commanded to distribute to others that which is required for his own necessities and those of his household; nor even to give away what is reasonably required to keep up becomingly his condition of life; for no one ought to live unbecomingly. But when necessity has been supplied, and one's position fairly considered, it is a duty to give to the indigent out of that which is over. It is a duty, not of justice (except in extreme cases), but of Christian charity—a duty which is not enforced by human laws.

"But the laws and judgment of men must give place to the laws and judgment of Christ, the true God; Who in many ways urges on His followers the practice of almsgiving....

"Whoever, therefore, has received from the Divine bounty a large share of blessings, whether they be external and corporal, or gifts of the mind, has received them for the purpose of using them for perfecting his own nature, and, at the same time, that he may employ them, as the minister of God's Providence, for the benefit of others.

13. "If a workman's wages be sufficient to enable him to maintain himself, his wife, and his children in reasonable comfort, he will not find it difficult, if he is a sensible man, to study economy; and he will not fail, by cutting down expenses, to put by a little property. Nature and reason would urge him to do this.

"We have seen that this great labor question cannot be solved except by assuming as a principle that private ownership must be held sacred and inviolable. The law, therefore, should favor ownership, and its policy should be to induce as many people as possible to become owners.

"Many excellent results will follow from this; and first of all, property will certainly become more equitably divided. For the effect of civil change and revolution has been to divide society into two widely different castes. On the one side there is the party which holds the power because it holds the wealth; which has in its grasp all labor and all trade; which manipulates for its own benefit and its own purposes all the sources of supply and which is powerfully represented in the councils of the State itself.

"On the other side there is the needy and powerless multitude, sore and suffering, always ready for disturbance. If working people can be encouraged to look forward to obtaining a share in the land, the result will be that the gulf between vast wealth and deep poverty will be bridged over, and the two orders will be brought nearer together.

"Another consequence will be the greater abundance of the fruits of the earth. Men always work harder and more readily when they work on that which is their own; nay, they learn to love the very soil which yields in response to the labor of their hands, not only food to eat, but an abundance of the good things for themselves and those that are dear to them. It is evident how such a spirit of willing labor would add to the produce of the earth and to the wealth of the community.

"And a third advantage would arise from this: men would cling to the country in which they were born; for no one would exchange his country for a foreign land if his own afforded him the means of living a tolerable and happy life.

"These three important benefits, however, can only be expected on the condition that a man's means be not drained and exhausted by excessive taxation. The right to possess private property is from nature, not from man; and the State has only the right to regulate its use in the interests of the public good, but by no means to abolish it altogether. The State is, therefore, unjust and cruel, if, in the name of taxation, it deprives the private owner of more than is just." (*The Condition of Labor*)

From Pope Pius XI we have the following:

14. "Let it be made clear beyond all doubt that neither Leo XIII, nor those theologians who have taught under the guidance and direction of the Church, have ever denied or called in question the two-fold aspect of ownership, which is individual or social accordingly as it regards individuals or concerns the common good.

"Their unanimous contention has always been that the right to own private property has been given to man by nature or rather by the Creator Himself, not only in order that individuals may be able to provide for their own needs and those of their families, but also that by means of it, the goods which the Creator has destined for the human race may truly serve this purpose. Now these ends cannot be secured unless some definite and stable order is maintained.

"There is, therefore, a double danger to be avoided. On the one hand, if the social and public aspect of ownership be denied or minimized, the logical consequence is Individualism, as it is called; on the other hand, the rejection or diminution of its private and individual character necessarily leads to some form of collectivism....

"That we may keep within bounds the controversies which have arisen concerning ownership and the duties attaching to it, We reassert in the first place the fundamental principle laid down by Leo XIII, that the right of property must be distinguished from its use.

"It belongs to what is called commutative justice faithfully to respect the possessions of others, not encroaching on the rights of another and thus exceeding one's rights of ownership. The putting of one's own possessions to proper use, however, does not fall under this form of justice, but under certain other virtues and therefore it is 'a duty not enforced by courts of justice.'

"Hence it is idle to contend that the right of ownership and its proper use are bounded by the same limits; and it is even less true that the very misuse or even the non-use of ownership destroys or forfeits the right itself." (Pope Pius XI, *The Reconstruction of the Social Order*)

15. Note in the three following excerpts from Pope Pius's encyclical on *The Reconstruction of the Social Order*, how he repeats variously the point that *good order* in society necessitates the division of property—that is, justifies the private holding of property. He says:

(a) "Now these ends [providing for one's personal and family needs] cannot be secured unless some definite and stable order is maintained."

(b) "Now the Natural Law, or rather, God's Will manifested by it, i.e., the Natural Law, demands that right order be observed in the application of natural resources to human needs; and this order consists in everything having its proper owner."

(c) "The division of goods, which is effected by private ownership is ordained by nature itself and has for its purpose that created things may minister to man's need in orderly and stable fashion."

16. See the chapter on human law (chapter 7), the *jus gentium*, in connection with good order in society and the division of goods.

Summary

1. Ownership is the moral right to have, to use, and to dispose of something as one's own. Property is the thing over which this dominion is exercised.

2. God has absolute dominion over all things. He is the Master of the universe. Man has a dominion over things as to the use of the things required for the sustenance of his body and for decent human living.

3. The world belongs to the race as a whole. Thus the universe and all it contains are for the benefit of the whole of mankind. This is what is meant when we say that man possesses the universe *in common*.

4. Man has the right to possess things as his own because man has a rational nature and is capable of supplying for his future needs from present abundance or from the labor of his hands. For this reason only intellectual beings have the right to possess.

5. Man's right to own springs from the needs of his nature. He must fill the needs of nature daily and thus it is his right to have a supply that never fails. Pope Leo says nature owes him this.

6. The right to possess in private is the right to claim something as one's own to the exclusion of everybody else. This right is a moral power to have, to use, and to dispose of things as one's own.

7. Man has the right to things, not only for present use, such as consumptive goods which perish in the use, but also the right to possess things for future use, such as productive possessions which do not perish in the use but remain for further use.

8. The basis of man's right to *private* possessions is the law of nature and the *jus gentium*. (See chapter 7.)

9. The right of property must be viewed in a twofold aspect; the right *to have* and the right *to use*. This corresponds to the twofold division of individual and social aspects of property.

10. St. Thomas expresses these aspects by the terms: to have privately, to use publicly.

11. Man may own not only the fruits of the land but even the land itself.

12. Occupation and industry are just titles to private ownership.

13. Ownership extends to the right to procure and to dispense things. It means, briefly, that one may buy, sell, donate, use, transfer, will by testament, or exchange things over which he has dominion.

14. A man's property is as much at his disposal as the wage he receives for his labor.

15. A man may dispose of his property as he wishes provided he work no injustice upon another or do anything contrary to the common good. As for the giving of alms a man is not obliged to give:

   (1) out of absolute necessity, that is, out of that which is so necessary for him that without it his life could not be sustained.

   (2) out of relative necessity, that is, out of that which is required for living according to his station in life.

16. A man is required, not by justice, except in extreme cases, but by charity to give out of that which is over and above his absolute and his relative necessities.

See the excerpt from St. Thomas on almsgiving among the original sources, no. 1, this chapter.

For Study and Discussion

1. Explain the difference between *ownership* and *property*.

2. Discuss the difference between the dominion of God and the dominion of man over the goods of the earth.

3. What is the distinction between *common* and *private* property? On what basis is the world said to be the common property of mankind?

4. Explain: only a rational being has the right of ownership.

5. Explain how the right of property is derived from man's needs and hence is traceable to and based on the natural law.
6. What is the difference between consumptive private property and productive private property? Give examples of each kind.
7. Explain the basis of man's right to *private* possessions.
8. What three arguments does St. Thomas give why possessions should be held privately?
9. Discuss: Man should be entitled to the earth, as well as to the fruits thereof. Give reasons. What is Pope Leo's argument on this matter?
10. Explain the extent of ownership.
11. Enumerate the various just claims to property. Explain each kind.
12. Explain how Pope Leo arrived at the conclusion that "a working man's little estate should be as completely at his own disposal as the wages he receives for his labor."
13. What is meant by *to have privately* and *to use publicly*? What is the difference between the individual and the social aspects of property?
14. Explain how one may dispose of his property. What is man's obligation with respect to almsgiving?
15. How does the Catholic doctrine of property answer the excesses of Liberalism and Communism?

For the Advanced Reader

St. Thomas:

An Apology for Religious Orders, pp. 168ff
Opusculum no. 66, chap. 9
Summa Contra Gentiles, vol. 3, chap. 30
Summa Theologica, vol. 8, pp. 256ff; vol. 10, pp. 221ff

Farrell, Walter:

A Companion to the Summa, III, pp. 204–210

McDonald, William:

The Social Value of Property, vol. 48, *Philosophical Studies*, C.U.A.

Papal Encyclicals:

Pope Leo XIII: *The Condition of Labor*
Pope Pius XI: *The Reconstruction of the Social Order*

Philosophy of the State, reprinted 1940 from 1939 proceedings of the American Catholic Philosophical Association: "Public Control of Private Property," pp. 191ff

23

Man Socially "Ordered"

───────────────────⟨∞⟩───────────────────

"Unless brains, capital and labor combine together for common effort, man's toil cannot produce due fruit." These words were written by Pope Pius XI. Can we find in them some reason for the economic distress so prevalent among the masses today and which caused the same Holy Father to call the present economic domination cruel and relentless in a ghastly way? The present order (we might more properly say the present disorder) of society is the logical result of the "rugged individualism" which Liberalistic philosophy bequeathed to the modern world.

Society Reordered

A third objective, therefore, of the papal program for social reconstruction is a new "ordering" of society. It means a new socially correct and morally correct re-adjustment of the levels or classes of society. It requires a more harmonious coordination of society's members. It necessitates a return from the social distortion which isolated member from member and paralyzed the common united effort of the social whole.

For man, you know, is by nature socially inclined. He needs now to be redirected, reordered to the social organism which became dismembered under the devastating philosophy of "individual liberty" prevalent during the past several centuries. We have already noted these words of Pope Pius:

> When We speak of the reform of the social order it is principally the State We have in mind ... because, on account of Individualism, things have come to such a pass that the highly developed social life which once flourished in a variety of prosperous institutions organically linked with each other, has been damaged and all but ruined, leaving thus virtually only individuals and the State. Social life lost entirely its organic form.

The only means, therefore, whereby the individual can be saved from that absolute State domination which is totalitarianism, is by a return to social life that is *organic*. That is a kind of social life which consists of a variety of independent and interdependent *organs* or institutions. Each unit plays its necessary part as an organ in the social organism and it thereby contributes to the attainment of society's goal.

The "Reordering"

We must recall in this place the definition of St. Thomas for order. He calls it, "the apt arrangement of a plurality of parts." The arrangement must be *apt*, that is, suited or fitted to the nature and needs of the parts which are being arranged.

There are first of all, a number of *parts*, and these, secondly, must be suitably arranged, for order consists precisely in this proper arrangement of the parts of a whole. Each part must occupy the position in the whole for which it is most suited. In a hotel, for instance, one is best suited to cook; another to run the elevators; another to be desk clerk; another to make the purchases; and still another to oversee the activities of all. If the chefs insisted upon running the elevators, and the bell boys insisted upon managing the hotel, there would be no order. The whole hotel life would be chaotic, confused. There is order only when each part plays the role for which it is suited and to which it has been assigned. It is that which constitutes the "apt arrangement" of different capacities.

In the social order as a whole, as well as in each of the various lesser social unities (or institutions), such as the family, the State, the Church, the school, the city, the economic realm, and the like, there must be suitable arrangement of persons and of institutions according to their capacities and goals. Things will not run smoothly unless all are thus "ordered." A machine breaks down if a screw becomes disordered. An army becomes a mob when it becomes disorganized.

The reordering of society, for which the papal plan for reconstruction calls, means that the various parts of society must be united in common effort for a common goal according to the capacities of the various members. That is the ideal of society, the end for which society exists, and the only adequate way in which it can effect man's greatest temporal good. The modern world, however, has witnessed a very decided swerving of society from its true purpose. Society as a whole is not at present attaining its purpose because the component parts of society have failed to make common effort for the common end. Individualism is to blame for it. It dismembered the social body. It made each individual a self-inflated individual with a personal goal out of harmony with the common goal. It struck off countless bypaths toward individual ends of an absolute character. It did not hold society and its parts to the main road, to the common pursuit of a common end.

It is as if, in the human body, the various organs and members which are commonly ordained to the good of the whole body, were each to strike out for themselves regardless of the well-being of the whole body. If the hand were to claim absolute independence of the rest of the body, what a state man would be in! How could we reconcile that independence with St. Thomas's insistence that, in place of certain animal equipment for easy living, man has been supplied with *reason and hands* to supply his daily needs? For a hand, if it should claim absolute independence of the rest of the body, would not work in harmony with reason for the good of the body. And how, then, could man's needs be met?

Again, if the heart, for instance, were to claim independence of the rest of the body, how long would the body survive? If the heart worked without regard for the organs which supplemented its work or which contributed to its activity, how long could the body stand up under the strain of this disorganization? Organs are ordained to each other and to the body as a whole. Only then is there organic unity. For then there is truly "a body" because there is collaboration and cooperation in singleness of purpose by a multiplicity of interdependent organs and members.

In the social body, it is similar. There we find a variety of organs and members, independent relatively, yet interdependent socially, namely: the individuals, the family, the State, the Church, economic groups, and the like. The cure for present conditions must be found in the redirection of these members of society one to the other and of each to the whole. "The good of each and the good of all" is an expression of Pope Pius's which states the true aim of the social body. This cure is an answer to the Communistic aim of leveling society. Pope Leo, you recall, insisted that society could not be conceived nor could it exist without levels. By *levels* is meant inequalities in conditions resulting from diversity of talents. It means that variety of contributions which the members of society make, each making the contribution which he is best fitted by nature to make. These natural inequalities necessitate an "ordering" of the parts to the whole in the social body, an ordering of the lesser to the higher, of the imperfect and the proximate, to the perfect and the ultimate.

Reordering society, therefore, necessitates (1) the recognition of the inequalities themselves, and of the naturalness of these inequalities; (2) the just distribution of contributions and of burdens so that each part of the whole will play the role he is best fitted to play *in view of the good of all and the good of each*. This makes for healthy members in a healthy body. This constitutes an "apt arrangement of a plurality of parts" in the social order. This effects social unity in a social organism.

The Guild System

Human society at one time was characterized by a kind of organic unity which we might here designate as *corporativeness*. Let us take a brief, a very brief, look back into history.

Agriculture and hunting were the early pursuits of man. Man had to live and preserve his life. Nearest to his hand were the soil and animal life, as means to his physical end. These met his most elementary needs. In his leisure time man developed skills in artistry of a variety of kinds. Man's hands then worked for things other than the bare necessities of life. Men drew, carved, molded, hammered, wove. With the development of the nations, other pursuits in addition to agriculture and hunting occupied members of the race. Men became *makers* of things. Tools were crude at first, then later they became more and more refined. Output in the beginning was limited and none too perfect. With increased experience there arose a delicacy and exquisiteness in the products of the artisans which defy machines to match.

By the Middle Ages the workers who were engaged in the crafts, being already united in common interests, formed themselves into groups for better production, for the protection and the extension of their craft, and for the well-being of its workers. Merchants likewise combined, as did nearly all workers having common interests. This combination of workers united in a *common* line of work became known by the name of the *guild*. The aim of the guilds was to regulate *industry* as they used the term; not the large-scale machine production that we know, but the small-scale industry of the arts and crafts of the Middle Ages. Their aim was to secure a better livelihood for their members. They not only controlled industry but maintained schools, libraries, hospitals, and like institutions for their members. They were social organs, cooperating with other institutions such as the family, the State, and the Church, and organically united to them in a system of social institutions harmoniously co-acting as a social body for the good of all and the good of each.

When William the Conqueror invaded England, the merchant guilds were already existing. In France merchant guilds and craft guilds existed from the earliest years of the eleventh century. The guild system spread throughout the continent of Europe. Its history can be traced from the eleventh century through to the close of the eighteenth, though its most prosperous period extended from the twelfth to the fourteenth centuries. At the height of the effectiveness of the guild system there was scarcely an industry which escaped its control.

Then the Black Plague struck. It devastated Europe when the fourteenth century had run about half its course. It carried off thousands upon thousands of laborers. Those that remained were greatly in demand. The demand exceeded the supply and the price of labor rose. It was then, as an effect of the Plague on industry, that a weakening began in the guilds' control of industry. Labor became a bit independent and restive under the regulations imposed by the guilds. Within the century whose closing years witnessed the discovery of America, labor was drawing more and more from the influence of the guilds.

Then came a plague worse than the Black Death which had stalked across Europe in the middle of the fourteenth century. The "plague" was a religious one: the Protestant Revolt begun by Martin Luther early in the sixteenth century. (Luther's dates are 1483–1546.) The break with lawfully constituted authority which marked the origin, doctrine, and history of the Protestant Revolt found ready sympathy among many working men who had already begun to withdraw themselves from the control of the guilds.

Guilds Permeated by Religion

The chief point to bear in mind in speaking of the guilds of the Middle Ages is that they flourished in a religious atmosphere. The age of the rise and growth of the guilds was the Age of Faith. Religion and morality played their unifying and purifying roles in the guild system. It was an age when men recognized "others" as "brothers"; it was the age before Protestantism in any form had appeared on the scene. The social body of those centuries was strong and the members of that body had not yet been infected with the evil of individualism. That the guilds did not survive to modern days can be accounted for in a number of ways. The question is beyond the scope of the present work. The Protestant Revolt, however, had much to do with the death of them in England. The religious atmosphere to which they had been accustomed lost its purity. The king instead of the pope was declared the official head of the Church. The will of the king instead of the will of God was acclaimed the only course of duty for the subjects. The immutable moral principles of which the Church of Christ is the custodian were declared to be no longer the guides to right and wrong. Men, they said, were free to decide for themselves what was right and what was wrong.

Their Decline

With the spread of the Protestant Revolt throughout the countries of Europe, with the free interpretation of the Bible, with the belief that faith without good works was sufficient for salvation, with the divorce of morality from economics, and with the glorification of the individual under the Liberalistic philosophy of the period, the guilds broke down. Authority had become undermined. The true religion was repudiated. The guilds therefore lost the only immutable and sustaining foundations of their effectiveness. Economics, without religion and morality, does not remain "ordered" in its course toward "the good of all and the good of each." It tends rapidly to excessive individualism and domination.

Historians can and do give numerous other reasons for the decay of the guilds. For the most part, the reasons assigned are economic and political reasons. However, the real reason, if one judges fairly, is that men became irreligious and they became so mainly because of the effects of the Protestant Revolt. When religion and morality break down in a man's heart, or in the hearts of many men, disastrous results take place in the social body as well as in the individual person. Society must be permeated by morality. Justice must pervade the social relations. Charity must bind hearts together, or, in the state of fallen nature, the corruption resultant from men's selfish impulses are found in the organism. The germ of evil eats within the system. External causes, such as the French Revolution, as in the case of the guilds of France, merely break down the hollow shell.

That the guilds survived through at least seven hundred years — from before the Norman Conquest to after the American Revolutionary War — testifies to the fact that changing economic conditions did not cause their death blow. Certainly they had witnessed many and acute changes throughout their history. The guilds might have met the challenge of modern large-scale production had they retained the virility and unity which characterized them during the eleventh, twelfth, thirteenth, and fourteenth centuries. Through internal dissensions, jealousies, difficulties among the various guilds and within the guild units, disagreements between the masters and the workers, or in other words, through the poison of Liberalistic principles in industry, politics, and religion, the guild system broke down internally, and State legislation or political revolution merely interred them.

"At one period," writes Pope Pius XI,

> there existed a social order which, though by no means perfect in every respect corresponded nevertheless in a certain measure to right reason

according to the needs and conditions of the times. That this order has long since perished, is not due to the fact that it was incapable of development and adaptation to changing needs and circumstances, but rather to the wrong-doing of men. Men were hardened in excessive self-love and refused to extend that order, as was their duty, to the increasing numbers of the people; or else, deceived by the attractions of false liberty and other errors, they grew impatient of every restraint and endeavored to throw off all authority.

Behind Free Competition

There can be no question that the growing consciousness of the "I" to the exclusion of the "we" was no small factor in the breakdown of the guilds, despite the long array of economic causes which historians give. That this spirit of "I" rather than "we" later infected American industry there can be no doubt. The "I" spirit can be detected wherever there is unlimited competition. The later decades of nineteenth-century American history witnessed governmental legislation against it. Theodore Roosevelt has become known to schoolchildren equally under the cognomens the "Rough Rider" and the "Trust-Breaker." The aim of free competition was monopoly, and American history of the period named is replete with examples of monopolistic activities.

The period was also the period of early struggles of American labor for organization. The name of Samuel Gompers is prominent on the pages of history of that time. The labor organization movement was deemed necessary as a protection for the laborers against the monopolists, the money-men. There is no doubt that such organization is necessary for class interests. The evil attached to such movements is found in the hostility which characterizes the classes and accentuates the differences between them. The natural result of free competition, as we have noted before, is the rise of the classes which we term capital and labor. Now from this distinction of classes a new danger has grown. With the concentration of money in the hands of a few, came concentration of power. It is this economic dictatorship which holds man in its grasp today. Of it Pope Pius XI writes:

> In the first place, it is patent that in our days, not alone is wealth accumulated, but immense power and despotic economic domination is concentrated in the hands of a few, and that those few are frequently not the owners, but only the trustees and directors of invested funds, who administer them at their good pleasure.

This power becomes particularly irresistible when exercised by those who, because they hold and control money, are able also to govern credit and determine its allotment, for that reason supplying, so to speak, the life-blood to the entire economic body, and grasping, as it were, in their hands, the very soul of production, so that no one dares breathe against their will.

This accumulation of power, the characteristic note of the modern economic order, is a natural result of limitless free competition which permits the survival of those only who are the strongest, which often means those who fight most relentlessly, who pay least heed to the dictates of conscience.

This concentration of power has led to a threefold struggle for domination. First, there is the struggle for dictatorship in the economic sphere itself; then the fierce battle to acquire control of the State, so that its resources and authority may be abused in the economic struggles; finally, the clash between States themselves.

This is the situation in the social economic realm today and it is the remedying of this condition that constitutes the "reordering" of society of which we are speaking in this chapter.

What Is the Remedy?

The proper remedy to be applied in any situation depends upon the effects produced by the evil. What are the effects of the domination, first, of the individual over society, and secondly, of concentrated money and power over the individual? The answer, in general terms, is *the dismemberment of the social body.*

Organs and members of the social body are no longer free to act *naturally* according to their capacity and talents. Human beings stand beside machines for eight hours a day. They watch the mechanism to see that the product comes forth as it should. That is their job, hour by hour, day by day. There is no development of the intellect; no exercise of the will; no share in the management; no share, or little, in either the profits or the ownership. They stand by their machines forty hours a week and then go home on payday with an envelope. It contains money — a material means of meeting necessary material needs. That is all. The routine is the same week by week. If business is slack, they are laid off. Perhaps the business closes down. Then they are out of work. And through it all, they must be voiceless. They work readily when there is work to be done; they stay away reluctantly when there is no work. The ownership, the management, the profits are all beyond them. The opportunity for exercising intellect or will is slight. The workers are dependent upon the organized control *of money* and *power* and *management* from above them, and which has them in its grasp.

Now labor was meant to perfect man as man. It was meant to develop *all his powers*. The ideal situation for doing this is found in that form of economic society in which the wage contract is modified to some extent so as to form what Pope Pius XI calls a kind of partnership between employer and worker. In this form the wage earners are made *sharers of some kind* in the ownership, or the management, or the profits. It would mean that to a just, though limited, extent, all who work in a particular type of work, would be entitled to a share in managing the business, in owning the business, or in sharing the surplus profits.

According to this plan, the now bitterly opposed classes would be bound together. It would not mean that the chef (of our hotel illustration given previously) would be running the elevators or the bell boys the hotel. Rather it would mean that they would become more personalized organs and less depersonalized units in the system, through some manner of representation, shareholding, and dividends. The whole system would be arranged hierarchically, according to capacities. Chefs would remain chefs and bell boys, bell boys, but everybody in the system, from chef to manager, would be directing his energies and natural capacities for the good of the whole and the good of each member. They would have, at the same time, a personal interest in the prosperity of the enterprise through personal participation in its ownership, management, or profits. In this case, the organs would be "ordered" to the good of the enterprise through their own healthy functioning in collaboration and cooperation with one another and with the whole. In other words, there would be corporativeness in society — there would be a *social organism*.

Economic Reorganization

We indicated earlier in this chapter that Pope Pius XI declared that the breakdown of the once-flourishing organically operating social body has left, to all practical purposes, only the individual and the State. The logical consequence in time would be direct and absolute State domination over the individual — which is precisely what must be avoided. As an alternative of this State domination, there is the economic dictatorship which at the present time dominates the economic realm. This, too, must not be tolerated if society is to be healed of its wounds and pursue its true course.

Neither domination by the State nor domination by wealth and power will create an organized social order happily harmonized in its strivings for the good of all and the good of each. The remedy lies, initially, in the organization of "brains, capital, and labor" in common action rather than in the continued opposition which at present characterizes them in the labor market. Pope Pius writes:

> The demand and supply of labor divides men on the labor market into two classes, as into two camps, and the bargaining between these parties transforms this labor market into an arena where the two armies are engaged in combat. To this grave disorder, which is leading society to ruin, a remedy must evidently be applied as speedily as possible. But there cannot be question of any perfect cure, unless this opposition be done away with, and well-ordered members of the social body come into being anew, namely, vocational groups, binding men together not according to the position they occupy in the labor market but according to the diverse functions which they exercise in society.

The condition, therefore, of any perfect cure of a society, the condition of its being redirected to its true goal, lies in the elimination of class opposition (not of the classes!) and the reorganizing of economic societies on the basis of the function they perform rather than of distinctions between capital and labor.

Economic Organization Legitimate

Considering the probable age of the world, or considering at least the history of the human race, it can justly be said that the age of industry is decidedly young. The Industrial Revolution, comparatively speaking, was not so long ago in the age of the human race. The American Revolutionary War was fought during those years which witnessed the change from old-type production to new-type production. The water power loom and cotton gin were invented after the close of the war we fought for our independence. Howe's sewing machine and McCormick's reaper came more than half a century after the adoption of the Constitution of the United States. So you can readily see that the problem of monopoly, of labor organization, and of economic dictatorship are relatively new problems in the history of the human race.

Nevertheless in 1891 — within a man's memory of the invention of Hoe's rotary press, of Morse's telegraph, of Field's ocean cable, of Bell's telephone, of Bessemer's discovery of the steel process, of Carnegie's foundation of the great steel mills — Pope Leo XIII, as the spokesman of the Catholic Church, enunciated the basic principles which should regulate economic enterprises in the modern setting of large-scale output and highly socialized production. His principles, as we have already seen, are rooted in right reason and in religion. They draw their validity from God and the law of God. The remarkable thing about Pope Leo's pronouncements is that they were enunciated with such authority and without fear of error so early in the large-scale industrial epoch. And yet this ought not to be surprising, since fundamental principles of human nature and the natural law are as immutable as the eternal law of God upon which nature and its laws draw for their origin and sole sufficient support.

Among the basic principles which we find enumerated by Pope Leo is the right of working men to organize. It is a right which can be traced back to nature — to man's natural impulse to live in society. The working man's right to organize in order to better his condition is not so fundamental a right as the rights of marriage, offspring, property, education, labor, and a just wage. We do not mean that it is less *natural*, but that it is less *necessary* to human nature. Now the family is a most necessary human association because it is so closely connected with the existence and development of the ever-replenished newer members of the human race. Working men's associations are less necessary because they are not universally necessary but only under certain conditions and in certain periods of human history.

Working men's associations, nevertheless, are true societies. They are not complete or perfect societies, nor can they be called public societies. The State is a true, a perfect, and a public society. Working men's associations are true, but imperfect (i.e., incomplete) and private societies. The former has the common good as its goal; the latter has the individual's good as its proximate goal. As a true society, therefore, springing from the natural desire of man to associate with others in common effort for the advance of common interests, working men's associations cannot be absolutely forbidden *as such* by the State, for they have the same origin as the State itself. Pope Leo expresses this clearly when he says:

> Particular societies, then, although they exist within the State, and are each a part of the State, nevertheless cannot be prohibited by the State absolutely and as such. For to enter into "society" of this kind is the natural right of man; and the State must protect natural rights, not destroy them; and if it forbids its citizens to form associations, it contradicts the very principle of its own existence; for both they and it exist in virtue of the same principle, viz., the natural propensity of man to live in society.

To safeguard the common good against undesirable associations of this kind, and in virtue of its right and duty to promote the common welfare, the State may subject such associations to a certain amount of regulation, within reasonable limits and in keeping with the rights and duties of all concerned. "Let the State watch over these societies of citizens united together in the exercise of their right," says Pope Leo, "but let it not thrust itself into their peculiar concerns and their organization, for things move and live by the soul within them, and they may be killed by the grasp of a hand from without."

Need and Advantage of Organization

Pope Leo's keen observation during the early period of free competition and growing monopolies led him to recognize the evils of the growing rift between workmen and their employers. He asserted repeatedly the principle that capital cannot do without labor, nor labor without capital. He fearlessly championed the cause of the laboring man. He indicated his rights as well as his duties. He encouraged workers to form unions according to their trade. He declared the innate right of working men to form such unions. Finally, he taught them how to do it and defended them in so doing.

There are frequent references in the encyclicals of Popes Leo XIII and Pius XI to conditions which show the necessity of labor organizations in this our epoch of industrialism. Man's individual weakness and wealth's concentrated power, in general language, sum up the reasons for the desirability of organization. The Holy Fathers speak of the "needy and powerless multitude, sore and suffering," and urge that their condition be improved. On the other hand, in condemning concentrated wealth, it is pointed out by the popes that wealth has "in its grasp all labor and all trade," and that it "manipulates for its own benefit and its own purposes all the sources of supply."

It is not difficult to understand that working men, being free to form associations, are free, also, to decide upon the form which these associations shall take. This principle is true when applied to the formation of civil society. It is equally true in the formation of the lesser societies, provided *always* that no harm be done to others individually or to others socially, that is, in reference to the common good. Pope Pius, reaffirming this principle which had been laid down by Pope Leo in his encyclical on *The Christian Constitution of States*, remarks: "It is hardly necessary to note that what Pope Leo XIII taught concerning the form of political government can, in due measure, be applied also to vocational groups. Here, too, men may choose whatever form they please, provided that both justice and the common good be taken into account."

Not only are workmen's organizations free to exist, but they are free to establish rules and regulations which, if not out of harmony with the common good, are conducive to the attainment of the purposes of these lesser societies. The principle again in question is the right of individuals to pursue their private advantage "provided that both justice and the common good be taken into account." "These vocational groups," remarks Pope Pius XI, "in a true sense autonomous [i.e., self-governing] are considered by many to be, if not essential to civil society, at least its natural and spontaneous development."

These organizations of working men, of farmers, of craftsmen, and of humbler classes including wage earners of all kinds, if universally organized, would constitute types of social institutions or social organs. This would reorganize human society into that organic unity, the loss of which has resulted logically from the philosophy of unlimited freedom in individual pursuits. The loss of this organic unity, Pope Pius says, has left "only individuals and the State." This is, as we suggested previously, an undesirable thing. It constitutes an unnatural and dangerous approach to the absorption of the individual by the State, to totalitarianism in other words. But of its very nature "the true aim of all social activity," says Pope Pius XI, "should be to help individual members of the social body, but *never to destroy* or *absorb them.*"

Advantages of Labor Organization

We have seen that man's individual weakness in the presence of wealth's concentration of power and exercise of control of trade and credit, is logically the reason for working men's organizations. We indicated the private character of such societies, as different from the public character and role of civil society. We are ready, therefore, to hear in the words of Pope Leo, that they should be "so organized and governed as to furnish the best and most suitable means for attaining what is aimed at, namely, *for helping each individual member to better his conditions to the utmost in body, in mind and in property.*"

These words express generally the advantages derived — or that can be derived — from working men's associations. Seeking specific advantages included under the general term "better his condition," we might note these: (1) the infusion of a spirit of justice into all relationships between labor and capital; (2) the imposition of a desirable kind and degree of self-restraint and moderation both on the part of capital and of labor; (3) a harmonization of divergent interests among the natural "levels" of human society; (4) the creation or the promotion of means of honorable and profitable employment; (5) the just regulation of wages with a view not only to private advantage of employer and worker but also to the common good of the State; (6) an intensification of happiness, contentment, and prosperity in general in the State.

Administration of Labor Associations

To effect their purpose, these societies must necessarily be just, firm, prudent, and upright in their government and activities. Without these characteristics, it would be impossible to achieve unity of purpose or harmonious co-action. They should be free, as we said previously, to govern themselves according to their end and the proper means thereto. The rules and regulations which they adopt must not exceed the end and means of their particular type of association. We learned early in this book, you recall, that every authority is limited by the purpose (i.e., the end) of the society over which it exercises the right to rule. So working men's associations are limited by their purpose. Among the things which are considered proper matter for the exercise of authority in these economic societies are hours and wages, nature and conditions of the labor to be done, internal discipline of members and officers, and similar affairs.

In member-to-member relations, amiability and sincere good will should characterize the associations. Just as the ruler in political society ought not to act through private benefit, so, too, in the administration of economic associations, the officers must act justly and prudently, administering the funds honestly and performing the tasks of their office without detriment to the true good of the members or injustice to anyone.

In legislating in those matters which pertain to its goal and the proper means thereto, the rights and duties of the employer as well as of the worker must receive adequate consideration. To say all the foregoing briefly and simply, the administration of working men's associations must be conducive to the good of the individuals, whether employer or worker, guided by commutative justice, and with special emphasis on fostering conditions of "a better life" for the working man.

Religion and Morality the Foundation

If the aim of the working men's associations be the "better condition of body, mind, and property," it becomes immediately evident that religion and morality must be their guiding norms. How would the condition of a man be bettered if he lost his soul? Of what advantage would an increase in intellectual knowledge or material wealth be, if that meant the loss of the intellectual vision of God and the unending possession of the Eternal and Supreme Being? "For what shall it profit a man, if he gain the whole world, and suffer the loss of his soul? Or what shall a man give in exchange for his soul?" (Mark 8:36–37).

For this reason, Pope Leo lays down the principle that religious instruction should hold the foremost place in working men's associations, and that, by instruction and by practices of piety and of morality, workmen may know and perform their duty toward God, toward neighbor, and toward self. The role of religion and of morality in social organization will be discussed in our next and final chapter.

No Detailed Scheme Given

Pope Leo states the impossibility of outlining a detailed scheme for workmen's associations beyond the general essential characteristics given above. Each nation would have to work out for itself, on the above religious and moral principles, the detailed application of them to specific situations of time, place, progress, size, and extent of the trades and occupations to be organized, past and present practices, as well as of the experience, knowledge, and skill of the persons to be organized. In other words, the definite details of organization depend on the national character and needs of the people. Any form, so long as it be not opposed to the common good and the true well-being of the individual, and provided it be based on true morality and religion, is deemed a satisfactory type of working men's organization.

Earlier in this chapter we quoted Pope Pius XI to show (1) that he attributed the present sad state of human society to the loss of its organic unity, and (2) that he sees the remedy in a twofold social enterprise: the abolition of class hatred, and the renewal of an "ordered society." Corporative society, like the working men's organizations, cannot be outlined in detail. Pope Pius makes no such attempt. He indicates the need for it, tells its advantages, and lays down the moral principles upon which it should be founded and governed, but beyond that he does not go. We shall attempt to lay down these principles as they are found in the encyclical on *The Reconstruction of the Social Order* and make some attempt at indicating how they might be applied to those conditions of labor and industry with which we, in our day and age, are rather familiar.

The Proposed Corporative Society

The basis of the corporative society, which is proposed by Pope Pius XI, is the proper "ordering" of all the members of society. In speaking of the opposition which divides men on the labor market into two classes as into two camps,

Pope Pius introduces his plan for binding them together and thus taking the *first step* toward a corporative society, a true social order. "A true and genuine social order," he says, "*demands various members of society, joined together by a common bond*" (my emphasis). Here is his general plan for organization (my emphasis):

> To this grave disorder [namely, the hostility between capital and labor as between two armies engaged in combat] which is leading society to ruin, a remedy must evidently be applied as speedily as possible. But there cannot be question of any perfect cure except this opposition be done away with and *well-ordered* members of the social body come into being anew, namely, vocational groups, binding men together, not according to the position they occupy in the labor market, but according to the diverse functions which they exercise in society.

The important point in the plan is that the men will not continue to be divided as they are at present on the labor market, that is, into laborer and capitalist. Instead, they will be joined according to the vocation they follow; that is, to the occupation in which they are engaged. In other words, *all* the members of any industry will be united in a single organization, whether the members be the men who supply the money, the men who direct the activities, or the men who labor with their "hands." Thus brains, capital, and labor will be combined in common effort.

There would then be a hierarchy of these functional societies, or *organs*, and they, taken together, would constitute the whole social-economic *organism*. Each organ would be a unit in itself with its own function. It would be self-directive, that is, self-governing according to its own function. Each unit would have a relation to similarly self-governing units exercising different functions, and thus the "body of organs," or the *organism*, would constitute *corporative society*. The unique function of each unit, the intimate relation each bears to other units, and the unity of operation of the whole system, resembles the activities of the human organs and the unified activity of the whole human organism. That accounts for the term *corporate* society, taken from the Latin term, *corpus*, the body.

Concretely, what does all this explanation mean? Well, this — the various functions or services rendered in social-economic affairs include such diverse industries as steel, coal, textile, and so forth. They include, also, public, private, and domestic services. Farmers, miners, foresters, and lumbermen, as well as professional men, and other economic units of modern society also constitute social functions or services. Each of these would have a distinct

unit of organization. All the doctors would be organized; all the steel workers; all the textile workers; all of any and of every function or service. By *all*
we mean just that, namely, everyone connected with any given service, or
industry — directors, managers, clerks, laborers, all bound together into one
organization, "ordered" according to their capacity and contribution, and
forming a hierarchical society, from the lowest to the highest in every given
industry and work. This is a *vertical* or column-like arrangement of the workers in a single industry or line of work. It puts all men of a single type of work
into one organization. It puts in another and distinct organization, all the men
engaged in another type of work. It puts into still another group men of still
another class. All are organized into their distinctive units.

This differs from an arrangement or grouping of workers whereby they are
classed according to "level" of society to which they belong. This classification
corresponds to "layers" horizontally arranged, one lower than the other. The
directors would form a distinct level or strata. The capitalists would form a
second distinct strata of society. The wage earners, both low-salaried clerks
and wage earners properly so-called, would form the lowest levels or strata
of society. Each would (and do in practice) constitute a distinct class, with
diversified interests. There results frequent opposition between them.

This is the situation of which both Pope Leo and Pope Pius speak when
they call attention to the opposition or conflict between the classes on the labor
market. To break down the opposition, while still maintaining the possibility
of *natural* harmonious interaction between the classes, Pope Pius offers his
suggestion: (1) to combine brains, capital, and labor together for common effort; (2) in a contract of partnership or modified wage contract, to make wage
earners sharers in some sort in the ownership or the management, or the profits.

This is the "vertical" arrangement of which we spoke, and in which all
natural "levels" (brains, capital, labor) are combined in a single organization
for common pursuit of common interests. In the arrangement which we are
here calling the *vertical ordering*, *all* members of a given industry or service,
whether they be the directors or the least of the wage earners, would be found
in the same organization ranked or *ordered* according to what they do.

Each local unit, as, for instance, the steel workers, would consist of the
capitalists, the directors, the clerks, and the laborers united in a single organization of the workers of the steel industry. These in turn unite with similar
local groups elsewhere and form a regional unit. The various regional units,
through freely chosen representatives, would form the national association.
Representatives from each national occupational group (or guild) would

form a council representing all the industries of the nation. This would be the supreme council. The national and supreme councils could then impose upon industry, the professions and services, those wages, hours, conditions, and so forth which have been agreed upon by the employers and the employed in the lesser autonomous groups. The aim of the national and the supreme councils would be to keep as nearly uniform as possible throughout the country wages, hours, and prices. Then one industry or one section of the country would not suffer from unemployment caused by insufficient incomes in other industries. Neither would they suffer from lack of equality in prices or purchasing power.

Now when this would be carried out, not in this or that industry, but in every social and economic group, including also governmental circles, there would be a number of "industrial societies," "professional societies," "governmental societies," and the like, self-governing within their spheres. The organization does not end there any more than the body consists only of a number of organs. The body must be *an organism* or a unity of organs operating for a common end, namely, the health of the whole body. So, too, these smaller separate industrial and other social-economic units would be inter-organized with others of a similar kind to form a larger industrial society, until all the plants and companies of a single industry come under the influence of these societies. The local units combine, as we said, in a single, larger unit; these combine into regional units; they combine into a national unit. Each unit, local, or regional, or national, is self-directive while maintaining, at the same time, interrelations with all other units in the one industry and through the national organization with all the other industries, professions, and the like.

The interaction of all these local, regional, and national units of the industries, professions, services, and similar social-economic groups constitutes an organism. They are directed by a national council which unifies the activities of all, heading them toward the good of all and the good of each. Thus organized and inter-organized, collaborating and cooperating, the directors of the various lines of work, know, and plan together what is best for the social-economic order as a whole. The result would be a *corporative* society.

Pope Pius XI says this:

> True and genuine social order demands various members of society, joined together by a common bond. Such a bond of union is provided, on the one hand, by the common effort of employers and employees of one and the same group joining forces to produce goods or give service;

on the other hand, by the common good which all groups should unite to promote, each in its own sphere, with friendly harmony.

This system of vocational societies or occupational groups — these twentieth-century guilds — would not call for the abolition of employers' unions, labor unions, collective bargaining, and the like forms and measures with which we are familiar. Within each modern guild as we have described it above, there would be an employers' unit as well as labor units, but they would need to be somewhat reconstructed to permit of greater mutual cooperation. Pope Pius writes: "Cases in which interests of employers and employees call for special care and protection against opposing interests, separate deliberations will take place in their respective assemblies and separate votes will be taken as the matter may require."

When organization is complete along these lines, when the *industrial societies* or social organs exist in all phases of the social-economic life, and are directed in their activities toward the common good, then we shall have an escape from individualistic regimes of competition. We shall escape, too, from concentration of wealth and power, that is, economic dictatorship. Unless some such plan is gotten under way and earnestly fostered for the good of all and the good of each, there will be no escape from these two evils other than direct and absolute governmental control. But this, too, would be wholly undesirable and unnatural.

Government Control of Economics

There is a basic principle of philosophy which states that the higher ought not to undertake to perform what can well be done by the lower. Very concretely, we would not expect an executive to put the stamps on his business letters, nor would we expect the principal of a school to sweep the classrooms and tend to the furnace. Executives have their own work to do — a higher type of work, and if they were to meddle in the work of the lower members, of their subordinates, it would mean that the work of the higher would be neglected. The lesser members would be forced to idleness or uselessly employed. The result would be detrimental to the whole society over which the executive is superior.

Now the State has its particular work to do: namely, to advance the common good so that it might shed upon all individuals the fruits of the wealth of the community as a whole. There is no doubt that the condition of economic groups reflects on the common good, so that, insofar as they hinder or advance the common good, the State must concern itself with economic societies.

On the other hand, were the State to delve into the administration of these economic groups and undertake to direct its details, it would be acting out of its sphere. Were it to attempt to manage them, were it to concern itself with the details of their conduct, it would be doing what a lower order is capable and willing to do.

Therefore, the State must not "run" industry. It must not give up its purely governmental administration of the goods of the commonwealth and enter into the sphere of business. Each so-called member of the corporative society outlined in the preceding pages ought to be allowed freely to adopt "such organization and rules as may best conduce to the attainment of their respective ends." Such rules would be those regulations affecting wages, salaries, prices, profits, and the like. The State should lend assistance to these economic groups through its legislation, law enforcement, and other administrative functions which promote economic well-being. This, however, must not amount to assuming control of business.

Pope Pius warns of this in his encyclical on *The Reconstruction of the Social Order*. After having described an attempt made to organize a corporative society (said to have been the one made in Italy not many years ago), the Holy Father adds:

> We feel bound to add that to our knowledge there are some who fear that the State is substituting itself in the place of private initiative instead of limiting itself to necessary and sufficient help and assistance. It is feared that the new syndical and corporative institution possesses an excessively bureaucratic and political character, and that, notwithstanding the general advantages referred to above, it risks serving particular political aims rather than contributing to the initiation of a better social order.

The "particular political aims" undoubtedly were those of the Fascist regime which was at the time strengthening its hold on all phases of Italian life.

State Ownership of Anything?

We might here pause long enough to remark that in some instances it is not only proper but imperative for the State to "go into business." This does not contradict the statement made previously that it should not do so — ordinarily. However there are some enterprises too great for private ownership and controls. These should be under public ownership and control. Among such projects known to you might be mentioned the huge dams recently constructed or now under construction by the government. To leave these in the hands of private corporations could endanger the public welfare, affecting, as they do, such wide areas and controlling the water and power supply of so many people. Pope Pius justly remarks: "It is rightly contended that certain forms of property must be reserved to the State, since they carry with them an opportunity of domination too great to be left to private individuals without injury to the community at large. Just demands and desires of this kind contain nothing opposed to Christian truth."

The State and Organization

Pope Pius XI reviews the breakdown of the social body caused by the evil of individualism. He notes that nothing has taken the place of the guilds, and that the State has burdened itself with problems which were once borne by lesser associations. This has brought upon the State so many affairs and duties that it can no longer, without detriment to its own particular end, manage these extraneous things. He says, "Social life has lost entirely its organic form. The State, which now was encumbered with all the burdens once borne by associations rendered extinct by it, was in consequence submerged and overwhelmed by an infinity of affairs and duties." (Here he has reference to the fact that the guilds were legally abolished through governmental action.)

Then he continues: "It is indeed true, as history clearly proves, that owing to the change in social conditions, much that was formerly done by small bodies can nowadays be accomplished only by large corporations." (His reference, of course, is to the large-scale production which has displaced the small-scale industry of the past.) "Nonetheless, just as it is wrong to withdraw from the individual and commit to the community at large what private enterprise and industry can accomplish, so too it is an injustice, a grave evil, and a disturbance of right order for a larger and higher organization to arrogate to itself functions which can be performed efficiently by smaller and lower bodies." (Examples of this would be to withdraw from the father the care of his offspring, and from private business the management of its affairs.)

> The State should leave to these smaller groups the settlement of business of minor importance. It will thus carry out with greater freedom, power, and success the tasks belonging to it, because it alone can effectively accomplish these, directing, watching, stimulating and restraining, as circumstances suggest or necessity demands.
>
> Let those in power, therefore, be convinced that the more faithfully this principle be followed, and a graded hierarchical order exist between

the various subsidiary organizations, the more excellent will be both the authority and the efficiency of the social organization as a whole and the happier and more prosperous the condition of the State.

This puts the case quite clearly. The State must not become an administrator in economic affairs. It must refrain from economic administration under penalty of failing to achieve its own purpose through unnecessary assumption of the work of lesser societies. It must not substitute itself for private initiative. If it does so, the result will be such great administrative perplexity that all orders of society and the whole social order as such will be injured. This does not deny to the State the right to interfere when necessity demands it. It does not deny the right to control certain very great enterprises of an economic character. We have already admitted that right. In fact, we declared it a duty of the State to do so. The limits, as you know, are determined by the common good, provided that no injustice be done to anybody. Economic dictatorship, however, hampers the progress of individuals. It also retards seriously the progress of the common good. The State, therefore, in virtue of its end, must interfere to abolish economic dictatorships. The point we wish to stress is this: that its interference is just, provided it be only so far as is necessary to correct the disorder and apply a remedy. It does not consist in the State's taking over the economic sphere, for of those things it is not the duly appointed authority. The work of the State, on the whole, is to permit these lesser societies to function provided they do not act contrary to the common good. If they act contrary to the common good, the State must correct the abuse, but not absorb the lesser society and arrogate to itself the tasks of the lower order. "Free competition," says Pope Pius, "and still, more economic domination, must be kept within just and definite limits, and must be brought under the effective control of the public authority, *in matters appertaining to this latter's purpose*" (my emphasis).

There are several places in the encyclical on *The Reconstruction of the Social Order* in which Pope Pius declares the benefits which accrue to the State and the social body from a graded hierarchical order. This principle is in direct opposition to the Communist principle of no levels, no hierarchy of orders, no ruling power but the Communist party.

A word might be said at this place that, until the modern "guilds" could become organized, until the corporative society could run smoothly under its own power, the State would have to do more than it would do later when the proposed lesser occupational groups finally became organized. The State would, first of all, have to overcome the two evils which at present affect society: individualism, which remains to a certain limited extent, and economic dominance, which quite completely has grasp of the social-economic order. When these, under governmental legislation, have loosened their hold upon society, then the lesser societies, as the occupational groups, would begin to function and grow under their own power. It is not the work of a day or a year. It is something into which we would have to grow over a number of years, experimenting along this and that line, but always holding before our eyes the one general aim: the good of all and the good of each through collaboration and cooperation of each and every unit of society.

Now corporative society as we have attempted to explain it here is not totalitarianism. On the contrary, Corporatism is opposed to totalitarianism in its very essence. Under the corporative system, the lesser groups would be granted self-government in all their affairs, always, however, being subject to the common good. This power of self-government would be greatest in the smallest groups, and the higher the society in the economic hierarchy, the less domination it would have in the details of the lesser units. The national council would direct all toward the interest of all, leaving to the lesser groups the right to make laws suitable to their needs.

However, in totalitarianism, all self-government is taken from the lesser units of society and centered in the highest. The chief function of the State under totalitarianism is domination. Under a corporative society as we are explaining it, the chief function of the State with regard to these groups is one of safeguarding the conditions required for the full collaboration of the various parts. Direct State action is not desirable, except only insofar as it is necessary for the preservation of the common good. Direct action ordinarily is the work of the occupational group — the "guild" of modern times.

Corporative society, then, consists in the organization of industries, services, pursuits, professions, labor, capital, and so forth, into guilds or autonomous *organs*. These organs, through cooperation and co-action for the good of all and the good of each, constitute the organism which we have called the *social-economic order*. This is the order to which the Holy Father refers when he says: "All the institutions of public and social life must be imbued with the spirit of justice, and this justice must above all be truly operative, must build up a juridical and social order able to pervade all economic activity."

Justice, therefore, must be the foundation of the reordered social life. Justice must underlie the laws which are made to establish and direct the new order to the common good. But when all that will have been accomplished, when the corporative society will have been organized anew, there will be a body, but a soul will be needed to vivify it. The soul of the social body is charity. "Social Charity should be the soul of this order, and the duty of the State will be to protect and defend it effectively. This task the State will perform the more readily if it frees itself from those burdens which are not properly its own."

Advantages of Corporatism

What are the advantages of a physically healthful body? There are several: ease of action, inclination to work efficiently, harmony among the members, a general spirit of initiative, a better outlook on life, and last, but not least, a spirit of cooperation and helpfulness which sheer good health originates in one.

Transferred to the social-economic order, a healthy corporative society has similar benefits. All parts are in harmony. The various activities functioning for the good of each and the good of all bring a certain facility, a smoothness of operation. With this comes joy in the striving. The combined efforts and the growth which results therefrom create a general spirit of initiative. This results in the production of a sufficiency of the goods of nature. These will be transformed and perfected by the technical knowledge and skill found in modern industry. They will be equitably distributed through the channels of an ordered economic society. Thus they will promote the well-being of each and of all. They will bring to the individual, through the common good, the decent human existence for which the papal plan for reconstruction so earnestly pleads.

The formation of a modern type of guild, fashioned after the manner of operation of the human body, will combine brains, capital, and labor to the end that man's labor will bear its due fruit.

The Future Task

In closing, let it be noted again that the encyclicals do not outline *in detail* any plan for a corporative order. Varying circumstances and conditions of people and of society as a whole must be taken into consideration. Details of economics will have to be worked out by experts in that line. Details of government, of industrial organization, of morality, and of all phases of social living will have to be worked out by experts in the various fields. The work calls for wholehearted, sincere, and constant cooperation among all agencies in the social order. It will require much study, years of slow growth, and unwearying devotion to the cause.

The goal of a modern corporative State is not only an ideal, but an attainable goal. It becomes more and more possible of attainment in proportion as men turn more and more to God, to religion, to morality. As Pope Pius says (my emphasis):

> We believe that to attain a better social order for the true and permanent advantage of the commonwealth, there is need *before and above all else* of the blessing of God, and, in the second place, of the cooperation of all men of good will. We believe, moreover, as a necessary consequence, that the end intended will be the more certainly attained, the greater the contribution furnished by men of technical, commercial, and social aptitude, and, more still, by Christian principles and their application....
>
> However, all that we have taught about reconstructing and perfecting the social order will be of no avail without a reform of morals.

To effect, therefore, the basic solution of present social disorders, it is not sufficient to reorder man socially but, more fundamentally, man must be morally redirected to God, his supreme good and only adequate goal.

Some Original Sources

The encyclicals of Popes Leo and Pius contain so much that is pertinent to modern conditions that we shall confine our attention to their encyclicals in seeking original sources for this chapter. Some of the following extracts have been mentioned before. They are given here in sequence as they occurred in the encyclicals so that we can better see their relation to other ideas as they have been presented by the Holy Fathers.

The following is an unabridged account of vocational groups taken directly from the encyclical on *The Reconstruction of the Social Order.*

1. "What We have written regarding a right distribution of property and a just scale of wages is concerned directly with the individual, and deals only indirectly with the social order. To this latter, however, Our Predecessor, Leo XIII, devoted special thought and care in his efforts to reconstruct and perfect it according to the principles of sound philosophy and the sublime precepts of the Gospel.

"A happy beginning has here been made. But in order that what has been well begun may be rendered stable, that what has not yet been accomplished may now be achieved, and that still richer and brighter blessings may descend upon mankind, two things are particularly necessary: the reform of the social order and the correction of morals.

"When We speak of the reform of the social order it is principally the State We have in mind. Not indeed that all salvation is to be hoped for from its intervention, but because of the evil of Individualism, as We called it, things have come to such a pass that the highly developed social life which once flourished in a variety of prosperous institutions organically linked with each other, has been damaged and all but ruined, leaving thus virtually only individuals and the State. Social life lost entirely its organic form. The State, which now was encumbered with all the burdens once borne by associations rendered extinct by it, was in consequence submerged and overwhelmed by an infinity of affairs and duties.

"It is indeed true, as history clearly proves, that owing to the change in social conditions, much that was formerly done by small bodies can nowadays be accomplished only by larger corporations. Nonetheless, just as it is wrong to withdraw from the individual and commit to the community at large what private enterprise and industry can accomplish, so too it is an injustice, a grave evil and a disturbance of right order for a larger and higher organization to arrogate to itself functions which can be performed efficiently by smaller and lower bodies. This is a fundamental principle of social philosophy, unshaken and unchangeable, and it retains its full truth today. Of its very nature the true aim of all social activity should be to help individual members of the social body, but never to destroy or absorb them.

"The State should leave to these smaller groups the settlement of business of minor importance. It will thus carry out with greater freedom, power and success the tasks belonging to it, because it alone can effectively accomplish these, directing, watching, stimulating and restraining, as circumstances suggest or necessity demands. Let those in power, therefore, be convinced that the more faithfully this principle be followed, and a graded hierarchical order exists between the various subsidiary organizations, the more excellent will be both the authority and the efficiency of the social organization as a whole and the happier and more prosperous the condition of the State.

"Now this is the primary duty of the State and of all good citizens; to abolish conflict between classes with divergent interests, and thus foster and promote harmony between the various ranks of society.

"The aim of social legislation must therefore be the reestablishment of vocational groups. Society today still remains in a strained and therefore unstable and uncertain states, being founded on classes with contradictory interests and hence opposed to each other, and consequently prone to enmity and strife.

"Labor, indeed, as has been well said by Our Predecessor in his encyclical, is not a mere chattel, since the human dignity of the working man must be recognized in it, and consequently it cannot be bought and sold like any piece of merchandise. Nonetheless the demand and supply of labor divides men on the labor market into two classes, as into two camps, and the bargaining between these parties transforms this labor market into an arena where the two armies are engaged in combat.

"To this grave disorder which is leading society to ruin, a remedy must evidently be applied as speedily as possible. But there cannot be question of any perfect cure, except this opposition be done away with, and well ordered members of the social body come into being anew, vocational groups, that is, binding men together not according to the position they occupy in the labor market, but according to the diverse functions which they exercise in society.

"For as nature induces those who dwell in close proximity to unite into municipalities, so those who practice the same trade or profession, economic or otherwise, combine into vocational groups. These groups, in a true sense autonomous, are considered by many to be, if not essential to civil society, at least its natural and spontaneous development.

"Order, as the Angelic Doctor well defines it, is unity arising from the apt arrangement of a plurality of objects; hence, true and genuine social order demands various members of society, joined together by a common bond. Such a bond of union is provided on the one hand by the common effort of employers and employees of one and the same group joining forces to produce goods or give service; on the other hand, by the common good which all groups should unite to promote, each in its own sphere, with friendly harmony.

"Now this union will become powerful and efficacious in proportion to the fidelity with which the individuals and the groups strive to discharge their professional duties and to excel in them. From this it is easy to conclude that in these associations the common interest of the whole group must predominate: and among the interests, the most important is the directing of the activities of the group to the common good.

"Regarding cases in which interests of employers and employees call for special care and protection against opposing interests, separate deliberation will take place in their respective assemblies and separate votes will be taken as the matter may require.

"It is hardly necessary to note that what Leo XIII taught concerning the form of political government can, in due measure, be applied also to vocational groups. Here, too, men may choose whatever form they please, provided that both justice and the common good be taken into account.

"Just as the citizens of the same municipality are wont to form associations with diverse aims, which various individuals are free to join or not, similarly, those who are engaged in the same trade or profession will form free associations among themselves, for purposes connected with their occupations.

"Our Predecessor explained clearly and lucidly the nature of free associations. We are content, therefore, to emphasize this one point: not only is man free to institute these unions which are of a private character, but he has the right to adopt such organization and such rules as may best conduce to the attainment of their respective objects.

"The same liberty must be claimed for the founding of associations which extend beyond the limits of a single trade. Let those free associations which already flourish and produce salutary fruits make it the goal of their endeavors, in accordance with Christian social doctrine, to prepare the way and to do their part towards the realization of that ideal type of vocational groups which we have mentioned above."

2. "All that We have taught about reconstructing and perfecting the social order will be of no avail without a reform of manners. Of this, history affords the clearest evidence. At one period there existed a social order which, though by no means perfect in every respect, corresponded nevertheless in a certain measure to right reason according to the needs and conditions of the times. That this order has long since perished is not due to the fact that it was incapable of development and adaptation to changing needs and circumstances, but rather to the wrong-doing of men.

"Men were hardened in excessive self-love and refused to extend that order, as was their duty, to the increasing numbers of the people; or else, deceived by the attractions of false liberty and other errors, they grew impatient of every restraint and endeavored to throw off all authority." (From the same encyclical of Pope Pius XI)

Let us hear now from Pope Leo XIII on this important matter. All the following extracts are from his encyclical on *The Condition of Labor*.

3. "If Christian precepts prevail, the two classes [capital and labor] will not only be united in the bonds of friendship, but also those of brotherly love.

"For they will understand and feel that all men are the children of a common father, that is, of God; that all have the same end, which is God Himself, Who alone can make either men or angels absolutely and perfectly happy; that all and each are redeemed by Jesus Christ, and raised to the dignity of children of God, and are thus united in brotherly ties both with each other and with Jesus Christ; that the blessings of nature and the gifts of grace belong in common to the whole human race, and that to all, except those who are unworthy, is promised the inheritance of the Kingdom of Heaven."

Pope Leo, in discussing the requirements for a better social order, says (my emphasis):

4. "Employers and workmen may themselves effect much in the matter of which We treat, by means of those institutions and organizations which afford opportune assistance to those in need, and which draw the two orders more closely together.

"Among these may be enumerated: societies for mutual help; various foundations, established by private persons for providing for the workman, and for his widow or his orphans, in sudden calamity, in sickness, and in the event of death; and what are called 'patronages' or institutions for the care of boys and girls, for young people, and also for those of more mature age.

"The most important of all are Workmen's Associations; for these virtually include all the rest. History attests what excellent results were affected by the artisans' guilds of a former day. They were the means not only of many advantages to the workmen, but in no small degree of the advancement of art.

"Such associations should be adapted to the requirement of the age in which we live—an age of great instruction, of different customs, and of more numerous requirements in daily life.

"It is gratifying to know that there are actually in existence not a few societies of this nature, consisting either of workingmen alone, or of workmen and employers together; but it were greatly to be desired that they should multiply and became more effective.

"A natural impulse unites men in civil society; and it is this also which makes them band themselves together in association of citizen with citizen; associations which, it is true, cannot be called societies in the complete sense of the word, but which are societies nevertheless.

"These lesser societies and the society which constitutes the State differ in many things, because their immediate purpose and end is different.

"Civil society exists for the common good and therefore is concerned with the interests of all in general, and with the individual interests in their due place and proportion. Hence it is called *public* society....

"But the societies which are formed in the bosom of the State are called *private* and justly so, because their immediate purpose is the private advantage of the associates.

"Particular societies, then, although they exist within the State, are each a part of the State, nevertheless cannot be prohibited by the State absolutely and as such. For to enter into society of this kind is the natural right of man; and the State must protect natural rights and not destroy them; and if it forbids its citizens to form associations, it contradicts the very principle of its own existence; for both they and it exist in virtue of the same principle, viz., the natural propensity of man to live in society.

"There are times, no doubt, when it is right that the law should interfere to prevent association; as when men join together for purposes which are evidently bad, unjust, or dangerous to the State.

"In such cases, the public authority may justly forbid the formation of associations, and may dissolve them when they already exist. But every precaution should be taken not to violate the rights of individuals, and not to make unreasonable regulations under the pretense of public benefit. For laws only bind when they are in accordance with right reason, and therefore with the Eternal Law of God.

5. "At this moment the condition of the working population is the question of the hour; and nothing can be of higher interest to all classes of the State than that it should be rightly and reasonably decided. But it will be easy for Christian workingmen to decide it aright if they form associations, choose wise guides, and follow the same path which with so much advantage to themselves and the commonwealth was trod by their fathers before them. Prejudice, it is true, is mighty and so is the love of money; but if the sense of what is just and right be not destroyed by depravity of

heart, their fellow-citizens are sure to be won over to a kindly feeling towards men whom they see to be so industrious and so modest, who so unmistakably prefer honesty to lucre, and the sacredness of duty to all other considerations.

"And another great advantage would result from the state of things We are describing; there would be so much more hope and possibility of recalling to a sense of their duty those workingmen who have either given up their faith altogether, or whose lives are at variance with its precepts. These men, in most cases, feel that they have been fooled by empty promises and deceived by the false appearances. They cannot but perceive that their grasping employers too often treat them with the greatest inhumanity, and hardly care for them beyond the profit their labors bring; and if they belong to an association, it is probably one in which there exists, in place of charity and love, that intestine strife which always accompanies unresigned and irreligious poverty." (*The Condition of Labor*)

Summary

1. A third objective of the papal program for social reconstruction is the establishment of a new order of society. Society has lost its organic form, social unity has weakened as a consequence, and individuals and institutions alike have become individualistic rather than social-minded.

2. *Reordering* means a rearrangement of the social parts—of individuals and institutions—so that each plays its role in the light of social justice and the common good.

3. Individualism, promoted by Liberalistic philosophy, is in great measure responsible for the breakdown of social unity. Its cry was, "The good of self!" whereas a true society must uphold the principle, "The good of each and the good of all."

4. There are "levels" in human society, inasmuch as inequalities exist among men. They are due to diversity of talents. Hence society is hierarchical, having lesser parts and greater parts. When these "parts" are suitably arranged according to their talents and conditions and contributions, they are *ordered*. Order is the unity which arises from the apt arrangement of a plurality of parts.

5. An ordered society, known as the guild system, existed during the Middle Ages. It was an organic society. Through organizations of masters and of workers, they regulated the social-economic life of the times. Their aim was to secure a better livelihood for their members.

6. The history of the guild system is closely bound up with the history of the Middle Ages of England and continental Europe. For approximately eight centuries the guilds existed: from the early part of the eleventh to the closing days of the eighteenth centuries.

7. The guilds were founded on religious principles. So long as they retained their religious and moral practices, they flourished. The height of their power was in the thirteenth and fourteenth centuries—the Age of Faith. St. Thomas lived in the thirteenth century.

8. When religion and morality weakened in their hold on men's will, when the Protestant Revolt devastated the hearts of so many princes and peasants, the guilds declined.

9. Factors purely economic contributed their part to the death of the guilds. Factors purely political contributed likewise. But the fact remains—with the loss of morality and religion, the very life went out of the guilds.

10. In America as elsewhere, the spirit of Liberalism, namely, free, unlimited competition, became widespread. In the economic realm monopolies became the order of the day. Economics was declared to be outside the moral realm. Freedom, to increase one's wealth by whatever means were at hand, was declared the rule of economics.

11. The logical outcome of individualism was complete disruption of social unity. A further development was the amassing of immense fortunes in the hands of a few. This led to a struggle for domination.

12. Control of power—the economic dictatorship of our time—has helped further to disrupt the social order. It is against this evil that men of good will must direct their attention if they would save society.

13. The dismemberment of the social body, initiated by individualism and completed (or nearly so) by concentrated money and power, is the world's great evil in view of the social nature of man and society's aim and purpose.

14. The remedy for the evil consists in a rebuilding of an organic society. Member must be ordained to member, parts to the whole, and particular ends to the general end.

15. An initial step in this social reorganization is to do away with the conflict between capital and labor. This can be effected by organizations in which "brains, capital, and labor" are united for common effort in view of their common good.

16. The Holy Father advocates the formation of vocational groups which "bind men together, not according to the position they occupy in the labor market but according to the diverse functions which they exercise in society."

17. Economic organizations, such as labor unions, are entirely legitimate and wholly in accord with man's social nature. Were a State to deny absolutely the right of men to organize, it would be denying the very principle of its own existence. Man is naturally inclined to society.

18. Man's individual weakness and wealth's concentrated power are unequal forces. To protect the weakness of man from the strength of concentrated power, it is desirable, nay at times even necessary, for men to organize.

19. The aim of such organization should be, as Pope Leo expressed it, "to help each individual member to better his condition to the utmost in body, in mind and in property."

20. Religion and morality must be the foundation stones of organizations of working men and of employers. Religion teaches to each group their rights and their duties, and urges them to act with justice.

21. A corporative society, or a social order that is organic, wherein all members and institutions work for the good of each and the good of all, is a most desirable social order. Though it is suggested in the papal encyclicals, no detailed scheme has been given for their formation. None could be given, since times, conditions, and circumstances must all be considered as they differ from country to country. Only a general idea could be proposed. It must be left to corps of economists, moralists, political experts, statesmen, and the like to draw up the details.

22. The plan calls for the organization of all lesser units of the social order into "organs." These are in a sense autonomous within their own sphere. They are ordained to the good of the whole social order as organs always are in an organism.

23. In the matter of governmental supervision, the government ought not to interfere unduly in economic matters. That would take the State into a field which is not its own. It would give to the State duties which it is not qualified to fulfill. The State should allow the lesser social organs freedom of activity in the attainment of their end.

24. The State may direct, watch, stimulate, and restrain these lesser organs as circumstances suggest or necessity demands. Under ordinary circumstances, that is the only rightful role of the State with regard to workmen's organizations.

For Study and Discussion

1. Discuss the need for a new order of society. Why may the present order be said to have failed?

2. What had the philosophy of individualism to do with the destruction of the present social order?

3. What is an *ordered* society? Explain why society cannot be leveled.

4. Explain the analogy between the human body as an organism and the organic structure of a corporative social order.

5. Discuss the guild system. Why was it an organic social order? What part did religion and morality play in the guilds?

6. Explain how free competition naturally led to concentration of wealth and of power.

7. Pope Leo wrote his famous *Labor* encyclical in 1891. How were economic events shaping themselves at that time in the United States? How much earlier than that did workmen in the United States begin to organize? Select several highlights of American business development of the last quarter of the nineteenth century. What bearing had Pope Leo's encyclical on them?

8. Pope Leo wrote his encyclical on labor in the fourteenth year of his pontificate. What events might he have watched in the development of business in the United States during the first fourteen years of his reign?

9. How can wage earners be made sharers "in some sort in the ownership, or the management, or the profits"?

10. Discuss the nature and the advantages of the vocational groups spoken of by Pope Pius XI.

11. Why must the elimination of the opposition between the classes be a constant aim of social reformers?

12. Discuss the basis upon which man has the right to organize. What makes organization desirable and at times even necessary?

13. What should be the attitude of the State with regard to private societies within its bosom? Discuss the question, considering first, ordinary circumstances; secondly, considering extraordinary circumstances.

14. Why should working men's associations be free within limited fields of action? What should be included in the scope of their activity? By what limits ought they to be bound?

15. Discuss the advantages of working men's associations (1) to the worker; (2) to the industry; (3) to the public; (4) to the society as a whole.

16. Why must religion and morality be the foundation stones of associations of workers or of employers?

17. Discuss: A true and genuine social order demands that the various members of society be joined together by a common bond.

18. Explain how "brains, capital, and labor can be combined in common effort."

19. Discuss:
    • Should government control economics?
    • Is public ownership of anything desirable?
    • What should be government's attitude toward labor unions?

20. How is a corporative society different from totalitarian social orders?

21. What are the advantages of a corporative society? What parts do justice and charity play in the corporative social order?

22. What are the possibilities for a successful formation of modern guilds?

Christian Social Principles

For the Advanced Reader

Nell-Breuning and Dempsey:
Reorganization of Social Economy

Papal Encyclicals:
Pope Leo XIII: *The Condition of Labor*
Pope Pius XI: *The Reconstruction of the Social Order*

Philosophy of the State, reprinted 1940, from 1939 proceedings of the American Catholic Philosophical Association, "The Corporative State," pp. 66–93

24

Man and Society Morally Renewed

—◦∞◦—

Throughout these pages of *Christian Social Principles* we have studied (1) man as an individual, (2) society as man's natural environment, (3) man as he lives in the various necessary societies of the social order, (4) man as he labors to secure the necessities of life for himself and his dependents, and lastly, man as he ought to be directed anew toward his destiny in the solidarity of an organic society. There remains now but one topic for brief treatment: namely the moral renewal of man and of society.

Human Nature Is Moral

The two terms *human nature* and *moral nature* cannot be separated under penalty of distorting the view of man which is the Christian view. To deny the morality of his nature would be equivalent to reducing man to the level of the non-thinking, non-loving lower natures. We must either admit that man is rational, and therefore responsible for his actions, or we must deny his rationality and hold him irresponsible for his actions. But a true social order could not be maintained among irresponsible beings. This is evident even in family life when a member of the domestic circle is irresponsible. Irresponsibility of one member adds to the weight borne by the other members. It adds, too, to their inconvenience, annoyance, and anxiety. The best social order is one in which all the members recognize and share responsibilities.

Justice, which is the foundation of social living, is that constant, habitual, firm determination to give to another what is due to him. But this presupposes a sense of obligation, a recognition of rights and duties, but this is possible only to rational beings. We learned earlier, you recall, that only beings possessed of reason and a deliberate will can be *obliged*. All other beings are *driven*. Only rational beings can know the meaning of *ought*. Human nature, therefore, being rational, is moral, and if a man would deny his morality he must likewise deny his humanity. But that would be no escape, for however much a man may deny that he is morally responsible for his actions, the fact remains: he is responsible because he is powerless to transmute his given nature. He can do nothing about it. His nature stands as God created it — a rational nature with the power to know the true and to choose or reject the good. As such he stands accountable for his deliberate actions.

Man is a moral being whether we view him in the bosom of his family, in the affairs of his workshop or office, in the private pursuits of his individual good, or in the activities of his civic and social life. For wherever a man goes, he carries along with him his human nature; he brings into play his reason and his will. In all his deliberate actions, the light of reason directs him toward the good of his nature. The desires of his will urge him to the fulfillment of the good of his nature. Whether a man sits behind a director's desk, operates a machine, cleans the streets, shoulders a gun, or guides a ship safely to port, he is accountable for his actions. He is everywhere a moral being. He is praiseworthy or blameworthy in all his deliberate actions, for he is a moral being. He is bound by the moral law and subject to its standards wherever he is and whatever he does provided it be done with a deliberate will. Upon his obedience to the moral law depends man's eternal happiness, for, as Pope Pius XI writes: "It is the Moral Law alone which commands us to seek in all our conduct our supreme and final end, and to strive directly in our specific actions for those ends which nature, or rather, the Author of nature, has established for them, duly subordinating the particular ends to the general end."

The statement is clear. The moral law applies to "all our conduct." It commands that we not only seek our final end but that we strive to attain the particular ends which God has ordained for specific actions. It means that in the acquisition of wealth we bear in mind and strive for the true end of wealth: provision of life's needs and charity for the poor. It means that whether we labor or whether we play, we keep before us the true purpose of these things and strive earnestly to attain it. To "subordinate the particular ends" of one's activity to the general end is to recognize the proportion between what is of time and what is of eternity. It means, too, to discern the difference between an intermediate goal and a final goal. The moral law commands us to seek our ultimate goal in all our activities. This is to choose the good, the truly good. It means the subjection of all our deliberate actions to the dictates of reason: Do good. Avoid evil.

Morality Must Be Renewed

A renewal of morality is the only salutary cure for the social-economic disorders which harass the world. These disorders have been summed up quite generally by Pope Pius XI as follows: "Concentration of power has led to a threefold struggle for domination ... (1) for dictatorship in the economic sphere; (2) for control of the State that its resources and authority might be abused in the economic struggles; (3) the clash between States themselves." The statement is an accurate one. Today's evils can be traced directly or indirectly to one or other of these causes; in some instances, to all of them. It enables us to see that any genuine, thorough social-economic "reordering" must be based on moral principles universal in application. Moral influence must extend beyond the individual and beyond the family. It must penetrate society. It must include also economic, political, and international relations.

It seems unnecessary to indicate the fact that morality declines wherever and whenever God is denied or is thrust from His rightful place as Supreme Ruler of the universe. It is evident that when one denies the lawgiver, no such thing as law is admitted. One does not deny a cause but admit an effect. Those who find morality inconvenient do not say, "There is no moral law." They say, rather, "There is no lawgiver" which means, in effect, "There is no one to whom I am responsible for my deeds." The conclusion is evident: there are no standards for judging, no norms of morality. This is how the modern world has sought to escape the restrictions of the moral law. It denied God or God's dominion, and declared itself free. Its "freedom" is a hollow freedom because it is severed from the sole source of true freedom. Only the renewal of morality can give the death blow to licentiousness and restore the freedom of the children of God.

The logical consequence of the wholesale denial of a universal norm of morality has been the rise of individual norms for judging conduct. Chief among them today are the standards of "convenience," of "usefulness," and of "advantage." According to these standards, if it is convenient for one to break civil laws, then it is right for him to do so. If it is of advantage to cheat the working man, then it is right to do so. If it serves the purpose of the laborer to defraud his employer, it is right for him to do so. The effect of such utterly false norms of human behavior is not difficult to see. For unless the standards for judging be universal — as universal and unvarying as the twelve inches that make the foot — there would be no yardstick of justice.

Suppose you went to buy a yard of cloth. You would insist upon thirty-six inches, wouldn't you? Would you be satisfied to pay for a yard but receive only thirty inches of the cloth? Now if the standard of lengths or weights or money were left to the individual buyers and sellers, universal confusion would reign. One might hold that a dollar, for example, is equivalent to any number of dimes when he *buys* goods from another, but equivalent only to two dimes when he *sells* goods to another. Standards must be fixed. Weights and measures and money must have recognized and unvarying equivalents; words must have determined meanings (or why use a dictionary?); norms or standards of right and wrong must likewise have a fixity and universality proper to them.

Under the standard whereby usefulness or advantage is the measure of truth or of right, what would be right for one is wrong for another. A man greedy for wealth shouts "Right" regardless of the means he employs to increase his possessions. He shouts "Wrong" at a competitor who tries to increase his wealth by use of the former's tactics. Our present social order has been brought to its unhappy state in part by individual standards of right and wrong. The universal norm, based on God's eternal law, must be reestablished for no number or degree or kind of individual norms of human behavior can substitute for the divinely ordained norms which are rooted ultimately in the immutability of God Himself.

Pope Pius XII, in writing of the drift toward universal chaos which is so marked in modern society, says,

> Before all else, it is certain that the radical and ultimate cause of the evils which We deplore in modern society is the denial and rejection of a universal norm of morality as well for individual and social life as for international relations. We mean the disregard, so common nowadays, and the forgetfulness of the Natural Law itself, which has its foundation in God, Almighty Creator and Father of all, supreme and absolute Lawgiver, all-wise and just Judge of human actions. When God is hated, every basis of morality is undermined; the voice of conscience is stilled, or at any rate, grows very faint — that voice which teaches even to the illiterate and to uncivilized tribes what is good and what is bad, what lawful, what forbidden, and makes men feel themselves responsible for their actions to a Supreme Judge.

These words are from the writings of Pope Pius XII.

Stemming the tide of immorality alone is not sufficient. When one has been lost and is wandering in a wrong direction or is devoid of any true direction, it is not enough merely to stop. One must make the return to the right road.

Once upon the right road, one must follow its direction, otherwise the goal will not be reached. So in the social order, it is the task of society not alone to cease acting unmorally, but to return wholeheartedly to the practice of morality. It must effect a return to the divine, universal standards of right and wrong. Society must, in other words, return to God. The return will not be easy. Much rebuilding must be done; damage must be repaired; wills must be strengthened; vision must be cleared; hearts must become generous and unselfish. Justice must be established. With justice, must come charity. The task is not one of a day nor the work of a few. Society en masse must seek its true course; must make its way to the feet of the heavenly Father and there acknowledge, as did the Prodigal, its sin, its dependence, its filial duties. Then, in the embrace of its Father, society will find succor and support in the eternal truth, the strict justice, the profound peace, and the merciful love of the immortal God.

"With the weakening of faith in God and in Jesus Christ," writes Pope Pius XII, "and the darkening in men's minds of the light of moral principles, there disappeared the indispensable foundation of the stability and quiet of that internal and external, private and public order which alone can support and safeguard the prosperity of States." That indispensable foundation of social prosperity and individual happiness is the twofold basis of religion and morality: a strengthening of faith and a renewal of morals.

Public Morality Renewed

As the individuals and the family are, so must the State be. It follows that morality in private living must precede the practice of morality in public affairs. In other words, society as such cannot be moral unless men individually are moral, for as the parts are, so will the whole be. The return to morality must begin, therefore; first of all in the hearts of the individual persons who comprise the social whole. But it must not remain in that limited sphere of private living. It must work outward into the social order generally, so that not alone in the individual members of society but in society's institutions may be found that true morality which alone can lead both men and society to the goals established for them by God.

In this moral leavening, religion must play a foremost part. Religion is the expression of man's dependence upon God. It belongs to the virtue of justice, inasmuch as man owes to God, his Maker, an acknowledgement of his dependence. Religion recognizes God's rights and directs man and society in the proper ways of rendering to God His due. Pope Leo wrote: "The primary thing needful is to return to real Christianity in the absence of which all the plans and devices of the wisest will be of little avail." Pope Pius XI, in commenting on Pope Leo's statement that society can be healed in no way except by a return to Christian life and practices, adds this: "Christianity alone can apply an efficacious remedy for the excessive solicitude for transitory things, which is the origin of all vices. When men are fascinated and completely absorbed in the things of the World, it alone can draw away their attention and turn it to Heaven."

Private Morality

Free competition, as we have seen, stimulated in men the passions of greed, selfishness, avarice, and arrogance and fed them to disregard the demands of justice and the promptings of charity. To heal society, men must refrain from those things which keep its wounds open. Consequently, the virtuous life must be the goal of the individuals which comprise human society. They must rise above the fascination of wealth and power and must seek their only true goal in things beyond the temporal, beyond the material, beyond themselves. To do this, however, a certain amount of earthly goods is required, inasmuch as one cannot readily seek things eternal when one's dependents are economically insecure and suffering from want of the necessities of life. A father who is harassed in securing sufficient means to keep alive his family has little inclination or time to pay attention to the one thing necessary: the salvation of his immortal soul. Bodies have to be clothed and fed and sheltered. As economic dictatorship presses more heavily on the laboring class, making their life ever more difficult, spiritual concerns are easily forgotten. When "making ends meet" consumes all the time and wastes all the energies of the body and mind, God is forgotten. Hence to a certain extent, freedom from anxiety is a condition of virtuous, religious, happy human living. It is a condition of true seeking and finding in material things the appropriate means to a better life. It cannot be denied that a sufficiency of the things necessary for decent human living better disposes a man toward God and religion than does extreme poverty. Pope Pius writes: "The conditions of social and economic life are such that vast multitudes of men can only with great difficulty pay attention to that one thing necessary, namely their eternal salvation."

Social and Political Morality

Though morality exists primarily in individual hearts, it does not exist there exclusively. Corporations, civil authority, *moral persons* — groups of individuals acting as a unity — are all obliged by the moral law: as are isolated individuals acting on their own responsibility. Pope Pius XI writes:

"All the institutions of public and social life must be imbued with the spirit of justice.... Social charity must be the soul of the social order ... and the duty of the State will be to protect and defend it effectively."

One social order has failed. Another must be set up. After it has been established, it must be preserved in the fulfillment of its true purpose. Now for this desirable and necessary renewal and preservation, the institutions of public and social life must not only be imbued with a Christian spirit, but they must direct their activities in close accord with its teachings. They must be not only hearers of the Word, but doers also. "The public institutions of the nations must be such," writes Pope Pius XI, "as to make the whole of human society conform to the common good, that is, to the standard of social justice."

In his encyclical on *The Reconstruction of the Social Order*, this Holy Father shows how even lawful regulations imposed upon economic societies (corporations) by constituted civil authority have been evaded and have produced abominable abuses. He proceeds to mention ways in which unscrupulous men, disregarding the demands of social justice and the common good, have made their appeals to the lowest of human passions and have turned the gratification of these passions into their own gain.

Outstanding among the prevalent unscrupulous enterprises contrary to the individual and the common good might be mentioned *smutty* literature and indecent moving pictures. These are put on the market for general consumption without regard to the damage done by them. They falsely portray life, love, honor, nobility, marriage, family life, and goodness. The immorality of such pictures and literature has called into being such associations as The Legion of Decency and Committees for the Suppression of Indecent Literature. These are founded and fostered by the Church to protect the morals of individuals and of society as a whole.

Pope Pius XI, in the encyclical last mentioned, denounces the exploitation of public and private morality for gain. He declares that public authority is accountable for its failure to avert such evil practices. He says — and remember he is speaking of civil authority —

A stern insistence on the Moral Law, enforced with vigor by civil authority, could have dispelled or perhaps averted these enormous evils. This, however, was too often lamentably wanting. For at the time when the new social order was beginning [i.e., after the destruction of the guilds] the doctrine of Rationalism had already taken firm hold of large numbers, and an economic science alien to the true Moral Law had soon arisen, hence it followed that free rein was given to human avarice.

It follows, therefore, that society and social institutions must not only be imbued with the proper spirit of justice and charity, but also that that spirit must find its way into social and public action in view of the common good. Morality is more than an individual concern in social living.

Morality in Economics

Labor is a divinely ordained means by which man supplies his daily needs. It is a means to man's end; it is a way by which he attains to the necessary degree of temporal well-being which is so conducive to religious and moral living. That degree of temporal well-being is, as we have seen, "decent comfort." Now when men find themselves at the mercy of unscrupulous economic lords who rob them of their very lifeblood, they are prone to seek their livelihood by whatever means they can. Hence labor, which was meant to perfect man, often degrades him. Pope Pius XI writes:

"With the leaders of business abandoning the true path, it is not surprising that in every country multitudes of working men, too, sank into the same morass: all the more so, because very many employers treated their workmen as mere tools, without any concern for the welfare of their souls — indeed, without the slightest thought of higher interests." After mentioning the perils to Christian morality which beset individual workmen and families under deplorable working and housing conditions, the Holy Father continues:

> How universally has the true Christian spirit become impaired, which formerly produced such lofty sentiments even in uncultured and illiterate men. In place of that Christian spirit, man's one solicitude is to obtain his daily bread in any way he can. And so bodily labor, which was decreed by Providence for the good of man's body and soul even after original sin, has everywhere been changed into an instrument of strange perversion: for dead matter leaves the factory ennobled and transformed, where men are corrupted and degraded.

The final thought in these words of Pope Pius deserves special consideration. "Dead matter" enters the factory. Perhaps it is lumber. Perhaps it is leather, or cotton, or wool, or raw material of any kind. Upon this "dead matter" man expends the energies of his mind and his body. Machines, designed by man's mind and made by man's hands, transform the raw product. A new value is given to the material. It assumes a new form and renders a new service. By contact with human personality and human inventiveness, the "dead matter leaves the factory ennobled and transformed."

In contrast with this perfecting process, men not infrequently are degraded at their labor. According to God's plan, however, man should be perfected in body and in soul by his work. But economic dictatorship, holding the reins, has corrupted many men. Modern economic conditions "lay more snares than ever for human frailty." For as a result of an economic system which divorced itself from the true moral foundations of God's law, "a much greater number than ever before, solely concerned with adding to their wealth by any means whatsoever, sought their own selfish interests above all things." Then Pope Pius adds: "They had no scruple in committing the gravest injustice against others. Those who entered first upon this broad way leading to destruction, easily found many imitators of their iniquity because of their manifest success, their extravagant display of wealth, and their derision of the scruples of more delicate consciences, and the crushing of more cautious competitors." And all this corrupts men. Men are degraded when they are used as mere tools for the production of wealth to be amassed in the hands of the leaders of business. Man has spiritual concerns which are of greater importance than the making of money. To consider the working man apart from his spiritual interests, to treat him only as a means of satisfying greed, is to violate his most sacred rights. Pope Leo writes (my emphasis):

> If the owners of property must be made secure, the workman, too, has property and possessions in which he must be protected, and *first of all*, there are his spiritual and mental interests. Life on earth, however good and desirable in itself, is not the final purpose for which man is created; it is only the way and the means of that attainment of truth, and that practice of goodness in which the full life of the soul consists.... No man may outrage with impunity that human dignity which God himself treats with reverence, nor stand in the way of that higher life which is the preparation for the eternal life of Heaven. Nay, more; a man has here no power over himself. To consent to any treatment which is calculated to defeat the end and purpose of his being is beyond his right; he cannot give up his soul to servitude; for it is not man's own rights which are here in question, but the rights of God, most sacred and inviolable. (Pope Leo on *Labor*)

But we know that economic dictatorship has outraged the dignity of all too many workers, and men who are thus degraded fall to a level below that of the "dead matter" upon which they labor, for the latter "leaves the factory ennobled and transformed," while he who labors on it frequently is corrupted and degraded.

Public Morality: International in Scope

You will recall that Pope Pius enumerated three fields wherein the struggle for domination was waging fierce battle. He mentioned the economic realm, the political realm (the State), and the clash between states. Of the latter struggle he says: "This arises from two causes: (1) Because the nations apply their power and political influence, regardless of circumstances, to promote the economic advantages of their citizens; and (2) because, vice versa, economic forces and economic domination are used to decide political controversies between peoples (nations)."

In practice the nations realize they are interdependent. No one would deny the reality of the increasing volume of world trade prior to 1939. There is no self-sufficient nation. The social nature of man manifests itself as well in world relations as in lesser societies. But despite the recognized and admitted dependence of nation upon nation, they clash. As economic dictatorship is the cause in the realm of industry, so economic imperialism causes the disorders on an international scale. To enter into the details of economic imperialism is beyond our purpose. We mention the evil in order to round out fully the thought of Pope Pius in suggesting the remedies for the social-economic disorders. With reference to the renewal of morality on the international plane, he points out that "the public institutions of the nations must be such as to make the whole of human society conform to the common good, i.e., to the standard of social justice." This means, not the common good of this or that individual nation, but the common good of the human race — of the world of nations.

Does it not seem strange that the closer the nations are brought together through modern means of transportation and communication, the farther they tend from unity in common human interests? Despite the unity of human nature, what barriers of race and country can be thrown up to exclude peoples from sharing in the resources of the earth, and hence from bettering their condition!

Charity Necessary for Union

The reuniting of the peoples of the earth must be done through the virtue of charity. Economic goods draw men apart; religious goods — the virtues — draw men together. Even were men to succeed in establishing an economic order of worldwide proportions based on the virtue of justice, charity would still be needed. For justice removes the obstacles to peace, whereas charity establishes a union of hearts in peace. Justice alone is not sufficient because it is not the role of justice to bind men together. "Justice alone," says Pope Pius XI,

> even though most faithfully observed, can remove indeed the cause of social strife, but can never bring about a union of hearts and minds. Yet this union, binding men together, is the main principle of stability in all institutions, no matter how perfect they may seem, which aim at establishing social peace and promoting mutual aid.... Then only will it be possible to unite all in harmonious striving for the common good, when all sections of society have the intimate conviction that they are members of a single family and children of the same Heavenly Father, and further, that they are "one body in Christ and everyone members one of another"; then the rich and others in power will change their former negligence of their poorer brethren into solicitous and effective regard; will listen with kindly feeling to their just complaints, and will readily forgive them the faults and mistakes they possibly make.

Charity permeating human society on a worldwide scale — what an ideal! It is the ideal of Christ who said, "Thou shalt love thy neighbor as thyself" (Mark 12:31). To effect such a society, no other spirit but that of Christ can bring about the necessary change of heart. It will demand the putting off of the old man and the putting on of the new. It will be a task beyond man's unaided efforts. It demands the help of God, the infusion of His Spirit, a steady inflowing of divine grace. It demands, for human society, the moral law, religion, and the Church of Christ.

The Church Must Enter

Pope Pius XI remarks in his encyclical on *Atheistic Communism*: "For the preservation of the moral order neither the laws and sanctions of the temporal power are sufficient, nor is the beauty of virtue and the expounding of its necessity. Religious authority must enter in to enlighten the mind, to direct the will, and to strengthen human frailty by the assistance of divine grace. Such an authority is found nowhere except in the Church instituted by Christ the Lord." Pope Leo fearlessly declared fifty years ago that "no practical solution of these questions will ever be found without the assistance of religion and the Church." Again he says: "Religion alone can destroy the evil at its root," hence "all men must be persuaded that the primary thing needful is to return to real Christianity, in the absence of which all the plans and devices of the wisest will be of little avail."

Conclusion

With this chapter we conclude our study of man and society. We have learned a number of basic principles upon which rest the good of man and of society. It is our hope that these principles — seeds of knowledge and motives for acting — will be productive of fruit. We hope they will lead the reader beyond the field of "knowing" into the field of "doing," so that knowledge will lead to acting; so that the intellectual virtues will be perfected by the moral virtues. Then men will not only know what God wants them to do, but they will live as God wants them to live. When they find an ever-increasing activity of the theological virtues within them, when, with the increasing indwelling of the Holy Spirit, the gifts and fruits become established in their souls, then they will have attained the goal of Christian education. They will be true Christians, perfect men of character, who find in Christ the ideal of their lives.

It is to such men of character that the Church looks for apostles, lay and religious, to assist her in her mission to renew completely human society. Towards this ideal, earnest reader, will you not constantly strive?

Some Original Sources

For this chapter we shall confine our sources to the encyclicals, especially to Pope Pius's wherein he outlines the remedy for the social ills. He says in his encyclical on *The Reconstruction of the Social Order*:

1. "Just as the unity of human society cannot be built upon class warfare, so the proper ordering of economic affairs cannot, be left to free competition alone.

"From this source have proceeded in the past all the errors of the 'Individualistic' school. This school, ignorant or forgetful of the social and moral aspects of economic matters, teaches that the State should refrain in theory and practice from interfering therein, because these possess in free competition and open markets a principle of self-direction better able to control them than any created intellect.

"Free competition, however, though within certain limits just and productive of good results, cannot be the ruling principle of the economic world. This has been abundantly proved by the consequences that have followed from the free rein given to these dangerous individualistic ideals.

"It is therefore very necessary that economic affairs be once more subjected to and governed by a true and effective guiding principle. Still less can this function be exercised by the economic supremacy which within recent times has taken the place of free competition: for this is a headstrong and vehement power, which if it is to prove beneficial to mankind, needs to be curbed and governed by itself.

"More lofty and noble principles must therefore be sought in order to control this supremacy sternly and uncompromisingly: to wit, social justice and social charity.

"To that end all the institutions of public and social life must be imbued with the spirit of justice, and this justice must above all be truly operative. It must build up a juridical and social order able to pervade all economic activity. Social charity should be the soul of this order and the duty of the State will be to protect and defend it effectively. This task it will perform the more readily if it free itself from those burdens which, as we have already declared, are not properly its own.

"Further, it would be well if the various nations in common counsel and endeavour strove to promote a healthy economic cooperation by prudent pacts and institutions, since in economic matters they are largely dependent one upon the other, and need one another's help.

"Then if the members of the social body be thus reformed, and if the true directive principle of social and economic activity be thus reestablished, it will be possible to say, in a sense, of this body what the Apostle said of the Mystical Body of Christ: 'The whole body, being compacted and fitly joined together, by what every joint supplieth, according to the operation in the measure of every part, maketh increase of the body, unto the edifying of itself in charity.'"

One final quotation concerning the remedies to be applied to economic life. It, too, is from Pope Pius XI.

2. "All those versed in social matters demand a rationalization of economic life which will introduce sound and true order. But this order, which We ourselves desire and make every effort to promote, will necessarily be quite faulty and imperfect, unless all man's activities harmoniously unite to imitate and, as far as is humanly possible, attain the marvellous unity of the divine plan.

"This is the perfect order which the Church preaches, with intense earnestness, and which right reason demands: which places God as the first and supreme end of all created activity, and regards all created goods as mere instruments under God, to be used only in so far as they help towards the attainment of our supreme end.

"It is not to be imagined that remunerative occupations are thereby belittled or deemed less consonant with human dignity. On the contrary, we are taught to recognize and reverence in them the manifest will of God the Creator, Who placed man upon earth to work it and use it in various ways in order to supply his needs.

Christian Social Principles

"Those who are engaged in production are not forbidden to increase their fortunes in a lawful and just manner: indeed it is just that he who renders service to society and develops its wealth should himself have his proportionate share of the increased public riches, provided always that he respects the laws of God and the rights of his neighbor, and uses his property in accord with faith and right reason.

"If these principles be observed by all, everywhere and at all times, not merely the production and acquisition of goods, but also the use of wealth, now so often uncontrolled, will within a short time, be brought back again to the standards of equity and just distribution.

"Mere sordid selfishness, which is the disgrace and the great crime of the present age, will be opposed in very deed by the kindly and forcible law of Christian moderation, whereby man is commanded to seek first the Kingdom of God and His justice, confiding in God's liberality and definite promise that temporal goods also, so far as he has need of them, will be added unto him." (*The Reconstruction of the Social Order*)

3. From Pope Leo's encyclical on *Christian Popular Action* we have the following:

"We spoke ... of virtue and religion. Now it is the opinion of some, and it has been caught up by the masses, that the social question, as they call it, is merely economic. The precise opposite is the truth. It is first of all moral and religious, and for that reason its solution is to be expected mainly from the Moral Law and the pronouncements of religion.

"For suppose that the productiveness of capital was doubled, that the hours of labor were shortened, that food was reduced in prices; yet if the wage earner, as frequently happens, listens to teaching which destroys his reverence for God, and which corrupts his morals, and if he acts upon this teaching, his labor will necessarily be degraded and his earnings diminish.

"It is found by practical experience that many a workman lives poorly and miserably, in spite of shorter hours and higher wages, because his character is at fault and because religion has no hold upon him.

"Without the instincts which Christian religion implants and keeps alive, without providence, self-control, thrift, endurance and other natural qualities, you may try your hardest, but you cannot prosper.

"That is why in encouraging Catholics to form associations that might better the lot of the working class, or in furthering other designs of this kind, We have never failed at the same time to warn them that such things must not be attempted without the sanction of religion, without including it in their plans and calling on its aid." (*Christian Popular Action*)

Summary

1. Man's natural equipment—his intellectual nature—makes him responsible for his deliberate actions. Man is moral.

2. Morality must characterize the activities of all human beings if the acts are to be properly called *human acts.*

3. Not only a man as an individual, but men combined in social units, are bound by the moral law. Political government, therefore, is obliged to obey the moral law. So, too, are corporations and social institutions of any kind, bound to obey the moral law.

4. It is a wholehearted return to the standards of the moral law, upon which a right social order depends, that the Holy Father prescribes as the sole adequate remedy for present world disorder and distress.

5. Norms of morality must be universal in scope, stable, and founded upon God's eternal law. A moral code, less than universally applicable, could not direct humanity to its proper goal.

6. Religion must mould the heart and mind and will of human beings, making them see the one thing necessary—their eternal salvation.

7. Standards of morality must be respected and applied in government, in industry, and in other economic pursuits engaged in by men, alone or collectively. The virtues of justice and charity must be the body and the soul of the true Christian social order.

8. Social institutions must strive to make the whole of human society conform to the common good, that is, to the standards of social virtue: justice, charity, and peace.

9. Economic societies and leaders of industry must be animated by the spirit of Christianity, so that by the self-same activity "dead matter" will not be perfected while men are corrupted and degraded.

10. In international affairs, nations should be animated by the thought that all are common brothers of a common Father; all are redeemed by the Precious Blood of Christ; all are members—actually or potentially—of Christ's Mystical Body.

11. The Church must enter into the social-economic realm. Her mission requires it. Without religion to enlighten the mind, to direct the will and to strengthen human frailty, the laws and sanctions of the temporal power would be of little avail.

12. Religion and morality can destroy the evils and restore virtue to society. Without religion and morality the efforts even of the wisest will be in vain.

For Study and Discussion

1. Explain: human nature is moral nature.

2. Defend this principle: a man is bound by the moral law in all his actions, that is, in public as well as in private, in individual as well as in social pursuits.

3. Discuss the need of a universal norm of morality. Why are usefulness, advantage, or convenience inadequate norms of human behavior?

4. What is meant when it is said that "morality must be renewed" in social life?

5. Why are the State, economic associations, boards of directors, and other social units bound to obey the moral law?

6. What is the role of the Church and of religion in the renewal of morality?

7. Explain the statement: "Dead matter leaves the factory ennobled, whereas men are corrupted and degraded."

8. Why are the measures and sanctions of the temporal power alone not sufficient to hold society to its true course?

9. Discuss the reasons given by Pope Pius XI for the clash between states.

10. Explain: justice alone can never bring about a union of hearts and minds.

For the Advanced Reader

Nell-Breuning and Dempsey:
   Reorganization of Social Economy

Sheen, Fulton J.:
   Whence Come Wars, chap. 2

Papal Encyclicals:
   Pope Leo XIII: *The Condition of Labor*
                  Christian Popular Action
   Pope Pius XI: *The Reconstruction of the Social Order*

Man in Economic Society

Man is a laborer. By both nature and necessity, he is called to work. Nature equips man with reason and hands to procure the necessities of life. By personal labor man provides himself with those things he needs to preserve his life. Man has a natural right to labor. It is a right based on his fundamental needs. In return for his labor man is entitled to sufficient means to provide for himself and his dependents, maintaining them in decent comfort. He is entitled to sufficient supply of this world's goods to enable him to live a virtuous life.

Man's labor is both personal and social. By his labor man procures not only his livelihood, but he augments the wealth of the State. For this reason man is entitled to more than mere livelihood — to more than that which will keep alive his body. In virtue of his social contribution, he should receive sufficient means to ensure economic security throughout his life. Because man's labor is *necessary*, employers have a moral obligation to pay morally just wages. The wage must be sufficient for decent existence not alone for the laborer but for his family. To better the condition of the laboring man, Pope Pius XI advocates a just sharing, by the workmen, in the ownership, the management, or the profits of an industry or occupation.

A wider distribution of property, says Pope Pius, will tend to distribute more evenly the great accumulation of wealth now in the hands of a few. With the greater distribution of wealth will come the breakdown of concentrated power which results from concentrated wealth.

The right to possess flows from man's nature and his needs. Man's needs recur daily, hence he is entitled to a perpetual right to the things required to fulfill his needs. Man has the right to possess things not only for temporary use but also in permanent possession. This includes not only the right to the resources of the earth but even to the land itself. As man's labor is both individual and social, so is the right to possess. The right to own must not be confused with the unrestricted use of one's goods. Justice and the common good must never be violated in the exercise of one's right to his goods. Civil authority is justified when it intervenes to prevent disturbances to the common good and the social body through the abuse of private possessions.

Individualism, the logical consequence of Liberalistic philosophy, contributed greatly to the destruction of social unity and the social body as a whole. Society should be reconstructed as an organism, a unified whole, a system of organs united in common action for a common goal. Pope Pius XI suggests a plan of vocational or occupational groups as a first step toward a modern corporative society.

No social order, indeed no lesser organ in an organic social order, can long endure or pursue its goal without religion and morality. Only in religion, morality, and in God can *duty* be envisioned as the correlative of *right*. A social order built on rights only must perish. Rights and duties, hand in hand, recognized and exercised, can promote true temporal progress. But rights and duties both require spiritual soil from which to spring, and thus they come from God, the Pure Spirit, and they perfect man in his soul made to the image and likeness of God.

A return to religion, to morality, to God on the part of all mankind, alone will reorder human society and reform human conduct.

Book Suggestions

To attempt to list all the books on the subject of social principles would be a difficult task. There are many excellent books on the subject. Current periodicals carry much literature on social problems. The author makes no effort to suggest all the possible material available. Any up-to-date library will supply titles and authors.

The encyclicals used in this work are from translations published by the America Press, the Paulist Press, the N.C.W.C., and Fr. Wynne's work. It is earnestly hoped that the encyclicals will become better known to the masses. The many excellent translations offered by Catholic publishers are a big step in that direction.

For the works of St. Thomas, the translation of the *Summas* of St. Thomas, undertaken by the English Dominican Fathers and published by Burns, Oates, and Washbourne, London, is highly recommended. References to it appear throughout this work. So, too, is the English translation of *De Regimine Principum*, under the title *On the Governance of Rulers*, by Gerald B. Phelan of St. Michael's College, Toronto, Canada, to be recommended. In *An Apology for Religious Orders*, published by Benziger, St. Thomas gives many of his principles of social philosophy.

For one who is hesitant about going into St. Thomas's works without a guide, there is the excellent series of books by Fr. Walter Farrell, O.P.: *A Companion to the Summa*, volumes 1, 2, and 3 being now available. Fr. Farrell speaks of his volumes as "an easy guide-book to Saint Thomas's greatest work." One would profit much from reading and studying these volumes.

Innumerable pamphlets dealing with the social order are procurable from the N.C.W.C., the Paulist Press, the Queen's Work, and other publishers.

Catholic literature is increasingly coming to the fore combating the cheap propagandizing of the enemies of truth. Of divine truth the Church alone is the divinely appointed custodian. A visit to any Catholic library or publishing house will acquaint the reader with very fine Catholic books on the subject of social problems and the Christian solution to them.

Sophia Institute

Sophia Institute is a nonprofit institution that seeks to nurture the spiritual, moral, and cultural life of souls and to spread the Gospel of Christ in conformity with the authentic teachings of the Roman Catholic Church.

Sophia Institute Press fulfills this mission by offering translations, reprints, and new publications that afford readers a rich source of the enduring wisdom of mankind.

Sophia Institute also operates the popular online resource Catholic-Exchange.com. *Catholic Exchange* provides world news from a Catholic perspective as well as daily devotionals and articles that will help readers to grow in holiness and live a life consistent with the teachings of the Church.

In 2013, Sophia Institute launched Sophia Institute for Teachers to renew and rebuild Catholic culture through service to Catholic education. With the goal of nurturing the spiritual, moral, and cultural life of souls, and an abiding respect for the role and work of teachers, we strive to provide materials and programs that are at once enlightening to the mind and ennobling to the heart; faithful and complete, as well as useful and practical.

Sophia Institute gratefully recognizes the Solidarity Association for preserving and encouraging the growth of our apostolate over the course of many years. Without their generous and timely support, this book would not be in your hands.

www.SophiaInstitute.com
www.CatholicExchange.com
www.SophiaInstituteforTeachers.org